VOLUME II

Research on Sentencing: The Search for Reform

Alfred Blumstein, Jacqueline Cohen, Susan E. Martin, and Michael H. Tonry, *Editors*

Panel on Sentencing Research

Committee on Research on Law Enforcement and the Administration of Justice

Commission on Behavioral and Social Sciences and Education

National Research Council

NATIONAL ACADEMY PRESS
Washington, D.C.   1983

Prepared under grant #80-IJ-CX-0067 from the National Institute of Justice, U.S. Department of Justice. Points of view do not necessarily represent the official position or policies of the U.S. Department of Justice.

Library of Congress Cataloging in Publication Data
Main entry under title:

Research on sentencing.

Bibliography : v. 2, p.
1. Sentences (Criminal procedure)—United States.
2. Sentences (Criminal procedure)—United States—
States. I. Blumstein, Alfred.   II. National Research
Council (U.S.). Panel on Sentencing Research.
KF9685.R38   1983   345.73'0772   83–4048
                          347.305772
International Standard Book Number 0-309-03383-7

Available from

NATIONAL ACADEMY PRESS
2101 Constitution Avenue, NW
Washington, DC 20418

Printed in the United States of America

PANEL ON SENTENCING RESEARCH

ALFRED BLUMSTEIN (*Chair*), School of Urban and Public Affairs, Carnegie-Mellon University

SYLVIA BACON, Superior Court of the District of Columbia

RICHARD A. BERK, Department of Sociology, University of California, Santa Barbara

JONATHAN D. CASPER, Department of Political Science, University of Illinois, Urbana

JOHN C. COFFEE, JR., School of Law, Columbia University

SHARI S. DIAMOND, Department of Psychology, University of Illinois, Chicago Circle

FRANKLIN M. FISHER, Department of Economics, Massachusetts Institute of Technology

DON M. GOTTFREDSON, School of Criminal Justice, Rutgers University

JOSEPH B. KADANE, Department of Statistics, Carnegie-Mellon University

NORVAL MORRIS, Law School, University of Chicago

DAVID J. ROTHMAN, Department of History, Columbia University

RUTH L. RUSHEN, Department of Corrections, Sacramento, California

JAMES Q. WILSON, Department of Government, Harvard University

SUSAN E. MARTIN, *Study Director*

DIANE L. GOLDMAN, *Administrative Secretary*

JACQUELINE COHEN, *Consultant,* School of Urban and Public Affairs, Carnegie-Mellon University

MICHAEL H. TONRY, *Consultant,* School of Law, University of Maryland

COMMITTEE ON RESEARCH ON LAW ENFORCEMENT AND THE ADMINISTRATION OF JUSTICE

ALFRED BLUMSTEIN (*Chair*), School of Urban and Public Affairs, Carnegie-Mellon University

LEE P. BROWN, Chief of Police, Houston, Texas

JOSEPH B. KADANE, Department of Statistics, Carnegie-Mellon University

SAMUEL KRISLOV, Department of Political Science and Law School, University of Minnesota

RICHARD LEMPERT, School of Law, Cornell University

NORVAL MORRIS, Law School, University of Chicago

RICHARD D. SCHWARTZ, College of Law, Syracuse University

LEE B. SECHREST, Center for Research in the Utilization of Social Knowledge, Institute for Social Research, University of Michigan

JUNE STARR, Department of Anthropology, State University of New York, Stony Brook

JACK B. WEINSTEIN, U.S. District Court, Brooklyn, New York

JAMES Q. WILSON, Department of Government, Harvard University

ANN WITTE, Department of Economics, University of North Carolina

MARVIN E. WOLFGANG, Department of Criminology, University of Pennsylvania

v

Contents

Contents
Volume I

Preface

The Panel on Sentencing Research is an outgrowth of the ferment that significantly affected sentencing practice in the 1970s. That ferment is reflected in a variety of sentencing "reforms," many of which had their roots in research, much of which involved technical questions of some complexity.

The Panel on Sentencing Research was established in September 1980 to review that research on sentencing and its impact. The panel was created in response to a request from the National Institute of Justice to the National Academy of Sciences, as a panel of the Committee on Research on Law Enforcement and the Administration of Justice of the Commission on Behavioral and Social Sciences and Education of the National Research Council. The panel's task was to assess the quality of the available research, to indicate how the application of research techniques could be improved, and to suggest directions for future research, especially that supported by the National Institute of Justice. To address this range of issues, the panel was composed of specialists representing a variety of academic disciplines, methodological approaches, and operational expertise in the criminal justice system.

The issue of sentencing is very broad, and so the panel very early had to limit the scope of its work. Much of the public concern over sentencing relates to its effects on crime, but those effects were explicitly excluded from the panel's efforts because two other panels of the Committee on Research on Law Enforcement and the Administration of Justice—the Panel on Research on Rehabilitative Techniques and the Panel on Research on Deterrent and Incapacitative Effects—had recently reviewed the research in their respective areas and identified directions for future research.

Sentencing also involves many complex philosophical questions relating to the role of punishment in society, to the appropriate form of punishment, and to the symbolic qualities of punishment. The panel inquired into these areas to provide a background perspective for its work, but viewed their resolution to involve predominantly normative, nonempirical considerations, and thus to fall outside the panel's research-related mandate. There are also many important issues surrounding the question of the sentencing of juveniles; however, since most of the recent sentencing research and reform have been directed at the adult criminal justice system, that has been the focus of the panel's attention.

In addressing its task, the panel directed its major attention to those issues on which a reasonable body of research already existed or for which new research held promise of making important new contributions. The panel commissioned several papers to synthesize the research in some areas that were particularly extensive, to explicate important methodological issues that limited the validity of existing research, and to identify particularly promising future research possibilities. These papers were presented at a conference the panel organized at Woods Hole, Massachusetts, on July 27-29, 1981. The discussion of those papers provided an important contribution to the panel's deliberations, and a number of the commissioned papers, revised in response to the panel's suggestions, constitute this volume. These papers, which represent the views of the individual authors rather than the panel, are published because the panel believes they make a valuable contribution to the literature on sentencing research.

The panel would like to express its deep appreciation for the extensive contributions by its staff. Susan Martin of the National Research Council served as study director and, as such, managed the affairs of the panel, and addressed many of the sociological issues involved in the work of the panel. As a consultant, Jacqueline Cohen of Carnegie-Mellon University had a primary responsibility for addressing the analytical issues in the research reviewed, but her skills and commitment resulted in many important contributions throughout the report. Michael Tonry of the University of Maryland School of Law, also as a consultant, contributed valuable perspectives on the many legal and philosophical considerations involved throughout the work of the panel. A final editing of the panel's report and the papers in Volume II was undertaken by Eugenia Grohman and Christine McShane, respectively, of the Commission on Behavioral and Social Sciences and Education, and their editorial skills are much appreciated. Diane Goldman at the National Research Council provided major administrative and secretarial support throughout the work of the panel, and her dedication was notable. Jane Beltz provided comparable support at Carnegie-Mellon University.

We would also like to express our appreciation to the National Institute of Justice. Robert Burkhart and Cheryl Martorana of the institute attended most of the meetings of the panel and were most helpful in providing .advice and information on the institute's program on sentencing research.

ALFRED BLUMSTEIN, *Chair*
Panel on Sentencing Research

Research on Sentencing: The Search for Reform

1

Making Sense of Sentencing: A Review and Critique of Sentencing Research

John Hagan and Kristin Bumiller

One of the few certain things about criminal sentencing is that it is an increasingly common subject of empirical research. The bibliography of this paper lists more than 40 studies of sentencing published in the past decade. These studies are notable not only for number but also for their diversity of methods and results. Although early studies of sentencing relied heavily on the use of contingency tables, a striking feature of the past decade has been the widespread application of multivariate techniques, including the development of structural equation models and log linear analyses of the sentencing process. The results have often been provocative, touching most sensitively on issues of racial discrimination in sentencing.

The results of recent studies are provocative not only because they raise important issues of equality before the law but also because they frequently appear to contradict one another. To cite only one recent example, while Eisenstein and Jacob (1977:v) conclude from a study of sentencing in Baltimore, Chicago, and Detroit that "blacks are not treated worse than whites . . . ," Lizotte (1978:577) uses some of the same data from Chicago to calculate that ". . . the 'cost' of being a black laborer is an additional 8.06 months of prison sentence. . . ." The purpose of this paper is to critically review these and other findings of sentencing research and to outline directions this research literature might usefully take in the future.

1

TWO INCIPIENT THEORIES OF SENTENCING

The literature on criminal sentencing is not guided by a dominant theory or set of theories. There have been attempts by sociologists to tie this literature to the debate between consensus and conflict perspectives (see Hagan et al., 1979; Chiricos and Waldo, 1975; Lizotte, 1978) and to link it to a labeling perspective on crime and deviance (Bernstein et al., 1977a). These perspectives do not have wide currency outside sociology, however, so only a small part of the literature can be tied directly to these theoretical frameworks. We argue in this paper that there are two incipient theoretical orientations implicit in the assumptions that sociolegal researchers bring to this area of work. We believe that an awareness of these two orientations--the individual-processual approach and the structural-contextual approach--is helpful to understanding developments in this research literature.

Early sentencing research observed bivariate relationships between attributes like race and sentencing outcomes (i.e., type and length of sentence). These studies (e.g., E. Johnson, 1957) were particularly concerned with demonstrating the differential use of the death penalty against blacks in the southern United States. These studies are important today as a significant source of historical-comparative data; however, legitimate questions have been raised about their tendency to equate correlation with cause in imputing sentencing differentials to discrimination, without controlling relevant "legal" variables (see Green, 1961; Wolfgang and Riedel, 1973). As subsequent studies began to take additional variables into account, initially with tabular techniques, what we call an individual-processual approach to sentencing research began to take form.

In the 1960s this research largely used contingency tables to test whether attributes like race remained significantly correlated with sentence outcome when type of offense and/or prior record were held constant. Although this research labored under the inherent liabilities of tabular techniques, particularly problems of controlling for more than one or two variables simultaneously, it served the important function (at least implicitly) of encouraging researchers to develop models of the sentencing process. For example, the burden of Edward Green's (1961, 1964) early and important work on sentencing was to argue that when "legal" variables like offense type and prior record are taken into account, the relationship between race and sentence disappears. Implicit in this argument is the assumption that prior record and current offense mediate (in a causal and sequential sense) the race-sentence relationship. Later arguments have focused on whether race linked patterns of offense type and prior record should be taken as reflecting differences in criminal behavior or as reflecting earlier experiences of differential treatment by legal authorities (for example, see Farrell and Swigert, 1978a). Both positions could be correct; what is important for our immediate purposes is that in either case it is assumed that offense type and prior record play a causally intervening role in the process by which judges reach sentencing decisions. Two different types of processes are involved, but each is an example of an individual-processual approach to the analysis and understanding of sentencing data.

Much of the sentencing research of the 1970s involved variations and elaborations of individual-processual models of the sentencing process. Most significant in the development of this approach was the introduction of a number of important "case-processing variables" into these models and the application of more sophisticated multivariate techniques in the effort to test the fit of these models with actual case data. Among the new variables considered were pretrial bail decisions (e.g., Bernstein et al., 1977a), plea and charging decisions (e.g., Hagan, 1975c), and the presentence recommendations of probation officers and prosecutors (e.g., Hagan, 1975b; Hagan et al., 1979). These studies made increasingly explicit the premise that sentencing is an end result of a decision-making process that involves offenders moving through a series of potentially important stages in a complex criminal justice system. Farrell and Swigert (1978a:442) make this point well: "The highly structured nature of the judicial system lends itself to a systematic analysis of legal processing. The discrete ordering of events--the social characteristics of the defendants prior to their entry into the system, their accumulated criminal histories, the type of legal representation, pretrial release, the mode of adjudication, and final disposition--constitutes a series of stages that allows the researcher to assert the causal sequence of relationships." Structural equation models and log linear techniques have provided the technology for modeling this complicated process.

Criminal sentencing is not only a matter of processing individuals through a criminal justice system. Both the individuals and the system occupy variable positions or locations within a social structure, so individual processing decisions can vary by social context. This point has been recognized implicitly in some past sentencing research, and it is made increasingly explicit in recent work. For example, the early studies of capital punishment often attempted to measure variation in the use of capital punishment against individuals across periods of time (E. Johnson, 1957), in different jurisdictions (Bedau, 1964, 1965), and according to whether the crime was interor intraracial (Wolfgang and Riedel, 1973) in character (i.e., interracial crimes represent a conflict across assumed status positions in American society). These studies also suffered from the limitations we have associated with the application of tabular techniques, and they were undertaken with little awareness of one another, thus limiting the full development of their contextual implications.

Since 1977, a number of studies have emerged that begin to exploit the possibilities of a structural-contextual approach. Combining data sets from several jurisdictions, Eisenstein and Jacob (1977), Levin (1977) and Balbus (1973) have linked variations in the political environment to sentencing behavior. Lizotte (1978) has identified the class as well as racial positions of individuals in the social structure and linked these to sentencing outcomes. Most recently Hagan et al. (1980) have distinguished proactive and reactive court organizations and considered their impact on the sentencing of white-collar offenders in 10 federal district courts, while Hagan (1982) has examined the consequences of corporate entities compared with individuals acting as victim-complainants in the criminal justice process. All of these studies add some feature of structural and contextual variation to their consideration of the individual processing that leads to sentencing decisions.

It should be emphasized that what we call the individual-processual and structural-contextual approaches are not mutually exclusive. Indeed, each of these approaches is increasingly persuasive as it includes variables emphasized in the other. For example, it is impossible to be sure whether a political

environment correlated with sentencing outcomes is a
cause of those differences in outcome unless the
variables considered in an individual-processual approach
are taken into account. Similarly, it is impossible to
know the generalizability of individual-processual
variables apart from structural and contextual considerations. Thus the limitations on combining these
approaches are clearly not conceptual but rather have to
do with the availability of comparable kinds of data
across contexts. We return to this problem several times
in the course of this paper, for it is central to the
advancement of this area of work. Meanwhile, we proceed
to a discussion of a variety of more specific problems
that plague the various kinds of sentencing research we
have introduced.

DEFINITIONAL PROBLEMS IN SENTENCING RESEARCH

Confusion of central concepts has often made the
collation of findings from sentencing studies difficult.
The most important of these problems has involved the
attempt to draw distinctions between legal and extralegal
factors in sentencing decisions. Much of the sentencing
research of the 1960s and early 1970s was premised on
such a distinction (see Green, 1961). The distinction
frequently drawn was that offense seriousness (as
indicated by the maximum sentence allowed by law) and
prior conviction record (often written into the law as a
basis for more severe sentences) were "legal" variables
and that race, sex, age, and other characteristics not
included in the law were "extralegal." Difficulties with
this distinction cut in at least two directions.

On one hand it has been noted that what are called
legal variables vary from jurisdiction to jurisdiction
(i.e., rankings of offense seriousness vary among
states), that what is legal at one stage of decision
making may not be at another (e.g., community ties may be
considered relevant for bail decisions and irrelevant at
sentencing), and that what is legal at the sentencing
stage (e.g., prior record) may be the product of
discrimination at earlier stages (e.g., by the police)
(see Bernstein et al., 1977b). On the other hand, it can
also be noted that what are called extralegal variables
are directly or indirectly built into some parts of the
criminal law. For example, probation statutes often
include consideration of the offender's age, and there

remain some state statutes (e.g., many prostitution laws) that justify differential treatment by sex. Many statutes encourage judicial consideration of an offender's employment record at various stages of the criminal justice process (see, for example, the language of the criminal code bill that passed the Senate Judiciary Committee in the first session of the 19th Congress), a factor that works disproportionately against black offenders. Even though the Fourteenth Amendment to the U.S. Constitution provides that "No state shall . . . deny to any person within its jurisdiction the equal protection of the laws," the law seems to provide plenty of latitude to do just that. In sum, the law is an ambiguous guide as to those factors that may legitimately influence sentencing decisions.

This issue of legitimacy is complicated further by the fact that it has empirical and moral as well as legal dimensions. The empirical dimension involves the issue of what the American public thinks should influence sentencing, while the moral dimension is concerned with what in some more ultimate sense actually should influence sentencing. We speak to the former rather than the latter issue in this paper, and we deal with it primarily in a contemporary context, focusing first on contemporary American judgments about influences on sentencing. We also note that such judgments may vary across time and place in the social structure (see Hagan and Albonetti, 1982). To offer a specific example, what are thought to be legitimate influences on sentences by most Americans today may be significantly different from what were thought to be legitimate influences earlier in this century in the South. Conceptions of what constitutes criminal justice change.

To acknowledge the moral and variable nature of what influences on sentencing are regarded as acceptable, we speak in this paper of legitimized and nonlegitimized, rather than of legal and extralegal influences on sentencing, and we regard the content of these categories as the product of ongoing social and legal processes. Legitimized and nonlegitimized influences are those within a given social structure and context that the public thinks should and should not affect sentence severity. Although there obviously is no method for unambiguously sorting all influences on sentencing into these two categories, social survey techniques are one important source of information on what influences are and are not regarded as legitimate by a surveyed population.

The top half of Table 1-1 presents data on public attitudes toward nine factors that may influence sentencing decisions. These data come from a national survey of American adults interviewed in 1977 to measure their perceptions of and experiences with local, state, and federal courts as well as their more general attitudes toward the administration of justice (see Inter-University Consortium for Political and Social Research, 1979). These data seem to indicate two rather different kinds of concerns. The first is that offenders with a prior record, offenders previously convicted of the same crime, and offenders convicted of a violent crime should receive tougher sentences than offenders who have done none of these things. Well over 80 percent of the respondents endorsed tougher sentencing of these kinds of offenders. The second concern is that whether an offender is well-to-do, poor, or of minority status should have no influence on sentencing; similar levels of support are apparent for this position. In terms of measured attitudes, it is clear that the American public regards prior record and type of offense as legitimate influences on sentencing and that they do not regard economic and ethnic characteristics as legitimate influences on sentencing.

The bottom half of Table 1-1 summarizes the responses of elite members of the community--i.e., judges, lawyers, community leaders--who were surveyed separately. A similar pattern is apparent. In the remainder of this paper we speak of the variables in Table 1-1 as legitimized and nonlegitimized influences on sentencing decisions. Of course, as we noted above, these data cannot resolve in any ultimate moral sense the issue of whether the legitimacy of variables such as prior record is or is not deserved. In addition, all relevant influences are not considered in this survey. For example, these data do not inform us as to public attitudes toward the influence on sentencing of an offender's employment record.

It is also important to note that the data presented in Table 1-1 indicate that the American public as well as some of its elite members believe that neither of its primary concerns is translated fully into the admin- istration of criminal justice in America. In general these data indicate that both groups _believe_ that legitimized factors do not result in sentences as severe

TABLE 1-1 Preferred and Perceived Influence of Nine Factors on Sentencing (in percent)

Influence	Public Survey						Elite Survey					
	Much Tougher	Little Tougher	No Influence	Little Lighter	Much Lighter	Number	Much Tougher	Little Tougher	No Influence	Little Lighter	Much Lighter	Number
Prior Record												
Preference	49.0	35.0	15.1	.6	.3	(1,916)	53.3	41.7	5.0	0	0	(1,059)
Perception	27.4	45.1	20.7	1.5	1.0	(1,847)	38.6	55.6	4.7	1.0	0	(1,054)
Well-To-Do												
Preference	6.1	6.0	82.9	3.0	1.9	(1,917)	1.6	5.4	91.0	1.0	1.0	(1,045)
Perception	4.1	7.3	29.5	36.4	1.8	(1,854)	.9	6.1	28.7	48.5	15.7	(1,061)
Victimless Crime												
Preference	2.0	5.7	57.5	27.2	7.5	(1,865)	.8	2.1	31.4	44.8	20.9	(1,067)
Perception	1.6	5.1	46.5	40.0	6.8	(1,788)	.2	1.8	21.3	64.7	12.0	(1,052)
Under 18												
Preference	2.2	5.5	51.1	33.9	7.5	(1,902)	.8	1.2	31.1	49.4	17.5	(1,054)
Perception	2.2	6.3	27.6	44.4	19.5	(1,845)	35.4	54.4	7.5	1.9	.8	(1,053)
Poor												
Preference	1.5	4.0	85.7	6.9	1.9	(1,913)	.2	.3	91.6	7.2	.7	(1,086)
Perception	5.0	25.8	54.7	12.0	2.5	(1,832)	2.5	25.2	53.3	17.4	1.7	(1,060)
Minority												
Preference	2.9	4.4	87.3	2.9	1.8	(1,916)	1.3	.3	96.1	1.8	.6	(1,086)
Perception	7.1	26.7	48.3	13.5	4.3	(1,848)	3.8	30.8	48.7	14.7	2.1	(1,058)
Violent Crime												
Preference	70.7	17.6	9.9	.6	.2	(1,911)	85.8	12.4	1.9	0	0	(1,084)
Perception	46.3	36.9	14.7	1.6	.5	(1,844)	69.5	27.7	2.4	.4	0	(1,068)
Same Crime												
Preference	67.2	23.5	7.7	.5	.4	(1,916)	74.6	23.4	1.2	.6	.2	(1,088)
Perception	38.7	40.4	18.6	1.8	.5	(1,854)	45.8	49.4	4.0	.8	0	(1,072)
Crime Unplanned												
Preference	5.8	13.8	45.1	30.2	3.2	(1,893)	1.4	5.3	20.3	65.6	7.3	(1,067)
Perception	4.7	12.8	34.8	40.2	7.5	(1,822)	1.0	4.7	13.7	70.4	10.3	(1,053)

SOURCE: Adapted from Inter-University Consortium for Political and Social Research (1979).

as they should be, and that nonlegitimized factors have an influence on sentences that they should not have. For example, while over 80 percent of the respondents thought being well-to-do should have no influence on sentencing, fewer than 30 percent thought this was actually the case. There is good evidence that a substantial part of the American public perceives its system of criminal justice to be unjust, at least to some degree. Table 1-2 makes the additional point that black Americans are particularly likely to perceive minority offenders as receiving tougher sentences than whites (see also Hagan and Albonetti, 1982). The Pearson's r for this relationship is .18. This may not be surprising, but it does help to focus the concerns of this review.

The latter finding leads to the final concern of this section: Past research has confused discussions of discretion, disparity, and discrimination in sentencing. For our purposes we regard discretion as the latitude of decision provided by law to someone in imposing a sentence; we regard discrimination as a pattern of sentencing regarded as unfair, disadvantaging, and prejudicial in origin; and we regard disparity as a form of unequal treatment that is often of unexplained cause and is at least incongruous, if not unfair and disadvantaging, in consequence. An illustration of the confusion that can occur in the use of these terms is Farrell and Swigert's conclusion (1978a:450) from an important study of the impact of prior offense record on sentencing that "the use of a prior record as meaningful information in the disposition of a criminal case

TABLE 1-2 Perceived Influence of Minority Status on Sentencing by Race of Respondent

| Race | Influence | | | | | |
	Much Lighter	Little Lighter	No Influence	Little Tougher	Much Tougher	Total
White	4.7	14.7	49.0	26.3	5.4	
	(76)	(237)	(791)	(424)	(87)	1,615
Black	1.7	3.9	40.4	32.6	21.3	
	(3)	(7)	(72)	(58)	(38)	178

NOTE: Gamma = .45; Pearson's r = .18.

compounds the discretion of prior adjudications." This use of the term <u>discretion</u> renders the conclusion of this study unclear: Do the authors mean only that the latitude of decision available to authorities has been increased in a legally acceptable manner? The context suggests that what is really meant is that reliance on prior record as a factor in sentencing institutionalizes a form of <u>discrimination</u>. In any case, our purpose in defining these terms is to make our use of them as unambiguous as possible.

METHODOLOGICAL PROBLEMS IN SENTENCING RESEARCH

Ideally, social science research is a cummulative enterprise: Research problems are refined in their definition, increasing amounts of data are brought to bear, findings accumulate, and knowledge increases. The reality of sentencing research falls far short of this ideal. In this section we consider some of the methodological sources of this shortfall.

Alternative Measures of Sentence Severity

One problem in the cummulation of results from sentencing studies is that they operationalize the dependent variable--sentence--in a variety of ways. The only clear area of agreement on this issue seems to be an implicit consensus that sentences can be ordered in terms of severity; the type of ordering applied, however, varies considerably from study to study. These orderings range from a basic binary division between those offenders sentenced to prison versus those who are not (see, for example, Clarke and Koch, 1976) to Uhlman and Walker's 93-point scale that attempts to differentiate in considerable detail ". . . between and among degrees of deprivation of individual freedom and the varying severity of nonprison sanctions" (1980:327 and Appendix). Somewhere between these two approaches is the position taken by Hagan et al. (1979:516), who operationalize the concept of sentence severity by using two different binary codings of the same set of sentence outcomes. The first coding separates prison sentences from all others, while the second coding separates the most lenient disposition in their data set, deferred sentences, from all others. The assumption, confirmed in their subsequent analysis, is that if there is a single dimension of severity, then we should expect to find similar effects of opposite signs when the two codings are used to examine the determinants of sentencing. Our purpose is not to favor one or another of the preceding approaches, but to make clear the diversity of dependent measures that have been used in sentencing studies. In order to cumulate findings from these studies, it is necessary to adopt a common standard, or variety of standards, to be used in some meaningful way across studies. Reanalysis of the original data may be the only definitive way of doing this.

Sampling Problems

Another problem that complicates the cumulation of results from sentencing studies is the variety of court settings and stages in the criminal justice system at which this research is done. Sentencing studies have been done in federal, state, and municipal courts, drawing samples from locations in the system as early as prosecutors' offices and as late as corrections institutions. There are good arguments for drawing samples from all of these settings and stages. Hagan et al. (1980) argue that federal court samples are important because they include larger numbers of white-collar offenders than lower courts, while Feeley (1979) argues that studies of municipal courts are needed because 90-95 percent of all cases are handled in these lower courts, with the result that "Next to the police, the lower criminal courts play the most important role in forming citizen impressions of the American system of criminal justice" (p. xv).

With similar conviction, arguments are made for collecting data relevant to sentencing decisions at various stages of the criminal justice system. On one hand it is suggested that focusing exclusively on offenders sentenced to prison allows consideration of a homogeneous set of dispositions that can be compared in a straightforward way. On the other hand it is suggested that considering a broader range of offenders, to whom various kinds of sentences and other kinds of sanctions are attached, may reduce problems of bias resulting from nonrandom selection processes that may characterize the criminal justice system, from the earliest stages of detection through the imposition of final dispositions.

This problem of sample selection bias is dealt with in detail by Klepper et al. (in this volume). We have reason to raise this issue at several points below.

Measurement of Legitimized Influences on Criminal Sentencing

What we have called legitimized influences on criminal sentencing--for example, type of offense and prior record--should be expected to be strongly related to sentence outcomes. In practice this expectation confronts at least two problems: (1) accurate measurement of these influences and (2) determining how strong a relationship constitutes compliance with public wishes. These problems may be related in that the more measurement error there is, the weaker the observed relationships are likely to be. The issue of measurement error is of further significance in that determining the net influence of illegitimate variables requires effectively holding constant legitimized influences. This cannot be done, of course, without appropriate measurement. We now turn to a discussion of some of the measurements applied.

Type of offense has been measured in sentencing studies in a variety of ways, with an equivalent variety of results. The early tabular studies, like that of Green (1961), measured type of offense in terms of legal categorizations, such as burglary and robbery; these different crimes were then considered separately. This tradition has endured (see LaFree, 1980; Bernstein et al., 1977a), but with the increasing popularity of the linear assumptions of regression analysis, researchers have begun to use scales of offense seriousness. One approach takes the maximum sentence allowed by law for an offense as a measure of statutory seriousness (e.g., Hagan et al., 1980). Another approach applies the Sellin-Wolfgang (1964) seriousness scale, based on several aspects of the crime and its victim (Hagan, 1982). A third approach asks judges to indicate how serious they perceive a particular offense presented for sentencing to be (Hogarth, 1971). A fourth approach uses survey responses from the public as to the type and length of sentences they would apply to particular offense descriptions (Blumstein and Cohen, 1980). Although this is not a full enumeration of the types of offense measures that have been applied, these four measures alone have produced quite different results, increasing in the size of their correlation with sentence outcomes in approximately the order they are presented. The findings of prior research may be in part a result of the types of offense measures applied, leaving no clear indication as to what the strength of this legitimized influence actually is. It also must be said that none of these measurement approaches is clearly right or wrong; each approach represents a different, defensible way of conceiving offense seriousness. The concept of offense seriousness is one that indeterminate sentencing laws leave ambiguous, since they allow both public and judicial views to have an effect through the discretion judges have in determining offense seriousness. There may be no definitively correct way of measuring this concept.

Similar problems emerge in the measurement of prior record. A variety of alternative measures have been used: presence and absence of prior arrests and/or convictions, number of prior arrests and/or convictions, presence or number of prior felony convictions, most serious prior conviction charge, conviction on the same charge previously, and most serious prior disposition. Again, the type of measure used makes a difference. For example, Wolfgang et al. (1972:227) find in an analysis of juvenile court dispositions that the severity of the prior disposition exerts a substantial influence on outcome. This version of a prior record measure has not been used in adult sentencing studies, and the measures that have been used yield a complicated pattern of results (see Hagan, 1974a).

It should also be noted that there are other conceivably legitimate influences on sentencing decisions that have not been included in previous studies. For example, criminal intent, particularly the degree of intent, may be a legitimate consideration at sentencing. Similarly, the type, quality, and quantity of evidence may play a role in sentencing that the public may judge legitimate. Finally, it may be that the sheer bloodiness of a crime may influence sentencing in ways that abstract measures of offense seriousness do not suggest. Again, these other plausibly legitimate influences may be particularly important insofar as they mediate, and thereby serve to justify, the influence of the non-legitimized variables we consider next. Probably in contrast to those who study sentencing professionally, the public seems to be equally concerned with the

influence of legitimized and nonlegitimized factors in
sentencing. One purpose of this section is to give equal
priority in measurement to this concern.

Measurement of Nonlegitimized Influences on Sentencing

Most, if not all, of the nonlegitimized factors
considered in sentencing studies have their base in
social science research, yet the measurement of these
factors has often not kept pace with their
conceptualization and operationalization in other
spheres. This is most conspicuously the case in terms of
measures of social class and status. Although we cannot
reproduce the history of these measures here (but see
Featherman, 1980; Wright, 1980; Kalleberg and Sorensen,
1979), we can note that little of their diversity,
subtlety, or sophistication is reflected in contemporary
sentencing studies. For example, the most widely
disseminated form of these measures is based on the work
of Blau and Duncan (1967) and their model of status
attainment. Social scientists of this tradition have
assumed that the rate of social mobility is so high in
societies like our own that, rather than being characterized in terms of any particular grouping,
individuals are located more meaningfully along a ranked
socioeconomic continuum. The measures of occupational
standing used in this tradition assume a graduated
continuum with no clear discontinuities (see Duncan,
1961; Treiman, 1977).

Insofar as sentencing research has incorporated
stratification measures, which are fundamental to issues
of equality before the law, it has adopted the type of
measure of occupational standing just described. The
most systematic example of this is a study by Chiricos
and Waldo (1975) of socioeconomic status and criminal
sentencing in a large sample of incarcerated offenders.
These researchers carefully applied a measure of
occupational standing (Nam and Powers, 1968; U.S. Bureau
of the Census, 1963) and perceptively note several of the
problems that application of this kind of measure
involves (758-759n). The most significant of these
problems are the skewness of prison populations toward
the low end of the socioeconomic continuum and a lack of
certainty about how this kind of skewed distribution
should be handled.

One response is to argue that socioeconomic status actually is a discrete rather than a continuous variable (Hopkins, 1977); the great mass of incarcerated offenders then falls into a "lower class" and perhaps a few represent a "middle or upper class counterpart." Chiricos and Waldo (1975) demonstrate that measurements based on this continuum approach, manipulated in a variety of ways, yield neither consistent nor significant correlations with length of prison sentences. A common response to this kind of outcome in the stratification literature is to argue that the continuum measure itself, from which these divisions are drawn, is problematic in its conceptualization.

The base of the problem, it is suggested, is that mobility and income determination are neither as open nor as fluid as a continuum conceptualization suggests. It therefore is argued that what is needed is a "relational" rather than a "gradational" measure of class position; that is, a measure based on "common positions within the social relations of production" (Wright, 1980:326). This approach distinguishes one class from another largely on the basis of two criteria: ownership of the means of production and purchase of the labor power of others. A second and related approach distinguishes classes on the basis of their relation to authority. This approach, based on the work of Dahrendorf, is concerned with whether authority is exercised over the work of others. Combining these two models, Robinson and Kelley (1979) have conceptualized and measured class positions as a collection of discrete categories. In an analysis of national survey data drawn from the United States and Great Britain, Robinson and Kelley are able to show that all three of the models we have discussed make an independent contribution to the explanation of men's income. The implication is that each of these models could contribute to the explanation of variations in criminal sentencing as well; however, these types of distinctions have not been drawn in the sentencing literature.

Another type of nonlegitimized influence that has been considered sporadically in sentencing research is the relationship between the victim and the offender. Early studies concentrated on the race of the offender and the victim (e.g., Garfinkel, 1949). As we note later in this review, there is convincing historical evidence of discrimination in some offender-offense combinations; however, victim-offender relationships are considerably

more complicated than this type of analysis suggests.
For one thing, all victims and offenders obviously are
not either black or white; we know little about American
Indian, Spanish-speaking, and other kinds of victims and
offenders who also are involved in large numbers in the
criminal justice systems of this country. More
specifically, we do not know how patterns of interracial,
intraracial, and victimless crimes vary across these
groups or the implications of this for criminal
sentencing. Cutting across these ethnic categories, we
also do not know how the relative class positions of
victims and offenders (see Black, 1976) and the intimacy
versus impersonality of victim-offender relationships may
influence sentencing decisions. Finally, we know little
about the role of the courts, at either adjudication or
sentencing, in resolving family disputes in this
country. The characteristics of victims and offenders,
and the relationships between them, are a largely
uncharted area of sentencing research.

Measurement of Contextual Effects

The last of the methodological problems we discuss is
perhaps the one that will be of most concern in the near
future. As sentencing studies focus increasingly on
structural and contextual aspects of sentencing,
methodologically they must address the problems of
demonstrating contextual effects. There are two primary
problems involved: The first is that of demonstrating
that differences in sentencing patterns result from the
aggregative properties of a setting rather than from
characteristics of the people selectively aggregated into
that setting; the second is that of demonstrating which
among a collection of intercorrelated contextual
variables, measured or unmeasured, is responsible for the
residual differences among the settings. We consider
these problems in sequence.

The first problem is essentially an issue of
composition: How do we show that there are differences
in the sentencing patterns of different settings once
their differing composition is taken into account?
Although sentencing research has not yet progressed to
this point, the common approach to demonstrating
contextual effects on a dependent variable is to examine
the influence of a contextual variable that represents an
aspect of group variation, while controlling for all

those characteristics by which aggregative units differ
in their composition and are known to be correlated with
and antecedent to the dependent variable. In a manner
that Hauser (1970:14) skeptically calls the "method of
residues," residual covariation of the contextual
variable with the dependent variable is then identified
as the effect of the context. Hauser points out that
gross aggregate differences in a dependent variable are
usually small when compared with the total variability of
that variable, and that when other independent variables
that must be controlled are held constant, aggregate
differences in levels of the dependent variable are
diminished further. This point should be kept in mind
when considering the variation explained "contextually"
in aggregate studies of jurisdictional differences in
sentencing.

There is also the problem of correctly interpreting
these contextual effects. As Hauser points out, the
choice of a variable to represent a context is arbitrary
in the sense that most contextual variables are
intercorrelated and thus can generate similar residual
differences among groups. The problem is that the
particular contextual variable chosen affects the
interpretation of residual group differences.
Furthermore, this interpretation will usually rest on
equally arbitrary assumptions about the effects of
unmeasured variables. For example, in a national
sentencing study one can readily imagine the use of
region as a contextual variable, with residual
differences associated with this variable being
interpreted as the product of differences in regional
culture. A problem with this interpretation, however, is
that regional culture is unlikely to be measured
directly. The interpretation of a contextual effect,
then, can be no more secure than the measurements on
which it is based, and these measurements are often
indirect in character.

Finally, it should be noted that time as well as place
can be a source of contextual variation. As we will see
below, Thomson and Zingraff (1981) and Hagan and
Bernstein (1979) have demonstrated that the practice of
aggregating sentencing data over time to construct larger
data sets can mask important shifts in sentencing
patterns. Similarly, Greenberg (1977:175) notes that
sentencing practices may be sensitive to long-term social
trends, such as the growing number of blacks in the
judiciary and increased public concern about racial

discrimination. Although this type of contextual
analysis must confront issues such as those outlined
above, data covering lengthy periods or measured at
regular intervals can be modeled using a time-series
approach (Box and Jenkins, 1970). These techniques,
applied to sentencing data, hold the promise of
statistically identifying long-term deterministic trends
and intervention effects attributable to important social
events. Unfortunately these kinds of data have not yet
been put to this type of use in the study of sentencing.
Without such work we must rely on independent studies
done at different points in time as well as in different
jurisdictions to learn what we can about the influence of
variations in social context on sentencing decisions.

THE PROBLEM OF CUMULATION

The preceding section has reviewed in some detail the
problems involved in reaching cumulative conclusions from
existing sentencing research. Although less can be done
than we would like, some important cumulative conclusions
can be reached. The path to these conclusions begins
with a narrowing of the problems and possibilities to be
pursued.

An obvious first step is an identification of studies
to be considered. We identified existing sentencing
studies by reviewing bibliographies (e.g., Hagan, 1974a)
and searching Sociological Abstracts, Crime and
Delinquency Abstracts, and Legal Abstracts. Appendix A
is our attempt to summarize all of the nonredundant
(i.e., some published studies use the same data in only
marginally different ways) American studies that include
empirical data on sentencing. As will soon be apparent,
many of these studies do not present data in a form that
facilitates our cumulative goal.

Ideally a comprehensive cumulation of what we know
from the empirical literature on sentencing would involve
the generation of precise statements about the influence
of the different kinds of variables that have been
included:

(1)   Offense Attributes: Offense seriousness,
      offense type, number of offenses charged, degree
      of harm inflicted, weapon use.
(2)   Offender Attributes: Race-ethnicity, sex, age,
      social class and employment status, education,

(3)   marital status, drug/alcohol dependence, prior
criminal record.
(3)   Case-Processing Attributes: Bail status,
attorney type, plea, presentence report,
recommendations of prosecutors and probation
officers.
(4)   Contextual Attributes: Court characteristics,
case load, identity of judge, community
characteristics, social change over time.

Unfortunately most of these variables are not
consistently measured and considered in the sentencing
literature. And many of these studies do not present
their data in a form that can be readily cumulated with
other studies for the purposes of reanalysis. For
example, some studies report only mean scores that cannot
be accumulated across studies (e.g., Tiffany et al.,
1975; Perry, 1977; Levin, 1972), other studies using
correlation and regression techniques frequently do not
report zero-order correlations (e.g., Nardulli, 1979;
Chiricos and Waldo, 1975; Kelly, 1976; Eisenstein and
Jacob, 1977), and studies based on multivariate
categorical techniques often do not report comparable
statistics or a full cross-tabulation of their variables
(e.g., Unnever et al., 1980; Burke and Turk, 1975; Uhlman
and Walker, 1979, 1980; Thomson and Zingraff, 1981).
This point is not made as a criticism of these studies;
they were not done for the purpose of facilitating our
review. The cumulation of these data sets in a central
data bank would allow those interested in reanalysis to
overcome some of these problems. Lacking immediate
access to these data sets, we must work with what is
provided in the form of published results.

The possibilities that published results provide vary
according to the attribute considered. For example, the
best prospects for cumulation involve consideration of
the offender's race: 51 studies reach conclusions about
the relationship between the offender's race and sentence
(these studies are described in greater detail in
Appendix A). No other attribute benefits from such a
large pool from which to draw conclusions. For this as
well as for other attributes, however, there remains the
issue of how cumulative conclusions can best be drawn.
The most common approach to this problem takes a
narrative form, in which the reviewer uses his or her own
judgment to weigh the findings against one another. We
too rely on judgment, but we first organize our

consideration of the studies in a way that allows us to
more systematically and objectively reach some
preliminary conclusions, and to more usefully narrow our
attention to some of the most important recent studies of
race and sentencing.

RACE AND SENTENCING

In this section we will use the 51 studies with findings
on race and sentencing to reach conclusions about racial
disparities in sentencing (summaries of these studies are
provided in Appendix A). Our strategy is first to group
the available studies according to whether the analysis
presented (1) uses data from before 1969 or from 1969 and
after, (2) includes controls for the severity or type of
offense and the presence of a prior criminal record, and
(3) concludes with a finding of racial discrimination in
sentencing. The 1969 date is somewhat arbitrary but
intended to provide a division in time after which the
possible effects of the civil rights movement of the
1960s would be likely to have been felt. If a study
overlaps these time periods, it is placed in the category
of greater overlap. As we noted above, studies control
for offense seriousness and prior record in a number of
ways; consistent with the individual-processual approach
described above, our classification requires that some
control for both variables be present. Finally, our
classification of whether discrimination is found is
liberal (both methodologically and politically) in the
sense that if the study reports a specified condition in
which a nonspurious and statistically significant
disparity in outcome by race is found, the study is
categorized as revealing evidence of discrimination.

The results of the above cross-classification are
presented in Table 1-3. Several noteworthy trends in
studies of race and sentencing are apparent in this
table. The most conspicuous of these trends is the
increased tendency to control for the effects of offense
and prior record: 44 percent of the studies included
these controls through 1968, and 76.9 percent of the
studies contained such controls from 1969 on. While in
both time periods studies with these controls have fewer
findings of discrimination than studies without such
controls, this does not lead in the second time period to
any marked decline in the tendency to conclude that
discrimination has occurred. Indeed, studies from the

TABLE 1-3   Cross-Classification of Control for Offense and Prior Record by Finding of Racial Discrimination and Time Period

	To 1968			1969 on		
	No Discrimination	Discrimination	Total	No Discrimination	Discrimination	Total
No Control for Offense and Record	21.4% (3)[a]	78.6% (11)[b]	56.0% (14)	33.4% (2)[c]	66.6% (4)[d]	23.1% (6)
Control for Offense and Record	72.7% (8)[e]	27.3% (3)[f]	44.0% (11)	50.0% (10)[g]	50.0% (10)[h]	76.9% (20)
Total	44.0% (11)	56.0% (14)	100.0% (25)	46.2% (12)	53.8% (14)	100.0% (26)

[a]Bedau, 1965; Bensing and Schroeder, 1960; Conklin, 1972.
[b]Bedau, 1964; Bowers, 1974; Bullock, 1961; Garfinkel, 1949; Gerard and Terry, 1970; Johnson, 1957; Martin, 1934; Partington, 1965; Wolf, 1964; Wolfgang et al., 1962; Wolfgang and Reidel, 1973.
[c]Atkinson and Newman, 1970; Perry, 1977.
[d]Cargan and Coates, 1974; Uhlman, 1979; Zalman et al., 1979; Zimring et al., 1976.
[e]Baab and Furgeson, 1968; Burke and Turk, 1975; Farrell and Swigert, 1978b; Green, 1961, 1964; Judson et al., 1969; Levin, 1972; Mileski, 1971.
[f]Lemert and Rosberg, 1948; Nagel, 1969; Tiffany et al., 1975.
[g]Bernstein et al., 1977a; Chiricos and Waldo, 1975; Clarke and Koch, 1977; Eisenstein and Jacob, 1977; Feeley, 1979; Hagan et al., 1979; Hagan et al., 1980; McCarthy, 1979; Pope, 1975a; Shane-Dubow, 1979.
[h]Clarke and Koch, 1977; Gibson, 1978; Hagan and Bernstein, 1979; Kelly, 1976; LaFree, 1980; Lizotte, 1978; Myers, 1979; Pope, 1975b; Thomson and Zingraff, 1981; Unnever et al., 1980.

second time period that control for offense and record are more likely than those from the first period (with similar controls) to find discrimination (50 percent compared with 27.3 percent). Although studies from the second period are still evenly divided between those that do and do not find discrimination, the fact that an increased proportion of these studies conclude discrimination deserves an explanation.

One possible explanation we elaborate below is that, as researchers have increased their use of multivariate techniques facilitating the control of legitimized variables like offense and prior record, they also have focused more selectively on those structural and contextual conditions that are most likely to result in racial discrimination. We make this point below by individually considering the 10 studies based on data from 1969 on that find evidence of racial discrimination with offense and record controlled. It is important before turning to this discussion to repeat that the

studies from this period are evenly divided in their
findings, half finding no evidence of discrimination by
race. Some comparative consideration is given later to
the studies that find no racial discrimination; however,
our primary attention is given to those that do.

Clarke and Koch (1977)

This study analyzes the sentences imposed on 683
defendants convicted of 860 felony counts between August
1974 and August 1976 in Alaska. A unique feature of this
study is the attention it gives to specific groupings of
offenses, including violent crimes (such as rape,
robbery, and assault with a dangerous weapon), crimes of
theft or unlawful entry (such as burglary and larceny),
crimes of deceit (such as fraud, forgery, and
embezzlement), and drug felonies (such as possession of
heroin or sale of marijuana). The dependent variable for
this analysis is length of sentence in months; offenders
receiving no active sentence (e.g., a suspended sentence
and probation) were coded zero.

The data are analyzed in two stages: First, analysis
of variance is used to eliminate nonsignificant
correlates of sentence length; second, multiple
regression is used to determine the independent
contribution of the surviving variables to the
explanation of sentence length. A binary coding of race
allows the authors to estimate from their regression
results that being black in and of itself contributes a
substantial 11.9 months to drug felony sentences, and a
somewhat less dramatic 6.5 months to sentences for crimes
of theft or unlawful entry. Clarke and Koch note that
"This independent 'blackness factor' survived . . .
statistical tests and was shown to increase the severity
of sentences entirely aside from such considerations as
employment history, educational level, occupation,
income, prior criminal history, and probation or parole
status" (p. v). Race was not found to be a significant
factor in crimes of violence or in frauds, forgeries, or
embezzlements. The authors conclude from this that ". . .
sentencing drug offenders was more subjective (and thus
more susceptible to 'individualization' on questionable
grounds) than sentencing those who committed felonies
against persons or property" (p. 36). In the language of
our earlier discussion, drug offenses may represent a
structural context in which racial discrimination is

particularly likely to occur. Ethnic and racial
hostility has long been thought to be a factor in
American drug policy (Musto, 1973; Bonnie and Whitebread,
1974), and the manifestation of this hostility in
sentencing patterns might therefore be expected.

Gibson (1978)

This study focuses on 11 judges who sentenced 1,219
felony cases in the superior court of Fulton County
(Atlanta, Georgia) from March 1968 to October 1970. A
unique feature of this study is its attention to the
sentencing behavior of individual judges. The index of
discrimination in sentencing used attempts to capture the
differential severity of sentences imposed by individual
judges to black and white offenders net of legitimized
criteria. The results reveal differences among judges
that are masked in the aggregate. Gibson concludes that
". . . blacks are the victims of discrimination by some
judges but the beneficiaries of discrimination by others"
(p. 470). Gibson uses interview responses to show that
the antiblack judges are tied strongly to traditional
southern culture, concerned about crime, prejudiced
against blacks, and relatively punitive in their
sentencing philosophies; in addition they tend to rely
more heavily on the defendant's attitude and prior record
in making their sentencing decisions.

Gibson is cautious in framing his conclusions, noting
the limitations that a sample of 11 judges, only three of
whom were clearly discriminatory, imposes. Nonetheless,
it is interesting to note a parallel between this and a
Canadian study by Hagan (1975a): namely, that the
finding of discrimination is specific to a subset of
judges considered. Only in this context is a culturally
based finding of discrimination revealed.

Hagan and Bernstein (1979)

Using data from the 14-year period 1963-1976, this study
analyzes the sentences imposed on 238 persons for
selective service violations in one of America's largest
cities. Unique features of this study are its identification of two different social and political contexts
in which these cases were sentenced and an examination of
the influence of race within these contexts independent

of other legitimized factors. An initial, "coercive" period, from 1963 through 1968, was characterized by large numbers of antidraft demonstrations, by editorials that admonished resisters to accept gracefully the punishments that were imposed, and by a predominant reliance of judges on the use of imprisonment. A later "cooptive" period, from 1969 through 1976, was characterized by a sharp reduction in antidraft demonstrations, by editorials that challenged the use of severe sanctions for some types of resisters, and by a new willingness on the part of judges to expand the use of probation.

Subsequent analyses using the decision to imprison as the dependent variable show that in the early period of coercive control, black resisters were more likely than white resisters to be imprisoned. In contrast, during the period of cooptive control, white resisters were more likely than black resisters to be imprisoned. A similar pattern was observed in that Jehovah's Witnesses were more likely than others to be imprisoned in the earlier period and more likely than others to be given probation in the later period. These findings are interpreted in terms of the suggestions of Simmel, Merton, and Coser that when political dissent becomes widespread, majority group members can present an even greater threat than minority group members to governing authority. The authors show that it was draft resisters who were both white and activist who were singled out for the most severe sanctioning during the era of cooptive control; they were most likely to be imprisoned during a period in which imprisonment had declined dramatically. Like Gibson, Hagan and Bernstein note that the observed racial differences would not have been found had the data not been disaggregated, in this case by social and political context.

Kelly (1976)

The sample for this study consists of 385 offenders incarcerated for burglary and 356 offenders incarcerated for homicide in Oklahoma corrections institutions as of March 1974. The unique feature of this study is its focus on two specific offense categories; length of sentence is the dependent variable. The results of this research indicate that net of legitimized criteria in

Oklahoma, black offenders receive longer sentences than whites for burglary. Blacks do not receive significantly longer sentences for homicide than whites, but Mexican-American and Indian offenders do receive shorter sentences than whites convicted of this offense. Although these findings are context-specific, as Kelly (p. 248) notes, "the racial and ethnic differences by crime type are difficult to explain."

LaFree (1980)

The sample for this study consists of 881 suspects charged with "forcible sex offenses" in a large midwestern city between January 1970 and December 1975. Two unique features of this study are (1) its focus on the racial composition of the victim-defendant dyad rather than on attributes of the defendant or victim taken separately and (2) its consideration of a series of official processing decisions in these cases, from initial police reports to final dispositions. A variety of dependent measures are used. "To the extent that relationships between men and women in America are still defined by race-specific rules of sexual access," LaFree (p. 843) argues, "an implicit ordering of official reactions to sexual assault by race of the victim and offender is suggested."

Results of a stepwise multiple regression analysis confirm this expectation: compared with other defendants, black men who assaulted white women received (1) more serious charges and (2) longer sentences and were more likely to (3) have their cases filed as felonies, (4) receive executed sentences, and (5) be incarcerated in the state penitentiary. Overall, the inclusion of racial composition substantially improves the prediction of outcomes, the greatest increases occurring for later sentencing outcomes. These findings are certainly not unique to this study: Even stronger relationships between racial composition of the victim-defendant dyad and sentencing are apparent in studies focusing on rape cases in earlier eras (see Wolfgang and Reidel, 1973; Partington, 1965). The long history of black-white sexual segregation in the United States makes sexual assault cases one of the most likely structural contexts in which racial discrimination will be found.

Lizotte (1978)

This study had an initial sample of 816 criminal cases processed by the Chicago trial courts in 1971. Two unique features are: (1) an examination of an explicit model of discrimination in the criminal justice system that posits both direct and indirect effects of race and (2) a consideration of the combined effects of race and class position on sentencing. Length of imprisonment was used as the dependent variable, and inactive sentences were coded as zero.

Although Lizotte finds no direct effect of race net of other variables on sentencing, he does find an indirect effect operating through the failure to make bail that results in black offenders receiving prison sentences 4.3 months longer than whites. More striking, however, are the results of the combined consideration Lizotte gives to race and class positions in his analysis. Lizotte estimates the mean sentence length received by black and white laborers compared with white proprietors, net of all other measured legitimized and nonlegitimized variables. Although there are only 15 proprietors (all white) available for this part of the analysis, and the findings should therefore be treated cautiously, it nonetheless is striking that the resulting estimated "cost" of being a black laborer is an additional 8.06 months of prison sentence, while for white laborers it is an estimated 27.89 months. Lizotte (p. 578) concludes that "this might suggest that in the criminal court system one's position in the 'division of labor' is a more pervasive basis for discrimination than race." In any case, Lizotte has succeeded in showing that race and class positions combine to form an interesting structural context in which to examine differences in sentence outcomes (see also Hagan and Albonetti, 1982).

Myers (1979)

This study considers the cases of 205 offenders who victimized specifiable individuals and were convicted at trial and sentenced between January 1974 and June 1976. Two features of this study deserve note: (1) its consideration of the racial composition of the victim-offender dyad and (2) its examination of the mediating role that the recommendations of probation officers can play in the sentencing process. These two features of

Myers' research are connected, in that although the racial composition of the victim-offender dyad did not notably affect sentencing directly, it did have a significant effect indirectly, through probation officers' recommendations. The ultimate effect was greater leniency for blacks convicted of victimizing blacks compared with white-white and black-white dyads, net of other legitimized factors. The decision to imprison was the dependant measure for this analysis. As Myers (p. 530) notes, the subset of cases considered in this analysis represents a small minority of all cases sentenced: Most cases do not go to trial, and the restriction to cases with specified individual victims further narrows the focus. Nonetheless, the indicated role of probation officers' recommendations and their liability to bias has been noted before (see Hagan, 1975b; Unnever et al., 1980, below), and we have discussed the influence of racial composition above (e.g., LaFree, 1980). Both of these variables may identify structural contexts in which the likelihood of racial discrimination is increased.

Pope (1975)

This study is based on 32,694 offenders sentenced in 12 counties in California between 1969 and 1971. Unique features of this study are (1) its separate consideration of sentencing decisions in urban and rural counties and (2) its separate use of type (e.g., probation, jail, prison) and length (i.e., length of confinement or probation) of sentence as dependent variables. The technique used to take account of legitimized influences in this analysis is test factor standardization. When type of sentence is the dependent measure, the results of this analysis indicate that rural courts sentence blacks more severely than whites. Blacks sentenced by rural courts, for example, were substantially more likely to be confined and less likely to obtain a probation disposition. Bivariate differences by race in urban areas disappeared when legitimized influences were taken into account. When length of sentence was used as the dependent measure, no racial differences were evident for either urban or rural areas. The latter finding may be a consequence of sample selection bias. In any case, the former finding of discrimination in rural but not urban settings has a parallel in at least one other, Canadian

study (Hagan, 1977). Rural court settings may mark
another structural context in which discrimination is
likely to occur.

Thomson and Zingraff (1981)

The sample for this study consists of all males sentenced
in one southeastern state for armed robbery during 1969
(N=251), 1973 (N=441), and 1977 (N=502). Length of
prison sentence is the dependent measure. The selection
of these discrete time periods is the unique feature of
this study. Thomson and Zingraff present evidence that
over the last decade (1) the public's fear of crime and
negative evaluation of court performance have increased,
(2) judicial legislation geared to making the offender
more accountable has emerged, and (3) robbery has become
more interracial in character. They hypothesize that
racial discrimination in robbery should be more likely in
recent years. Using log linear techniques, Thomson and
Zingraff find evidence that this is indeed the case.
While no evidence of racial discrimination is found for
all three years combined, in 1977 it is found that whites
incarcerated for armed robbery had a greater than average
chance of receiving the least severe sentence, and that
nonwhites had a greater than average chance of receiving
a moderately severe sentence. Members of each racial
group had average chances of receiving the most severe
sentence. It is possible that a focus on only the length
of sentence given incarcerated offenders poses problems
of sample selection bias that mute the strength of these
findings (see Thomson and Zingraff, 1981:873 on this
point). The point is still effectively made that context
makes a difference. In this case, the context of concern
involves the factor of racial composition as well as the
surrounding social and political environment.

Unnever, Frazier, and Henretta (1980)

The sample for this study is 229 cases adjudicated and
followed by a presentence investigation in a six-county
judicial district in Florida between June 1, 1972, and
May 31, 1973. The unique feature of this study is its
exclusive attention to cases on which presentence reports
were prepared. In a LOGIT analysis of the data net of
other legitimized and nonlegitimized influences, the odds

ratio corresponding to the chances of probation compared
with prison for whites is predicted to be 2.3 times that
for blacks. Unnever et al. also find that when a control
is introduced for the inclusion of probation officer's
recommendations in the final disposition equation, the
effect of race is reduced substantially. The
implication, as noted above in Myers' study (1979; see
also Hagan, 1975b), is that the incorporation of
probation officers in the sentencing process can result
in discrimination by race. We have made the point
elsewhere (Hagan et al., 1979) that the historical
process by which probation officers were included in the
sentencing process represents a structural change in the
American courts with significant symbolic consequences.
This study illustrates that the implications of this
structural change can be instrumental as well, in this
case with racial consequences.

We have talked in some detail about recent studies
that have found evidence of racial discrimination and
about the structural and contextual conditions that may
give rise to these findings. It is important to note as
well that one of those studies that does not find
evidence of racial discrimination since 1969 does report
class-linked disparities in sentencing. This study
(Clarke and Koch, 1976) analyzes the experiences of 798
burglary and larceny defendants in the criminal courts of
Mecklenburg County, North Carolina, in 1971. Clarke and
Koch report that both income and race have a substantial
first-order relationship to whether a defendant goes to
prison, but while income continues to show at least a
small effect on this outcome when other variables are
taken into account, race does not. It is also shown that
most of the effect of income on sentence is mediated by
two variables: bail status and defense counsel. In the
county under study, the only alternative to pretrial
detention for most defendants was bail bond, which meant
depositing in cash the full amount of the bond set for
the offense charged or obtaining a professional bondsman
as surety in exchange for a nonreturnable fee. An
assigned counsel system was used in the county to provide
private representation for defendants who could not
retain private counsel. Clarke and Koch (pp. 83-84)
found that in the county considered ". . . most of the
influence of income on the likelihood of imprisonment
among the defendants studied is explained by poorer
opportunity of the low-income defendant for bail and his

greater likelihood of having a court assigned, rather than privately retained attorney."

Clarke and Koch (p. 37) are rather explicit in concluding from their data that race is of "little or no importance" in determining whether criminal defendants go to prison. Furthermore, they cautiously resist saying whether any kind of discrimination at all has occurred. They speak instead of "unequal opportunity" associated with income (p. 85). As we have noted earlier in this paper, this inequality of opportunity is built into bail statutes that make employment a legal criterion in bail decisions. There also may be limits to how far the state can or should go in making assigned counsel the equivalent of the most expensive and most able of private counsel. In any case, we have not categorized this study as one finding evidence of racial discrimination. What this study does show, however, as have several other studies that consider similar variables (see Lizotte, 1978; Farrell and Swigert, 1978a), is that there are a variety of processual factors, such as the denial of bail and assigned counsel, that can disadvantage offenders who are black or of lower socioeconomic status in the sentencing process. We are now in a position to draw some conclusions.

DISCUSSION AND CONCLUSIONS

The study of sentencing, particularly as it is influenced by the factor of race, is changing. Perhaps most notable among the changes is the increasing tendency for studies of race and sentencing to consider in their designs, at a minimum, the additional legitimized influences of offense seriousness and prior record. Less than half of the studies using data from before 1968 included controls for these variables, while more than three-quarters of the later studies did so. We have argued that the inclusion of such variables marks the beginning of an individual-processual approach in sentencing research. Models based on this approach have steadily expanded the number of variables they consider, commonly including today factors such as bail status, defense counsel, and plea in addition to prior record and offense. As we have seen, all these variables in various ways have been found to mediate the influence of race and socioeconomic status on sentencing (Lizotte, 1978; Clarke and Koch, 1976; Farrell and Swigert, 1978a).

Interestingly, the increased tendency to control for legitimized variables in sentencing studies has not resulted in fewer findings of racial discrimination. In fact, the more recent studies that include these controls are more likely to report discrimination than the older studies with similar controls; the recent studies are equally divided between those that do and do not conclude discrimination. The challenge is to explain why some studies find discrimination while others do not, and why among those studies including controls for legitimized variables the proportion finding discrimination has shown signs of increasing. Our explanation is that with increasing sensitivity, those researchers who find evidence of discrimination have specified for study structural contexts in which discrimination by race is most likely to occur. This type of work marks the emergence of what we have called a structural-contextual approach in sentencing research. It also can be noted that this approach has roots in an earlier period.

In the earlier part of this century a large number of studies both with and without controls for offense and prior record found evidence of racial discrimination in the use of the death penalty, particularly in the South (Bedau, 1964; E. Johnson, 1957; Wolf, 1964; Wolfgang et al., 1962; Wolfgang and Reidel, 1973). Notwithstanding their incomplete control of legitimized variables, many of these studies found such large relationships between race and sentence outcome that it is difficult to imagine that further control would have eliminated evidence of racial discrimination (e.g., Wolfgang and Reidel, 1973; Hagan, 1974a). The use of the death penalty early in this century in the South represents one structural context in which racial discrimination seems clearly to have occurred; however, the declining use of the death penalty in this century has diminished the importance of this context for our immediate concerns. Thus we have focused most of our attention in this review on more recent studies.

Studies with data sets drawn over the last decade have identified a number of structural contexts in which racial discrimination seems to persist. A number of these studies reveal racial discrimination, for example: in rural but not in urban settings (Pope, 1975a; Hagan, 1977); among judges with culturally linked prejudicial attitudes (Gibson, 1978; Hagan, 1975a); for crimes like rape (LaFree, 1980) and robbery (Thomson and Zingraff, 1981) that are interracial (see also Myers, 1979); among highly politicized crimes (e.g., drug felonies, Clark and Koch, 1977) and settings (e.g., draft evasion during the antiwar movement, Hagan and Bernstein, 1979); in cases in which probation officers offer presentence recommen-dations (Myers, 1979; Unnever et al., 1980; Hagan, 1975b); and in conditions that mark the intersection of race and class positions in American society (Lizotte, 1978). In contrast, studies of the last decade that have not found discrimination have focused frequently on settings in which discrimination by race may be least likely to be expected, for example, in large urban jurisdictions (e.g., Bernstein et al., 1977a; Hagan et al., 1980; Eisenstein and Jacob, 1977; McCarthy, 1979; Hagan et al., 1979) and/or in courts that handle large numbers of misdemeanor cases (e.g., Feeley, 1979). These large volume, highly bureaucratized settings, highly characteristic of the American practice of criminal justice, may simply be too constrained by their high visibility, lack of time, and strained resources to allow direct discrimination by race. Said differently, these court settings may be too important symbolically and too bureaucratic organizationally to allow overt discrimination as a frequent occurrence.

Several caveats should be added to our discussion of the significance of structural context in sentencing research. First, it is important to note that the strength of the relationships reported in the recent studies is often not large, in spite of differences in statistical significance. While a few recent studies under specified conditions estimate that black offenders receive sentences of as much as six months to a year longer than white offenders (Lizotte, 1978; Clark and Koch, 1977), the differences found are usually less substantial. In this sense the studies we have reviewed are not as far apart as they otherwise might seem. With the several exceptions noted above, the studies of race and sentencing done over the past decade collectively indicate that the relationship between race and sentence outcomes is relatively weak. To confirm this point, we calculated a bivariate measure of the relationship between race and sentence (either a gamma or Pearson's r) for each of 31 studies with reanalyzable data; the results appear in Appendix A. This bivariate measure represents in linear terms the total effect (direct and indirect) that race could have on sentence in these studies. The measures calculated for the more recent of these studies reveal that this relationship is generally weak. Indeed, the relationships for recent studies generally are weaker than the relationship noted early in this paper between the race of surveyed respondents and their tendency to believe that the courts discriminate by race.

The weakness of the race-sentence relationship is not necessarily surprising. An important feature of the individual-processual approach is its conceptualization of race as an exogenous variable exercising its influence through an extended causal chain that includes such intervening variables as offense type, prior record, bail status, and recommendations by various control agents. Since we ordinarily expect that the largest correlations will occur between adjacent variables in such a chain, and since all of these correlations are assumed to be less than perfect, we should therefore expect that the smallest correlations will occur between those variables that are furthest removed from each other in the causal chain (Blalock, 1964): i.e., race and sentence. It is also important to note that the influence that race may have on earlier decisions such as pretrial detention may be even more punishing that the final sentence imposed (see Feeley, 1979). Meanwhile, the increasing attention that has been given to this causal chain has confirmed that other variables do have a regular and important impact on sentence. In fact, there is considerable evidence to confirm that the closer one gets to sentence in such causal chains, the stronger the observed correlations become. Thus it has been noted that presentence recommendations by probation officers and prosecutors exhibit a substantial relationship to sentence (Hagan, 1975b, 1977; Hagan et al., 1979; Myers, 1979; Unnever et al., 1980) and that judges' perceptions of offense seriousness and offender culpability are very strongly related to sentence (Hogarth, 1971). Indeed, in the latter case the relationships are so strong that one may reasonable begin to question the conceptual and methodological separateness of the independent and dependent variables. Nonetheless, the pattern of relationships is consistent with the type of causal chains implied by the individual-processual approach.

This approach to the issue of race and sentencing is also important because it can alert us to the ways in which mediating variables like employment can be incorporated in a disadvantaging way into the sentencing process. We have noted that employment has a legally mandated role to play in bail decisions and that unemployment, partially because of its role in the denial of release at the bail stage, may have a legitimized influence on sentence. This ambiguity in the class-linked role of bail in sentencing decisions may help to explain how researchers, sometimes working with the same data (Eisenstein and Jacob, 1977; Lizotte, 1978) and sometimes finding similar patterns in different data (compare Lizotte, 1978, with Clark and Koch, 1977) can reach quite different conclusions about whether racial discrimination has occurred. By clarifying these kinds of linkages, the individual-processual approach can make these issues explicit and open up to scrutiny the way in which race and class-linked mediating variables like employment and bail status can become legitimized influences on sentencing.

Having indicated in several ways the importance of the individual-processual approach and its contributions to research on race and sentencing, we end by reemphasizing the crucial role of a structural-contextual approach in stimulating and organizing future work. There is an understandable tendency in following an individual-processual approach to see all issues of race and sentencing in microlevel terms that emphasize the stages through which individual cases are processed, ignoring the location of individual cases and the courts in which they are processed in the larger social world. This is not to say that studying the consequences of processing cases through various stages of a criminal justice system is unimportant. We noted early in this paper that the selection of samples at different stages of the criminal justice process can lead to important differences in findings and their interpretations.

Furthermore, research promises to become increasingly sophisticated as this issue is addressed as a problem of sample selection bias (see Klepper et al., in this volume). This kind of approach draws our attention to the fact that insofar as at each stage of the court process cases are selected for, and deselected from, further consideration on a nonrandom basis, the sample of cases transmitted to the next stage will be further removed in some systematic way from the original population of concern. The implication is that data sets drawn at late stages of the criminal justice system may produce biased estimates of influences, including that of race, on sentencing. This may even be one reason why the measured influence of race on sentencing is small. Once one begins to consider what these nonrandom sources of

sample selection are, one has to admit that among them
are the variable characteristics of the settings in which
the selection processes occur. Indeed, variation in the
selection process across variable structural contexts is
an intriguing and important topic for study. Ignoring
this kind of structural variation would simply constitute
a macrolevel source of sample selection bias.

The important research on race and sentencing of the
future will involve individual-processual analyses of the
sentencing process that are also able to take the types
of structural and contextual variation we have discussed
into account. This research will require data that allow
consideration not only of the characteristics of
individuals and their cases as they move through the
criminal justice system, but also of the structural and
contextual conditions in which they are processed; in
other words, data collected on individual offenders
across stages and settings. This kind of data is costly
to collect but necessary for full consideration of the
types of theoretical issues we have raised. Sentencing
is an outcome of the contextualized processes in which it
occurs.

TABLE A-1 Empirical Studies of Sentencing in the United States

Study	Years and Location	Sample Size and Type	Sentence Measure	Offense Attributes	Offender Attributes	Case-Processing Attributes	Contextual Attributes	Association of Race and Sentence[a]	n	General Findings
Atkinson and Newman (1970)	1969, Midwestern city	674 misdemeanor to felony cases	sentence type	crime type	residence, age, birthplace, race, sex, employment	counsel presence	judge	G = -.35	410	lenience for younger persons, women, homeowners, employed, and slight lenience for blacks; variations among judges
Baab and Furgeson (1968)	1966, 4 areas of Texas	1,720 felonies	type and length of sentence	crime type	prior record, age, marital status, sex, education, race	judge-jury plea, counsel, pretrial detention	court	r = .00	1,720	pretrial detention, presence of counsel, and trial court all influence sentence; prior record, offense type, and sex are also influential
Bedau (1964)	1907-1956, New Jersey	232 persons sentenced to death	execution versus commutation	crime type	sex, prior record, race, nativity, age, occupation	mandatory versus discretionary death penalty, appeal	county, year	G = .36	191	differential treatment by race more prominent in earlier years; blacks have benefited least from jury discretion and gained from appellate courts; being male, felony murder, and prior record influence outcomes
Bedau (1965)	1903-1964, Oregon	92 persons sentenced	execution versus commutation	crime type	race, native-born, age, occupation, prior record, victim characteristics	counsel, mandatory versus discretionary death penalty, appeal	county, year	G = .10	81	death sentences received by nonwhites follow the general pattern found for native-born whites

Study	Sample/Location	Sample size	Dependent variable	Offense	Independent variables	Control	Other controls	Statistic	N	Findings
Bensing and Schroeder (1960)	1947-1953, Cuyahoga County, Ohio	462 felonious homicides	probation versus other sanctions	homicide type	race, sex, age	type of adjudication	--	G = .06	462	no statistical evidence of race discrimination
Bernstein, Kelly, and Doyle (1977a)	1974-1975, New York City	1,213 felonies	sentence severity scale	severity, type, and numbers of arraignment and arrest charges, possesion of weapons, resisting arrest	race, ethnicity, age, employment, prior record, time since arrest	pretrial release status, reduction of charges	--	r = .05	1,213	age, education, employment stability, marital status have small effects, with whites receiving slightly longer sentences than blacks
Bowers (1974)	1864-1967, all executions in United States with data available	5,707 executions	distributions of persons executed	offense type	race, age	appeals prior to executions	region, period, mandatory versus discretionary death penalty	--	--	blacks particularly in the South were executed for less serious crimes--notably rape--than whites
Bullock (1961)	1958, Texas	3,644 burglary, rape, and murder cases	sentence length dichotomized	offense type	race	plea	region, degree of urbanization	G = .08	3,644	black offenders were apparently underpenalized for one type of offense and overpenalized for another
Burke and Turk (1975)	1964, Indianapolis	3,941 male arrests	no court through prison	offense type	age, race, occupational status, prior incarceration	--	--	--	--	class-linked behavior variations rather than discriminatory treatment create differences in dispositions
Cargan and Coates (1974)	1971-1972, Montgomery County, Ohio, common pleas court	721 convictions	sentence severity scale	crime type	race	--	judge	G = .04	721	overall, there is little sentencing disparity by race, but judges differ significantly in their sentencing of blacks and whites

TABLE A-1 (Cont.)

Study	Years and Location	Sample Size and Type	Sentence Measure	Offense Attributes	Offender Attributes	Case-Processing Attributes	Contextual Attributes	Association of Race and Sentence[a]	n	General Findings
Chiricos and Waldo (1975)	1967-1970, North and South Carolina, Florida	10,488 inmates	sentence length	offense severity	socioeconomic status, race, prior record, age	--	urbanization	--	--	correlation analysis between socioeconomic status and sentence length for specific crimes yields few significant relationships
Clarke and Koch (1976)	1971, North Carolina	798 burglary, breaking and entering, and larceny cases	prison versus other sanctions	offense type, arrest time	age, race, income, employment, prior arrests	--	--	$G = .31$	798	income influences chances of receiving prison sentence, while race, employment, and age have no important effects; offense charged and prior record are important influences
Clarke and Koch (1977)	1974-1976, Alaska	860 felony counts against 683 defendants	sentence length	offense type	socioeconomic status, record	basis of conviction	--	--	--	drug offenses were distinguishable from all other offense classes in that many socioeconomic considerations not related to degree of culpability or prior criminal history contributed substantially to sentence length
Conklin (1972)	1964 and 1968	405 robbery cases	sentence type	loss, injury, and role of victim	race, prior record, age	--	court	$G = .21$ $G = -.14$	77 93	race has weak and inconsistent relationship with disposition; more important are district in which tried, prior incarceration, and role of victim

Study	Year, place	Sample	Dependent measure					Statistic	N	Findings
Cook (1979)	1972, United States	1,852 draft offenders and 304 judges	sentence severity scale	--	--	plea	number of draft cases, judge characteristics, population, political environment	--	--	public opinion explains more of the variation in sentencing than case attributes
Eisenstein and Jacob (1977)	1972-1973, Baltimore, Chicago, and Detroit	2,809 indicted defendants	type and length of sentence	offense type and evidence strength	grouped defendant characteristics	mode and stage of disposition	identity of courtroom	--	--	identity of courtroom and offense charged explain most in all three cities
Farrell and Swigert (1978a, 1978b)	1955-1973, Northeastern United States	444 murder cases	conviction severity	--	age, race, sex, prior conviction severity, occupational prestige	private attorney, bail, jury, trial, legal resources	--	r = .03	444	lower-class defendants, independent of prior record, receive more severe dispositions; explanations of effects of social status need to take into account the stereotype "effects of criminal conceptions on legal treatment"
Feeley (1979)	1932, New Haven	843 circuit court cases	sentence severity scale	offense seriousness, number, and charge type	sex, race, age, victim, record	plea, attorney, number of appearances, bail status	judge, type of prosecutor	--	--	differences in sentences are not attributable to the seriousness of the charge, record, race, sex, or age
Garfinkel (1949)	1930-1940, North Carolina	1,067 homicides	type and length of sentence	severity of conviction charge	race of offenders and victims	--	--	G = -.22	1,067	intraracial homicides involving blacks victimizing whites meet with differential severity; interracial homicides result in differential leniency
Gerard and Terry (1970)	1962, 3 Missouri counties	203 convictions	sentence type	offense	race, age	bail, jury, verdict, attorney type	--	G = .27	203	for homicide, rape, and burglary an equal proportion of whites and blacks sent to prison; for every other less serious crime type, a higher proportion of blacks receive prison sentences

TABLE A-1 (Cont.)

Study	Years and Location	Sample Size and Type	Sentence Measure	Offense Attributes	Offender Attributes	Case-Processing Attributes	Contextual Attributes	Association of Race and Sentence[a]	n	General Findings
Gibson (1978)	1968-1970, Atlanta	1,219 felony indictments	sentence severity—above and below mean	offense seriousness	prior record, race	--	individual judge, attorney	G = .03	984	with separate "index of discrimination" for each judge, 3 of 11 judges treat blacks more severely
Green (1961)	1956-1957, Philadelphia	1,437 misdemeanors and felonies	sentence severity scale of categories	offense, number of indictments	sex, race, age, prior record	plea	prosecutor, judge	G = .03	1,425	patterns of criminal behavior mediate any influence of sex, age, or race on sentence; disparity among judges great in cases of intermediate gravity
Green (1964)	1956-1957, Philadelphia	116 robberies, 291 burglaries	type and length of sentence	offense type	race of offender and victim, number of indictments, prior convictions	--	--	G = .16	275	sentence differences by race of offender function of behavioral differences
Hagan and Bernstein (1979)	1963-1976, American city	238 draft cases	sentence type	offense	race, education, record, resistance	plea, presentence report	judge, time period	--	--	blacks received more severe punishment than whites during coercive era, less severe treatment during cooptive era
Hagan, Hewitt, and Alwin (1979)[b]	1973, King County, Washington	1,832 felonies	sentence severity	offense severity, prior record, weapon or violence	sex, race, work history, family integration	bail, plea, prosecutor's and probation officer's recommendation	--	G = .21	505	race effects are indirect; being female, white, having stable work history and family ties decrease the likelihood of incarceration; offense characteristic with the largest effect is prior record

Study	Years, Place	Sample	Dependent Variable	Offense Controls	Offender Variables	Process Variables	Other	Statistic	N	Findings
Hagan, Nagel, and Albonetti (1980)	1974-1977, 10 federal district courts	6,562 misdemeanors and felonies	sentence severity scale	statutory seriousness, number of charges	race, sex, age, employment, prior record	plea, charge reduction	districts categorized as proactive and reactive	r = -.04 r = -.08	694 5,868	proactive districts exhibit a unique leniency in the sentencing of college-educated white-collar criminals that is related to earlier plea and charging decisions
Hall and Simkus (1975)	1966-1972, Western state	1,745 probationary sentences for felonies	types of probation	offense type	prior felonies, sex, juvenile record, age, education, employment, occupation, marital status, ethnicity, dependents	--	judge	--	--	Native Americans (Indians) are more likely to receive sentences (incarceration) with higher degree of stigmatization
E. Johnson (1957)	1909-1954, North Carolina	650 convicted offenders on death row	execution	offense type	race, occupation	--	--	G = .30	650	blacks more likely to be executed than whites, but some narrowing of gap over time
Judson et al. (1969)	1958-1966, California	238 first-degree murder cases	life versus death sentence	--	race, age, education, sex, motive, occupation, employment, prior record	defense used, testimony, publicity, jury composition, length of deliberation, counsel	place of trial, year of trial	G = -.14	209	blue-collar offenders get worse treatment than white-collar offenders; prior criminal record is a very strong influence on outcome; no bias by race of offender and victim
Kelly (1976)	1974, Oklahoma	2,090 convicts	sentence length	crime type	age, marital status, education, prior record	plea, type of defense, attorney	--	--	--	racial differences greater for burglary than homicide
LaFree (1980)	1970-1975, large Midwestern city	881 forcible sex offenses	sentence type and length	offense type, eyewitness, weapon	racial composition, criminal record, age	--	--	--	--	lenience for black suspect-black victim and differential severity for black suspect-black victim

TABLE A-1 (Cont.)

Study	Years and Location	Sample Size and Type	Sentence Measure	Offense Attributes	Offender Attributes	Case-Processing Attributes	Contextual Attributes	Association of Race and Sentence[a]	n	General Findings
Lemert and Rosberg (1948)	1938, Los Angeles County	914 felonies	sentence type	offense type	race, prior record	--	--	$G = .54$	504	blacks receive longer sentences than whites, particularly when stereotyped as criminals (i.e., prior record); Mexicans receive more severe treatment for auto theft, the crime for which they are most frequently convicted
Levin (1972)	1959–1965, Minneapolis 1960–1965, Pittsburgh respectively	2,513 and 4,324 cases respectively	percent probation and length of incarceration	--	race, age, prior record	plea	local culture	--	--	sentencing decisions are more favorable to blacks in Pittsburgh than in Minneapolis--absolutely and relatively to whites
Lizotte (1978)	1971, Chicago	816 trial court cases	sentence length	offense seriousness	race, occupation, prior record	bail amount, success of legal counsel	--	$r = .03$	816	nonwhites and those of lower occupational prestige are less likely to make bail, resulting in longer prison sentence
Martin (1934)	1930, 25 counties in Texas	927 felonies	sentence type	property versus person offenses	race, sex, age, education, nativity, occupation, marital status	--	--	$G = .44$	823	blacks receive more severe treatment, as do young offenders and those with prior records
McCarthy, Sheflin, and Barraco (1979)	1976–1977, New Jersey	15,000 cases	type and length of sentence	offense type	prior record, race, employment, family history	plea, recommendations	--	--	--	racially different but otherwise similar offenders convicted of similar offenses receive similar sentences

Study										
Myers (1979)	1974-1976, Indianapolis	980 felonies involving individual offenders	sentence type	conviction charge, offender-victim characteristics	sex, age, prior record, racial composition	probation officer's recommendation, counsel type, pretrial release	--	--	--	lighter sentences for blacks convicted of victimizing blacks in comparison to white versus white and black versus white dispositions
Mileski (1971)	1969, midsized Eastern city	292 lower court cases	sentence type	offense seriousness	race, prior record	--	--	--	--	race differences for disposition in intoxication cases follow no consistent pattern that could be called discriminatory
Nagel (1969)	50 states, federal courts	2,930 larceny and assault cases	sentence type	offense type	race, record	--	--	--	--	--
Nardulli (1979)	1972-1973, Chicago	429 trial court dispositions	sentences by plea and trial	offense seriousness	socioeconomic status, arrest record	trial type, indictment delay, motions requested, plea bargaining	judge and prosecutor	--	--	overall, those who go to trial are more severely sanctioned, with jury trials leading to more severe sanctions than bench trials; offense and prior record are important influences
Pattington (1965)	1908-1963, Virginia	1,513 rape cases	type and length of sentence	offense type	race of offender and victim	appeal	year of sentence	G = .43	1,513	blacks received more severe treatment
Pattridge and Eldridge (1974)	1974, second circuit district judges	1,442 judges	simulation of 20 criminal cases	--	addict, prior conviction, blue or white collar	probation recommendations, trial or guilty plea	district, judge	--	--	no significant differences by recommendation, addiction, method of conviction, or socioeconomic status; significant difference by prior record
Perry (1977)	1972, United States	naval and marine offenders	sentence length	class of offense	race	--	--	--	--	no significant black-white differential in any of the four offense cases examined

TABLE A-1 (Cont.)

Study	Years and Location	Sample Size and Type	Sentence Measure	Offense Attributes	Offender Attributes	Case-Processing Attributes	Contextual Attributes	Association of Race and Sentence[a]	n	General Findings
Pope (1975a)	1969-1971, 12 California counties	5,184 burglary, 3,155 assault cases	sentence type	offense type	race, sex, age, prior record, criminal status	--	urban versus rural, lower versus superior court	G = -.03	4,362	prior record and criminal status and, to a lesser extent, sex were most closely associated with sentence outcome, whereas racial differences proved negligible after controlling for prior record
Pope (1975b)	1969-1971, 12 California counties	32,694 lower and superior court cases	type and length of sentence	offense type	sex, race, age, prior record, criminal status	--	urban versus rural, lower versus superior court	G = .16	16,849	rural courts tend to sentence blacks more severely than whites at both lower and superior court levels
Rhodes (1976)	1970, U.S. district courts in Minnesota	--	sentence severity	--	percent under 21, prior record	--	prosecutor's resources, availability of counsel, court delay, district	--	--	there is an inverse relationship between the volume of plea bargaining and the severity of sentences for guilty pleas
Shane-Dubow (1979)	1974-1975, Wisconsin	2,627 felonies	type and length of sentence	offense type, weapon, victim	race, sex, age, education, employment, prior record	attorney, bail status, recommendations	county	--	--	district attorney recommendation, judges, and record most influential in determining sentence severity
Thomson and Zingraff (1981)	1969, 1973, and 1977, Southeastern state	251, 441, and 502 armed robbery cases	length of sentence	--	race, prior incarceration, education, occupation	number of cases	time, jurisdiction	--	--	when disaggregated by years in 1977 both prior incarceration and race have direct effects on sentence length

Study	Sample	Dependent variable	Offense variables	Defendant variables	Process variables	Decision-maker	Statistic	N	Findings
Tiffany, Avichai, and Peters (1975)	1967-1968, federal courts	1,248 federal trial cases	sentence severity scale	offense type	age, race, prior record	counsel type, conviction type	--	--	--	race has impact on sentence for first offenders only; offense seriousness and prior record have strong effects
Uhlman (1979)c	1968-1974, Northeastern urban center	18,772 trial court dispositions	sentence severity scale	offense severity, number of charges	race	bail amount, bail status, counsel, method of disposition	judge	G = .10	30,492	race differences with other variables held constant; charge has strong effect and bail status is an important mediator of class/status effects
Unnever, Frazier, and Henretta (1980)	1972-1973, 6-county Florida judicial district	229 cases with pre-sentence report	sentence severity	offense severity	age, race, sex, employment, marital status, education, prior record	recommendations of police, district attorney, and probation officer	--	--	--	race, youth, and unemployment have effects with other variables controlled; arrest severity but not prior record have significaint effect after controlling for other variables
Wolf (1964)	1937-1961, New Jersey	159 capital crimes	life versus death sentence	offense type, weapon	race, age	--	--	G = .35	159	blacks receive harsher treatment than whites, even when other variables controlled
Wolfgang and Reidel (1973)	1945-1965, Southern states	1,265 rape cases	death versus other sentences	various offense character-istics	age, prior record, employment, victim characteristics	plea, counsel	states	G = .86	1,265	death sentences imposed on blacks more frequently than whites, particularly blacks with white victims
Wolfgang et al. (1962)	1914-1958, Pennsylvania	439 offenders on death row	executed versus commuted	murder type	age, race, nativity, occupation	counsel type, reason for commutation	--	G = .32	410	blacks have not received equal consideration for commutation of the death penalty
Zalman et al. (1979)	1977, Michigan	6,000 felonies	type and length of sentence	offense type, weapon, motive, victim injury	race, education	attorney, recommendations of probation officers	judge	--	--	results indicate the presence of disparity in felony sentencing by race and geographical area

TABLE A-1 (Cont.)

Study	Years and Location	Sample Size and Type	Sentence Measure	Offense Attributes	Offender Attributes	Case-Processing Attributes	Contextual Attributes	Association of Race and Sentence[a]	n	General Findings
Zimring, Eigen, and O'Malley (1976)	1970, Philadelphia	170 murder cases	minimum sentence	--	race	plea, jury	--	G = .70	36	black defendants who murder white victims receive life or death sentences twice as often as black defendants with black victims

[a]Bivariate measure of the association of race and sentence (either a gamma or Pearson's r).
[b]See also Lotz and Hewitt (1977).
[c]See also Uhlman and Walker (1979, 1980).

REFERENCES

Atkinson, David N., and Dale A. Newman
    1970 Judicial attitudes and defendant attributes:
          some consequences for municipal court
          decision-making. Journal of Public Law 19:68-87.
Baab, G.A., and W.R. Furgeson, Jr.
    1968 Texas sentencing practices: a statistical
          study. Texas Law Review 45:471-503.
Balbus, Isaac D.
    1973 The Dialectics of Legal Repression: Black
          Rebels Before the American Criminal Courts. New
          York: Russell Sage Foundation.
Bedau, Hugo Adam
    1964 Death sentences in New Jersey. Rutgers Law
          Review 19:1-2.
    1965 Capital punishment in Oregon 1903-1964. Oregon
          Law Review 45:1-39.
Bensing, Robert C., and Oliver J. Schroeder
    1960 Homicide in an Urban Community. Springfield,
          Ill.: Charles Thomas.
Bernstein, Ilene Nagel, William R. Kelly, and Patricia A.
Doyle
    1977a Societal reaction to deviants: the case of
          criminal defendants. American Sociological
          Review 42:743-755.
Bernstein, Ilene Nagel, Edward Kick, Jan T. Lehng, and
Barbara Schultz
    1977b Charge reduction: an intermediary stage in the
          process of labelling. Social Force
          56(2):362-384.
Black, Donald
    1976 The Behavior of Law. New York: Academic Press.
Blalock, Hubert
    1964 Causal Inferences in Nonexperimental Research.
          New York: Norton.
Blau, Peter, and Otis D. Duncan
    1967 The American Occupational Structure. New York:
          Wiley.
Blumstein, Alfred, and Jacqueline Cohen
    1980 Sentencing of convicted offenders: an analysis
          of the public's view. Law & Society Review
          14(2):223-261.
Bonnie, Richard, and Charles Whitebread
    1974 The Marihuana Conviction: A History of
          Marihuana Prohibition in the United States.
          Charlottesville: University Press of Virginia.

Bowers, William J.
  1974 Executions in America. Lexington, Mass.: D.C.
        Heath.
Box, George E.P., and Gwilym M. Jenkins
  1970 Time Series Analysis: Forecasting and Control.
        San Francisco: Holden-Day.
Bullock, H.A.
  1961 Significance of the racial factor in the length
        of prison sentences. Journal of Criminal Law,
        Criminology and Police Science 52:411-417.
Burke, Peter, and Austin T. Turk
  1975 Factors affecting postarrest dispositions: a
        model for analysis. Social Problems 22:313-332.
Cargan, Leonard, and Mary A. Coates
  1974 Indeterminate sentence and judicial bias. Crime
        & Delinquency 20:144-56.
Chiricos, Theodore G., and Gordon P. Waldo
  1975 Socioeconomic status and criminal sentencing:
        an empirical assessment of a conflict
        proposition. American Sociological Review
        40:753-772.
Clarke, Stevens H., and Gary G. Koch
  1976 The influence of income and other factors on
        whether criminal defendants go to prison. Law &
        Society Review 11:57-92.
  1977 Alaska Felony Sentencing Patterns: A
        Multivariate Statistical Analysis. Alaska
        Judicial Council, Anchorage.
Conklin, John E.
  1972 Robbery and the Criminal Justice System.
        Philadelphia: Lippincott.
Cook, Beverly B.
  1979 Public opinion and federal judicial policy.
        American Journal of Political Science 21:567-600.
Duncan, Otis D.
  1961 A socioeconomic index for all occupations. Pp.
        109-138 in A.J. Reiss, Jr., O.D. Duncan, P.K.
        Hatt, and C.C. North, eds., Occupations and
        Social Status. Glencoe, Ill.: Free Press.
Eisenstein, James, and Herbert Jacob
  1977 Felony Justice. Boston: Little, Brown.
Farrell, Ronald A., and Victoria Lynn Swigert
  1978a Prior offense as a self-fulfilling prophecy.
        Law & Society Review 12:437-453.
  1978b Legal disposition of inter-group and intra-group
        homicides. Sociological Quarterly 19:565-576.

49

Featherman, David
  1980 Social stratification and mobility: two decades
        of cumulative social science. American
        Behavioral Scientist 24(3):364-385.
Feeley, Malcolm M.
  1979 The Process is the Punishment: Handling Cases
        in a Lower Criminal Court. New York: Russell
        Sage Foundation.
Garfinkel, Harold
  1949 Research note on inter- and intra-racial
        homicides. Social Forces 27:369-381.
Gerard, Jules, and T.R. Terry
  1970 Discrimination against Negroes in the
        administration of criminal law in Missouri.
        Washington University Law Quarterly 1970:415-437.
Gibson, James L.
  1978 Race as a determinant of criminal sentences: a
        methodological critique and a case study. Law &
        Society Review 12:455-478.
Green, Edward
  1961 Judicial Attitudes in Sentencing: A Study of
        the Factors Underlying the Sentencing Practices
        of the Criminal Court of Philadelphia. Vol. 15,
        Cambridge Studies in Criminology. London:
        Macmillan.
  1964 Inter- and intra-racial crime relative to
        sentencing. Journal of Criminal Law,
        Criminology and Police Science 55:348-358.
Greenberg, David F.
  1977 Socioeconomic status and criminal sentences: is
        there an association? American Sociological
        Review 42:174-176.
Hagan, John
  1974a Extra-legal attributes and criminal sentencing:
        an assessment of a sociological viewpoint. Law
        & Society Review 8(spring):357-383.
  1974b Criminal justice and native people: a study of
        incarceration in a Canadian province. Canadian
        Review of Sociology and Anthropology. Special
        issue published in conjunction with the
        International Sociological Association Meetings
        (August):220-238.
  1975a Law, order and sentencing: a study of attitude
        in action. Sociometry 38(2):374-384.
  1975b The social and legal construction of criminal
        justice: a study of the pre-sentencing
        process. Social Problems 22(5):620-637.

1975c Parameters of criminal prosecution: an application of path analysis to a problem of criminal justice. Journal of Criminal Law, Criminology and Police Science 65:536-544.

1977 Criminal justice in rural and urban communities: a study of the bureaucratization of justice. Social Forces 55(3):597-612.

1982 The corporate advantage: a study of the involvement of corporate and individual victims in the criminal justice system. Social Forces 60(4):993-1022.

Hagan, John, and Celesta Albonetti
1982 Race, class and the perception of criminal injustice in America. American Journal of Sociology 88(2):329-355.

Hagan, John, and Ilene Bernstein
1979 Conflict in context: the sanctioning of draft resisters, 1963-76. Social Problems 27:109-122.

Hagan, John, John Hewitt, and Duane Alwin
1979 Ceremonial justice: crime and punishment in a loosely coupled system. Social Forces 58(2):506-527.

Hagan, John, Ilene Nagel, and Celesta Albonetti
1980 The differential sentencing of white collar offenders in ten federal district courts. American Sociological Review 45(October):802-820.

Hall, E.L., and A.A. Simkus
1975 Inequality in the types of sentences received by native Americans and whites. Criminology 13:199-222.

Hauser, Robert
1970 Context and consex: a cautionary tale. American Journal of Sociology 75:645-664.

Hogarth, John
1971 Sentencing as a Human Process. Toronto: University of Toronto Press.

Hopkins, Andrew
1977 Is there a class bias in criminal sanctioning? American Sociological Review 42:176-177.

Inter-University Consortium for Political and Social Research
1979 Public Image of the Courts, 1977: General Publics Data. Ann Arbor, Mich.: Inter-University Consortium for Political and Social Research.

Johnson, Elmer H.
1957 Selective forces in capital punishment. Social
Forces 36:165-169.
Judson, Charles J., James J. Pandell, Jack B. Owens,
James L. McIntosh, and Dale L. Matschullat
1969 A study of the California penalty jury in first
degree murder cases. Stanford Law Review
21:1297-1431.
Kalleberg, Arne, and Aage B. Sorensen
1979 The sociology of labor markets. Annual Review
of Sociology 5:351-379.
Kelly, Henry E.
1976 Comparison of defense strategy and race as
influences in differential sentencing.
Criminology 14:241-249.
LaFree, Gary
1980 The effect of sexual stratification by race on
official reactions to rape. American
Sociological Review 45:842-854.
Lemert, Edwin M., and Judy Rosberg
1948 The Administration of Justice to Minority Groups
in L.A. County. Berkeley, Calif.: University
of California Press.
Levin, Martin A.
1972 Urban politics and judicial behavior. Journal
of Legal Studies 1:220-221.
1977 Urban Politics and the Criminal Courts.
Chicago: University of Chicago Press.
Lizotte, Alan J.
1978 Extra-legal factors in Chicago's criminal
courts: testing the conflict model of criminal
justice. Social Problems 25:564-580.
Lotz, Roy, and John D. Hewitt
1977 The influence of legally irrelevant factors on
felony sentencing. Sociological Inquiry
47:39-48.
Martin, Roscoe
1934 The Defendant and Criminal Justice. Bulletin
No. 34-37. Bureau of Research in the Social
Sciences, University of Texas.
McCarthy, J.P., N. Sheflin, and J.J. Barraco
1979 Report on the Sentencing Guidelines Project to
the Administrative Director of the Courts: On
the Relationship Between Race and Sentencing.
Sentencing Guidelines Project, State of New
Jersey Administrative Office of the Courts,
Trenton.

Mileski, Maureen
    1971 Courtroom encounters: an observation of a lower
          criminal court. Law & Society Review 5:473-538.
Musto, David
    1973 The American Disease. New Haven, Conn.: Yale
          University Press.
Myers, Martha A.
    1979 Offended parties and official reactions:
          victims and the sentencing of criminal
          defendants. Sociological Quarterly 20:529-540.
Nagel, Stuart
    1969 The Legal Process From a Behavioral
          Perspective. Homewood, Ill.: Dorsey Press.
Nam, C.B., and M. Powers
    1968 Changes in the relative status level of workers
          in the United States, 1950-1960. Social Forces
          47:158-170.
Nardulli, Peter
    1979 The Courtroom Elite. New York: Ballinger.
Partington, Donald
    1965 The incidence of the death penalty for rape in
          Virginia. Washington and Lee Law Review
          22:43-75.
Partridge, Anthony, and William B. Eldridge
    1974 Second Circuit Sentencing Study: A Report to
          the Judges of the Second Circuit. FJC No.
          74-4. Washington, D.C.: The Federal Judicial
          Center.
Perry, R.W.
    1977 Justice system and sentencing: the importance
          of race in the military. Criminology 15:225-234.
Pope, Carl E.
    1975a Sentencing of California Felony Offenders.
          National Criminal Justice Information and
          Statistics Service. Washington, D.C.: U.S.
          Department of Justice.
    1975b The Judicial Processing of Assault and Burglary
          Offenders in Selected California Counties.
          National Criminal Justice Information Statistics
          Service. Washington, D.C.: U.S. Department of
          Justice.
Rhodes, William M.
    1976 The economics of criminal courts: a theoretical
          and empirical investigation. Journal of Legal
          Studies 5:311-340.

Robinson, Robert V., and Jonathan Kelley
1979 Class as conceived by Marx and Dahrendorf:
effects on income inequality and politics in the
United States and Great Britain. American
Sociological Review 44:38-58.
Sellin, Thorsten, and Marvin E. Wolfgang
1964 The Measurement of Delinquency. New York:
Wiley.
Shane-Dubow, Sandra
1979 Felony Sentencing in Wisconsin. Wisconsin
Center for Public Policy (Mimeo).
Thomson, Randall J., and Matthew T. Zingraff
1981 Detecting sentence disparity: some problems and
evidence. American Journal of Sociology
86:869-880.
Tiffany, Lawrence, Yakov Avichai, and Geoffrey W. Peters
1975 A statistical analysis of sentencing in federal
courts: defendants convicted after trial,
1967-1968. The Journal of Legal Studies
4:369-390.
Treiman, D.
1977 Occupational Prestige in Comparative
Perspective. New York: Academic Press.
Uhlman, Thomas M.
1979 Racial Justice: Black Judges and Defendants in
an Urban Trial Court. Lexington, Mass.:
Lexington Books.
Uhlman, Thomas M., and N. Darlene Walker
1979 A plea is no bargain: the impact of case
disposition on sentencing. Social Science
Quarterly 60:218-324.
1980 "He takes some of my time; I take some of his:"
an analysis of judicial sentencing patterns in
jury cases. Law & Society Review 14:323-341.
U.S. Bureau of the Census
1963 Methodology and Scores of Socioeconomic Status.
Working Paper No. 15. Washington, D.C.: U.S.
Department of Commerce.
Unnever, James D., Charles Frazier, and John C. Henretta
1980 Race differences in criminal sentencing.
Sociological Quarterly 21:197-207.
Wolf, Edwin D.
1964 Abstract of analysis of jury sentencing in
capital cases. Rutgers Law Review 19:56-64.

Wolfgang, Marvin E., and Marc Reidel
  1973 Race, judicial discretion, and the death
        penalty. The Annals of the American Academy of
        Political and Social Science 407:119-133.
Wolfgang, Marvin E., Robert Figlio, and Thorsten Sellin
  1972 Delinquency in a Birth Cohort. Chicago:
        University of Chicago Press.
Wolfgang, Marvin E., Arlene Kelly, and Hans C. Nolde
  1962 Comparison of the executed and commuted among
        admissions to death row. Journal of Criminal
        Law, Criminology and Police Science 53:301-311.
Wright, Erik Olin
  1980 Varieties of Marxist conceptions of class
        structure. Politics and Society 9(3):299-322.
Zalman, Marvin, Charles W. Ostrom, Jr., Phillip
Guilliams, and Garret Peaslee
  1979 Sentencing in Michigan: Report on the Michigan
        Felony Sentencing Project. Michigan State Court
        Administrative Office, Lansing.
Zimring, Franklin E., Joel Eigen, and Sheila O'Malley
  1976 Punishing homicide in Philadelphia:
        perspectives on the death penalty. University
        of Chicago Law Review 43:227-252.

2

Discrimination in the Criminal Justice System: A Critical Appraisal of the Literature

Steven Klepper, Daniel Nagin, and Luke-Jon Tierney

INTRODUCTION

Discrimination in the criminal justice system is an issue of substantial social concern. The discretionary powers of the principal actors--the police, prosecutors, and judges--are considerable and allow ample latitude for unfair treatment of persons of a specific race or social background. A large empirical literature has emerged concerning the extent of discrimination in the criminal justice process. These studies examine separately or in combination the effect of race or social class on the likelihood of arrest, prosecution, bail, conviction, and the type and severity of sentence. The findings of the studies are by no means consistent. Some find evidence of discrimination while others do not.

In this paper we argue that there are major flaws in the literature we have reviewed that limit its usefulness for making inferences about the extent of discrimination in the criminal justice system. We also suggest research strategies to remedy these weaknesses. Our critique and suggestions are prompted by a review of 10 papers, chosen by the panel on the basis of their salience in the literature and their quality, as well as a number of additional papers.

While our paper is based on a review of a small sample of studies, we are confident that our conclusions apply generally to the larger literature. First, to some degree our criticisms apply to all of the studies reviewed, which makes it unlikely that they do not apply to the larger literature. Second, implementation of several of our recommendations requires the use of statistical methods that have only recently been developed and are not yet widely employed. Third, implementation of these statistical procedures requires the use of modeling approaches that have not been widely adopted in the criminological and sociological literature.

Our review suggests three major remediable flaws in the literature:

(1) The Absence of Formal Models of Processing Decisions in the Criminal Justice System Case disposition--whether it is dismissal, acquittal, conviction, or sentencing--is the consequence of the interplay of a diverse set of actors, each with individual objectives. Even if a disposition does not directly involve one of these actors, expectations about their actions if they were to become involved may affect decisions. For example, a prosecutor may choose to dismiss a case based on the expectation that a judge will do the same if the case is prosecuted. Similarly, a defendant may choose to accept a plea bargain on the basis of an expectation of the likelihood of conviction at a jury trial and the sentence if convicted.

In order to model decisions at each stage of the criminal justice system, a theory of the important decision criteria of each of the major actors and their interaction is required. Without such a theory, estimating equations are likely to be misspecified, which in turn is likely to result in serious biases in the estimated effects of included variables and an inability to discern the effects of more subtle influences. The latter is particularly pertinent to measuring the effects of social class and race because their influence, while possibly of sufficient magnitude to warrant concern, are probably less important in affecting disposition than clearly legally relevant variables like case quality and the seriousness of the crime. Perhaps even more important is that without a well-structured theory, inferences about the role of social status and other factors at each processing stage may be extremely misleading. For example, an observation that social status affects sentences in negotiated pleas may not reflect prosecutorial bias but rather the biases of judges or juries. We regard this point as crucial because implementation of policies to rectify any undesirable effects of race and social status on disposition requires a knowledge of the stage(s) of the criminal justice system at which these factors are important.

(2) <u>Sample Selection Biases Resulting from Screening and Processing Decisions</u> The criminal justice system has been likened to a leaky sieve. In Washington, D.C., for example, of every 100 felony arrests only 13 result in felony convictions. Of the remaining 87, 16 result in misdemeanor convictions. Nearly all the rest are rejected for further processing at an initial screening or subsequently dismissed by a prosecutor, judge, or grand jury. Of those convicted only about 32 percent are incarcerated (Forst et al., 1977). Thus, cases that reach the sentencing stage are a very select group that typically represent only a small proportion of the population of "similar" cases (e.g., same arrest charges) that originally entered the system. Moreover, even those cases entering the system via an arrest are themselves a selected sample of crimes. In most major metropolitan areas, clearance rates (crimes solved by the police, typically by the arrest of a suspect) hover around 20 percent. This low clearance rate principally reflects the absence of any suspect but is also affected by the exercise of arrest discretion by the police.

By the very nature of the system, analyses of the determinants of sentence must be executed on a selected sample of cases, namely those that have resulted in conviction. Since the selection process is by no means random, it may induce serious biases in parameter estimates of included variables. Such biases may, for example, result in an inappropriate conclusion that racial considerations influence sentencing decisions when in fact they do not. Recently developed econometric procedures can be employed in some circumstances to cope with the biases induced by sample selection.

(3) <u>Use of Arbitrary Scales to Measure Qualitatively Different Dispositions</u> A case may be disposed by dismissal or acquittal. For convictions, possible sentences include fines, probation, and prison or some combination of these at a specified amount or duration. Many of the papers we reviewed employ arbitrary rules for measuring these qualitatively different outcomes. The index that results serves as the basis (e.g., the dependent variable in a regression model) for an analysis of the correlates of "severity of outcome." While the scales that are applied are not patently unreasonable, serious questions remain about the degree to which

findings are simply an artifact of an artificial scale.
We are particularly concerned that use of these arbitrary
scales may conceal the importance of subtle influences
that could be measured if such scales were not used.

ORGANIZATION OF THE PAPER

While the approaches we suggest for coping with these
problems will improve the quality of statistical
inference about discrimination, we are under no illusion
that their adoption will yield definitive results. The
combination of our relative ignorance about the factors
determining case-processing decisions and the problems of
using nonexperimental data ensure that definitive
findings will not be forthcoming soon. In response to
the inherent limitation of studies based on nonexperimental data, we have included a section on the use of
experiments to measure discrimination in the criminal
justice system. This section discusses the limitation of
experiments, approaches for minimizing these limitations,
and strategies for combining experimental and nonexperimental data.

The paper is organized as follows. We begin with a
review of statistical issues that arise in the analysis
of binary data. Next we discuss the so-called sample
selection phenomenon and elaborate on its effects. We
then develop a model of the criminal justice system.
Next we review selected studies in the context of the
sample selection phenomenon and the model developed. We
then discuss alternative models of the sentencing
decision that do not require the use of arbitrary
severity indices. Next we discuss experimental
approaches to measuring discrimination. We conclude with
a summary of our major points.

THE ANALYSIS OF BINARY VARIABLES

Many decisions in the criminal justice system involve
binary outcomes, such as the prosecutor's choice to
dismiss or prosecute a case or the jury's decision to
find the defendant guilty or innocent. It is common
practice to define a binary y such that $y = 1$ if one
outcome (say, a verdict of guilty) occurs and $y = 0$
otherwise. In a number of the studies we reviewed, the
relationship between the likelihood of the event $y = 1$

and a vector of variables $\underline{x}$ is examined by regressing y on $\underline{x}$. The purpose of this section is to point out some hazards of this approach and to describe an alternative approach that we employ in subsequent sections.

We begin with a discussion of the classical regression model. The model assumes that a random variable y can be related to a vector of variables $\underline{x}$ by

$$y_i = \underline{x}_i'\underline{\beta} + \varepsilon_i \qquad i = 1, \ldots, N, \qquad (1)$$

where column vectors are underlined, $\underline{x}_1$ is the K x 1 vector of regressors for the ith observation in a sample of size N, $\underline{\beta}$ is a K x 1 vector of unknown parameters, and ε_i is the disturbance or error associated with the ith observation. The errors $\varepsilon_1, \ldots, \varepsilon_N$ are assumed to be independent with zero mean and common variance σ^2. The regressors $\underline{x}_1, \ldots, \underline{x}_N$ are often assumed to be nonstochastic, although they may also be assumed to be random variables that are independent of the errors $\varepsilon_1, \ldots, \varepsilon_N$.

These assumptions imply that the conditional distribution of y given $\underline{x}$ is such that

$$E(y_i|\underline{x}_i) = \underline{x}_i'\underline{\beta} \qquad (2)$$

and

$$V(y_i|\underline{x}_i) = \sigma^2 . \qquad (3)$$

Equations (2) and (3) state that for each $\underline{x}_i$, the distribution of y_i given $\underline{x}_i$ is such that $E(y_i|\underline{x}_i)$ is linear in $\underline{x}_i$ and $V(y_i|\underline{x}_i)$ is constant for all i. Under these assumptions, it is well known that ordinary least squares provide consistent and unbiased estimates of the coefficient vector $\underline{\beta}$.

The assumptions of the classical regression model are appropriate in cases in which the dependent variable has a large, approximately continuous range of possible values. However, in the case of a binary variable, many of the assumptions are no longer tenable. Suppose y is a binary variable that takes on only the values of zero and one. Let $p(\underline{x})$ equal the probability that y = 1 given $\underline{x}$. Then it is easy to demonstrate that

$$E(y_i|\underline{x}_i) = p(\underline{x}_i) , \qquad (4)$$

and

$$\text{Var}(y_i | \underline{x}_i) = p(\underline{x}_i)[1 - p(\underline{x}_i)] . \tag{5}$$

Equation (4) indicates that the conditional expectation of y given $\underline{x}$ is equal to the conditional probability that y equals one given $\underline{x}$. If the range of the observed $\underline{x}$ values is very small, then it may be appropriate to approximate $p(\underline{x})$ by $\underline{x}'\underline{\beta}$. In this case, ordinary least squares will consistently estimate $\underline{\beta}$. However, equation (5) indicates that $V(y_i | \underline{x}_i)$ is not the same for all i. This implies that ordinary least-squares estimates are inefficient and the standard hypothesis tests are invalid. These problems can be corrected by using standard techniques for adjusting for heteroskedasticity. If, however, the range of the $\underline{x}$ values is large, then the fact that $p(\underline{x})$ can take on only values between zero and one (it is a probability) implies that it cannot be approximated by a linear function of $\underline{x}$.[1] In this case ordinary least-squares estimates are consistent, and the inconsistency may be very severe.

To illustrate this point, consider the linear probability model:

$$p(\underline{x}) = \begin{array}{ll} \underline{x}'\underline{\beta} & \text{if } 0 \le \underline{x}'\underline{\beta} \le 1 \\ 0 & \text{if } \underline{x}'\underline{\beta} < 0 \\ 1 & \text{if } \underline{x}'\underline{\beta} > 1 . \end{array} \tag{6}$$

Figure 2-1 displays the form of $p(\underline{x})$ for the case in which $\underline{x}$ is a scalar. Also shown is a set of hypothetical observations that might arise in which a number of the x-values fall outside the range where $p(\underline{x})$ is linearly increasing. The dashed line depicts the model that would be estimated by ordinary least squares. By choosing enough observations with very high or very low x-values, the slope of the model estimated by ordinary least squares can be made arbitrarily small. This difficulty can be avoided by fitting the linear probability model specified in equation (6) using nonlinear least squares. However, this introduces severe computational problems. Therefore, it is useful to consider alternative models.

Most models for binary variables that have been proposed in the statistical literature can be written as

$$p(\underline{x}) = F(\underline{x}'\underline{\beta}) , \tag{7}$$

where F is a continuous, nondecreasing function with $F(-\infty) = 0$ and $F(+\infty) = 1$, i.e., F is a continuous distribution function. The choice of a particular form

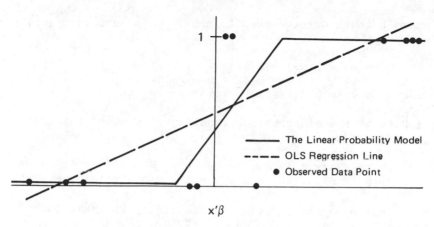

FIGURE 2-1   The Bias in Ordinary Least-Squares Estimation

for F is usually somewhat arbitrary and should be taken
in the same spirit as the assumptions of linearity and
normally distributed errors in simple regression models.
The most popular models of this form are the linear
probability model discussed above, which is obtained by
setting

$$F(z) = \begin{array}{ll} 0 & \text{if } z < 0 \\ z & \text{if } 0 \leq z \leq 1 \\ 1 & \text{if } z > 1 \ , \end{array}$$

the PROBIT model, where $F(z)$ is set equal to the
cumulative standard normal distribution function, and the
LOGIT model, with $F(z) = e^z/(1 + e^z)$.

Models of this form can be motivated in a number of
ways. We employ one such motivation repeatedly in the
following sections. Let $y*$ represent a latent,
unobserved variable that can vary between plus and minus
infinity. The latent variable $y*$ is assumed to be
related to $\underline{x}$ by the standard regression function

$$y_i* = \underline{x}_i'\underline{\beta} + \varepsilon_i \ , \tag{8}$$

where ε_i is an unobserved disturbance with mean zero and
constant variance σ^2. The dichotomous variable y is then
assumed to be related to $y*$ by

$$y_i = \begin{array}{ll} 1 & \text{if } y_i* \geq b \\ 0 & \text{if } y_i* < b \ , \end{array} \tag{9}$$

where b is an unknown cutoff level. Using equation (8),
this implies

$$p(y_i = 1|\underline{x}_i) = p(\underline{x}_i'\underline{\beta} + \varepsilon_i \geq b)$$
$$= p(\varepsilon_i \geq b - \underline{x}_i'\underline{\beta}) \ .$$
$$p(y_i = 0|\underline{x}_i) = 1 - p(\varepsilon_i \geq b - \underline{x}_i'\underline{\beta}) \ .$$

If $F(\cdot)$ is the distribution function of ε, then this can
be alternatively stated as

$$p(y_i = 1|\underline{x}_i) \equiv p(\underline{x}_i) = F(b - \underline{x}_i'\underline{\beta}) \tag{10a}$$
$$p(y_i = 0|\underline{x}_i) \equiv 1 - p(\underline{x}_i) = 1 - F(b - \underline{x}_i'\underline{\beta}) \ . \tag{10b}$$

Note that equation (10) is in essentially the same form
as equation (7).

The unknown parameters of the model are the vector of
coefficients $\underline{\beta}$, the variance σ^2, and the cutoff level b.
It can be shown that neither σ^2 nor b can be estimated
because they are not uniquely defined.[2] But the
coefficient vector $\underline{\beta}$ can be estimated directly from a
sample of observations on the binary variable y and $\underline{x}$.
One widely employed estimation procedure is called
maximum likelihood estimation. It has a number of
desirable features for cases in which a relatively large
sample of observations is available on $(y, \underline{x})$. For the
LOGIT and PROBIT models, specially designed computer
algorithms for calculating the maximum likelihood
estimator and its estimated standard errors in large
samples are available. For a more complete discussion of
estimation and other issues in binary variable models,
see Goldberger (1964:248-251) and Cox (1970).

To get a better idea of how this approach can be used
to model events that occur in the criminal justice
system, consider the example of a jury determining
whether a defendant is guilty. The jury hears the
evidence, which can be summarized in terms of various
attributes of the case, such as the number of
eyewitnesses, whether a weapon belonging to the defendant
was recovered, etc. Suppose that the investigator can
observe some of these attributes, perhaps from court
records, and can quantify them in terms of a numerical
vector $\underline{x} \equiv (x_1, x_2, \ldots, x_K)'$. Other attributes of
the case, such as the credibility of the witnesses, are
not recorded in court records and hence cannot be
observed by the investigator. Let their composite
influence be represented by ε. The jury then might be
viewed as computing an index $y^* = \underline{x}'\underline{\beta} + \varepsilon$ measuring the

strength of the case against the defendant. The
observable factors x_1, x_2, . . . , x_K are given weights
of β_1, β_2, . . . , β_K, respectively relative to the
weight assigned to ε. The jury then determines whether to
convict the defendant on the strength of the evidence,
measured by y^*, by comparing y^* to a level b and
declaring the defendant guilty if $y^* \geq b$ and not guilty
otherwise. The critical level b is presumed to be
determined according to the interpretation of the notion
"beyond a reasonable doubt."

The statistical problem is to determine the factors
the jury takes into account and their relative
importance. Among other matters, the investigator might
be interested in testing whether juries discriminate
against certain types of defendants, in which case the
personal characteristics of the defendant might be
included in x. The problem facing the investigator is
that he or she observes the vector of case attributes x
and whether the defendant is convicted, but not y^* and
ε. To estimate $\underline{\beta}$ using this information, the jury's
decision process can be modeled as

$$
\begin{aligned}
I_i = 1 \quad & \text{if } y_i^* = \underline{x_i}'\underline{\beta} + \varepsilon_i \geq b \\
0 \quad & \text{if } y_i^* = \underline{x_i}'\underline{\beta} + \varepsilon_i < b \ ,
\end{aligned}
$$

where I is a binary variable that equals one for
conviction and zero otherwise. The vector of
coefficients $\underline{\beta}$ are the parameters of interest. This is
in precisely the same form as equations (8) and (9).
Hence the weights β_1, β_2, . . . , β_K can be estimated
directly using the approach discussed above. A similar
approach is taken in the subsequent sections to model
other decisions in the criminal justice system that
involve binary outcomes.

SELECTION

Selection Bias

The criminal justice process can be thought of as a
series of stages, each involving a different set of
actors. The first stage involves the detection of a
crime, followed by communication of the crime to the
police, arrest, prosecution, trial, and sentencing. The
literature indicates that the various actors involved at
each stage make calculated decisions about the types of

crimes that are processed to the next stage. For
example, studies of the prosecutor indicate that less
serious crimes and those with weak evidence are more
likely to be dismissed following arrest. These same two
characteristics appear to influence the decision by the
police to make an arrest, while the quality of the
evidence certainly affects the likelihood that a jury
will render a verdict of guilty and pass a case on to the
sentencing stage. Other factors, such as the prior
record and socioeconomic status of the criminal, also
appear to play a role in some of the stages.

As a result of deliberate actions of the various
actors in the system, the crimes that reach each
successive stage in the system after the first are not
representative of the broader population of crimes.
Samples used to study the various stages in the system
are thus selected according to certain characteristics.
This does not itself pose a problem for the
investigator. A potential problem does arise, however,
from the combination of the sample selection process and
the fact that some of the features of a case that affect
the way it is processed cannot be observed by the
investigator. For example, prosecutors and judges may
possess a great deal of qualitative evidence about a case
that the investigator cannot observe from court records.
In other instances, the investigator may not observe
other, less qualitative types of evidence, such as
whether the criminal used a weapon. The combination of
screening and incomplete measurement implies that
criminals reaching the later processing stages are not
representative of the unobservable (to the investigator)
as well as the observable features of the population of
cases entering the system. This introduces the
possibility of sample selection bias.

The type of biases that may arise can be illustrated
best with an example. Consider the sentencing of
convicted criminals. Suppose that the various actors in
the system discriminate against individuals with low
socioeconomic status (SES) as well as individuals
committing more serious crimes. (The latter form of
"discrimination" may be socially desirable.) Then
consider high-SES individuals who are convicted of a
crime. Holding the effect of factors that are observable
to the investigator constant, such individuals would
ordinarily have a lower probability of reaching the
sentencing stage (given the hypothetical assumption of

discrimination). If they have been convicted, then, holding constant the effect of the factors observable to the investigator, they must be unrepresentative concerning the factors unobservable to the investigator that contribute to reaching the sentencing stage. For example, they may have exhibited a greater degree of premeditation than low-SES individuals who have been convicted, or a greater fraction of them may have used a weapon than low-SES convicted criminals. (The degree of premeditation and weapon use are assumed to be unobservable to the investigator.)

This may cause problems when the investigator tries to determine the factors influencing the sentencing decision. Suppose that SES does not affect sentencing, but seriousness of the crime does. By the above argument, if discrimination exists against low-SES individuals at the earlier stages of the criminal justice system, then, ceteris paribus, high-SES convicted criminals will be above average on both the observable and unobservable dimensions of the seriousness of a crime. Judges are assumed to observe both sets of factors and to take both into account when deciding on a sentence. The investigator, however, can observe only one set of dimensions. Even after taking account of the observable differences in the cases of highand low-SES criminals, the investigator will still find that high-SES criminals receive longer sentences. This will suggest that judges discriminate against high-SES individuals, even though there is no discrimination at the sentencing stage and there is discrimination against low-SES individuals at the stages preceding sentencing.

More generally, this example points out that if there does exist discrimination against low-SES individuals at the sentencing stage, then the biases induced by sample selection might mask the true extent of the discrimination. It is conceivable that the biases might even create the illusion of reverse discrimination at the sentencing stage, when in reality discrimination against low-SES individuals is present at all stages. The biases induced by sample selection are of course more general than the example--they might occur at any stage in the system following the first screening stage, and they might distort the effect of any of the observable features of a crime. This suggests that it is essential to try to account for the effects of sample selection in order to make reliable inferences about the various processing stages in the criminal justice system.

Heckman (1979) has proposed a model of the selection process that provides some direction in controlling for selection bias. Heckman's model is composed of two components:

$$y_i = \underline{x_i}'\underline{\beta} + \varepsilon_i \tag{11}$$

and

$$I_i = 1 \quad \text{if } I_i^* = \underline{z_i}'\underline{\gamma} + u_i \geq 0$$
$$0 \quad \text{if } I_i^* = \underline{z_i}'\underline{\gamma} + u_i < 0 , \tag{12}$$

where $E[\varepsilon_i] = E[u_i] = 0$ for all i,

$$E[\varepsilon_i\varepsilon_j] = \sigma_\varepsilon^2 \quad \text{if i equals j}$$
$$ = 0 \quad \text{if i does not equal j,}$$
$$E[u_iu_j] = \sigma_u^2 \quad \text{if i equals j}$$
$$ = 0 \quad \text{if i does not equal j,}$$

and

$$E[u_i\varepsilon_j] = \text{Cov}(u,\varepsilon) \quad \text{if i equals j}$$
$$ = 0 \quad \text{if i does not equal j.}$$

Equation (11) is the regression equation of interest: $\underline{x}$ is a K x 1 vector of nonstochastic regressors, $\underline{\beta}$ is a K x 1 vector of coefficients, and ε is an unobserved disturbance, where the subscript i denotes the ith observation in the sample. The problem is to estimate $\underline{\beta}$ from a sample of observations that has been selected according to equation (12). The binary variable I indicates whether an observation is included in the sample, with I = 1 representing inclusion. The indicator I is generated by an unobserved latent variable I*, which is the sum of $\underline{z}'\underline{\gamma}$ and u, where $\underline{z}$ is an L x 1 vector of nonstochastic variables, $\underline{\gamma}$ is an L x 1 vector of unknown parameters, and u is an unobserved disturbance with zero mean and variance σ_u^2. If I* $\geq$ 0, then I = 1 and the observation is included in the sample; otherwise the observation is excluded. The key specification of the model involves the assumption that ε_i and u_i need not be uncorrelated, which reflects the idea that the same unobservable factors that affect the process of interest may also affect the probability that an observation will be included in the sample.

To see how this model applies to the criminal justice literature, consider again the sentencing example. If

the regression equation relates the sentence received to
a set of observed variables, then it can be estimated
only for a sample of criminals who have been convicted.
As noted earlier, this sample is likely to be selected
according to certain characteristics. The specification
of I in the example would then relate the probability of
conviction to a set of observable characteristics z and a
set of characteristics unobservable to the investigator,
represented by the disturbance u. The literature
suggests that some of the factors influencing whether a
criminal act ultimately results in a conviction, such as
the seriousness of the crime, will also affect the
sentence length. This suggests that z and x will contain
common variables. It also suggests that to the extent
that some of the dimensions of the seriousness of a case
cannot be observed by the investigator, ε and u will be
composed of similar factors. Hence it might be expected
that the cov(ε,u) would be positive. Thus Heckman's
characterization of the selection problem naturally lends
itself to modeling the selection that occurs in the
criminal justice system.

Heckman's model can be used to probe the biases that
result from selection. Note, first, that if selection
was not operative and a random sample of observations was
available on y, then $E(y|\underline{x},\underline{z}) = \underline{x}'\underline{\beta}$ and the regression of
y on $\underline{x}$ would consistently estimate $\underline{\beta}$. However, since y
is observed only when $I_i = b$, the expected value of y
given $\underline{x}$ and $\underline{z}$ and $I_i = 1$ is

$$E(y_i|\underline{x}_i,\underline{z}_i, I_i = 1) = \underline{x}_i'\underline{\beta} + E(\varepsilon_i|\underline{x}_i,\underline{z}_i, I_i = 1)$$

$$= \underline{x}_i'\underline{\beta} + E(\varepsilon_i|u_i \geq -\underline{z}_i'\underline{\gamma}) , \qquad (13)$$

where the last equality follows from the definition of
I_i. Since the unconditional mean of ε is zero, it
follows immediately that if ε and u are correlated then
the last term in equation (13) will not equal zero.
Defining $G(\Gamma) = E[\varepsilon|u \geq \Gamma]$, we can rewrite equation (13)
as

$$E[y_i|\underline{x}_i,\underline{z}_i, I_i = 1] = \underline{x}_i'\underline{\beta} + G(-\underline{z}_i'\underline{\gamma}) . \qquad (14)$$

For most reasonable joint distributions for ε and u,
including the normal, $G(\Gamma)$ will be monotonic in Γ, with
the sign of $dG(\Gamma)/d\Gamma$ depending on the sign of cov(ε,u).
This follows from the observation that for most joint

distributions, increasing ε_i will increase the expected value of ε_i given $u_i \geq \Gamma$ if $cov(\varepsilon, u) > 0$ and decrease it if $cov(\varepsilon, u) < 0$.

Equation (14) thus implies that the regression of y on $\underline{x}$ will not consistently estimate $\underline{\beta}$ unless $\underline{x}$ and $G(-\underline{z}'\underline{\gamma})$ are uncorrelated. In many applications in the criminal justice area, it is untenable to expect $\underline{x}$ and $G(-\underline{z}'\underline{\gamma})$ to be uncorrelated. For example, we noted earlier in the sentencing example that $\underline{x}$ and $\underline{z}$ are likely to contain common variables, which makes it extremely unlikely that $\underline{x}$ and $G(-\underline{z}'\underline{\gamma})$ are uncorrelated. In other applications the presence of discrimination at multiple stages of the criminal justice system will also cause $\underline{x}$ and $\underline{z}$ to overlap.

A few simplifying assumptions will help clarify the nature of the biases when $\underline{x}$ and $\underline{z}$ do overlap. First, suppose that ε_i can be written as a linear function of u_i plus an independent disturbance:

$$\varepsilon_i = [cov(\varepsilon, u)/Var(u)]u_i + w_i = (\rho\sigma_\varepsilon/\sigma_u)u_i + w_i \ , \qquad (15)$$

where w_i is a random disturbance with zero mean and variance σ_w^2 that is independent of u_i and all other disturbance terms and ρ is the correlation coefficient between ε and u.[3] This representation follows immediately if ε and u are assumed to be normally distributed. Second, assume that u is uniformly distributed over $[-1/2, 1/2]$ and that $\underline{z}_i'\underline{\gamma}$ falls in this interval for all observations in our sample. Then

$$E(\varepsilon_i|\underline{x}_i, \underline{z}_i, I_i = 1) = .5\sqrt{3}\rho\sigma_\varepsilon - \sqrt{3}\rho\sigma_\varepsilon\underline{z}_i'\underline{\gamma}$$
$$E(y_i|\underline{x}_i, z_i, I_i = 1) = \underline{x}_i'\underline{\beta} + .5\sqrt{3}\rho\sigma_\varepsilon - \sqrt{3}\rho\sigma_\varepsilon\underline{z}_i'\underline{\gamma}$$
$$V(y_i|\underline{x}_i, \underline{z}_i, I_i = 1) = \sigma_\varepsilon^2(1 - \rho^2) + \rho^2\sigma_\varepsilon^2(.5 + \underline{z}_i'\underline{\gamma})^2 \ ,$$

which implies that for observations for which $I_i = 1$, y_i can be written as

$$y_i = \underline{x}_i'\underline{\beta} + .5\sqrt{3}\rho\sigma_\varepsilon - \sqrt{3}\rho\sigma_\varepsilon\underline{z}_i'\underline{\gamma} + \eta_i \ , \qquad (16)$$

where $E[\eta_i] = 0$, and

$$Var(\eta_i) = \sigma_\varepsilon^2(1 - \rho^2) + \rho^2\sigma_\varepsilon^2(.5 + \underline{z}_i'\underline{\gamma})^2 \ . \qquad (17)$$

Consider the important special case in which $\underline{z}$ is a subset of the regressors in $\underline{x}$. Let $\underline{x} = (\underline{z}|\underline{x}^*)'$ and $\beta = (\underline{\beta}^0|\underline{\beta}^*)'$. Then equation (16) can be rewritten as

$$y_i = .5\sqrt{3}\rho\sigma_\epsilon + \underline{z}_i'(\underline{\beta}^O - \sqrt{3}\rho\sigma_\epsilon\underline{\gamma}) + \underline{x}_i*'\underline{\beta}* + \eta_i \ . \quad (18)$$

This implies that the regression of y on $\underline{x}$ will consistently estimate $(\underline{\beta}^O - \sqrt{3}\rho\sigma_\epsilon\underline{\gamma}|\underline{\beta}*)$ for the coefficients of the nonconstant regressors. Thus if $x_j = z_j$ is one of the common regressors, then the regression of y on $\underline{x}$ will consistently estimate $\beta_j - \sqrt{3}\rho\sigma_\epsilon\gamma_j$ for the coefficient of x_j. This coefficient is a composite of β_j, the coefficient of x_j in the regression equation, and γ_j, the coefficient of x_j in the selection equation.

Returning to the sentencing example, if discrimination on the basis of SES is present at all stages of the criminal justice system, including the sentencing stage, then SES will appear as a variable in both the regression and selection equations. The regression of y on $\underline{x}$ will then consistently estimate a coefficient for SES that equals β_j, its true effect in the sentencing equation, minus $\sqrt{3}\rho\sigma_\epsilon$ times γ_j, the coefficient of SES in the selection equation. If discrimination is operative at all stages, then $\beta_j < 0$ and $\gamma_j < 0$. It was assumed that $\rho > 0$, and $\sigma_\epsilon \geq 0$ by definition. Hence the coefficient of SES that is consistently estimated by the regression of y on $\underline{x}$ will be greater than or equal to β_j and will be positive if $-\sqrt{3}\rho\sigma_\epsilon\gamma_j > -\beta_j$. Thus this regression is biased toward understating the true extent of discrimination at the sentencing stage and may in fact suggest the presence of reverse discrimination at the sentencing stage if discrimination exists at the earlier stages. The magnitude of the bias depends on the amount of discrimination occurring at the earlier stages, as measured by γ_j, and the variation of the common unmeasured forces in the regression and selection equations, as measured by $cov(\epsilon,u)/var(u)$. These results accord with the conclusions drawn earlier from the heuristic discussion of selection bias at the sentencing stage.

These results carry over to the case in which $\underline{z}$ is not a subset of $\underline{x}$ but the variables in $\underline{z}$ that do not coincide with those in $\underline{x}$ are uncorrelated with $\underline{x}$. If the nonoverlapping variables are correlated with $\underline{x}$ then the ordinary least-squares regression of $\underline{y}$ on $\underline{x}$ will be further biased by the omission of these relevant regressors.

In conclusion, selection bias may distort the role that some variables play at, say, the sentencing stage, or it may suggest a role for some variables at the sentencing stage that is largely a reflection of the

opposite role they play at an earlier stage. To the
extent that selection bias is operative, it clearly makes
inferences about where and how a factor plays a role in
the criminal justice system more difficult.

It is important to stress that selection bias does not
arise from a correlation in the population of all crimes
between the unobserved features of a crime that influence
the way it is processed through the criminal justice
system and those features that are observed. In the
terminology of the Heckman model, we have assumed that $\underline{x}$
and ϵ are uncorrelated. It is only in the selected
population of crimes from which we sample that a
correlation is induced between the observed and
unobserved factors affecting the processing of a crime.
It is this induced correlation that gives rise to sample
selection bias. If ϵ does contain factors that are
correlated with $\underline{x}$, then this may introduce additional
problems; these are discussed in Garber et al. (in this
volume).

Selection Bias at Different Processing Stages of the Criminal Justice System

Discrimination in sentencing can be manifested in many
different ways. Some researchers have examined whether a
greater fraction of arrestees with certain characteristics are sent to prison. Others have focused on the
severity of punishment received by convictees with
various characteristics. Still others have examined
whether individuals sentenced to prison receive longer
sentences according to certain characteristics.

Each of these studies involves a different population
of crimes. Some sample from the population of crimes
that lead to arrest, some sample from the crimes that
lead to conviction, and others sample from the crimes
that lead to imprisonment. Clearly, the sample of crimes
that lead to imprisonment is the most selected sample,
while the sample of crimes leading to arrest is the least
selected. It is natural to ask whether the distortions
induced by sample selection are greater for those studies
using the more selected samples.

This question can be analyzed in the context of the
following simplified model:

$$y_{1i} = \alpha + \beta S_i + \gamma_1 x_i + w_{1i} \tag{19}$$
$$y_{2i} = \alpha + \beta S_i + \gamma_2 x_i + w_{2i} \tag{20}$$

$$y_{3i} = \alpha + \beta S_i + \gamma_3 x_i + w_{3i} , \qquad (21)$$

where it is assumed that y_{2i} is observed only if $y_{1i} \geq 0$ and y_{3i} is observed only if $y_{1i} \geq 0$ and $y_{2i} \geq 0$. To make the model concrete, let y_{1i} be an index measuring the likelihood of conviction for each crime i (that is, the probability that a crime will be reported, lead to arrest, prosecution, and conviction), y_{2i} an index measuring the likelihood of imprisonment given conviction, and y_{3i} an index of the severity of punishment given imprisonment. Selection arises in that y_{2i} is observed only if case i results in a conviction, while y_{3i} is observed only if case i leads to both conviction and imprisonment.[4] Following the conventions used in the previous section, $y_{1i} \geq 0$ corresponds to the case in which crime i leads to a conviction and $y_{2i} \geq 0$ corresponds to the case in which a conviction leads to imprisonment. It is assumed that the sign of y_{1i} is observed but its value is unobserved. For simplicity of exposition, it is assumed that y_{2i} is observed for purposes of estimating equation (20) but that only the sign rather than the value of y_{2i} is observed for purposes of estimating equation (21). This corresponds to the conventions used in the previous section.

The three equations describe respectively the determinants of conviction, imprisonment given conviction, and punishment given conviction and imprisonment. To isolate the biases induced by selection, each equation is assumed to be composed of the same four factors: a constant regressor, a regressor S, which measures the characteristic on which discrimination occurs, an unobservable variable x, which commonly enters each equation, and a disturbance, which represents the effects of all other unobservable factors specifically affecting each of the three stages. The presence of the unobserved factor x in each equation is what gives rise to a nonzero covariance between the unobserved variables entering each of the three equations. The disturbances w_j, $j = 1, 2, 3$ are assumed to be independent of each other and all other variables in the model.

In order to isolate the effects of selection, two assumptions are made. First, it is assumed that the constant and the coefficient of S, denoted by α and β respectively, are the same in equations (19), (20), and (21). Second, it is assumed that $\text{Var}(\gamma_j x + w_j)$ is the same for all $j = 1, 2, 3$. The assumption that the coefficient of S and $Var(\gamma_j x + w_j)$ are the same in each of the equations ensures that the fraction of variation in y_j attributable to S is the same in all three equations. In turn, this ensures that the effects of discrimination, which can be measured by β if the y_j (j = 1, 2, 3) are observed, and by $\beta/Var(\gamma_j x + w_j)$ if only the binary outcomes indicating whether the $y_j \geq 0$ (j = 1, 2, 3) are observed, are comparable across equations. The assumption that α is the same in each equation, coupled with the other assumptions, ensures that the standard for selection is the same in all three equations. The only things that can vary across equations are the γ_j and the $Var(w_j)$. They determine the size of the covariance between the common unobserved components of each of the equations as well as the fraction of variation in $\gamma_j x + w_j$ that is attributable to x.

Selection bias occurs because y_{2i} and y_{3i} are observed in selected instances and the same unobservable factor affects each of y_1, y_2, y_3. We are interested in comparing the magnitude of the inconsistency in the estimate of the coefficient of S from the regression of y_2 on S versus the regression of y_3 on S. The regression of y_2 on S will not consistently estimate β because in the population from which observations on y_2 and y_3 are drawn, $E(\gamma_2 x + w_2|S, y_1 \geq 0)$ and $E(\gamma_3 x + w_3|S, y_1 \geq 0, y_2 \geq 0)$ are both not equal to zero. In particular, if we assume that S is binary, for example $S_i = 1$ if the ith defendant is black and $S_i = 0$ otherwise, then it is easy to show that these conditional expectations can be written as

$$E[\gamma_2 x + w_2|S, y_1 \geq 0] = \theta_2 S$$

and

$$E[\gamma_3 x + w_3|S, y_1 \geq 0, y_2 \geq 0] = \theta_3 S ,$$

where

$$\theta_2 = E(\gamma_2 x + w_2|S = 1, y_1 \geq 0) \\ - E(\gamma_2 x + w_2|S = 0, y_1 \geq 0) , \tag{22}$$

and

$$\theta_2 = E(\gamma_3 x + w_3|S = 1, y_1 \geq 0, y_2 \geq 0) \\ - E(\gamma_3 x + w_3|S = 0, y_1 \geq 0, y_2 \geq 0) . \tag{23}$$

Following the logic in the previous subsection, it is straightforward to demonstrate that θ_2 and θ_3 are the inconsistencies in the estimates of the coefficient of S in the regressions of y_2 on S and y_3 on S respectively (in the selected populations). Thus we are interested in the relative values of θ_2 and θ_3. Substituting for the conditions $y_1 \geq 0$ and $y_2 \geq 0$ in equation (22) and exploiting the fact that the w_j, $j = 1, 2, 3$, are independent, we find that

$$\theta_2 = \gamma_2 \{ E[x \mid \gamma_1 x + w_1 \geq -(\alpha + \beta)] - E[x \mid \gamma_1 x + w_1 \geq -\alpha] \}$$

and

$$\theta_3 = \gamma_3 \{ E[x \mid \gamma_1 x + w_1 \geq -(\alpha + \beta), \gamma_2 x + w_2 \geq -(\alpha + \beta)] - E[x \mid \gamma_1 x + w_1 \geq -\alpha, \gamma_2 x + w_2 \geq -\alpha] \} .$$

These two expressions can be interpreted as follows. If $\beta > 0$ then equation (19) indicates that y_{1i} is larger for blacks (i.e., S = 1 for blacks) than for whites, ceteris paribus. Since $y_{1i} \geq 0$ is a necessary and sufficient condition to pass to the imprisonment stage, this implies that it is harder for whites to pass to the next stage than for blacks. The whites who do pass to the next stage must on average have a larger value of x than the blacks who pass to the next stage. The difference between the expected value of x for the blacks who reach the imprisonment stage and the whites who reach the imprisonment stage is equal to θ_2, the inconsistency in the regression of y_2 on S using the selected sample. Similarly, θ_3 equals the difference between the expected value of x of the blacks who reach the punishment stage and the whites who reach the same stage. The question we wish to address is whether θ_3 is more negative than θ_2--i.e., whether the bias due to selection rises as the sample is repeatedly selected according to the same standard.

It turns out that the answer to this question depends on the magnitude of the coefficients γ_1, γ_2, and γ_3. Consider the extreme case in which $\gamma_1 = 0$ and γ_2, $\gamma_3 > 0$. Then it is easy to demonstrate that the regression of y_2 on S will consistently estimate β, while the regression of y_3 on S will consistently underestimate β. Thus in this extreme case, $|\theta_3| > |\theta_2| = 0$. Since the biases are continuous functions of the γ_j's, this implies, more generally, that $|\theta_3| > |\theta_2|$ whenever γ_1 is small compared with γ_2 and γ_3.

The coefficient γ_1 might be expected to be relatively small compared with γ_2 and γ_3 if, for example, equation (19) represents the likelihood of a crime leading to conviction and equations (20) and (21) represent imprisonment and sentence length, respectively. The likelihood that a crime leads to a conviction depends principally on the seriousness of the offense and the quality of the evidence. The imprisonment and punishment decisions depend primarily on the seriousness of the offense. The variable x in equations (19-21) might then be interpreted as the unobservable components of the seriousness of the offense. The fact that the role of seriousness at the conviction stage depends on the quality of the evidence (variations in seriousness are likely to have little effect on the likelihood of conviction if the quality of the evidence is either very bad or very good), whereas for the most part it operates unconditionally at the imprisonment and punishment stages, suggests that γ_1 is less than γ_2 and γ_3.

Thus if γ_1 is small relative to γ_2 and γ_3, we expect that the regression of sentence length on race, SES, income, etc. as well as other factors will indicate less discrimination than the regression of the likelihood of imprisonment on the same or similar factors. Depending on the coefficients of S in these equations, this suggests that (if γ_1 is small relative to γ_2 and γ_3) regressions using samples of individuals sentenced to prison might have the greatest chance of (spuriously) finding reverse discrimination relative to regressions using less selected populations, when in reality the same amount of discrimination occurs at each stage. More generally, it might be expected that we would estimate a greater amount of discrimination at the imprisonment stage than at the punishment stage given imprisonment. We shall return to this prediction when we review various studies of both the imprisonment decision and the punishment decision given imprisonment.

It must be pointed out, however, that these conclusions do not hold for all possible values of γ_1, γ_2, and γ_3. For example, if $\gamma_1 = \gamma_2 = \gamma_3$, x is uniformly distributed, and if the range of w_1 and w_2 is suitably restricted, then $\theta_2 = \theta_3$; this is shown in the appendix to this paper. If x is normally distributed, then $\theta_3 - \theta_2$ might be either positive or negative, depending on the values of α, β, $Var(x)$, and $Var(w_j)$. The intuitive rationale for this result is that the

second round of selection that occurs at equation (20) is
operating on two different populations—i.e., the blacks
who have reached equation (20) have not passed through as
stiff a screen as the whites who have reached equation
(20). Putting the blacks through an additional screen,
albeit not as stiff a screen as the whites, may still
have a greater effect on the blacks than the whites,
because the population of blacks to which the screen is
applied is not as selected as the respective population
of whites. Whether this is true depends critically on
the distribution of x and the various parameters of the
model.

Procedures to Deal with Selection Bias

If sample selection bias is operative, it is essential to
consider how its effects might be isolated in order to
estimate the true extent of discrimination in the
criminal justice system. This section outlines some
approaches to dealing with the selection problem.

The first approach involves placing bounds on the
parameters of the regression equation of interest to take
account of the effects of selection bias. Consider the
most difficult estimation problem—the case in which the
vector of variables z, the regressors in the selection
equation, are a subset of the variables in the regression
equation. Suppose that ρ, the correlation coefficient
of ϵ and u, is known a priori. Then equation (17)
indicates that η, the disturbance in the regression of
y on x (using the selected sample), has a variance that
is a function of only two sets of unknowns—σ_ϵ and γ. If
data are available to estimate the selection equation,
then γ can be consistently estimated using the estimation
procedure described above. This information is
sufficient to generate a consistent estimate of σ_ϵ (see
Olsen, 1980). Coupled with a consistent estimate of γ,
this is sufficient to purge the coefficient estimates
from the regression of y on x of the inconsistencies
induced by selection. This can be done using the
relationship between the coefficients consistently
estimated by the regression of y on x and the true
coefficient vector β described in equation (18).
Consistent estimates of β can then be computed for each
maintained value of ρ. Allowing ρ to vary from -1 to
+1 will then trace a bounded set of estimates that
bracket the estimate of β that would be generated if ρ

was known a priori. In addition, confidence intervals
for the extreme points of the bracketed set of estimates
could be used to measure the uncertainty in the estimates.

The bounds on the estimated value of $\underline{\beta}$ (given ρ) could
be further narrowed if the investigator possessed a
priori knowledge concerning the values of ρ, σ_ϵ, $\underline{\gamma}$,
and/or $\underline{\beta}$. The most likely candidate for such a priori
knowledge that would be widely shared by the readership
of the prospective data summary would be ρ. In many
instances, the researcher may be able to perform
experiments to learn about the value of ρ (this topic is
discussed in more detail below). A formal Bayesian
analysis could be helpful in deriving a posterior
distribution on $\underline{\beta}$ that takes account of the
investigator's uncertainty concerning the value of ρ.
While these approaches clearly do not provide a single
point estimate of $\underline{\beta}$, they may be quite helpful in
narrowing the uncertainty about $\underline{\beta}$ created by the presence
of sample selection.

A second approach that can be pursued involves the use
of exclusion restrictions to yield a consistent point
estimate of $\underline{\beta}$. The bounding approach does not require
the investigator to specify which of the variables
included in the estimated regression equation are
included because they are important in the selection of
the sample as distinct from the regression equation of
interest. Equation (16) indicates that variables that
enter the selection equation but not the regression
equation of interest will have a nonzero coefficient in
the regression equation if a selected sample is used to
estimate the regression equation. But if the
investigator is willing to specify that at least one of
the included variables is included only because of its
role in the selection of the sample, then it is possible
to get a consistent estimate of $\underline{\beta}$ even in the presence of
sample selection. Examining equation (18), it is clear
that if a regressor, say z_j, is included in the estimated
regression only because of its role in the selection
equation, then the regression of y on $\underline{x}$ will consistently
estimate $-\sqrt{3}\rho\sigma_\epsilon\gamma_j$ for the coefficient of z_j. If data are
available to estimate the parameters of the selection
equation, this will be sufficient to get a consistent
estimate of $\rho\sigma_\epsilon$. Equation (18) indicates that this is
sufficient to get a consistent estimate of the entire
coefficient vector $\underline{\beta}$. This procedure can be generalized
straightforwardly to handle multiple exclusion
restrictions (see Heckman, 1979, and Olsen, 1980).

It is important to stress that the critical assumption that identifies $\underline{\beta}$ is the assumption that one of the z_j's affects the observed y's only through the selection process. The imposition of such a restriction should not be taken lightly; it should be done only if the investigator is convinced that it is essentially correct, i.e., that z_j has very little influence on the nonselected y values. If the investigator has considerable uncertainty about the value of the coefficient of z_j in the nonselected regression, then this specification uncertainty should be incorporated into the analysis and should not be ignored by imposing an arbitrary exclusion restriction. Failure to do so may yield extremely unreliable estimates of $\underline{\beta}$.

The third approach involves dealing directly with the factors giving rise to the selection bias. As we noted earlier, selection bias arises only if some of the factors affecting both the selection of the sample and the regression process of interest cannot be observed. This suggests that an attempt to measure some of these factors, by means of, for example, interviews of the relevant individuals involved in each of the cases in the sample, would reduce the magnitude of the selection bias. Experiments might be helpful in identifying the most prominent factors giving rise to a nonzero covariance between the unobserved factors affecting both selection and the regression process of interest. A related strategy involves specifying other variables besides the dependent variables in the selection and regression equations that are also affected by the unobserved factors that give rise to selection bias. This approach is pursued in Garber et al. (in this volume).

Finally, another approach, proposed by Heckman (1979), can be used to get a consistent estimate of $\underline{\beta}$ in all cases, including the case in which the investigator is not willing to impose any exclusion restrictions on the selection variables. For the case in which the regressor in the selection and regression equations are the same, identification of $\underline{\beta}$ effectively rests on specifying a different functional form for the relationship between the probability that an observation is included in the sample and the vector of regressors $\underline{x}$ and the relationship between $\underline{x}$ and the process of interest (as represented by y) (Olsen, 1980). This approach is quite sensitive, however, to the specific functional forms chosen (see Goldberger, 1980). When one or more exclusion restrictions are exploited, Olsen's findings suggest that Heckman's approach yields a very similar coefficient estimate to an alternative approach suggested by Olsen (1980).

In practice, then, three basic approaches can be adopted to control for selection bias. The ideal approach is to measure the relevant factors well enough to eliminate the nonzero covariance between the disturbances in the selection and the regression equations. This will eliminate the sample selection bias entirely. If this is not possible, then the investigator can attempt to find an additional variable that is also affected by the unobserved factors giving rise to the nonzero covariance between the selection and the regression disturbances. If this approach cannot be implemented, then the investigator can consider the imposition of an exclusion restriction on the model. If none of these approaches can be implemented satisfactorily, then the investigator can always resort to the bounding approach. While this approach does not yield a consistent estimate of the regression coefficient vector, it will indicate the potential magnitude of the selection bias.

It should be noted that both the exclusion and the bounding approaches require the investigator to estimate the parameters of the selection equation. This equation cannot be estimated unless data are available on the cases not reaching the stage of interest (as well as on the cases that do reach the stage of interest). In the case of the sentencing stage of criminal justice system, this means that data must be available at the very least on the crimes that are not reported and the crimes that are reported but do not lead to an arrest. These data are rarely if ever available. Unless the investigator is willing to introduce considerable a priori information, the best the researcher can do under these circumstances is to control for the selection that takes place at the stages at which data are available. If there is a considerable amount of discrimination at the reporting and arrest stages, the available procedures may still yield unreliable estimates of the extent of discrimination. In particular, they will yield downwardly biased estimates of the extent of discrimination at the sentencing stage even if procedures are introduced to take account of selection bias occurring after the arrest stage. Thus the selection problem cannot be controlled for completely unless data are available for a random sample of all crimes committed. In the absence of such data, selection bias will occur unless there is no discrimination at the reporting and arrest stages.

A MODEL OF THE CRIMINAL JUSTICE SYSTEM

The processing of cases through the criminal justice system is a complex process, involving a number of different actors, each with individual objectives. In order to make inferences about the role of extralegal factors in the various stages of processing, it is essential to have a model of the criminal justice system. This is not to say that there is no room for an inductive, empirically based analysis, but rather that the analyst cannot remain wholly agnostic about the objectives of the different actors, the factors affecting their decisions, and the role of institutional constraints. Our primary purpose in this section is to construct a model of the criminal justice system that will help us judge the plausibility of the inferences made by previous researchers concerning the role of extralegal factors in case disposition.

We begin with a background discussion of several of the key aspects of case processing. The discussion serves as the basis for the formal specifications that follow.

Background Discussion of the Model

The model is a formal characterization of the interrelationship of four significant aspects of case processing in the criminal justice system: (1) the decision to prosecute; (2) plea bargaining; (3) trial;[5] and (4) sentencing. We abstract considerably from the full complexity of the system, ignoring such elements as the bail decision and the choice of attorney.

Trial and Sentencing

While trial by jury (or judge) is a hallmark of the American criminal justice system, it is not the predominant mode for reaching disposition. Table 2-1 shows the percentage of indictments that were adjudicated

by trial in the district court of Washington, D.C., in
1971. Only about a quarter of the indictments resulted
in trial, and about half of these resulting in
convictions. The other three-quarters of the indictments
were either dismissed by the prosecutor or were settled
by a guilty plea. The most common form of disposition
was a guilty plea.

The statistics in Table 2-1 overstate the frequency of
trials (and guilty pleas) because the figures are based
on indicted offenses. Not included are cases dismissed
at initial screening or dismissed prior to indictment.
Rejection rates at these preindictment phases can be very
high. For example, in the Washington, D.C., superior
court (which is different from the district court) only
16 percent of arrests were indicted and prosecuted as
felonies in 1974 (Forst et al., 1977).

Table 2-1 also reveals that trials are more frequent
in cases involving more serious offenses. For example,
over 50 percent of the homicides are disposed by trial
compared with a 13 percent rate for larceny. The figures
in Table 2-1 also suggest that conviction rates at trial
appear to be inversely correlated with seriousness.
While the statistics in Table 2-1 are for only one,

TABLE 2-1 Mode of Disposition by Crime Type--Washington,
D.C. District Court, 1971

Crime Type	Disposition by Trial (Percent)	Conviction Rate (Percent)	Disposition by Guilty Plea (Percent)
Homicide	50.3	50.0	31.6
Robbery	28.2	66.0	58.7
Assault	34.6	71.4	45.0
Burglary	20.3	68.6	52.3
Larceny	13.0	80.0	69.8
Auto Theft	17.1	75.0	74.3
All Dispositions	24.1	56.5	57.1

SOURCE: Administration Office of the United States Courts
(1971:98).

perhaps atypical, court, similar patterns are observed in the 89 federal district courts and in a sample of nonfederal courts examined by Landes (1971).

The statistics in Table 2-1 on conviction rates suggest conviction at trial is by no means certain. Various studies of the conviction process for different offenses indicate that, not surprisingly, the quality of the evidence is the most important factor affecting the likelihood of conviction. LaFree (1980) finds that in rape cases, the likelihood of conviction is directly related to the strength of the prosecution's case and inversely related to the strength of the defense's case. The findings of Forst et al. (1977) and Forst and Brosi (1977), while not directly applicable because their estimation data set includes guilty pleas, also illustrate the important influence of case quality on the likelihood of conviction.

Probably the single most important factor affecting the sentence of those convicted is the seriousness of the offense. This is clearly revealed in statutory specification of penalties and in statistics on the likelihood of incarceration and time served by offense type. Factors such as weapon use, victim provocation, and victim/offender relationship, all of which may be interpreted as components of seriousness, also appear to influence sentence (see for example LaFree, 1980; Cook and Nagin, 1979; and Zimring et al., 1976).

Another well-documented factor affecting sentence is the offender's prior record. Many statutes formally specify prior record as a criterion for imposing harsher punishment (e.g., in California) and numerous statistical studies strongly suggest that offenders with more extensive criminal histories are more harshly punished. An important question that is not addressed in this paper is the appropriate way to measure prior record. This issue is analyzed in Garber et al. (in this volume).

Finally, it appears that persons convicted at trial are sentenced more harshly than those who plead guilty. Table 2-2 shows for the district court of Washington, D.C., the percentage of defendants sentenced to prison contingent on whether the defendant is convicted at trial or through a plea of guilty. The statistics reveal that the likelihood of a prison sentence is substantially greater for those who are convicted at trial. This difference can be interpreted as an indication of the leniency afforded to defendants who are willing to acknowledge their guilt. We will suggest and develop an

TABLE 2-2 Percentage of Convictees Sentenced to Prison by Mode of Conviction: District Court of Washington, D.C., 1971

	Percent Given Prison Sentence	
Crime	Convicted by Guilty Plea	Convicted at Trial
Homicide	68.2	38.6
Robbery	80.5	94.1
Assault	46.5	55.0
Burglary and Larceny	68.3	80.6
All Cases	65.3	82.8

SOURCE: Administrative Office of the United States Courts (1971).

alternative explanation of this result that is based on the nature of the plea bargaining process.

Plea Bargaining

Plea bargaining involves a prosecutor's offering to the defendant special consideration in return for a plea of guilty. The consideration may be a promise to recommend a sentence to the judge that is acceptable to the defendant or, alternatively, a promise to drop or reduce charges or both. The former is called sentence bargaining, and the latter charge bargaining. While clearly different, there is an essential equivalence in both types of bargaining. The defendant pleads guilty with the expectation of receiving a lighter sentence than if convicted at trial. While judges typically are not directly involved in these negotiations and in some jurisdictions are legally prohibited from doing so, the defendant's expectation about sentence if he pleads must typically be borne out. Otherwise, the plea bargaining process would not persist.

The high rate of guilty pleas shown in Table 2-1 suggests that plea bargaining is a common practice in the Washington, D.C., district court. Of course, not all these guilty pleas are necessarily the result of plea bargains. Some proportion is undoubtedly guilty pleas that were tendered without negotiation. There are no official statistics on the proportion of convictions resulting from guilty pleas. But most observers believe plea bargaining is common. For example, Farrel and Swigert (1978:46) state: "In fact, more than 90% of all convictions involve negotiations of a guilty plea between defense and prosecution."

Plea bargaining is an established and much used institution in the U.S. criminal courts for several reasons. First, prosecutorial and judicial resources are insufficient to adjudicate all cases by trial. Plea bargaining enables the prosecutor to conserve scarce resources. Second, according to some, the practice of plea bargaining is related to the limited resources of public defenders. Overburdened public defenders may encourage their clients to plea bargain to avoid the time demands of preparing and presenting a case for trial. Third, plea bargaining may be motivated by the desire of the defendant to avoid the risk of severe punishment if convicted at trial and perhaps secondarily to economize on defense fees and to avoid the time cost of going to trial.[6]

The essential aspect of the plea bargaining process is the negotiation of a "deal" that is acceptable to both the prosecutor and the defendant (and, indirectly, to the judge). In our model a key parameter in the negotiations is the expected sentence at trial--that is, the probability of conviction at trial times the expected sentence if convicted. This suggests that if the defendant's perceptions of the likelihood of conviction and/or the expected sentence if convicted are less than those of the prosecutor, then a bargain may not be struck and the case will be adjudicated at trial.

The Decision to Charge

The decision to charge[7] is a prosecutorial decision that is most commonly made in response to the arrest of a suspect or the filing of a complaint. Case dropouts at this initial juncture are extremely high. Forst et al. (1977) report that 21 percent of the arrests brought to Washington, D.C., superior court in 1974 were rejected at an initial screening. Another 29 percent were subsequently dismissed by the prosecutor. Dropout rates at this stage appear to vary considerably by crime type. For example, Reiss (1975) reports that in the Washington, D.C., superior court, the dropout rate for homicide arrests was only 4 percent, whereas for aggravated assault it was 23 percent.

The discretionary power of the prosecutor at this stage in the criminal process is considerable and, of course, of substantial importance to the potential defendant. If extralegal factors play a major role in determining case disposition, their most important influence may be at this highly discretionary and low-visibility decision point.

While extralegal considerations may affect the charging decision, clearly relevant factors also have a major influence. The decision to prosecute appears to be primarily influenced by case quality, seriousness of the alleged offense, and defendant's prior record. In an excellent study of federal prosecutors in the northern district of Illinois, Frase (1978) analyzed the reasons given for rejecting complaints filed for prosecution. In 22 percent of the rejections, insufficiency of evidence and/or witnesses was cited. In another 42 percent of the rejections, the alleged offense was characterized as too trivial for prosecution (e.g., a small amount of contraband was involved). Finally, 16 percent of the rejections cited the accused as having no prior criminal record as the rationale for not accepting the case. These findings are consistent with those of Greenwood et al. (1973), Reiss (1975), and Forst et al. (1977).

The Model of the Decision to Prosecute, Plea Bargaining, and Conviction and Sentencing

The model is composed of two basic equations. The first equation relates the probability of conviction at trial, P, to a set of observable and unobservable factors:

$$P = f(\underline{q}, \underline{x}) + \epsilon_1 + u . \tag{24}$$

The vector $\underline{q}$ is composed of an observable set of attributes of the case that define the quality of the evidence. Factors such as the number of eyewitnesses, the amount of tangible evidence, and verification of the defendant's alibi are components of $\underline{q}$. The vector $\underline{x}$ is composed of a set of observable extralegal case characteristics, such as the race of the defendant and

the race of the victim. It is included to account for
any discrimination that may be present in the conviction
process. The last two terms in equation (24), ε_1 and u,
are two independent classical disturbances. The
disturbance ε_1 represents the influence of factors that
are not observed by the investigator but are assumed to
be known to both the defendant and the prosecutor. The
disturbance u summarizes the influence of factors that
prior to the trial are known only to the defendant. Such
factors might include the defendant's knowledge of the
vulnerability of his or her alibi, agreements made with
codefendants on the specifics of their testimony, the
nature of the testimony that will be provided by defense
witnesses, etc. The presence of u in equation (24)
implies that this information will become known at the
trial and hence influence P. The asymmetry in the
knowledge of u on the part of the defendant and the
prosecutor plays an important role in the plea bargaining
model that follows.

The second equation relates the sentence given
conviction, S, to a set of observable and unobservable
factors:

$$S = h(\underline{e},\underline{x}) + \varepsilon_2 . \tag{25}$$

We assume that there is only one sentencing option
available, which the judge specifies at a level S. (In a
later section we pose a model that more fully captures
the range of options actually available.) The vector $\underline{e}$
represents various observable aspects of event
seriousness, such as charge, weapon use, victim
provocation, etc. To avoid unnecessary notation, we also
include legally relevant characteristics of the
defendant, such as prior record, in $\underline{e}$. The vector $\underline{x}$ is
included in equation (25) to account for any
discrimination that is present in sentencing. The final
term, ε_2, is a classical disturbance that represents the
influence of factors not observed by the investigator
that are assumed to be known to both the defendant and
the prosecutor.

These two equations form the basis of our model of
prosecutorial decision making and the plea bargaining
process. Our model of prosecutorial decision making
borrows from Landes (1971). We assume that the objective
of the prosecutor is to maximize the expected punishment
received in cases available for prosecution subject to a
constraint on the availability of prosecutorial

resources. It generalizes the Landes model, first, by being more explicit about the sources of randomness and, second, by including the decision to charge within the model framework.

We begin by defining a variable D, where

$$D = 0 \text{ if the case is dismissed,}[8]$$
$$= 1 \text{ if the case leads to a pleaded settlement,}$$
$$= 2 \text{ if the case goes to trial.}$$

Prosecutorial decision making is assumed to be determined by an index SP, where

$$SP = \{[h(\underline{e},\underline{x}) + \epsilon_2][f(\underline{q},\underline{x}) + \epsilon_1]\}[1 + m(\underline{x})] - \lambda RP$$
$$= [S(P - u)][1 + m(\underline{x})] - \lambda RP . \tag{26}$$

In cases that are not dismissed, SP is the sentence that the prosecutor will offer in plea negotiations. The term $S(P - u)$ is the prosecutor's perception of the expected sentence. Its presence in SP reflects the assumed prosecutorial objective of maximizing expected punishment. Note that since the term u is not observed by the prosecutor, it is not included in the prosecutor's estimate of expected sentence at trial. Ignore for the moment the remaining terms in equation (26). Then given the assumed objective, the prosecutor will be indifferent between resolving the case by a negotiated plea with a sentence of $S(P - u)$ and disposing of the case at trial. This is because from the prosecutor's perspective, both modes of disposition result in an equivalent expected sentence for the defendant.

The other two terms in equation (26) are included to account for any bias on the part of the prosecutor and for any resource savings that will accrue to the prosecutor if the case is settled without a trial. The function $m(\underline{x})$ represents the bias of the prosecutor. If a defendant has characteristics that prompt leniency, then $m(\underline{x})$ will be less than zero, whereas a value of $m(\underline{x})$ greater than zero corresponds to prosecutorial discrimination against certain types of defendants. If the prosecutor does not discriminate at all, then $m(\underline{x})$ would be equal to zero for all $\underline{x}$. Discrimination is assumed to affect the expected sentence multiplicatively. This captures the idea that the prosecutor does not simply add or subtract a constant amount to the sentence offered in plea negotiations. Instead, he or she adjusts the offer in proportion to the sentence he or she would offer in the absence of discrimination. The final term in equation (26), λRP, is a "leniency bonus" the prosecutor is willing to offer in exchange for a plea of guilty. The term RP represents the prosecutorial resources that would be required if the case went to trial, and λ is the shadow price of the prosecutor's resources. The presence of this term reflects the constraint on prosecutorial resources.

We assume that a case will be dismissed if SP < 0. Intuitively, SP < 0 implies that the expected sentence at trial less the shadow price of the resources expended in prosecution is negative. Assuming that the prosecutor's objective is to maximize expected punishment, it is rational for the prosecutor to dismiss the case and not proceed into plea negotiations when SP < 0. This implies that the probability a case is dismissed is

$$\text{Prob}(D = 0) = \text{Prob}(SP < 0)$$
$$= \text{Prob}(S[P - u][1 + m(\underline{x})] < \lambda RP) \ . \quad (27)$$

We assume that all cases that are not dismissed enter into plea negotiations. Whether the negotiations result in a negotiated plea depends on the decision rule of the defendant. The defendant is assumed to consider the prosecutor's offer, SP, in light of his own perceptions of the expected sentence at trial and perhaps secondarily his estimate of any savings in legal fees and time required to prepare for trial if he accepts the prosecutor's offer. Accordingly, we define a variable SP, which is the maximum negotiated offer acceptable to the defendant, where

$$SP = S^{\bullet}P + \theta RD = [h(\underline{e},\underline{x}) + \varepsilon_2][f(\underline{q},\underline{x}) + \varepsilon_1 + u]$$
$$+ \theta RD \ . \quad (28)$$

The term $S^{\bullet}P$ is the defendant's perception of expected sentence if he goes to trial. Note that it is different from the prosecutor's perception of expected sentence because the defendant, unlike the prosecutor, is aware of the factors included in the term u that will affect the probability of conviction at trial. Ignore for the moment the final term in equation (28). If we assume that the defendant is risk-neutral with regard to prison sentences, then he will be indifferent between taking his chances at trial and accepting a sentence equal to his perception of the expected sentence at trial. This is because both alternatives have an equivalent expected sentence. The term RD measures any savings in defense resources that will result from avoiding trial. The parameter θ measures the shadow price of defense resources. A value of θ strictly greater than zero implies that a defendant will be willing to accept a sentence greater than the expected sentence at trial in order to avoid expending the additional time and money required to prepare and present a case at trial.

For cases that are not dismissed, we assume that a negotiated plea will result if the prosecutor's offer, SP, is less than the defendant's maximum acceptable offer, SD. Otherwise, the case will be adjudicated at trial. Accordingly, the probability of a negotiated plea given the case is not dismissed is

$$
\begin{aligned}
\text{Prob}(D = 1 | D \neq 0) &= \text{Prob}(SP < SD) \\
&= \text{Prob}\left(m(\underline{x})[(u + \varepsilon_1)h(\underline{e},\underline{x}) + S^{\bullet}\varepsilon_2] \right. \\
&\quad - S^{\bullet}u[1 + m(\underline{x})] \\
&\quad \left. < \theta RD + \lambda RP - m(\underline{x})f(\underline{q},\underline{x})h(\underline{e},\underline{x})\right) \quad (29)
\end{aligned}
$$

and the probability of going to trial is

$$
\text{Prob}(D = 2 | D \neq 0) = 1 - \text{Prob}(D = 1 | D \neq 0) . \quad (30)
$$

Several predictions of this model are of interest. If prosecutors do not discriminate (i.e., $m(\underline{x}) = 0$ for all $\underline{x}$), the probability that a plea bargain will be struck simplifies to

$$
\text{Prob}(D = 1 | D \neq 0) = \text{Prob}(S^{\bullet}u < \theta RD + \lambda RP) . \quad (31)
$$

Observe that this expression does not include the probability of conviction at trial. Assuming that case quality, $\underline{q}$, does not affect sentence following conviction, the model predicts that the likelihood of conviction by plea is unaffected by factors of case quality known to both parties. This is a surprising result. It is a reflection of the assumption that the defendant and the prosecutor have similar perceptions of the effect of $\underline{q}$ on the probability of conviction. The implication of this observation is that if the factors affecting the likelihood of conviction are analyzed using a sample of dispositions that include negotiated pleas, the effects of case quality on conviction are likely to be understated. LaFree (1980) reports evidence for forcible sex offenses that is supportive of this prediction. He finds that for forcible sex offenses, case quality variables are considerably more important in explaining the probability of conviction given trial than in the probability of conviction for all cases, including those that are settled by guilty plea. More generally, the model suggests that for the purposes of estimation, dispositions resulting from trials should not be mixed with dispositions resulting from pleas because they are the outcomes of very different processes.

Absent prosecutorial discrimination, another interesting prediction of the model is that the larger the sentence given conviction at trial, the greater the likelihood that plea negotiations will fail and the case will go to trial. Observe that the term $\theta RD + \lambda RP$ in equation (31) is greater than zero. The probability that $S^{\cdot}u$ is greater than $\theta RD + \lambda RP$ is then an increasing function of S. The statistics in Table 2-1 are consistent with this prediction. The percentage of cases disposed by trial is greater the more serious the offense. For example, about 50 percent of all homicides are disposed by trial, whereas for larceny only 13 percent of the cases go to trial. The intuition of this result is straightforward. The difference between the prosecutor's and the defendant's perception of the expected sentence if the case goes to trial equals $S^{\cdot}u$. Recall that u measures factors affecting the probability of conviction that are known only to the defendant. The magnitude of this difference grows with increases in S, thus increasing the likelihood that the prosecutor's offer will not be acceptable to the defendant.

Before elaborating on some of the implications of the model, some caveats on the potential narrowness of the model will help place it in perspective. The model undeniably neglects a variety of factors that motivate prosecutors and defendants. It assumes risk neutrality on the part of prosecutors and defendants alike. Defendants in particular may be risk-averse, particularly if the sentence they might receive if convicted at trial is severe. Some defendants who believe they are innocent may also refuse to negotiate on principle. Likewise, prosecutors may flatly refuse to negotiate cases when the defendant is "notorious" or the case has received considerable public attention. In such cases the expected sentence if convicted at trial may not closely approximate the seriousness of the crime. However, the purpose of this model is not to provide a literal characterization of the motives and decision rules of the major actors in the criminal justice system. Rather its purpose is to provide some structure for interpreting the results in the literature and to provide a basis for making constructive suggestions for improving future research. In this regard several implications of the model are pertinent.

First, the model implies that the stages of the criminal justice system cannot be neatly separated and examined in isolation. Expectations about the outcome at later stages will affect prior processing decisions. For example, the model predicts that both the probability of the prosecutor's dismissing a case and the sentence offered by the prosecutor in plea negotiations are affected by expectations about the outcome of a trial. Thus, any bias on the part of judges or juries may be reflected in the dismissal decision and the plea bargaining process. The observation that decision making in the criminal justice system is affected by expectations about the actions of parties not directly involved in the decision is not a peculiarity of this model. Other plausible characterizations of decision making in the process would similarly incorporate the effects of expectations. For example, a prosecutor may choose to dismiss a case based on the expectation that a judge would dismiss the case if prosecuted.

Second, the model predicts that the sentence received in a negotiated plea will be the function of the product of the probability of conviction at trial and sentence given conviction. This implies that the sentence in a negotiated plea will be a function of the interaction of the seriousness of the offense and case quality.

Third, the model implies that an analysis of the determinants of conviction should not mix guilty pleas and trial convictions. The model suggests that the probability of the defendant's pleading guilty is not related to the attributes of case quality known to both the defendant and the prosecutor. In contrast, the probability of conviction at trial is assumed to be directly related to these attributes.

In the next section we elaborate on these issues in the context of studies we have reviewed.

REVIEW OF SELECTED STUDIES

Our review of the studies selected by the panel suggests that they generally suffer from three flaws: (1) the biases induced by sample selection are ignored; (2) model specifications do not adequately distinguish guilty pleas from trial convictions; and (3) acquittals and dismissals are inappropriately mixed with convictions. The consequences of these practices are discussed below.

Sample Selection Bias

Sample selection is a natural aspect of the criminal justice system. Cases are screened from the system at various stages. We have discussed the conditions under which this could lead to biased estimates of the extent of discrimination in sentencing. Three conditions were identified. First, the screening process had to be nonrandom. Second, it was necessary that there be some discrimination in at least one of the screening stages prior to sentencing. Third, some of the unobservable factors that play a role at the sentencing stage also had to play a role at an earlier screening stage. We argued that when these conditions were met, selection bias would generally contribute to an underestimate of discrimination at the sentencing stage.

There are a number of stages at which these conditions may be met. Table 2-3 lists these stages and the type of unobservable factors that may play a role in the screening decision.

TABLE 2-3   Screening Points in the Criminal Justice System

Factor State of Selection	Principal Type of Unobserved	
	Seriousness of the Offense	Quality of Evidence
Detection	X	
Arrest	X	X
Prosecution	X	X
Charge type	X	
Conviction		X
Sanction Type	X	

The stages itemized in Table 2-3 correspond to various decisions that must be made by one or more actors in the criminal justice system. Four of the decisions-- detection, arrest, prosecution, and conviction--are clear instances of sample selection in that a negative decision terminates case processing. The charge type and sanction type decisions are more subtle examples of sample selection. Unlike the other screening decisions listed in the table, the charge type and sanction type decisions do not result in case dropout. Instead, cases are sorted into various charge type and sanction type categories. Because the sorting decisions are based on case-specific factors, the selection is not random. This introduces the possibility of selection bias. For reasons elaborated below, we suspect that studies that analyze one type of sanction type and secondarily one charge type may be particularly vulnerable to selection bias.

The studies we reviewed employed samples that are selected to varying degrees. The nature of the sample used in each study is listed in Table 2-4. All the studies involve samples of cases that resulted in both detection and arrest. A number of the studies focus on cases that are further selected according to whether the cases resulted in prosecution, a specific charge, conviction, and/or like punishment. Two general comments can be made about these studies with regard to sample selection bias. First, if there exists discrimination at the detection and arrest stages (particularly the latter) then sample selection will cause all the studies to underestimate the magnitude of discrimination in sentencing. Second, if the extent of discrimination at each stage prior to sentencing is unknown, but discrimination is suspected at some of the stages, then the more selected the sample used to analyze the sentencing decisions, the greater the chance of selection bias.

Our analysis in the section on sample selection above provides specific guidelines on the factors affecting the magnitude of the bias in the estimate of discrimination in sentencing. The first factor involves the extent of discrimination at each point of selection. For example, if a sample of convictions is used, discrimination may have been a basis for selection at the detection stage, the arrest decision, the prosecution decision, the charge decision, and the conviction process. The greater the extent of discrimination at the various selection stages,

the larger will be the bias in the estimate of
discrimination at the sentencing stage, ceteris paribus.

The other two factors relate to the magnitude of the
covariance between the disturbance in the sentence length
equation and each of the disturbances in prior selection
equations. The magnitude of this covariance will be
affected by the investigator's success in measuring the
range of factors determining sentence. The more such
factors are measured, the smaller will be the role played
by unobservables, hence the smaller the covariance of the
unobserved influences. Consequently, studies that
account for a larger portion of the variation in sentence
in the selected sample are likely to be less subject to
selection bias.

The second factor affecting the magnitude of the
covariance is the extent to which specific unobservable
case or defendant characteristics commonly affect the
sentence length decision and prior selection decisions.
We argued above that the commonality of influences is
likely to be particularly large for the unobservable
factors affecting both the sentence length decision
(given the choice of sanction type) and the choice of
sanction type. Both decisions are primarily determined
by the seriousness of the offense and the defendant's
prior record. Seriousness of the offense is a
particularly difficult concept to measure. It has many
dimensions, few of which are typically observed by the
investigator. Consequently, selection bias is likely to
be particularly great for studies that use samples of
cases that resulted in like punishment. Such studies
might be expected to find the least evidence of
discrimination.

These arguments are applied below to the studies we
reviewed. The studies are concerned with two types of
discrimination, which we distinguish as direct and
indirect discrimination. Direct discrimination involves
a finding that sentence is affected by offender
characteristics such as race and/or SES after holding
constant other factors affecting sentence. Indirect
discrimination involves a finding that some of the
factors affecting sentence, such as whether the defendant
makes bail, are related to offender characteristics such
as race, income, etc. We concentrate on the former type
of discrimination. The studies are divided into two
groups according to whether they found direct
discrimination. We analyze the degree to which the
differences in the findings of the two sets of studies

TABLE 2-4   Summary of Selected Studies of Discrimination
in Sentencing

Study	Sample Following Arrest
Clarke and Koch (1976)	Individuals charged with burglary, breaking and entering, and larceny. They also considered separately the cases in their sample that led to conviction.
Lizotte (1977)	Union of 200 cases processed by 15 Chicago trial courts during a one-week period and a random sample of 596 Chicago trial cases in which a grand jury returned an indictment.
Hagan (1975)	A random sample of individuals arrested or a random sample of prosecutions.
Chiricos and Waldo (1975)	Individuals sentenced to prison for a diverse set of felonies.
Farrell and Swigert (1978)	Individuals charged with murder.
Gibson (1978)	Random sample of indictments on felony charges resulting in convictions.
Swigert and Farrell (1977)	Individuals charged with murder.
Tiffany, Avichai, and Peters (1976)	Individuals convicted at trial of bank robbery, auto theft, interstate transportation of forged securities, and miscellaneous forgery.
LaFree (1980)	Individuals charged with forcible sex offenses (but cases not leading to arrest and/or charge are also analyzed).

may be attributable to selection bias. This exercise is
at best suggestive--it is post hoc and it is made more
difficult because there are other problems with the
studies that may account for their findings. (Some of
these problems are discussed below.) Nevertheless, the
discussion of the various studies is suggestive of the
kind of problems sample selection can induce. It also

TABLE 2-4 (Cont.)

Mixture of Guilty Pleas and Trial Convictions	Mixture of Acquittals and Dismissals with Convictions	Nature of Findings Concerning Discrimination
Yes	Yes	Discrimination present against low income defendants in that they have a greater probability of being sentenced to prison, ceteris paribus. They infer, through, additional tests, that discrimination arises at the sentencing rather than the conviction stage.
Yes	Acquittals: Yes Dismissals: No (?)	No direct influence of occupation or race on prison sentence length found; indirect effects of race acting through bail and attorney choice found.
Yes	Acquittals: Yes Dismissals: Alternately included and excluded	No direct influence of race on the outcome of a case. Indirect effects of race on charge seriousness found.
No	No	No direct discrimination; if anything, reverse discrimination.
Yes	Yes	Direct discrimination on the basis of occupational prestige found. Indirect discrimination also found through the effect of occupational prestige on prior record.
Yes	No	No overall racial or SES discrimination found, but discrimination on the part of some judges found.
Yes	Yes	Discrimination on the basis of sex and occupational prestige found. Indirect discrimination on the basis of a normal primitive characterization also found.
No	No	Discrimination on the basis of race found, but only for cases where the defendant had no prior record.
Yes, but guilty pleas also examined separately	No	Discrimination found against black defendants when the victim is white at a number of processing stages, including the sentencing stage.

provides an explanation of why some studies might find evidence of discrimination while others do not.

The findings of the various studies concerning direct discrimination are listed in Table 2-4. Four studies found no evidence of direct discrimination, four found evidence of discrimination, and one found evidence of discrimination only for cases in which the defendant does not have a prior record. Some of the studies finding no evidence of direct discrimination did find some evidence of indirect discrimination. Overall, the results are mixed. We argued earlier that sample selection bias will generally cause an underestimate of the true extent of discrimination. This suggests that the studies that did not find evidence of discrimination may be more subject to sample selection bias than those studies that did find evidence of discrimination. This is the issue we address in the remainder of this subsection.

We first examine the four studies that found no evidence of discrimination. We begin with the study by Chiricos and Waldo (1975). This analysis deserves special attention because of its prominence in the literature and the quality of the study. Chiricos and Waldo analyzed the length of prison sentence for 17 offenses and further analyzed each offense separately for three different jurisdictions. Their findings suggest that if there is any discrimination in sentencing, it is in favor of lower-SES offenders.

The overwhelming nature of the evidence led them to conclude with considerable confidence that there is no discrimination in sentencing in the cases they analyzed. While their conclusion is certainly reasonable, sample selection is an alternative explanation for their findings that we feel is equally plausible. As we argued above, studies analyzing a specific type of sanction for a specific offense are particularly susceptible to selection bias. Thus it is possible that there may be considerable discrimination in sentencing in the sample of cases they analyze, even though their evidence seems to point overwhelmingly against it.

There is further evidence that is supportive of the argument that the Chiricos and Waldo findings are attributable to selection bias. In their regressions, Chiricos and Waldo explain on average about 9 percent of the variation in sentence length. This implies that their estimating equations include very few of the factors determining sentence length. This is precisely the situation in which selection bias is likely to be large. Furthermore, we argued that selection bias is larger the larger the amount of discrimination at stages preceding the sentence length decision. We emphasized that it is the amount of discrimination in the imprisonment decision that might be particularly important. Two of the studies that we reviewed examine discrimination in the imprisonment decision. Both studies found evidence of discrimination--Clarke and Koch (1976) for the case of larcenies and burglaries and LaFree (1980) for forcible sex offenses. These findings are supportive of our general argument that Chiricos and Waldo's findings may be attributable to selection bias.

Selection bias also provides an alternative interpretation of Gibson's findings. Gibson (1978) analyzed for specific offenses the sentence length for each of three sanction types. As with Chiricos and Waldo, this sort of sample specificity makes the analysis particularly vulnerable to selection bias. The specifics of Gibson's findings also suggest sample selection. Gibson examined the sentence length decision for a single jurisdiction outside Atlanta. He analyzed the decisions by all 11 judges in the district both individually and as a group. He found no discrimination for the group as a whole but did find that some judges imposed stiffer sentences on blacks than on other defendants.

The differences across judges appear to be related to their racial attitudes, religious preferences, and other factors that suggest discrimination. This is a curious finding. Overall, Gibson found no discrimination, but for individual judges he found substantial discrimination. The explanation he provides is that there is sufficient reverse discrimination on the part of some judges to offset the discrimination by others. Another explanation for this finding is that selection bias causes the extent of discrimination in sentencing by each judge to be underestimated but does not alter the relative ranking of the judges concerning discrimination in sentencing. This would occur if the factors causing selection bias are the same for all judges.[9]

Of the other two studies finding no discrimination, there is no apparent reason to think that selection bias contributed to their findings. Both studies used samples that are not especially selected and both examined a diverse set of charges (though this may tend to blur their results). Hagan (1975) analyzed racial discrimination against native Indians in the Canadian criminal justice system and Lizotte (1977) examined SES discrimination in the United States. However, both studies are plagued by other problems that obscure the effects of all factors on sentencing, including race, SES, etc. These problems are discussed below.

Thus of the four studies finding no discrimination, two may be particularly subject to selection bias. The

remaining question is whether there are good reasons to
suspect that the five studies that found evidence of
discrimination are less subject to selection bias. We
begin with Swigert and Farrell (1977) and Farrell and
Swigert (1978), both of which analyze the incidence of
discrimination in homicide cases. The two studies
analyzed a sample of arrests for homicide. Across the
nine studies we reviewed, only one other study (Hagan,
1975) used a sample of cases that are as "unselected" as
the sample analyzed by Farrell and Swigert. In contrast
to Hagan, however, Farrell and Swigert concentrated on
one type of crime. Because they considered the range of
charges available in homicide, they avoid the additional
selection bias that would arise if they concentrated on
only those homicides resulting in conviction for one type
of charge, such as first-degree murder. This enabled
them to concentrate on a single class of crimes without
artificially introducing an additional round of
selection. Presumably their concentration on a like set
of offenses made it easier to spot discrimination.

The sample they used--arrests for homicide--is
selected only in that the cases were detected and
resulted in arrest. Thus their estimates of
discrimination are subject to selection bias only if (1)
there is some discrimination at the detection and arrest
stages and (2) the sample of cases leading to arrest is
unrepresentative of the broader population of homicides.
Farrell and Swigert argue that the latter condition is
less likely to be satisfied for homicides than for most
crimes. They write (1978:439):

> As an offense type, criminal homicide provides a
> valuable opportunity for the study of legal
> treatment. Homicide defendants are more
> representative of persons who commit homicide than are
> defendants accused of any other crime of persons who
> commit that crime. The visibility of the offense and
> the high clearance rate of deaths due to homicide
> suggest that individuals charged with murder exemplify
> persons who actually commit murder; other offenses
> display a much greater disparity between crimes known
> to the police and arrests recorded.

This suggests that the magnitude of the bias induced
by selection at the detection and arrest stages is less
for homicide cases than for other types of offenses.
This, coupled with Farrell and Swigert's use of an

otherwise relatively unselected sample, may account for
the fact that they found evidence of discrimination while
other studies did not.

The third study that found evidence of discrimination
is Clarke and Koch (1976). They too examined a sample of
arrests (for burglary and larceny) and found that
individuals with lower income have a greater chance of
going to prison given arrest. Further analysis suggested
that the disadvantages sustained by low-income
individuals occurred not at the conviction stage but at
the imprisonment decision given conviction.[10] They
found that given conviction, low-income individuals had a
considerably greater chance of being sent to prison than
high-income individuals.

Clarke and Koch effectively found evidence of
discrimination among a sample of cases that resulted in
conviction. This sample is more selected than a sample
of arrests but is less selected than the samples used in
studies like those of Gibson (1978) and Chiricos and
Waldo (1975), in which the sample is composed of
convictions resulting in like punishment. In principle,
it is the least-selected sample that could be used to
analyze the determinants of sentencing if acquittals and
dismissals are not pooled with convictions. (We comment
critically later on the implications of pooling
nonconvictions with convictions.) For these reasons, we
expect that Clarke and Koch's findings are less subject
to selection bias than those of Gibson and Chiricos and
Waldo.

There are two other features of the Clarke and Koch
study that may also restrict the magnitude of the
selection bias. First, they did not analyze cases
charged with a specific offense. Instead, they analyzed
a sample of thefts with charges spanning the spectrum of
misdemeanor larceny to felonious burglary. This has the
advantage of mitigating the selection bias attributable
to the specific charging decision of the prosecutor.
Second, they did not find evidence of discrimination in
the process from arrest to conviction. This means that
the selection of the sample that occurs between arrest
and conviction is unlikely to bias the estimate of
discrimination in the equation explaining imprisonment
given conviction.

The fourth study finding evidence of discrimination is
LaFree (1980). LaFree examined the various stages from
arrest to sentence in the processing of forcible sex
offenses. Discrimination was examined in the context of

the combination of the race of the victim and the race of the defendant. LaFree found that cases involving black defendants and white victims are treated differently than intraracial assaults by whites and blacks (he has virtually no incidents in his sample involving white offenders and black victims). He found that holding all other observable factors constant, cases involving a black defendant and a white victim have a greater probability of resulting in imprisonment given conviction and on average receive a longer prison sentence given imprisonment.

LaFree interprets his findings as evidence of discrimination. However, there is an alternative interpretation of his findings. It has been noted by many researchers that a critical factor in rape cases is whether the victim knew the assailant. The racial composition of the victim-defendant dyad may be proxying for this factor. Whatever the interpretation of this variable, however, our arguments about selection are still applicable. We argued earlier that selection bias would reduce the estimate of discrimination at the sentencing stage among a sample of cases resulting in imprisonment if there was some type of discrimination occurring at the stages preceding sentencing. LaFree did find discrimination (i.e., a role for the race of the victim and defendant) in the decision to imprison given conviction. Following the argument we applied to Gibson (1978) and Chiricos and Waldo (1975), this should make it less likely to find discrimination in a sample of cases resulting in imprisonment. However, LaFree did find discrimination, whereas Gibson and Chiricos and Waldo did not. If our explanation of the Gibson and Chiricos and Waldo findings is correct, it is imperative that we explain why selection bias did not affect LaFree's findings to the extent that it affected those of Gibson and Chiricos and Waldo.

There are two possible explanations for the difference in LaFree's findings. First, LaFree used explanatory variables that account for a much larger fraction of the variation in sentence length given imprisonment than in the average regression performed by Chiricos and Waldo (Gibson does not report a comparable statistic). The R^2 in LaFree's regression equation for sentence length given imprisonment is .27 whereas the average R^2 for the comparable regressions in Chiricos and Waldo is .09. As we argued earlier, selection bias will be smaller the

more the investigator is able to measure the factors
affecting sentence length that also affect prior
decisions such as the imprisonment decision. The second
possible explanation for LaFree's findings is that the
magnitude of discrimination in sentencing given
imprisonment is so large that even selection bias could
not mask it completely. There is independent evidence
(see Wolfgang and Reidel, 1973) that there may be a great
deal of discrimination in rape cases in which the victim
is white and the defendant black. Both factors would
help to explain the difference between the findings of
Gibson and Chiricos and Waldo and those of LaFree.

The last study that does find some, albeit mixed,
evidence of discrimination is Tiffany et al. (1975). For
each of four crime types, they analyzed a sample of cases
resulting in conviction by trial. They found evidence of
racial discrimination among cases in which the defendant
had no prior record. Otherwise, they did not find any
general pattern of discrimination. With regard to
selection, their sample is more selected than most in
that they considered only cases resulting in conviction
via trial, but less selected than those of Gibson and
Chiricos and Waldo in that they did not restrict their
sample to cases resulting in like punishment. They
avoided this restriction by the use of an index that
arbitrarily scales different types of punishments such as
fines, probation, and prison sentences. Their findings
may be colored by the use of this arbitrary index, which
is an issue we discuss in greater length below. It is
difficult to say more about the role that selection bias
may have played in their findings.

Our discussion of selection bias is at best
suggestive, but it does illustrate the role that
selection bias may play in the various studies.
Generally, selection bias is likely to cause all the
studies to underestimate the magnitude of discrimination
in sentencing decisions. It may also be an important
factor in explaining the results of studies like those of
Gibson (1978) and Chiricos and Waldo (1975), which
analyzed cases for a specific offense resulting in like
punishment. We discussed above the various approaches
that might be useful in probing the sensitivity to
selection bias of the results of the various studies.
While these approaches may involve some additional
assumptions that might be controversial, they at least
provide a means of addressing the issues. We have tried
to argue in this subsection that the problem is

sufficiently serious that the use of these approaches might yield considerable dividends.

Mixing Guilty Pleas and Trial Convictions

The vast proportion of cases ending in conviction result from a negotiated guilty plea. Of the nine studies we reviewed, only one (Tiffany et al., 1975) explicitly excludes guilty pleas from the analysis. The other eight do not distinguish between guilty pleas and trial convictions or merely enter an additive dummy variable in a sentencing equation to account for the type of conviction. This implicitly incorporates the assumption that the relationship between sentence given conviction (or, more broadly, case outcome) and various observable features of the case is the same for guilty pleas and trial convictions, except perhaps for an additive constant. If this is not correct, then the estimating equations used in the various studies are misspecified. More important, guilty pleas generally dominate trial convictions in samples of convictions. Since the great proportion of guilty pleas are tendered as the result of plea bargaining, sentencing equations that are estimated on samples of all convictions primarily provide information about the factors affecting sentence in successful plea negotiations. The natural question this raises is what we learn from such exercises about the incidence of discrimination in sentencing.

The answer critically depends on the way the plea bargaining process is perceived to operate. And different models of the plea bargaining process suggest very different interpretations. None of the studies we reviewed introduces a model of the plea bargaining process, nor is there any single model that is widely accepted. Therefore, we have chosen to interpret the results of the various studies in terms of the model of the plea bargaining process we presented in the previous section. While this model is stylized, we feel that it captures many of the essential features of the plea bargaining process.

Suppose we find that in a sample of sentences comprised of or dominated by negotiated guilty pleas, black defendants receive stiffer sentences, holding all other factors constant. Our model suggests that there may be three very different explanations for this finding. First, it may reflect that judges discriminate against blacks. If black defendants anticipate that they are likely to receive a stiffer sentence than white defendants if convicted at trial, then the model suggests that blacks would be willing to accept a stiffer negotiated settlement than whites, holding all other factors constant. This explanation also presumes that the prosecutor actively exploits judicial bias in sentencing.

Another explanation for this finding is that the probability of conviction is higher for black defendants than for white defendants, holding all other factors constant, and that this is perceived by both the defendant and the prosecutor. This also causes both the prosecutor and the (black) defendant to have a higher expected sentence, thereby resulting in a stiffer negotiated sentence. Again, this requires the prosecutor to exploit the biases inherent in the system.

A third explanation for the finding is that the prosecutor directly discriminates against black defendants. We specified above that a case would result in a negotiated settlement whenever the prosecutor offered the defendant a settlement that was less than the sum of the defendant's expected sentence and a positive term reflecting the cost to the defendant of waging a trial. In many instances, the settlement that is acceptable to the defendant may be greater than the minimum settlement the prosecutor would be willing to offer (assuming no discrimination). This may provide the prosecutor with sufficient discretion to offer stiffer settlements to some types of defendants. In this explanation, it is the prosecutor and not the judge or jury that is the direct source of the discrimination.

Without separating guilty pleas from jury trial convictions in some way, it is not possible to distinguish between these three explanations. The only study that does make this distinction is Tiffany et al. (1975). However, even this study never addresses the issue of why some cases go to trial and others are settled by negotiation. In fact, it raises an additional issue that we have not considered: Among those defendants who choose to go to trial, why do some opt for a jury trial while others opt for a bench trial? In light of their findings that convictions in bench trials result in lesser sentences than convictions in jury trials for what appear to be comparable types of cases, it is perplexing that any defendant would ever opt for a jury trial. Until we understand the reasons that cases

are disposed of in different ways, even inferences that
are made from cases disposed of in a common way must be
treated with caution. As we noted in the previous
section, such cases represent a selected sample, which
introduces the possibility of selection bias.

Our model of the plea bargaining process also provides
some guidance on how the sentence received from a
negotiated settlement should be analyzed. The model
suggests that the sentence in negotiated guilty pleas is
a function of the seriousness of the offense and the
legal and extralegal characteristics of the defendant as
they interacted with the probability of conviction. This
implies that such sentences include information about
factors affecting the probability of conviction as well
as the factors affecting sentence length given
conviction. The multiplicative form of the interaction
provides some guidance on how this information might be
extracted.

This interaction also implies that for guilty pleas
the effect of variations in the seriousness of the
offense on sentence depends on the quality of the
evidence. In contrast, we assumed in the previous
section that the sentence received by those who are
convicted at trial is related only to the seriousness of
the offense and the characteristics of the defendant.
This suggests that mixing guilty pleas and trial
convictions introduces a misspecification into models of
the sentencing process. It is likely to blur the
relationship between sentence and both the seriousness of
the offense and the legal and extralegal characteristics
of the defendant, thus making it more difficult to assess
the true extent of discrimination in the criminal justice
system.

Mixing Outcomes

Several of the studies we reviewed test for discrimination by scaling the outcome of a case and relating this
scaled metric to various explanatory variables. The
scaled metric is formed by assigning scores to the
various possible outcomes, acquittals and dismissals at
one end of the scale and prison sentences at the other.
The scores are then regressed on factors that proxy for

the seriousness of the case, the quality of the evidence, the defendant's prior record, and various legal and extralegal factors.

Our model suggests that mixing different types of outcomes in this way is likely to blur the true extent of discrimination in the criminal justice system. The model suggests that (1) the factors affecting the likelihood of acquittal are different from the factors affecting the sentence decision given conviction at trial and (2) the factors affecting the likelihood of dismissal and the sentence decision given conviction via negotiated guilty plea are a mixture of the factors affecting the acquittal decision and the factors affecting the sentence decision (given conviction at trial). Thus condensing these different outcomes into one index effectively mixes together very different processes. Moreover, it makes it considerably more difficult to determine the source of discrimination if evidence in support of discrimination is found.

There is evidence in the various studies that is supportive of our view of the way the criminal justice system operates. LaFree (1980) found that in forcible sex offenses, the probability of conviction is primarily a function of the quality of the evidence, whereas the severity of punishment given conviction at trial is primarily related to the seriousness of the offense. In his study of the dismissal decision, Frase (1978) found that the probability of dismissal is primarily related to seriousness of the offense, the quality of the evidence, and the prior record of the defendant. The various studies we reviewed that focus on the sentencing decision given conviction confirm that the primary determinant of the sentencing decision is the seriousness of the offense. The evidence from the other studies is also consistent with the hypothesis that the various outcomes (following arrest) are the product of different processes.

The model we presented provides guidance on how the processes behind these different outcomes can be analyzed. As we noted earlier, it also provides guidance on how guilty pleas should be treated. The one issue we have not yet addressed is the implication of using an artificial index to scale the different types of sentences that are typically dispensed by judges. This practice, frequently used in the studies we reviewed, is the subject of the following section.

GENERALIZED MODELS OF SENTENCING

Criminal statutes typically empower judges to choose among a set of sentencing alternatives for a specified criminal act. Most commonly, these sentencing alternatives are prison, probation, fine, or some combination of these. For first-degree murder, execution is another sentencing option in an increasing number of states.

With few exceptions, criminal statutes also permit judges broad discretionary power in determining the type and length of sentence. This discretionary power is particularly broad in jurisdictiors with indeterminate sentencing statutes. Under such statutes, prison terms of a determinate length are not required and in some instances are prohibited. Instead, the judge is permitted or required to specify only a minimum and a maximum term. Within the bounds of the minimum and maximum sentence, parole boards have broad discretionary power to determine actual time served. Determinate and mandatory minimum sentencing statutes attempt to varying degrees to structure and limit sentencing discretion, but in most instances judges still have considerable latitude in specifying sentence.

The variety of sentencing options available to judges and the discretion they are permitted in choosing among them greatly complicates an analysis of sentencing behavior. The investigator must be attentive not only to the factors determining length of sentence but also to type of sentence. The multiple facets of the sentencing decision raise a number of difficult modeling and measurement problems, which are described below.

1. A common practice in sentencing studies is to collapse qualitatively different types of sentences into a single index of sentence severity. These sentence severity indices are in some respects uncomfortably arbitrary. Are there alternative approaches for analyzing sentencing decisions that do not require the investigator ex ante to impose a severity index?

2. In cases in which a judge does not impose a determinate sentence but instead specifies only a minimum and maximum sentence, how should such a sentence decision be characterized and modeled?

In this section we discuss two models of the sentence decision that do not rely on the use of an imposed

severity index. We also address the problem raised in
the second question.

Two Models of Sentencing Decisions

The model we have developed assumes that sentence
severity can be represented by a single index, S.
Several of the papers we have reviewed implicitly make
the same assumption. Tiffany et al. (1975) and Diamond
and Zeisel (1975) scaled sentences of different type and
length with slightly modified versions of a severity
index developed by the Federal Administrative Office of
the Courts (1973). This index is, with a few exceptions,
consistent with a lexicographic ordering of sanction
severity. Severity scores across sanction types (e.g.,
prison versus probation) typically do not overlap and
thus reflect an implicit ranking of sanction types from
least to most severe. Within sanction type, sentences
are ordered from least to most severe.

The ordering of the severity of sanction types is in
general intuitively reasonable. A suspended sentence is
scaled lower than supervised probation, and supervised
probation equal to or lower than an active prison term.
In some instances these orderings are open to reasonable
dispute (e.g., fines of any amount are assumed less
severe than supervised probation), but in our opinion the
major problems with collapsing sentences of different
types and degree into a single metric are not the
consequence of the assumed ordering of sanction
severity. Rather, our principal reservations about the
use of these scales stem from two issues. First, the
assumed cardinality of the scales is uncomfortably
arbitrary. For example, Tiffany et al. (1975) assign a
score of 2 to supervised probation of 13-36 months,
whereas prison sentences of 13-24 months and 49-60 months
are assigned scores of 7 and 14, respectively. Is a
prison sentence of 55 months twice as harsh as a sentence
of 20 months, and is a 20 month prison sentence 2.5 times
as harsh as a sentence of 18 months of supervised
probation?

The arbitrary cardinality of the scales may increase
the difficulty of detecting more subtle influences on
sentencing decisions by introducing (unnecessary) error
in the measurement of sentencing outcomes. It also makes
the interpretation of the magnitude of measured effects
more difficult because the unit of measurement has no

objective interpretation. Moreover, having collapsed sentence into a single metric, the investigator can only analyze variations in this index with a single-equation processing model. This constrains the decision on sanction type to be a function of the same factors that influence the decision on sentence length within each sanction type. It also greatly constrains the functional form of the two relationships.

In this section we develop two approaches for analyzing sentencing decisions that do not require the ex ante imposition of a severity scale for reducing qualitatively different sentences to a single metric. In the first approach, both the type and the length of the sentence are determined by the value of a single latent variable reflecting characteristics of the case and the offender. The second approach allows for the possibility that decisions on the type and the length of the sentence are made with different decision rules.

Latent Variable Model of Sentencing

Figure 2-2 is a graphical depiction of our latent variable model of sentencing. The vertical axis in the figure depicts the value of a latent variable, Z^*. We assume that Z^* is determined by

$$Z^* = \underline{\alpha}'\underline{e} + \underline{\beta}'\underline{x} + \epsilon, \tag{32}$$

where $\underline{e}$ is a vector of observed variables defining event seriousness and legally relevant defendant characteristics, $\underline{x}$ is a vector of observed extralegal characteristics of the defendant and victim, α and β are vectors of coefficients, and ϵ is an unobserved classical disturbance. The disturbance is assumed to measure the influence of various factors that are relevant to the judge in determining sentence but are not observed by the investigator.

The latent variable Z^* can be interpreted as an index measuring the judge's perception of the sentence merited in the case, with larger values of Z^* corresponding to more severe (or at least as severe) sentences. The coefficient vectors $\underline{\alpha}$ and $\underline{\beta}$ can be interpreted as weights that calibrate the importance of various observable case-specific factors in determining the sentence.

The sentence imposed is assumed to be related to Z^* as follows. Define a series of threshold parameters, T_j,

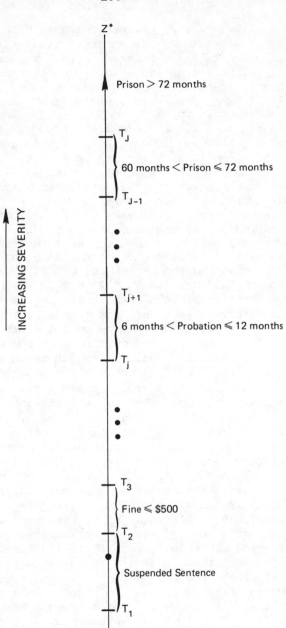

FIGURE 2-2   Latent Variable Model of Sentencing

$j = 1, 2, \ldots, J$, corresponding to each of J sentencing options presumed to be available to the judge. The T_j's are ordered so that T_1 corresponds to the least severe sentence and T_J to the most severe sentence. Sentencing option j is assumed to be chosen whenever $T_j \leq Z^* < T_{j+1}$, where T_{J+1} is definitionally set equal to infinity.

In Figure 2-1, the T_j's are denoted by horizontal slashes on the vertical axis. The T_j's define J sentencing options, which are ordered in Figure 2-2 from the least severe to the most severe. The ordering is based on the severity scale developed by the Federal Administrative Office of the Courts. The judge is assumed to compute the value of an index Z^* from case-specific information, some of which is observed by the investigator. He then compares the value of his index with the threshhold parameters denoted in the figure, choosing the sentencing option j with threshold parameter T_j for which $T_j \leq Z^* < T_{j+1}$.

Of interest are the parameters $\underline{\alpha}$, $\underline{\beta}$, and the T_j's. The coefficient vectors $\underline{\alpha}$ and $\underline{\beta}$ measure the effects of various case-specific factors on the sentence imposed. The threshold parameters coupled with $\underline{\alpha}$ and $\underline{\beta}$ define an implicit severity scale. The width between the T_j's coupled with $\underline{\alpha}$ and $\underline{\beta}$ determines the range of values of the explanatory variables in $\underline{e}$ and $\underline{x}$ that map into each sanction type. Both the coefficient vectors $\underline{\alpha}$ and $\underline{\beta}$ and the threshold parameters T_j, $j = 1, 2, \ldots, J$, can be estimated from a sample of observations on $\underline{e}$, $\underline{x}$, and the sentence imposed (given a rank ordering of the alternative sentences). A fuller discussion of this model, which is called the ordered PROBIT model for the case in which ε is assumed to be normally distributed, and the procedures available to estimate its parameters, can be found in Altman et al. (1981:Ch. 2).

The virtue of this latent variable model of the sentencing decision is that it does not require the analyst to impose an arbitrary scale to reduce sentences of different type and degree to a single metric. It only requires that the analyst be able to rank order the sentence options chosen according to a measure of severity. The threshold parameters, in conjunction with $\underline{\alpha}$ and $\underline{\beta}$, implicitly define a severity scale for offenses. Because these parameters are estimated from the data rather than imposed a priori, the implied severity scale is the one that best "fits" or "rationalizes" the sentences in the sample. It can be thought of as an estimate of the scale implicitly used by judges to translate case-specific information into actual sentences.

This type of model fits quite well into the framework we have developed. We assumed that there was only one sentencing option available to the judge, which he or she could set at a level S. The prosecutor and the defendant were assumed to make decisions based on their expectations about S and the probability of conviction. Such a model can easily be estimated by interpreting S to be the latent variable Z* defined above. We need only assume that the prosecutor and defendant operate on the basis of their perception of the expected sentence, the severity of the sentence (given conviction) being represented by the latent variable Z*.

An Alternative Model of the Sentencing Decision

While we believe the latent variable model is an improvement over the severity scale approach, it is perhaps an excessively restrictive conception of the sentencing decision. In particular, it is assumed that the choice of sanction type and length of sentence are both determined by the same latent index Z*. This implicitly assumes that the same factors that determine the sanction type also determine the length of sentence. It also constrains considerably the way the case-specific factors can affect the choice of sanction type and the choice of sentence length within the sanction type.

The model can be generalized considerably if we model the sentencing decision as a two-step decision, the first step corresponding to the choice of sanction type and the second step corresponding to the length of sentence given the sanction type. The first step can be modeled like the model discussed above. Define a latent variable R* as an index that determines the choice of sanction type. We assume that R* is generated by

$$R* = \underline{\gamma}'\underline{g} + v ,$$

where $\underline{g}$ is a vector of case-specific factors that affect the choice of sanction type, $\underline{\gamma}$ is a vector of coefficients (or weights), and v is an unobserved disturbance. The variable R* is then mapped into a choice of sanction type by a set of threshold parameters r_k, k = 1, 2, . . . , K, where K is the number of

sanction types available. As above, the choice of
sanction type depends on the value of R* relative to the
r_k. Given a sample of observations on $\underline{g}$ and the choice
of sanction type, we can estimate $\underline{\gamma}$ and the r_k, k = 1, 2,
. . . , K.

The second step can be modeled as a regression
equation. Let S_k represent the length of sentence for
sanction type k. Then S_k is assumed to be determined by

$$S_k = \underline{\theta}_k'\underline{h}_k + w_k ,$$

where $\underline{h}_k$ is a vector of variables that affect the length
of sentence for sanction type k, $\underline{\theta}_k$ is a vector of
coefficients for the kth sanction type equation, and w_k
is the disturbance for the kth sanction type equation.
The parameter vector $\underline{\theta}_k$ can be estimated given a sample
of observations on S_k and $\underline{h}_k$.

This type of model of the sentencing decision cannot
be easily adapted to the theoretical model we presented
in an earlier section. The fact that sentence severity
can no longer be characterized directly or indirectly by
a single metric S greatly complicates the model. If the
objectives of the prosecutor and defendant are to be
characterized in terms of a single metric of sentence
severity, then some mechanism for collapsing sentences of
different type and degree into this metric is necessary.
As previously discussed, the latent variable model of
sentencing provides this mechanism. The second model
provides no such mechanism.

The absence of such a mechanism is a result of the
second model's recursive characterization of the
sentencing process. The model does not require that all
case and defendant characteristics relevant to sentencing
be collapsed into a single metric that maps onto an
actual sentence. Indeed, the model is an explicit
disavowal of this conception of the sentencing process.
As a consequence, incorporation of this recursive model
of sentencing into the model developed earlier requires a
generalization of that model that takes account of the
multiplicity of sanctioning alternatives. The
prosecutor's objective of punishment maximization would
have to be specified in terms of a set of qualitatively
different penalty alternatives. Likewise, the
defendant's objective of minimizing his expected
punishment would have to be similarly specified.
Bargaining would have to take place concerning both the
sanction type and the sentence length. This is a much

more complicated process to model and is beyond the scope of this paper.

Modeling Indeterminate Sentences

In reviewing the literature on the effects of extralegal factors on case disposition, we have encountered an important and perplexing problem: How should indeterminate prison sentences be analyzed? As noted previously, in many jurisdictions judges are not required and are sometimes prohibited from imposing a prison term of a specified length. Instead they impose only a minimum and maximum term or in some instances simply remand the defendant to the custody of the Department of Corrections for a completely unspecified period. When the prison term is not specified exactly by the judge, actual time served is determined by a parole board or in some jurisdictions by the parole board with the consent of the sentencing judge.

Since the factors determining the length of sentence are an issue of particular concern, the use of appropriate models and statistical methodologies for analyzing indeterminate sentences deserves careful attention. To our knowledge, this issue has not been seriously addressed in the literature. Furthermore, in the studies reviewed, we found that the approaches used in dealing with this problem varied widely and that none was satisfactorily justified. For example, Chiricos and Waldo (1975) characterize an indeterminate sentence by the minimum term, Lizotte (1977) by the average of the minimum and maximum, and Tiffany et al. (1975) by the maximum. In no case do the authors provide a cogent justification for their measurement of a variable that is central to their analysis. Unfortunately, we cannot provide any specific suggestions for dealing with this problem. Its resolution requires a model of the objectives judges pursue in specifying the minimum and maximum sentence. While we have not been able to specify such a model, a discussion with one judge suggests that the following considerations may be useful in specifying a model.

1. The seriousness of the offense, the defendant's prior record, and his perceived threat to society may in the judge's opinion require at least some minimum term of incarceration.

2. If an individual on parole is convicted of another crime, he may be required to serve the remainder of his term for the crime for which he had been paroled. A high maximum may thus serve as a substantial deterrent to criminal behavior while on parole. The judge's view of the need for this deterrent may affect his specification of the maximum.

3. The judge may be very uncertain about the possibility that the defendant will reform. This uncertainty may be particularly great when the defendant has no prior record but has committed a serious crime. Uncertainty about the defendant's potential for reform may affect the spread between the minimum and the maximum.

We urge that immediate attention be given to development of a model of indeterminate sentencing. The absence of any such model is a major gap in the literature.

EXPERIMENTS IN SENTENCING RESEARCH

Designed experiments provide an alternative source of data for sentencing research. Most experiments in the literature are designed to analyze the behavior of judges. They present a group of judges with a set of case files and ask them the sentences they would impose (see Diamond and Zeisel, 1975; Partridge and Eldridge, 1974). The cases may be actual cases or artificially constructed ones designed to probe specific issues. Most studies tend to be interested in specific questions, such as the magnitude of discrimination and disparity in sentencing. We concentrate on these two issues in the discussion that follows.

The terms discrimination and disparity are somewhat vague. A more specific operational definition is provided by Kadane (personal communication, 1980):

Suppose two trials differ only in the race, sex or religion of the defendant (I like to think of them as plays or films in which the race, sex or religion of the actor playing the defendant differs, but the script is the same). Then any difference in sentencing we could call discrimination.

Suppose two trials differ only in the identity of the judge deciding the case. Then differences in the sentence could be called disparity.

This notion of disparity can be extended by noting
that identical cases tried by the same judge might result
in different sentences (one might imagine a judge trying
the same case repeatedly and having his recollection of
the previous trial erased before each new trial). This
form of disparity could be called within-judge
disparity. The form of disparity described by Kadane
might be called between-judge disparity.

These definitions emphasize that within-judge
disparity is inherently random. The severity of this
type of disparity might be quantified using a measure of
the amount of variation in this quantity, such as its
variance. The between-judge disparity is fixed for each
judge but varies randomly throughout the population of
all judges. Again, the severity of the problem is
reflected by the amount of variation in this quantity,
which might be measured by its variance. In the presence
of disparity, the amount of discrimination, as defined
above, is a randomly varying quantity as well. Its
severity can be captured using, say, the mean difference
between sentences in cases differing only in race, sex,
or SES of the defendant.

In view of the random nature of these phenomena, the
measurement of disparity and discrimination is inherently
a statistical problem. Ideally we would like to observe
different judges sentencing the same case (to measure
disparity between judges), the same judge sentencing a
case several times (to measure disparity within judges)
and the same judge sentencing the same cases with only
the race or sex of the defendant changed (to measure
discrimination). Data from such an experiment might be
analyzed using the additive mixed analysis of variance
model:

$$Y_{ijk} = \mu + v_i + \delta_j + c_k + \varepsilon_{ijk} , \qquad (33)$$

where Y_{ijk} is the sentence chosen in case i,j,k, v_i,
$i = 1, \ldots , I$, are the effects of the discriminatory
factors, δ_j, $j = 1, \ldots , J$, are the effects of the J
judges, c_k, $k = 1, \ldots , K$, are the effects of the K
basic cases, ε_{ijk} are the within-judge disparities for
each judgment, and μ is the overall mean sentence. The
factors v_i and c_k are fixed. The factors δ_j and ε_{ijk} are
assumed to be independent random variables with zero mean
and respective variances σ_δ^2 and σ_ε^2. Our interest
focuses on the levels of discrimination $v_1, \ldots , v_I$

and the amounts of disparity between judges, σ_δ^2, and within judges, σ_ϵ^2.[11]

For the case of nonexperimental data, the experimenter cannot control the cases that appear in court. Consequently, the cases studied for each level of the discriminatory factor and each judge are different. The model analogous to equation (33) that is appropriate for the analysis of nonexperimental data is

$$Y_{ijk} = \mu + v_i + \delta_j + c_{ijk} + \epsilon_{ijk} , \qquad (34)$$

where c_{ijk} is subscripted by i, j, and k to denote that it differs for each case. The parameters of this model cannot be estimated directly without imposing identifying restrictions on the c_{ijk}'s. The usual approach is to use some variables like seriousness of the offense, defendant's prior record, etc. to approximate the case effects. If we can write $c_{ijk} = g(x_{ijk}) + v_{ijk}$, where $g(\cdot)$ is a function that depends on some unknown parameters, $\underline{x}$ is a vector of case attributes, and v_{ijk} is a disturbance with variance σ_v^2, then equation (34) can be expressed as

$$Y_{ijk} = \mu + v_i + \delta_j + g(\underline{x}_{ijk}) + v_{ijk} + \epsilon_{ijk} .$$

If the errors v_{ijk} have mean zero and are independent of δ and ϵ_{ijk}, then all of parameters of the model are identified except σ_ϵ^2 and σ_v^2. However, $(\sigma_v^2 + \sigma_\epsilon^2)$, which provides an upper bound on both σ_v^2 and σ_ϵ^2, is identified. Unfortunately, due to selection effects and omitted variables, the assumption that $E[v_{ijk}] = 0$ is rarely justified; as a result, it is very difficult, if not impossible, to obtain consistent estimates of the parameters from these observations alone.

The problems in dealing with observational data are due primarily to the lack of comparability in the observed cases. This requires that the investigator control for differences in cases using observed attributes of the case. Some of the problems with this approach, such as sample selection, were discussed earlier; others are discussed in Garber et al. (in this volume). A reasonable alternative to using observational data is to create an environment that is similar to the courtroom in its essential features but that enables the investigator to control the cases that are considered. This is the idea behind sentencing experiments. If J judges consider K different cases, each at I levels of the discriminatory variable, then the imposed sentences might be written as

$$Y_{ijk} = \mu^* + \nu_i^* + \delta_j^* + c_k^* + \varepsilon_{ijk}^* . \qquad (35)$$

This model is of the same form as equation (33) and its parameters can easily be estimated. However, since the experimental setting is not identical to the court setting, the parameters, in particular the effects of the discriminatory variable $\nu_1^*, \ldots, \nu_I^*$ and the disparity variances σ_δ^2* and σ_ε^2*, may not be equal to the corresponding parameters in equation (33). This difficulty is often referred to as the problem of the external validity of the experiment.

There are three main challenges to the external validity of a sentencing experiment: Cases may not be complete or real enough to simulate actual cases, judges participating in the experiment may not be representative of judges as a whole, and judges' awareness that they are participating in an experiment might cause them to respond differently than they would in a courtroom. These problems and some possible remedies are discussed in turn.

In an experimental setting it is impossible to present judges with case information that is identical to the information they would have in a court setting. This is especially true if cases are summarized in terms of a limited number of pertinent variables. If judges do not receive all the information they need, then they may be unwilling to make a decision or, if forced to make a decision, they may use the information available along with their perceptions about the unavailable information. If these perceptions are correlated with the available information, then coefficient estimates may reflect the influence of this imputed information rather than the information that is provided. In particular, ν_i^* and ν_i, the effects of the discriminatory variable, may not be the same.

To minimize this problem, judges should be provided with information that is as close as possible to the information that would be available in a courtroom. Judges might attend selected court hearings or be shown video tapes of actual hearings. Video tapes have been used in a number of experimental studies of jury behavior. For artificially constructed cases (e g., cases that are constructed from actual ones by, say, changing the race of the defendant) actors might be used to act out the hearing. This could be done once and recorded on video tape or it could be done repeatedly with each judge in the experiment acting as the presiding judge.

The drawback of this approach is its high cost, both in time and money. Case files are less realistic but also easier and less expensive to use. It is not clear how much is actually lost if a well-designed case file is substituted for an actual or reenacted hearing. Preliminary experiments might be used to determine a reasonable format for presenting cases. Certain control questions designed to determine whether the information presented is adequate might be composed. For example, judges might be asked whether they felt that any additional information that might be available in court would change their decision. Several different questions might be asked, such as "What decision would you make based on the information you have?" and "What decision would you most likely make if you encountered this case in court?"

If the judges use the available information to construct subjective probability distributions over the possible values of the unavailable information, then these two questions address different aspects of these distributions. The answer to the second question would be the sentence associated with the mode of the subjective distribution, whereas, under quadratic loss, the first question would be answered with the sentence corresponding to the mean of that distribution. Thus in the presence of incomplete information, the answers to these questions might differ, whereas they would be the same if the necessary information was provided. Different answers can therefore be taken as an indication that the case information was not adequate (Manski and Nagin, 1981, discuss this point in the context of consumer choice surveys).

If an experiment is based on a subset of judges, then it is imperative that the subset be representative. In many sentencing experiments the participating judges are volunteers. Even when all judges in a particular jurisdiction participate in an experiment, nonresponse rates are often so high that participation in the experiment has to be viewed as essentially voluntary. As a result, judges who do participate are likely to be more conscious of existing problems and more interested in reducing them than the average judge. An experiment based on such a sample will tend to underestimate the

seriousness of these problems. To protect against this
kind of bias, an experimental format, such as personal
interviews, can be used to minimize the nonresponse rate.

Even if the cases presented to the judges are real
cases presented in their natural setting, the judges will
always be aware of the fact they are participating in an
experiment. Their decisions clearly will not have the
impact of decisions handed down in court, for a prison
sentence handed down in an experiment does not send
anyone to prison. As a result, judges may treat a
decision in an experiment less seriously than a decision
in court. To alleviate this problem, judges must be
provided with an incentive to treat experiments with the
same importance they would treat an actual case. For
example, decisions made by a panel of judges on an actual
case might be provided to the presiding judge before a
decision is rendered. This is done in the sentencing
council experiments discussed in Diamond and Zeisel
(1975).

The most serious problem in sentencing experiments is
the evaluative nature of the experiments themselves.
Most experiments are designed to collect data on a
specific problem, e.g., the extent of discrimination and
disparity in sentencing. This can rarely be concealed
from the judges participating in the experiment. As a
result, individual judges may try to ensure that they do
not deviate too far from perceived norms, thus leading to
an underestimate of the severity of the problem under
study.

This individual sensitivity to evaluation can be
reduced by keeping responses anonymous. However, the
fact that results of the experiments may be used by
critics of the judiciary to support changes in the system
may cause judges who want to maintain the status quo to
adjust their decisions to reduce the apparent severity of
the problems under study. This bias is likely to be
particularly severe if the experiment is an unusual event
rather than a routine matter. It may be reduced if
making decisions on experimental cases is required of all
jduges in a jurisdiction on a regular basis.

The reaction to the experimenter's intent may also be
reduced if the experimenter can deceive the judges as to
the purpose of the experiment. This requires a
convincing cover story and a carefully designed
questionnaire that does not reveal the true purpose of
the experiment. Deceptions of this type are often used
for similar reasons in psychological experiments,

although they raise serious ethical questions (see Rosenthal and Rosnow, 1969). Furthermore, in view of the narrow range of issues considered in most sentencing studies, it is not clear whether these deceptions will succeed. Thus it is unlikely that these biases can be eliminated completely.

If it is not possible to prevent the judges from adjusting their answers in an experiment, then it might be possible to control for these adjustments by modeling the process that generates them. Suppose, for example, that experimental cases have been constructed from actual cases by varying, say, the race of the defendant. In this case, using equations (33) and (35), for each k there is one pair i,j (the race of the actual defendant and the judge who heard the case) for which the actual decision is available. For the other i,j pairs only experimental observations exist. Thus for each k,

$$Y_{ijk} = \mu + v_i + \delta_j + c_k + \varepsilon_{ijk}$$

for one pair ij, and

$$Y_{ijk} = \mu^* + v_i^* + \delta_j^* + c_k^* + \varepsilon_{ijk}^*$$

otherwise. These observations might be combined by assuming that the overall mean sentence and the case effects are the same for the experimental and nonexperimental observations, i.e., $\mu^* = \mu$ and $c_k^* = c_k$, but that the effects of the discriminatory factor and the disparities in the experimental observations have been scaled down by the factors α, β, and γ, respectively. Thus $v_i^* = \alpha v_i$, $\delta_j^* = \beta \delta_j$, and $\varepsilon_{ijk}^* = \gamma \varepsilon_{ijk}$, where α, β, $\gamma > 0$ (and probably less than one). The observed court cases can then be used to calibrate the experimental responses.

This point illustrates one way in which experiments can be used in conjunction with nonexperimental data. Experiments can be used to validate results obtained from nonexperimental data or to provide alternative estimates with different biases. In particular, as noted above, observed court cases provide only an upper bound on the disparity within judges, whereas experiments (before adjustment) tend to underestimate this quantity. Simultaneous use of experiments and courtroom observations can thus provide bounds on the severity of disparity.

Experiments might also be used to deal with the selection problem. Wilkins et al. (1973) and others use experiments to analyze the details of the judges' decision processes, including the variables they use in making decisions and the order in which these variables are considered. Similar experiments could be performed with other members of the criminal justice system, such as the prosecutor. The results might provide information about the factors that contribute to the correlation between the unobserved variables in the different stages of the selection process. This information might help the investigator assess the magnitude of the correlation and determine which, if any, additional variables should be measured.

Experiments can be used to address a number of questions that cannot be answered using observational data. For example, judges might be asked to choose both a determinate sentence and a minimum and a maximum sentence for hypothetical cases. Their responses could be used to evaluate the implications of laws on determinate sentencing. Experiments can also provide information about cases that occur too infrequently in court for observational data to provide accurate results. Many studies, for example, have found it impossible to investigate the relationship between sentence and the defendant's sex because the number of women in their samples was negligible.

So far our discussion has been concerned with experiments for analyzing the behavior of judges. Other aspects of the criminal justice system can also be analyzed with experiments. For example, experiments could be designed to determine whether prosecutors act in a discriminatory fashion when deciding whether to prosecute a case. Experiments might also be useful aids for constructing models of the plea bargaining process.

In addition to providing data for analysis, experiments may also have a beneficial side effect, especially if they are conducted on a regular basis. Many judges and other members of the criminal justice system are sensitive to the problems of disparity and discrimination in sentencing. The results of regular controlled experiments might reduce disparity and discrimination by helping judges understand and calibrate their own decisions.

The major drawback to experiments is their cost. The problems associated with experimental data may seem easier to solve than the problems of observational data, but the cost of running experiments, both in money and in the demands they place on the judge's time, make it difficult to obtain samples that are large enough to provide very precise estimates of the parameters of interest. Thus it is unlikely that observational data, in which sample sizes are typically large, can be dispensed with entirely. The simultaneous use of both approaches, in which the particular advantages of each approach can be exploited, is an avenue that deserves more attention in future work.

CONCLUSIONS

We argued that the studies of discrimination in case disposition generally suffer from at least one of three major shortcomings: (1) the absence of formal models of the processing decisions in the criminal justice system, (2) failure to consider the sample selection biases that result from the many screening decisions in the criminal justice system, and (3) the use of arbitrary scales for scaling qualitatively different dispositions.

Most of our discussion of these problems focused on ways in which they can lead to underestimates of the severity of discrimination in the criminal justice system. Despite these problems, some studies do find evidence of discrimination. However, this should not be interpreted as suggesting that discrimination is actually present. There are many other problems, such as the omission of important variables possibly correlated with race or social status, that can lead to overestimates of the severity of discrimination. Some of these points are discussed in detail in Garber et al. (in this volume).

Each of the shortcomings enumerated above is, in principle, remediable. However, correcting them will require a formidable research agenda. Carefully specified models reflecting the essential motivations of the principal actors in the criminal justice system and the dynamics of their interplay are required. Furthermore, the data sets to be considered will have to be carefully chosen and perhaps combined with the results of designed experiments in order to mitigate the effects of sample selection. Novel and complex statistical techniques will be needed for the analysis. While these obstacles are formidable, we see no alternative to addressing these problems. If they continue to be neglected, then the extent of discrimination in the criminal justice system will continue to be mired in uncertainties so great that no generally accepted resolution will ever be reached.

APPENDIX

Proposition: If x is uniformly distributed then $\phi_1 = \phi_2$, where

$$\phi_1 \equiv E[x \mid x + w_1 \geq -(\alpha + \beta)] - E(x \mid x + w_1 \geq -\alpha) \quad \text{(A-1)}$$
$$\phi_2 \equiv E[x \mid x + w_1 \geq -(\alpha + \beta), \; x + w_2 \geq -(\alpha + \beta)]$$
$$- E(x \mid x + w_1 \geq -\alpha, \; x + w_2 \geq -\alpha) \; . \quad \text{(A-2)}$$

Proof: Equations (A-1) and (A-2) can be rewritten as

$$\phi_1 = E[x \mid x \geq -(\alpha + \beta) - w_1] - E(x \mid x \geq -\alpha - w_1) \quad \text{(A-3)}$$
$$\phi_2 = E[x \mid x \geq -(\alpha + \beta) - w_1, \; x \geq -(\alpha + \beta) - w_2]$$
$$- E(x \mid x \geq -\alpha - w_1, \; x \geq -\alpha - w_2) \; . \quad \text{(A-4)}$$

Let $f_1(\Gamma) \equiv p(-w_1 = \Gamma)$ and $f_2(\Gamma) \equiv p[\max(-w_1, -w_2) = \Gamma]$. Note that given w_1 and w_2, one of the two conditioning arguments in each of the two terms on the righthand side of equation (A-4) is redundant. Using this and $f_1(\Gamma)$ and $f_2(\Gamma)$ to integrate out w_1 and w_2, equations (A-3) and (A-4) can be written as

$$\phi_1 = \int \{E[x \mid x \geq -(\alpha + \beta) + \Gamma] - E(x \mid x \geq -\alpha + \Gamma)\} f_1(\Gamma) \, d\Gamma$$
$$\phi_2 = \int \{E[x \mid x \geq -(\alpha + \beta) + \Gamma] - E(x \mid x \geq -\alpha + \Gamma)\} f_2(\Gamma) \, d\Gamma ,$$

which implies

$$\phi_1 - \phi_2 = \int \{E[x \mid x \geq -(\alpha + \beta) + \Gamma]$$
$$- E(x \mid x \geq -\alpha + \Gamma)\} [f_1(\Gamma) - f_2(\Gamma)] \, d\Gamma \; . \quad \text{(A-5)}$$

Using the fact that if x is uniformly distributed, $E(x \mid x \geq \lambda) = (a + \lambda)/2$, where a is the maximum value x can assume, equation (A-5) implies

$$\phi_1 - \phi_2 = 1/2 \int -\beta [f_1(\Gamma) - f_2(\Gamma)] \, d\Gamma = 0 \; ,$$

where the second equality follows from the fact that $f_1(\Gamma)$ and $f_2(\Gamma)$ are proper probability density functions. This result generalizes trivially if x is multiplied by any scalar in the conditioning arguments in equations (A-1) and (A-2).

This establishes the assertion in the text that if x is uniformly distributed and $\gamma_1 = \gamma_2 = \gamma_3$ then $\theta_2 = \theta_3$.

NOTES

1. This is because a linear function of $\underline{x}$ is not constrained to lie between zero and one.

2. In the jargon of statistics, neither σ^2 nor b is identified (assuming, in the case of b, that $\underline{x}$ contains a constant regressor). This can be seen as follows. Multiply σ^2, b, and $\underline{\beta}$ by the same positive constant. Then $p(y_i = 1 | \underline{x})$ is unchanged. Hence it is not possible to estimate the levels of both $\underline{\beta}$ and σ^2. Instead, σ^2 is typically set equal to one for estimation purposes and $\underline{\beta}$ is effectively estimated relative to the arbitrary value assigned to σ^2. As for b, suppose that $\underline{x}$ contains a constant regressor. Then if $\underline{\beta}_1$, the constant term in the regression, and b are changed by the same amount, b - $\underline{x}_i'\underline{\beta}$, hence $F(b - \underline{x}_i'\underline{\beta})$ remains unchanged. As a result, for estimation purposes, b is typically set equal to zero and the cutoff level is subsumed into the constant.

3. The coefficient of u_i in this expression follows from the fact that if $E(y | z)$ is linear in z then y can be expressed as

$$y = \mu_z + [\text{Cov}(y,z)/\text{Var}(z)](z - \mu_z) + v ,$$

where $\mu_z \equiv E(z)$, $V(v) = \sigma_y^2(1 - \rho^2)$, $\rho = [\text{Cov}(y,z)/\sigma_y\sigma_z]$, $V(z) \equiv \sigma_z^2$, and $V(y) \equiv \sigma_y^2$.

4. The selection that occurs as a result of the imprisonment decision is somewhat different from other selection mechanisms we have discussed. The imprisonment decision is made by the judge who also determines the length of the sentence. The formal distinction between the imprisonment decision and the determination of the sentence length is thus somewhat artificial. Nevertheless, if the two decisions are viewed as separable, which is implicit in studies that investigate the sentence length for individuals that have been sent to prison, then the appropriate mathematical formulation of this process is the same as the one that would be appropriate if the decisions were made by separate individuals. As a result, the same model applies.

5. We do not distinguish between jury and bench trials. The model could easily be generalized to include this option, but such a generalization would only complicate

the discussion without further illuminating the points we wish to make.

6.   Another relevant factor is time spent in pretrial detention. Conditions in jail are frequently worse than in prison. If the defendant opts for a trial, the time spent in pretrial detention is likely to be increased.

7.   The decision to charge includes the choice of whether to prosecute and the choice of which charges to file given prosecution. We consider only the former choice.

8.   Dismissal can occur before or after charges have been filed. We treat dismissals that occur after charges have been filed as decisions not to charge. The term dismissal is restricted to instances in which the prosecutor declines to prosecute after an arrest has been made.

9.   The factors giving rise to selection bias involve the stages preceding the sentence length decision and thus are not related to the true extent of discrimination in the sentence length decision of each judge.

10.   However, we argue below that this finding may actually be the result of discrimination at the prosecution and/or conviction stage rather than in sentencing.

11.   The purpose of introducing this model is merely to fix ideas. The discussion could equally well be based on a more complicated ANOVA model, one in which the effects of the discriminatory factors are viewed as nested within judges, a binary model, a binary plus a conditional continuous model, or an ordered multiple response model.

REFERENCES

Administrative Office of the United States Courts
   1973   Federal Offenders in United States District
          Court, 1971. Washington, D.C.: Administrative
          Office of U.S. Courts.
Altman, E. I., R. A. Avery, R. A. Eisenbeis, and J. F.
Sinkey, Jr.
   1981   Application of Classification Techniques in
          Business, Banking, and Finance. Greenwich,
          Conn.: JAI Press.

Chiricos, T. G., and G. P. Waldo
  1975 Socioeconomic status and criminal sentencing:
        an empirical assessment of a conflict
        proposition. American Sociological Review
        40(December):753-772.
Clarke, S. H., and G. G. Koch
  1976 The influence of income and other factors on
        whether criminal defendants go to prison. Law &
        Society Review 11(1):59-92.
Cook, P. J., and D. S. Nagin
  1979 Does the Weapon Matter? An Evaluation of a
        Weapon-Emphasis Policy in the Prosecution of
        Violent Offenders. Washington, D.C.: Institute
        for Law and Social Research.
Cox, D. R.
  1970 Analysis of Binary Data. London: Methuen & Co.
Diamond, S. S., and H. Zeisel
  1975 Sentencing councils: a study of sentence
        disparity and its reduction. University of
        Chicago Law Review 43:109-149.
Farrell, R. A., and V. L. Swigert
  1978 Prior offense record as a self-fulfilling
        prophecy. Law and Society 12(Spring):437-453.
Forst, B., and K. Brosi
  1977 A theoretical and empirical analysis of the
        prosecutor. Journal of Legal Studies
        6(1):177-191.
Forst, B., J. Lucianovic, and S. J. Cox
  1977 What Happens After Arrest? A Court Perspective
        of Police Operations in the District of
        Columbia. Washington, D.C.: Institute for Law
        and Social Research.
Frase, R. S.
  1978 The decision to prosecute federal criminal
        charges: a quantitative study of prosecutorial
        discretion. University of Chicago Law Review
        47:246-330.
Gibson, J. L.
  1978 Race as a determinant of criminal sentences: a
        methodological critique and a case study. Law
        and Society Review 12(Spring):455-478.
Goldberger, A. S.
  1964 Econometric Theory. New York: John Wiley &
        Sons.
  1980 Abnormal Selection Bias. Unpublished
        manuscript. University of Wisconsin.

Greenwood, P., et al.
   1973   Prosecution of Adult Felony Defendants in Los
          Angeles County: A Policy Perspective. Santa
          Monica, Calif.: Rand Corporation.
Hagan, J.
   1975   Parameters of criminal prosecution: an
          application of path analysis to a problem of
          criminal justice. Journal of Criminal Law &
          Criminology 65(4):536-544.
Heckman, J. J.
   1979   Sample selection bias as a specification error.
          Econometrica 47(1):153-161.
LaFree, G. D.
   1980   The effect of sexual stratification by race on
          official reactions to rape. American
          Sociological Review 45(October):842-854.
Landes, W. M.
   1971   An economic analysis of the courts. Journal of
          Law and Economics 14:61-106.
Lizotte, A. J.
   1977   Extra-legal factors in Chicago's criminal
          courts: testing the conflict model of criminal
          justice. Social Problems 25(5):564-580.
Manski, C. F., and D. S. Nagin
   1981   Behavioral Intentions and Revealed Preference.
          Unpublished manuscript. Carnegie-Mellon
          University.
Olsen, R.
   1980   A least squares correction for selectivity
          bias. Econometrica 48:1815-1820.
Partridge, A., and W. G. Eldridge
   1974   The second circuit sentencing study: a report
          to the judges of the second circuit. Federal
          Judicial Center No. 74-4.
Reiss, A. J.
   1975   Public prosecutors and criminal prosecution in
          the United States of America. Juridical
          Review:1-21.
Rosenthal, R., and R. L. Rosnow, eds.
   1969   Artifacts in Behavioral Research. New York:
          Academic Press.
Swigert, V. L., and R. A. Farrell
   1977   Normal homicides and the law. American
          Sociological Review 42(February):16-32.
Tiffany, L. P., Y. Avichai, and G. W. Peters
   1975   A statistical analysis of sentencing in federal
          courts: defendants convicted after trial, 1967-
          1968. The Journal of Legal Studies 4:397-417.

128

Wilkins, L. J., D. U. Gottfredson, J. O. Robinson, and
C. A. Sadowsky
   1973   Information Selection and Use in Parole
          Decision-Making. NCCD Research Center, National
          Council on Crime and Delinquency, Davis, Calif.
Wolfgang, M. E., and M. Reidel
   1973   Race, judicial discretion, and the death
          penalty. The Annals of the American Academy of
          Political and Social Science 407(May):119-133.
Zimring, F. E., J. Eigen, and S. O'Malley
   1976   Punishing homicide in Philadelphia:
          perspectives on the death penalty. University
          of Chicago Law Review 43(2):227-252.

3

The Role of Extralegal Factors in Determining Criminal Case Disposition

Steven Garber, Steven Klepper,
and Daniel Nagin

INTRODUCTION

The major participants in the criminal justice process
exercise substantial discretion. An issue that has
received considerable attention is the degree to which
the existence of such discretion results in systematic
inequities in the disposition of criminal cases. In
particular, numerous empirical studies have examined the
extent to which members of racial minority groups and/or
disadvantaged social classes are treated more harshly
because of their race or socioeconomic status.

   Most of the empirical studies on case disposition use
regression and related statistical techniques.
Correlations between outcomes of the various processing
stages in the criminal justice system and measured case
and defendant characteristics are examined.
Discrimination is analyzed by testing for an empirical
association between extralegal characteristics, such as
race and socioeconomic status, and various decisions in
the criminal justice system, holding constant observable,
legally relevant case and defendant characteristics.

   A fundamental problem with this approach is that many
of the important factors affecting case disposition are

We thank Alfred Blumstein, Jacqueline Cohen, and Franklin
Fisher for their helpful comments.

129

extremely difficult to measure. In particular, the seriousness of an offense and the quality of the evidence, perhaps the two most important factors affecting case disposition, involve important elements for which researchers typically can observe no data. When seriousness and case quality are correlated with race and social status, the techniques currently being employed yield biased estimates of the effects of extralegal factors on case disposition.

This possibility is particularly troublesome for studies of discrimination in the criminal justice system because even if discrimination is present and of sufficient concern to warrant reform, extralegal factors are undoubtedly of secondary importance in explaining variations in case disposition. Under these circumstances, biases attributable to measurement error may dominate the estimated effects of extralegal factors. Thus inferences about the incidence of discrimination based on standard regression techniques may be seriously distorted and are unlikely to provide a reliable basis for policy reform.

One response to this problem is to measure more accurately the primary determinants of case disposition. However, the inherent unobservability of a number of the components of the primary determinants suggests strongly that this strategy is unlikely to resolve the ambiguities that plague existing studies. We propose an alternative approach known as structural equation modeling. It involves explicit mathematical representation of the fundamental mechanisms believed to generate the data. For the study of discrimination in the criminal justice system, it involves modeling the fundamental relationships linking observable case outcomes to both their observable and unobservable causes. If a sufficient number of decisions affected by the unobservable principal determinants of case disposition are observed, it is possible to control fully for forces that cannot be observed. It is then possible in principle to make inferences about the extent of discrimination that are not distorted by the inevitable lack of accurate measurements of the primary determinants of case disposition. The methods we propose are relatively complex, but we know of no simpler way to control for the effects of unobservable variables.

The paper is organized as follows. First we review nine recent and influential empirical studies of discrimination in the criminal justice system. The major purpose of the review is to provide motivation and background for the discussion that follows. In the next section we discuss statistical implications of the impossibility of measuring accurately the primary determinants of criminal case disposition. We then illustrate the import of these statistical issues by presenting alternative interpretations of various results reported in the literature. We then illustrate the proposed approach by presenting a structural equation model of criminal case disposition. We model nine decisions affecting the criminal process, taking explicit account of the measurement difficulties discussed. The next section is a discussion of the estimability of the parameters of our illustrative structural model and an example that illustrates how the effects of unobserved variables can be estimated. We then provide a heuristic discussion indicating how our illustrative model aids in the effort to obtain less ambiguous data summaries. In the next section we indicate briefly how future studies might take account simultaneously of the measurement issues emphasized here and the sample selection issues discussed in Klepper et al. (in this volume). The next section is a brief discussion of the trade-offs in specifying alternative structural models of the criminal justice system. The final section contains concluding remarks.

EMPIRICAL STUDIES OF DISCRIMINATION IN THE CRIMINAL JUSTICE SYSTEM

This section reviews nine recent and influential studies on the incidence of discrimination in the criminal justice system. The studies are of three kinds: studies of the choice of sentence given conviction, studies of case disposition[1] given arrest and/or indictment, and one longitudinal study of forcible sex offenses from arrest through sentencing. Some of the studies analyze samples combining dissimilar offenses, whereas others concentrate on specific offenses ranging from theft to murder.

We first discuss the studies of sentence given conviction and case disposition given arrest. This is followed by a review of studies on the various stages preceding sentencing, beginning with the conviction process and working backward to the choice of plea, release on and setting of bail, choice of legal representation, charge, and the decision to prosecute. Since only LaFree (1980a) examines separately the stages preceding sentencing, it was necessary to supplement the nine studies with a few additional studies of the stages preceding sentencing. We conclude with a summary of the major findings of the various studies.

Case Disposition and Sentencing Studies

The various studies of case disposition and sentencing focus on a small number of common forces. They include:

(1) Seriousness of the offense. Nearly all the studies include a measure of the charge to control for seriousness of the offense. The exceptions are Farrell and Swigert (1978), Swigert and Farrell (1977), and Chiricos and Waldo (1975), which concentrate on specific offenses.

Some of the studies also try to use characteristics of the offense to control more completely for seriousness. For example, Lizotte (1977:569) takes account of such factors as whether the defendant resisted arrest, the number of defendants, the sobriety of the defendant, injury to the victim, and the value of property taken. For forcible sex offenses, LaFree (1980a) considers such factors as whether a weapon was used and the type of offense (i.e., rape or attempted rape).

(2) Prior record. All of the studies include a variable to represent the criminal history of the defendant. Measures of prior record range from a dummy variable indicating whether the defendant was ever arrested to the total of the maximum statutory penalties of the defendant's prior convictions.

(3) Type of legal representation. A number of studies examine the choice of legal representation, distinguishing no attorney, a public defender, and privately retained counsel. The choice of legal representation is expected to affect primarily the probability of conviction and the sentence resulting from a plea bargain. Legal representation is not generally viewed as affecting sentence if the defendant is convicted at trial, although Tiffany et al. (1975) include a measure of legal representation in their sentencing study of defendants convicted at trial.

(4) Release on bail. A number of the studies include a variable indicating whether the defendant was released on bail. Being out on bail is expected to improve the defendant's ability to develop an effective defense, which is expected to be helpful both at trial and in plea bargaining.

(5) Type of conviction. Some of the studies that combine guilty pleas and trial convictions include an additive dummy variable denoting whether the defendant pleaded guilty. In studies of case disposition, a plea of guilty is generally expected to lead to a worse outcome in that it precludes acquittal. In studies of convictions, guilty pleas are generally assumed to be the result of plea bargains and hence are expected to result in lighter sentences, ceteris paribus.

(6) Miscellaneous factors. Some of the studies include the age of the defendant, whether the defendant is employed, and the type of county (urban versus rural) in which the defendant is convicted.

(7) Discriminatory or extralegal factors. Various characteristics of the defendant that are not legally relevant are included in all the studies. They include race, socioeconomic status (SES), sex, and the racial composition of the victim-defendant dyad. In addition, Clarke and Koch (1976) use the average income in the Census tract in which the defendant resides as a measure of the defendant's income, while other studies use SES as a proxy for income. Swigert and Farrell (1977) distinguish a characteristic they label "normal primitive" to denote particularly lower class, black defendants who are (stereotypically) thought to be disposed toward violent behavior.

The conclusions of the various studies of final case outcome can be summarized as follows. First, virtually all the studies that include a variable measuring the charge found that the seriousness of the offense is the most important factor affecting case outcome. This is most evident for studies that analyze only convictions. Second, all the studies conclude that the prior record of the defendant is important. Third, all the studies that include a variable denoting whether the defendant makes bail infer that it is an important factor in case outcome. Fourth, most of the studies that include legal representation found that it affects case outcome, but the nature of this effect varies considerably among the studies. Clarke and Koch (1976) and Tiffany et al. (1975) conclude that for some types of cases legal representation affects the sentence received, while Hagan (1975), Lizotte (1977), Farrell and Swigert (1978), and Swigert and Farrell (1977) infer that legal representation matters principally through making bail and secondarily through choice of plea. Fifth, type of conviction generally seems to be important: Defendants who plead guilty fare worse on average than those who plead not guilty (Hagan, 1975:541; Farrell and Swigert, 1978:449; Swigert and Farrell, 1977:26) but fare better than defendants who are convicted at trial (LaFree, 1980a:850).

The inferences concerning the role of extralegal characteristics differ considerably across the studies. One point of agreement is that if extralegal characteristics affect case outcome, their quantitative significance is small compared with the other factors discussed above. This view is consistent with Hagan's (1974) review of earlier studies. Most of the studies find a role for some extralegal characteristics, and different characteristics appear to be important in different studies. Swigert and Farrell (1977) and Farrell and Swigert (1978) infer that for murder cases, SES has a significant effect on case outcome, holding constant a number of other factors. LaFree (1980a) found that for forcible sex offenses, cases involving white victims and black defendants are generally treated more harshly. Clarke and Koch (1976) infer that for burglaries and larcenies, defendants with lower incomes are more likely to be imprisoned. They attribute most of this effect to the correlations between income and making bail and income and the choice of legal representation. Tiffany et al. (1975) found that for defendants with no prior record, blacks receive significantly more severe sentences, holding constant a number of other factors.

Some studies that did not find a direct role for extralegal characteristics in determining case disposition suggest an indirect role for such factors. Hagan's (1975) results suggest that individuals with lower socioeconomic status in Canada are charged with more serious offenses and that charge directly affects case outcome. Lizotte (1977) infers that race and SES play important roles in determining whether the defendant is released on bail, which in turn has an important effect on case outcome. Only the results of Gibson (1978) and Chiricos and Waldo (1975) suggest a role

neither for race nor SES, although Gibson does present
some evidence of racial discrimination on the part of
some judges.[2]

Overall the studies suggest that low-status blacks
fare worse in the criminal justice system than other
defendants. Below we examine the information provided by
the various studies concerning the extent to which this
disadvantage is attributable to events prior to the
sentencing decision.

The Conviction Process

LaFree (1980a, 1980b) focuses on factors affecting
conviction at trial for forcible sex offenses. None of
the other studies focuses directly on the conviction
process, although Clarke and Koch (1976) provide some
evidence concerning the conviction process for burglaries
and larcenies. Indirect evidence about the conviction
process is also provided by the studies of Lizotte
(1977), Hagan (1975), Farrell and Swigert (1978), and
Swigert and Farrell (1977), all of whom examined case
outcome following arrest or indictment.

The various studies emphasize two types of factors:
quality of the evidence and prior record of the
defendant. For forcible sex offenses, LaFree (1980b)
constructed measures of the quality of the prosecution
case and the quality of the defense case. He included
other variables, such as misconduct on the part of the
defendant and the victim's living arrangement, to proxy
for whether the alleged act was voluntary. Lizotte
(1977) also recognizes the importance of such factors.
He constructed an index that represents the availability
of 10 different types of evidence, including such factors
as the number of eye witnesses, length of time between
arrest and the incident, the recovery of a weapon, etc.
(Lizotte, 1977:568-9). Clarke and Koch (1976) also
constructed an admittedly crude measure of the quality of
the evidence using the length of time elapsed between the
offense and the arrest. LaFree (1980b) used a measure of
promptness of the report of the offense to the police.

Prior record is also cited in some of the studies.
LaFree (1980b:843) notes that despite legal procedures
intended to conceal from the jury the defendant's prior
record, it was often inferred by jurors from other
testimony or through the defendant's failure to testify.
Clarke and Koch (1976:72) conjecture that prior record

might affect the prosecutor's efforts to convict the defendant. Swigert and Farrell (1977) and Farrell and Swigert (1978) also consider the role of prior record in the conviction process.

The findings of the various studies suggest that both the quality of the evidence and the defendant's prior record affect the likelihood of conviction. LaFree (1980a, 1980b) infers that both factors are relevant in forcible sex offenses. Lizotte's (1977) results concerning the role of the quality of the evidence are inconclusive, but he attributes this to the equivocal nature of his index when applied to different types of crimes (Lizotte, 1977:57). Clarke and Koch (1976) found a minor role for the promptness of arrest and an insignificant effect of prior record, although their results are difficult to interpret since cases settled by guilty plea as well as at trial were considered jointly.

Only LaFree (1980a) examined the role of the race of the defendant in affecting the likelihood of conviction at trial. He did not find a significant role for race.

The Plea Decision

A number of the studies examined the choice of plea. None of the studies proposes an explicit theory of the plea bargaining process. The choice of plea is approached in an exploratory fashion, with different researchers examining the role of different factors.

LaFree's (1980b) analysis is the most detailed investigation of the plea decision. He found that the amount of evidence assembled by the defense is an important factor in the choice of plea, with the accumulation of more evidence lowering the probability of a guilty plea. Concerning the role of race, he found that black defendants were less likely to plead guilty, regardless of the race of the victim. He was unable to determine whether this is attributable to the attitude of the prosecutor or the defendant or both.

Hagan (1975) also analyzed the choice of plea. He concludes that defendants charged with more serious offenses and represented by private counsel are less likely to plead guilty. He found no role for race or SES.

The other study that considered the choice of plea is Swigert and Farrell (1977). They conclude that the single most important factor affecting the choice of plea is the perceived characteristics of the defendant, and those classified as normal primitive are more likely to plead guilty.

Release on Bail

Three factors are cited as affecting the decision to make bail: the amount of bail, the income of the defendant, and the defendant's legal representation.[3] The role of the first two factors is obvious. The role of legal representation is less obvious and differs across the studies that consider it.

The importance of bail amount is supported by Lizotte (1977:571). Clarke and Koch (1976:83) found that the defendant's income is an important factor in the ability to make bail. Lizotte (1977:571) provides evidence of a role for race and SES in making bail, which he interprets as proxies for the defendant's income. Lizotte (1977:572) and Swigert and Farrell (1977:25) found significant but somewhat opposite roles for legal representation.

Setting of Bail

Only Lizotte (1977) analyzed the setting of bail, although other studies contain speculation concerning the determinants of the bail amount. Lizotte (1977:571) found that seriousness of the offense, the defendant's prior record, and the defendant's legal representation influence the bail amount. Defendants represented by courtroom regulars and public defenders on average are required to post lower bonds. Lizotte (1977:566) offers, but is not able to test, the hypothesis that the quality of the evidence also affects the level of bail. He did not find a significant effect of race or SES on bail amount, although the results of Swigert and Farrell (1977:25) on making bail suggest possible discrimination against "normal primitives" in the determination of the level of bail.

Choice of Legal Representation

Defendants can choose either no attorney, a public defender, or a private attorney. (Lizotte further distinguishes between courtroom regular and nonregular private attornies.) This choice was studied by Lizotte (1977), Hagan (1975), Farrell and Swigert (1978), and Swigert and Farrell (1977). Four factors are cited: the seriousness of the offense, the prior record of the defendant, the quality of the evidence, and extralegal characteristics of the defendant. The seriousness of the offense and the prior record of the defendant are included as predictors of the sentence the defendant would receive if convicted. The quality of the evidence is included as a predictor of the probability of conviction. It is expected that the greater the probability of conviction and the more serious the offense, the greater the incentive of the defendant to retain higher-quality legal representation. A private attorney is assumed to mount the best defense and no attorney the worst. The primary extralegal character- istic that is expected to affect the choice of attorney is the defendant's income. Other characteristics of the defendant are included only to proxy for income when income is not observed.

The results of the various studies suggest that seriousness of the offense is the most important determinant of choice of attorney (Lizotte, 1977:570; Clarke and Koch, 1976:83; Hagan, 1975:541). None of the researchers was able to measure the quality of the evidence and hence none can test its effect on choice of attorney. However, Clarke and Koch (1976:83) found that case outcome and choice of attorney are highly corre- lated, those who choose no attorney having a much smaller probability of conviction and imprisonment. Prior record appears to affect the choice of attorney in Lizotte (1977) and, to a lesser degree, in Swigert and Farrell (1977): Those with more extensive prior records are more likely to choose either no attorney or a private nonregular attorney in Lizotte (1977:570) and a public defender in Swigert and Farrell (1977:23). Hagan's (1975:541) results, however, suggest that the effect of prior record is insignificant. As for extralegal characteristics of the defendant, the results of Clarke and Koch (1976:83) suggest a role for income, and Farrell and Swigert (1978:448) and Swigert and Farrell (1977:23-24) found a role for SES, which they interpret as a proxy for income. In contrast, Hagan (1975:541) and Lizotte (1977:571) found no role for race or SES in the choice of attorney.[4]

The Charge Decision

The charge decision was analyzed in detail only by LaFree
(1980a). The role of race (alone) was considered by
Hagan (1975). For forcible sex offenses, LaFree
(1980a:850) found that the type of offense (i.e.,
attempted rape or rape), the use of a weapon, and victim
preference are important elements of the charge
decision. These variables are interpreted primarily as
measures of the seriousness of the offense (LaFree,
1980a:852). LaFree (1980a:850) also found that the
racial composition of the victim-defendant dyad affects
the charge decision; cases involving a black defendant
and a white victim led to a more serious charge. Hagan
(1975:541) also found that SES is correlated with
charge: Individuals with lower SES were charged with
more serious crimes. Hagan did not control for other
factors (such as seriousness), presumably because of a
lack of data.

The Decision to Prosecute

The only study that focused on the decision to prosecute
is LaFree (1980a). He found that for forcible sex
offenses, the charge, the presence of witnesses, the use
of a weapon, and the defendant's age are important
determinants of the decision to prosecute. These
findings generally agree with Frase's (1980) detailed
investigation of the reasons given by U.S. attornies for
dismissals. Frase found that the three factors cited
most often for dismissing a case are the seriousness of
the offense, the quality of the evidence, and the
defendant's prior record.

LaFree (1980a:850) also found that the racial
composition of the victim-defendant dyad affects the
decision to prosecute; cases involving a white victim and
a black defendant less likely to be dismissed. Frase did
not consider the role of race or other extralegal
characteristics in his study.

Summary of the Major Findings

Virtually all the studies suggest that three factors are
of particular importance in the processing of cases

through the criminal justice system: the seriousness of the offense, the quality of the evidence, and the prior record of the defendant. These factors were measured in various ways. Seriousness of the offense is generally acknowledged to have a number of dimensions. Lizotte (1977) and LaFree (1980a) measured some of these dimensions, while most of the other studies used the charge as their only measure of seriousness (presumably because other measures are either not available or are too costly to compile). Some of the studies that concentrate on specific offenses (such as murder in Farrell and Swigert, 1978, and Swigert and Farrell, 1977) used no measure of seriousness at all.

Seriousness of the offense was generally found to play a role at a number of stages. It appears to be particularly relevant in the decision to prosecute, the charge, the size of bail, and the sentence (given conviction). It also appears to be an important factor affecting the defendant's choice of attorney.

The quality of the evidence also has many dimensions and was measured in various ways. LaFree (1980a) and Lizotte (1977) measured some of these dimensions, while others used the promptness of arrest as a crude proxy for the quality of the evidence. Most of the studies include no measure of the quality of the evidence, presumably because the relevant information is too costly to compile. The quality of the evidence appears to play an important role in the decision to prosecute, the choice of plea, and trial conviction.

Different researchers emphasize different aspects of prior record, the third primary factor. It too is multidimensional and is inferred to play an important role in the decision to prosecute, the size of the bail amount, sentencing, and (to some degree) conviction.

Other legal factors were also found to be important at some stages. Making bail consistently appears to affect case disposition. It presumably operates through the conviction process by affecting the defendant's ability to put together a successful defense. In some studies the quality of legal representation and the type of plea also seem to play a role.

Extralegal factors seem to affect outcomes at a number of stages, including the decision to prosecute, the charge decision, the choice of plea, making bail, and sentence. The only stage at which extralegal factors

have not been found to play a role is the trial
conviction stage--although only LaFree (1980a, 1980b)
studied convictions directly. A number of the studies
emphasize the cumulative nature of the role of extralegal
factors. By the time black and lower-status defendants
reach the sentencing stage, they are claimed to be at a
considerable disadvantage. They appear to face more
serious charges, be more often induced to plead guilty,
be less able to make bail and thus organize a successful
defense, and have restricted access to good legal
representation. All of these factors are believed to
affect sentence and more generally case disposition.
Swigert and Farrell (1977) also note that discrimination
can start a vicious cycle, with discrimination contributing to the creation and growth of a criminal record,
which in turn leads to harsher treatment in subsequent
encounters with the criminal justice system.

A number of the researchers discuss measures that
might be adopted to reduce the inequities they perceive
in the criminal justice system. These include reforms of
the bail system, constraints on the use of prosecutorial
discretion in plea bargaining, and various sentencing
reforms. Each of these reforms undoubtedly has some
undesirable aspects. A crucial question is whether there
really is sufficient evidence of discrimination to
consider seriously implementation of some of the
suggested reforms. In the following section we discuss
problems associated with the measurement of the key
forces that may substantially obscure the true extent of
discrimination in the criminal justice system. This
provides motivation for the modeling approach we propose,
illustrate, and develop in the following sections of the
paper.

BIASES INDUCED BY MEASUREMENT
ERROR AND OMITTED VARIABLES

The discussion above suggests that it is extremely
difficult to measure many of the principal determinants
of case disposition. In this section we discuss the
implications of measurement error and omitted variables
for inferences about the extent of discrimination in the
criminal justice system. Our discussion suggests that
failure to control adequately for the primary
determinants of case disposition may seriously distort

the true extent of discrimination. The discussion serves as the motivation for the model we propose.

The Statistical Consequences of Failing to Control Adequately for the Primary Determinants

We begin with a simple example. Suppose that we are interested in the following relationship:[5]

$$y = \beta x^* + \theta z + u \,, \tag{1}$$

where y = sentence (given conviction), x^* = seriousness of the offense, z = socioeconomic status of the accused, u = a random disturbance that is distributed independently of x^* and z, and β and θ = parameters to be estimated.

If we could observe a random sample of y, x^*, and z, the least-squares regression of y on x^* and z would yield unbiased and consistent[6] estimates of β and θ. Suppose, however, that seriousness of the offense cannot be measured and the researcher regresses sentence on SES alone. It is well known that this will generally cause the estimate of the coefficient of z to be biased and inconsistent for θ. In particular, the bias can be shown to equal αβ, where α is the coefficient of SES in the so-called auxiliary regression of seriousness on SES. Thus presuming that seriousness affects sentence (i.e., β does not equal 0), the omission of seriousness from equation (1) will lead to biased estimation of θ unless seriousness and SES are uncorrelated (i.e., unless α = 0).

The intuitive basis for this result is straightforward. Suppose that we do not control for seriousness and seriousness and SES are correlated. Under these circumstances, variations in sentence that are really due to variations in seriousness cannot be attributed to seriousness. Instead, they will be attributed to SES to the extent that SES and seriousness are correlated. In effect, regressions can only summarize correlations among observed variables: When seriousness is not measured, SES will proxy in part for seriousness and the coefficient of SES will in part reflect variations in sentence that are actually attributable to seriousness.

Thus, if sentence is regressed on SES alone, the coefficient of SES is properly interpreted as an estimate of $\theta + \alpha\beta$ rather than an estimate of θ alone. Suppose that more serious offenses are punished more severely, ceteris paribus. This implies that $\beta > 0$. In addition, suppose that seriousness and SES are negatively correlated, which implies that $\alpha < 0$. Then the coefficient of SES in the regression of sentence on SES will underestimate θ (i.e., $\alpha\beta$ is negative). Thus even if there is no discrimination (i.e., $\theta = 0$) or there is reverse discrimination (i.e., $\theta > 0$), it is conceivable that the regression of sentence on SES might be interpreted as suggesting the presence of discrimination. More generally, the omission of relevant factors like seriousness might cause the regression of case disposition on SES and other variables to suggest the presence of discrimination when no such discrimination exists. Alternatively, depending on the coefficients of the omitted variables and their correlation with SES, it is conceivable that the omission of relevant factors could cause the true extent of discrimination to be underestimated.

In many of the studies we reviewed, it is common practice to use an observed variable to proxy for a relevant variable that could not be observed. For example, suppose that a variable x is used to proxy for seriousness, where x is related to seriousness by

$$x = \delta x^* + \epsilon , \qquad\qquad (2)$$

where δ is an unknown coefficient and ϵ is a random disturbance that is independent of x^*, z, and u. The variable x is called a classical proxy and ϵ is referred to as the measurement error in x.[7] Suppose that x is used to "control" for x^* and y is regressed on x and z. Then it can be shown that the coefficient of z is properly interpreted as an estimate of $\theta + f\alpha\beta$ rather than θ where α is (again) the coefficient of SES in the regression of seriousness on SES and f equals the fraction of the independent (of z) variation in the proxy that is due to the measurement error.[8] Since f is between zero and one, this implies that the inclusion of the proxy in the regression of sentence on SES reduces the absolute magnitude of the bias from $\alpha\beta$ to $f\alpha\beta$.[9]

A bias remains, however, because the proxy does not fully control for the effects of seriousness, and SES still "picks up" some of the effect of seriousness on sentence that is not attributed to the proxy.

More generally, this suggests that if the primary determinants of case disposition are measured with error (or are not measured at all) in the studies we reviewed, then estimates of the effects of extralegal variables on case disposition will be biased. Of course, some measurement error is present in all regressions. The crucial question is whether the estimated coefficients of extralegal variables in the various studies are likely to reflect primarily discrimination or primarily statistical bias. The following discussion of the conditions under which the bias will be large relative to the true effect suggests that the estimates of the role of extralegal variables in the various studies may be seriously distorted.

For the case of one variable measured with error, it can be shown that the bias in the estimate of a correctly measured variable will be larger relative to its true coefficient:[10]

(1) The greater the fraction of the variation in the dependent variable attributable to the incorrectly measured variable;

(2) The smaller the fraction of the variation in the dependent variable attributable to the correctly measured variable;

(3) The greater the correlation between the correctly and incorrectly measured variables; and

(4) The greater the fraction of the variation in the incorrectly measured variable (holding constant the correctly measured variable) attributable to the measurement error.

Conditions (1) and (2) suggest that the bias in the estimates of the role of extralegal factors will be larger when extralegal factors play a relatively small role in affecting case disposition. The various studies suggest that the primary determinants of case disposition are the seriousness of the offense, the quality of the evidence, and prior record. While most of the studies suggest discrimination, they also suggest that if discrimination is present, it explains only a small fraction of variation in case disposition (see note 7). This does not imply that there isn't sufficient discrimination to warrant reform of the criminal justice system. Rather, it simply says that variations in case disposition can be explained primarily by clearly appropriate factors, such as seriousness of the offense.

145

Conditions (1) and (4) suggest that the bias in the estimates of the role of extralegal factors will be large when the primary determinants of case disposition are measured with considerable error. In the review in the previous section, we noted that two of the three primary determinants of case disposition—the seriousness of the offense and the quality of the evidence—are measured very crudely when they are measured at all. Both factors include many components that are difficult and/or costly to measure from available records. Combined with condition (3), this suggests that if seriousness of the offense and quality of the evidence are correlated with race and SES, the bias in the estimates of extralegal variables might dominate the true effects of extralegal variables on case disposition. In the subsection that follows, we explore the nature of these correlations.

Correlations Between the Primary Determinants and Extralegal Variables

Perhaps the most troublesome correlation between extralegal variables and the primary determinants of case disposition involves the seriousness of the offense. The literature reviewed above provides both theoretical and empirical reasons to expect seriousness of the offense to be correlated with race and SES. For example, Lizotte (1977) suggests two pertinent but quite different mechanisms. The first is the "labeling" mechanism associated with conflict theory. According to this view, society may perceive and therefore define some crimes to be more serious precisely because they are disproportionately committed by members of racial minorities and individuals with lower SES. The second mechanism is economic: Members of socially and economically disadvantaged groups may rationally choose to commit more serious offenses (particularly in samples of property crimes) precisely because their legitimate labor market opportunities are restricted. In addition, the "normal primitive" concept investigated by Swigert and Farrell (1977) could be interpreted as suggesting a cultural basis for correlation between seriousness and race and SES (see Swigert and Farrell, 1977:19).

Furthermore, various correlations are reported in the literature suggesting that seriousness is correlated with race and SES. Lizotte (1977) reports that SES and his index of seriousness are negatively correlated. Hagan

(1975) reports a negative correlation between SES and charge, which suggests a negative correlation between SES and seriousness unless (quite implausibly) charge is unrelated to seriousness. Another indication of correlation between seriousness and the race and income of the defendant is found in Clarke and Koch (1976). They found that estimates of the relationships between race and income and the likelihood of imprisonment were weakened when variables were added to control for seriousness and prior record. Finally, in a study of capital punishment in Dade County, Florida, Arkin (1980) found that among all murder cases, blacks were dispro-portionately involved in execution-style felony murders. Such offenses might reasonably be viewed as particularly serious relative to other murders.

There are at least three reasons that race and SES might be correlated with the quality of the evidence. First, members of racial minority groups and/or people with low SES who participate in criminal activities might on average be less competent than other criminals and thus tend to leave more incriminating evidence. Second, police and/or prosecutors might work harder to amass evidence against members of socially and economically disadvantaged groups. Finally, economic theories of crime suggest that individuals with restricted opportun-ities in legitimate labor markets might, because of this fact, be willing to undertake crimes involving higher probabilities of arrest and conviction. We could not find any evidence in the literature concerning the sign of the correlation between quality of the evidence and race and SES. This is presumably a reflection of the difficulty of constructing measures for quality of the evidence.

It seems well accepted that race and SES are corre-lated with prior record. This correlation does not seem problematic, however, because numerous aspects of prior record are generally observable to the investigator. Consequently, the fraction of variation in observable measures of prior record that is attributable to measure-ment error is likely to be quite small relative to the corresponding fractions for observable measures of seriousness and quality of the evidence. Condition (4) above suggests that under these circumstances, the measurement error in prior record will bias the estimates of the effects of extralegal factors considerably less than the measurement errors involved in seriousness and quality of the evidence.

Thus the possibility of nontrivial correlations of race and SES with seriousness of the offense and quality of the evidence seem to be the most troublesome. Further complications are introduced by the possibility that these correlations may differ for different types of crimes. As a result, the biases attributable to measurement error in seriousness and quality of the evidence might be critical in some cases and trivial in others. The biases might even work in opposite directions in different studies. This suggests that measurement error bias could substantially obscure the true incidence of discrimination in the criminal justice system. In the following subsection we present four examples of how measurement error bias might have distorted inferences in the literature about the incidence of discrimination in the criminal justice system.

Alternative Interpretations of
Results Reported in the Literature

The statistical perspective offered here suggests alternative interpretations of a number of the results reported in the review above. We discuss four such interpretations in this section in order to demonstrate the potential importance of taking account of measurement error.

First, consider Hagan's (1975) finding of a negative correlation between the initial charge and SES. One obvious explanation for this finding other than discrimination is that individuals with lower SES commit more serious crimes. Since Hagan does not control at all for seriousness, the analysis above suggests that SES may be "picking up" for some of the effects of seriousness. This is a simple example of omitted variable bias.

Second, a similar explanation can be provided for the finding by Swigert and Farrell (1977) and Farrell and Swigert (1978) that final case disposition and SES are negatively correlated in murder cases, holding constant a number of other factors, such as prior record, but not seriousness of the offense. Arkin's (1980) findings cited above support the hypothesis that individuals with lower SES commit more serious murders, which could explain Swigert and Farrell's and Farrell and Swigert's findings without appeal to discrimination.

A third example concerns the finding in a number of studies that defendants who are not released on bail experience less favorable case dispositions. This is

often cited as evidence of discrimination in that lower-
SES and black defendants are found to be less often
released on bail than other defendants, ceteris paribus.
Lizotte (1977) in particular emphasizes this finding. He
infers that failure to make bail hinders the development
of an effective defense.

An alternative explanation for this result is based on
the difficulty of measuring seriousness of the offense
and case quality. Lizotte's (1977) findings suggest that
the likelihood of making bail is highly related to the
bail amount. Lizotte (1977) also finds that bail amount
is directly related to a crude measure he constructs for
the seriousness of the offense. Thus it might be expected that on average, defendants who are not released on
bail commit more serious offenses. Suppose that making
bail does not have any causal effect on case disposition.
Consider a regression of case disposition on a proxy for
seriousness and a dummy variable for making bail. The
results above suggest that if making bail is negatively
related to seriousness and a proxy variable is used to
"control" for seriousness, then the estimate of the effect of making bail on case disposition will be biased
downward. Thus even if making bail has no causal effect
on case disposition, making bail will appear to contribute to a less severe disposition if seriousness is
measured with error.

A similar explanation may account for the finding in a
number of studies that defendants with higher-quality
legal representation experience more favorable case dispositions, holding constant a number of other legally
relevant factors. Suppose that higher-income individuals
commit less serious crimes and that the quality of legal
representation is highly (positively) correlated with
income. Then on average, defendants with higher-quality
legal represenation will have committed less serious
crimes. The results above suggest that, if case disposition is regressed on a proxy for seriousness and the quality of legal representation, then the coefficient of
legal representation may be negative even if legal representation has no effect on case disposition.

Each of our explanations for the four findings rests
on measurement error bias. One hypothesis--that seriousness is correlated with SES and race--coupled with measurement error in seriousness is sufficient to explain
all four findings. While not conclusive, this discussion
is suggestive of the extent to which measurement error
bias might account for some of the more prominent findings in the literature.

Future Research Directions

Our analysis suggests that biases due to measurement error may obscure the true incidence of discrimination in the criminal justice system. The most obvious response to this problem--better measurement of the primary determinants of case disposition--does not seem promising because of the inherent unobservability of a number of dimensions of seriousness of the offense and quality of the evidence. Thus further efforts that rely on crude proxies to control for seriousness of the offense and quality of the evidence are unlikely to provide a reliable basis for making inferences about discrimination in the criminal justice system. In the following sections we discuss an alternative approach that directly confronts the inherent unobservability of the primary determinants of case disposition.

AN ILLUSTRATIVE STRUCTURAL MODEL OF CRIMINAL CASE DISPOSITIONS

A natural response to the interpretation difficulties raised in the previous section is to model explicitly the various links among observable variables and the unobservable theoretical constructs that are hypothesized to be the primary determinants of case disposition. Such models are often described as "structural models involving latent variables" and have found applications in economics, political science, psychology, and sociology.[11] The effects of unobserved variables may be estimable if we can observe multiple variables (often called "indicators") whose values are postulated to be determined as functions of the unobservable variables. In this section we present a particular structural model that we believe to be plausible, consistent with the (often implicit) theorizing discussed above, and potentially capable of empirical implementation.

Structural equations are viewed as mathematical representations of the fundamental processes generating the data. Useful structural equation models are best formulated with explicit reference to a specific question of interest. We have chosen to model various aspects of criminal proceedings relating to individuals arrested for residential thefts who do not enter guilty pleas.[12]

The following notational conventions are employed. Outcomes of the criminal process (which are assumed to depend on the unobserved primary determinants) are denoted by y's with various subscripts (these are thought of as endogenous indicators of the latent variables). The latent variables are denoted by x*'s with various subscripts. Observed exogenous variables believed to have direct effects on the indicators are denoted by z's with various subscripts and observed exogenous variables believed to affect case disposition through the latent variables are denoted by x's with various subscripts.

We treat the three primary determinants of case disposition--seriousness, case quality, and prior record--as latent variables that are not observed. This does not suggest that it is impossible to measure some dimensions of each of these variables. Rather, it emphasizes that these variables can be measured only with considerable error relative to the other important determinants of case disposition. Part of our model, which we discuss at the end of this section, involves linking the three latent variables to their observable components.

Our structural equation model involves equations for nine indicators: (1) dismissal, (2) victim cooperation, (3) charge, (4) dollar level of bail, (5) release on bail, (6) type of legal representation, (7) conviction at trial, (8) presentence report recommendation, and (9) severity of punishment. We focus on these particular indicators for two reasons. First, the literature suggests that each is substantially influenced by one or more of the latent variables of interest: seriousness, case quality, and prior record. Second, each of these indicators either represents the outcome of an important juncture in the criminal justice system or is likely to have a major influence on a significant decision in it (e.g., the recommendation of the presentence report).

A number of these indicators can be observed only to a limited degree. For example, the dismissal decision is based on the prosecutor's desire to proceed, which we generally do not observe. Rather, we observe only whether the prosecutor decides to dismiss a case, which provides only limited information about the strength of the prosecutor's desires. For expositional convenience, we assume throughout that in instances such as the dismissal decision, we observe the indicator of interest. For example, we assume that in the case of the dismissal decision, we actually observe a continuous measure of the strength of the prosecutor's desire to prosecute. In later sections we consider complications that arise when such continuous measures are not available.

The structural model begins with the arrest of a suspect. Following the arrest, the first major function is the initial screening. The prosecution must decide whether to file charges or reject the case. In the event of an affirmative decision to press charges, the prosecutor may subsequently choose to nolle the charges.[13] We combine the rejection and nolle decisions into a single prosecutorial decision concerning whether to prosecute a case.

Studies suggest that the decision to prosecute or dismiss depends principally on the gravity of the offense, the quality of the evidence, and the record of prior criminal activity of the accused. Given the discretion the prosecutor can exercise at this stage, it is also possible that the decision to prosecute could be affected by discrimination. This suggests that the decision to prosecute can be specified as

$$y_1 = \beta_{11}x_1^* + \beta_{12}x_2^* + \beta_{13}x_3^* + \theta_{11}z_1 + \theta_{12}z_2 + u_1 , \quad (3)$$

where y_1 is an index variable that determines the probability that a case will be dismissed, x_1^* is the (unobserved) seriousness of the offense, x_2^* is the (unobserved) quality of the evidence, x_3^* is the (unobserved) prior record of the defendant, z_1 is the (observed) race of the defendant, z_2 is the (observed) wealth of the defendant, u_1 is an (unobserved) disturbance, and β_{11}, β_{12}, β_{13}, θ_{11}, and θ_{12} are parameters to be estimated.[14] The variables z_1 and z_2 are included to represent the possibility of discrimination.[15] The disturbance u_1 captures the effects of all factors that affect y_1 other than x_1^*, x_2^*, x_3^*, z_1, and z_2.

The second indicator is whether the victim cooperates with the prosecutor. The victim is often a pivotal figure in the preparation of the prosecution case. In some instances the victim may be able to identify the perpetrator and for the crime of residential theft is likely to be the person best able to identify property seized from the accused. Cooperating in the preparation of a criminal case can be very time-consuming and the likelihood of the victim's being willing to make this sacrifice is undoubtedly determined in part by the seriousness of the offense, x_1^*. Victims themselves may also exercise biases by being more willing to cooperate

if the accused is of a different race. Let y_2 be an
index variable that determines the probability that the
victim cooperates with the prosecution. We assume that
y_2 is determined by

$$y_2 = \beta_{21}x_1^* + \theta_{23}z_3 + u_2 , \qquad (4)$$

where x_1^* is as defined in the text below equation (3),
z_3 is a dichotomous variable taking the value one if the
victim and the accused are of different races and zero
otherwise, u_2 is a disturbance summarizing all relevant
factors besides x_1^* and z_3, and β_{21} and θ_{23} are
structural parameters to be estimated.

The third structural equation represents the
determinants of the severity of the charges filed against
the accused. For residential theft, the prosecutor may
be free to choose among a number of different charges
ranging from petit larceny to first degree burglary. We
expect that the principal case characteristics affecting
the choice of charge seriousness are the seriousness of
the offense and the defendant's prior record. We include
the latter because the evidence suggests that prosecutors
proceed more vigorously against defendants with prior
criminal records, particularly if the record is
extensive. As with the dismissal decision, the
prosecutor may be influenced by his racial and class
prejudices. These considerations suggest the following
specification of the determinants of charge seriousness:

$$y_3 = \beta_{31}x_1^* + \beta_{33}x_3^* + \theta_{31}z_1 + \theta_{32}z_2 + u_3 , \qquad (5)$$

where x_1^*, x_3^*, z_1, and z_2 are as defined in the text
below equation (3), y_3 is the severity of the charge(s)
filed against the accused, u_3 is a disturbance, and β_{31},
β_{33}, θ_{31}, and θ_{32} are structural coefficients to be
estimated. Thus the charge is assumed to depend on
seriousness, prior record, and race and class
considerations, but not on the quality of the evidence.

The bail-setting decision is typically made by a
magistrate. The stated purpose of bail is to ensure that
the accused appears for trial. The dollar amount of bail
is supposed to be set at a level that is sufficient to
ensure that the accused does not abscond.

The probability of the accused not appearing at trial
is generally thought to be related to the probability of
conviction and the expected sentence if convicted. Our

review of the literature suggests that the former is chiefly influenced by the quality of the evidence and the latter by the seriousness of the offense and the defendant's prior record. The bail amount is also supposed to be graduated to the defendant's income; wealthier defendants are required to post a larger bond to ensure appearance at trial. Finally, there is a possibility that judges discriminate against certain types of defendants in setting bail. These observations suggest that the bail amount, y_4, is influenced by all of the case and defendant characteristics previously defined. We relate y_4 to these variables by

$$y_4 = \beta_{41}x_1{}^* + \beta_{42}x_2{}^* + \beta_{43}x_3{}^* + \theta_{41}z_1 + \theta_{42}z_2 + u_4 \ , \quad (6)$$

where u_4 is a disturbance, β_{41}, β_{42}, β_{43}, θ_{41}, and θ_{42} are parameters to be estimated, and all other symbols are as defined above.

The fifth structural equation represents the accused's decision to make the payment required to be released on bail.[16] The likelihood of the accused being released on bail will be determined primarily by the amount of bail, y_4, and the defendant's wealth, measured by z_2. Let y_5 be an index variable determining the probability of the accused making bail. We assume y_5 is determined by

$$y_5 = \gamma_{54}y_4 + \theta_{52}z_2 + u_5 \ , \quad (7)$$

where u_5 is a disturbance term and γ_{54} and θ_{52} are parameters to be estimated.

A second decision made by the accused concerns the type of legal representation. Available options include no counsel, court-appointed counsel, and private attorney. The various studies we reviewed suggest that the choice of attorney is associated with the seriousness of the charge, the quality of the evidence, and the defendant's prior record. We would also expect this choice to be affected by the defendant's financial capabilities. This suggests the following representation for the quality of legal representation:

$$y_6 = \beta_{62}x_2{}^* + \beta_{63}x_3{}^* + \gamma_{63}y_3 + \theta_{62}z_2 + u_6 \ , \quad (8)$$

where y_6 is an index variable denoting the quality of the legal counsel chosen, u_6 is a disturbance, and

β_{62}, β_{63}, γ_{63}, and θ_{62} are structural coefficients to be estimated.

The next observable indicator is whether the accused is convicted at trial.[17] The literature suggests that the likelihood of conviction at trial is primarily determined by the quality of the evidence implicating the accused. In addition, the quality of legal representation may play an important role in affecting the likelihood of conviction. On the basis of these considerations we model the probability of conviction at trial by

$$y_7 = \beta_{74}x_4{}^* + \gamma_{76}y_6 + \theta_{71}z_1 + \theta_{72}z_2 + u_7 , \qquad (9)$$

where y_7 is an index variable determining the probability that the accused is convicted, $x_4{}^*$ is the quality of the evidence implicating the accused at the time of the trial,[18] u_7 is a disturbance term, and β_{74}, γ_{76}, θ_{71}, and θ_{72} are structural coefficients to be estimated. The variables z_1 and z_2 are included in equation (9) to allow for the possibility that juries discriminate on the basis of race or wealth.

The next structural equation specifies the determinants of the presentencing recommendation. Presentence reports may contain especially valuable information because in many instances they all but recommend the type of sentence the accused should receive. Presentence reports are often lengthy documents that emphasize the convicted criminal's psychological traits, prior criminal record, and the seriousness of the offense. This suggests the following specification for the presentence recommendation:

$$y_8 = \beta_{81}x_1{}^* + \beta_{83}x_3{}^* + \theta_{81}z_1 + \theta_{82}z_2 + u_8 , \qquad (10)$$

where y_8 is a variable measuring the severity of the sanction recommended by the presentence report, u_8 is a disturbance, and β_{81}, β_{83}, θ_{81}, and θ_{82} are parameters to be estimated. The severity of the presentence report is thus related to the seriousness of the offense ($x_1{}^*$) and prior record ($x_3{}^*$). The variables z_1 and z_2 are included in equation (10) to allow for discrimination at this state of the sentencing process.

The final outcome we consider is the severity of punishment. Perhaps the most important factor determining the severity of punishment is the seriousness of the charge for which the defendant is convicted. A

discussion with a judge in Pittsburgh and the results of
Swigert and Farrell (1977) suggests that the presentence
report may also be a major influence on the sentencing
decision. These considerations, along with the
possibility that judges may directly discriminate on the
basis of race and/or wealth, suggest the following
specification of the sentencing equation:

$$y_9 = \gamma_{93}y_3 + \gamma_{98}y_8 + \theta_{91}z_1 + \theta_{92}z_2 + u_9 , \qquad (11)$$

where y_9 is the severity of the sentence imposed on the
accused, u_9 is a disturbance, and γ_{93}, γ_{98}, θ_{91}, and
θ_{92} are structural coefficients to be estimated.
Sentence is thus assumed to depend directly on the charge
(y_3), the forcefulness of the presentence recommendation
(y_8), and the race (z_1) and wealth (z_2) of the
defendant. The seriousness of the offense and prior
record are allowed to affect sentence indirectly through
their influence on charge seriousness, y_3, and the
presentence recommendation, y_8.

The next four structural equations relate the
unobservables x_1^*, x_2^*, x_3^*, and x_4^* to observable
variables. This has two purposes. The first is to
structure the suspected correlations among race,
seriousness and case quality. This will allow us
explicitly to sort out potential sources of the various
reported correlations of race with case disposition.
Second, estimated parameters from these equations provide
important diagnostic information. Since the primary
variables believed to affect sentencing outcomes are
unobserved, it is worthwhile to structure the estimation
in order to be able to test whether the indicators are in
fact indicators of the theoretical variables specified.
This issue can be addressed by considering the conformity
of the estimated coefficients with a priori expectations
and more formally by statistical testing of implied
constraints on the estimated parameters.

We begin by specifying observable factors affecting
the seriousness of the offense, x_1^*. We relate x_1^*
to observables by

$$x_1^* = \delta_{11}z_1 + \delta_{1e}e + \underline{\alpha}_1'\underline{x}_1 + \varepsilon_1 , \qquad (12)$$

where z_1 is the race of the accused (as defined above), e
is the education of the accused, $\underline{x}_1$ is a $K_1 \times 1$ vector of
observable variables affecting seriousness but appearing
nowhere else in the model, ε_1 is a disturbance, and

δ_{11}, δ_{1e}, and $\underline{\alpha}_1$ are $K_1 + 2$ structural parameters to be estimated. The racial variable z_1 is included in equation (12) to allow for a correlation between race and seriousness.

Reasons to expect correlation between race and seriousness of the offense are discussed above. The education of the accused is included in equation (12) because people with less favorable opportunities in legitimate labor markets are likely to participate in more serious offenses.[19] The vector $\underline{x}_1$ includes measurable case characteristics that are conventionally thought to affect the perception of seriousness. For residential theft, this vector might include: (1) the value of the property taken, (2) whether the dwelling was occupied at the time of the crime, (3) whether there was forced entry, (4) whether the accused carried a weapon, (5) the age of the accused, etc.

The quality of the evidence prior to trial is specified as

$$x_2^* = \lambda y_2 + \delta_{21} z_1 + \delta_{2e} e + \underline{\alpha}_2' \underline{x}_2 + \epsilon_2 , \qquad (13)$$

where $\underline{x}_2^*$ is a $K_2 \times 1$ vector of observable variables affecting the quality of the evidence but appearing nowhere else in the model, ϵ_2 is a disturbance, and λ, δ_{21}, δ_{2e}, and $\underline{\alpha}_2$ are $K_2 + 3$ parameters to be estimated. As previously discussed, victim cooperation, y_2, is often critical for successful prosecution. Its inclusion as an observable cause of case quality reflects this view. Case quality will also be determined by observable variables such as: (1) the number of witnesses besides the victim, (2) whether the property was recovered, (3) whether the accused's fingerprints were found at the scene, (4) whether the accused was found with burglary tools, (5) whether the accused had an alibi, etc. These observables are included in $\underline{x}_2$. Race and education are included in equation (13) to control for common variation in x_1^* and x_2^*. Reasons to expect a correlation between race and case quality are discussed above. Education is included in equation (13) because all other things being equal, people with little education are likely to be less skillful even in illegitimate activities and hence may leave more incriminating evidence.

The prior record of the defendant consists of a number of dimensions. Generally, the information that is available to the judge concerning prior record can also be observed by the investigator. It is not clear, however, how this information is typically interpreted by the various decision makers in the criminal justice system. The various studies we reviewed emphasize different aspects of prior record. To reflect these uncertainties, we have chosen to model prior record as unobservable.[20] Our specification of prior record is

$$x_3{}^* = \underline{\alpha}_3{}'\underline{x}_3 + \varepsilon_3 \ , \tag{14}$$

where $\underline{x}_3$ is a $K_3 \times 1$ vector of observable variables determining the prior record of the accused, ε_3 is a disturbance, and $\underline{\alpha}_3$ contains K_3 parameters to be estimated. The components of the vector $\underline{x}_3$ might include the number of previous arrests (felony and misdemeanor separately), the number of previous convictions (felony and misdemeanor separately), previous time served, recency of previous offenses, whether the accused was on parole or probation at the time of the offense, etc. The disturbance ε_3 represents our uncertainty about the factors that determine prior record. Race and wealth are excluded from the equation for prior record because they are unrelated to our uncertainty concerning the determinants of prior record.

Finally, we specify an equation determining the quality of the evidence at the time of the trial, $x_4{}^*$. We distinguish between evidence quality at the time of the trial and prior to trial because some have conjectured that a defendant who is detained while awaiting trial is at a disadvantage in preparing a defense. This might be examined with the following specification of the quality of the evidence at the time of trial:

$$x_4{}^* = \eta y_5 + x_2{}^* + \varepsilon_4 \ , \tag{15}$$

where ε_4 is a disturbance and η is a parameter to be estimated.[21] Here y_5 indicates whether the accused was released on bail.[22]

The 13 equations (3) through (15) are the structural equations of the illustrative model of criminal case disposition. Specification of the model is finalized by specification of the stochastic properties of the disturbances $u_1, u_2, \ldots, u_9, \varepsilon_1, \varepsilon_2, \varepsilon_3,$ and ε_4.

The structural equations contain 13 disturbances: u_i ($i = 1, 2, \ldots, 9$), and ε_j ($j = 1, 2, 3, 4$). We assume that each u_i ($i = 1, 2, \ldots, 9$) has a zero mean, a constant variance denoted by ω_{ii} ($i = 1, 2, \ldots, 9$)

and is distributed independently of z_m (m = 1, 2, 3), e, ε_n (n = 1, 2, 3, 4), and the vectors $\underline{x}_n$ (n = 1, 2, 3). Equations (3) through (11) were specified so that any common determinants of every pair of indicators are explicitly taken into account. Accordingly, we assume that the covariance of u_i and $u_{i'}^1$ is zero for all i not equal to i'.

We assume that each ε_j (j = 1, 2, 3, 4) has a zero mean and is distributed independently of z_m (m = 1, 2, 3), e, and the vectors $\underline{x}_n$ (n = 1, 2, 3). Equations (12) through (15) were specified so that any common determinants of every pair of unobservable x*'s are explicitly taken into account. Accordingly, we assume that the covariance of ε_j and $\varepsilon_{j'}^1$ is zero for all j not equal to j'. Finally, in order to specify the scales of x_1*, x_2*, and x_3* we adopt the convenient normalizations $V(\varepsilon_1) = V(\varepsilon_2) = V(\varepsilon_3) = 1$. These normalizations and the coefficients of unity on x_2* in equation (15) remove the trivial indeterminacies due to the otherwise arbitrary units of measurement of x_1*, x_2*, x_3*, and x_4*.

ESTIMABILITY OF THE PARAMETERS OF THE ILLUSTRATIVE STRUCTURAL MODEL

The structural equation model we have presented involves coefficients with direct interpretations. In contrast, we argued in the previous section that the coefficients estimated in many of the studies we reviewed are best interpreted as mixtures of structural parameters. Such mixtures admit many different interpretations, often with very different policy implications. Our structural parameters, in contrast, yield direct tests of the incidence of discrimination in the criminal justice system. Hence an obviously important question is: Can the structural parameters of direct interest be estimated from observable data?

A structural parameter that can be estimated consistently is said to be identified. The structural parameters of the model presented above are the 40 + K_1 + K_2 + K_3 structural coefficients (i.e., 14 β's, 15 θ's, 5 γ's, 4 δ's, η, λ, and the K_1 + K_2 + K_3 elements of the vectors $\underline{\alpha}_1$, $\underline{\alpha}_2$, and $\underline{\alpha}_3$) and 10 unnormalized variances ω_{ii} (i = 1, 2, . . . , 9) and $V(\varepsilon_4)$. We have, in fact, verified that all of these parameters except ω_{77} and $V(\varepsilon_4)$ are identified.[23] This exercise, while straightforward, involves many tedious algebraic manipulations. Here we merely indicate the nature of the processes by which the identification status of the parameters was examined.

The issue of identification is conveniently examined by considering the reduced form of the model comprised of equations (3) through (15). The reduced-form equation for each indicator (y variable) is obtained by manipulating algebraically equations (3) through (15) to obtain expressions for the indicators solely as functions of observable exogenous variables (i.e., the z's, $\underline{x}$ vectors, and e) and disturbances (i.e., the u's and ε's). The reduced form for the system is the collection of the nine reduced-form equations.

The reduced-form system can be written most conveniently employing matrix notation. Let $\underline{y} \equiv (y_1, y_2, \ldots, y_9)'$ be the 9 x 1 vector containing the indicators of the structural model. Then the nine equations comprising the reduced form of equations (3) through (15) can be written compactly as

$$\underline{y} = \underline{\pi}_1 z_1 + \underline{\pi}_e e + \underline{\pi}_2 z_2 + \underline{\pi}_3 z_3 + \Pi_1 \underline{x}_1 + \Pi_2 \underline{x}_2 + \Pi_3 \underline{x}_3 + \underline{v}, \quad (16)$$

where:

$\underline{\pi}_1$ = a 9 x 1 vector containing the reduced-form coefficients of the race variable z_1 (i.e., the ith element of $\underline{\pi}_1$ is the coefficient of z_1 in the reduced-form equation for y_i),

$\underline{\pi}_e$ = a 9 x 1 vector containing the reduced-form coefficients of the education variable,

$\underline{\pi}_2$ = a 9 x 1 vector containing the reduced-form coefficients of z_2,

$\underline{\pi}_3$ = a 9 x 1 vector containing the reduced-form coefficients of z_3,

Π_1 = a 9 x K_1 matrix containing the reduced-form coefficients of the K_1 variables contained in the vector $\underline{x}_1$,

Π_2 = a 9 x K_2 matrix containing the reduced-form coefficients of the K_2 variables $\underline{x}_2$,

Π_3 = a 9 x K_3 matrix containing the reduced-form coefficients of the K_3 variables $\underline{x}_3$, and

$\underline{v}$ = a 9 x 1 vector of reduced-form disturbances.

The reduced-form coefficients (i.e., the elements of the π vectors and Π matrices) are specific, derivable functions of the structural coefficients. The reduced-form disturbances (i.e., the elements of $\underline{v}$) are specific, derivable functions of the structural parameters and the structural disturbances u_i (i = 1, 2, . . . , 9) and ε_j (j = 1, 2, 3, 4). The reduced-form coefficients are displayed in Table 3-1 and the reduced-form disturbances are displayed in Table 3-2.

The identification issue can be decomposed into the following two questions. Can the reduced-form coefficients and the variances and covariances of the reduced-form disturbances be consistently estimated from observable data? Assuming an affirmative answer, can the values of the structural parameters be deduced from knowledge of the values of these mixtures of the structural parameters? The first of these questions is statistical and the second purely algebraic.[24]

With regard to the first question, our assumptions concerning the u_i (i = 1, 2, . . . , 9) and ε_j (j = 1, 2, 3, 4), plus standard assumptions about the sampling process, imply that least-squares regressions of the indicators on the observed exogenous variables (i.e., the z's, $\underline{x}$ vectors, and e) yield consistent estimates of the elements of the π vectors and Π matrices.[25] In addition, the variances and covariances of the v's, which involve structural coefficients and the 10 unnormalized variances, can be consistently estimated from the reduced-form residuals.[26] In turn, it can be shown that these two sets of estimates are sufficient to solve uniquely for estimates of the structural parameters (with the exception of ω_{77} and $V(\varepsilon_4)$). Thus the parameters of the structural model (with the exception of ω_{77} and $V(\varepsilon_4)$) are identified.

To provide further insight into unobservable variable models generally and the identification issue in particular, consider the following simple model, which embodies the essential features of the reduced form of our illustrative model:[27]

$$y_1 = \theta_1 z + v_1 , \tag{17a}$$
$$y_2 = \theta_2 z + v_2 , \text{ and} \tag{17b}$$
$$y_3 = \theta_3 z + v_3 , \tag{17c}$$

where y_1, y_2, y_3, and z are observable and v_1, v_2, v_3 are unobservable. This model is a simplified version of the reduced form of our illustrative structural model. It contains an observable variable z and a set of unobservable disturbances v_1, v_2, and v_3.

To further the analogy between this simple model and the reduced form of our structural model, two additional

TABLE 3-1 Reduced-Form Coefficients for the Illustrative Structural Model

Indicator	Coefficients of: z_1	e	$\underline{x}_1$	$\underline{x}_2$	$\underline{x}_3$	z_2	z_3
y_1	$\delta_{11}(\lambda\beta_{12}\beta_{21}+\beta_{11})+\beta_{12}\delta_{21}+\theta_{11}$	$\delta_{1e}(\lambda\beta_{12}\beta_{21}+\beta_{11})+\beta_{12}\delta_{2e}$	$(\lambda\beta_{12}+\beta_{11})\underline{\alpha}_1'$	$\beta_{12}\underline{\alpha}_2'$	$\beta_{12}\underline{\alpha}_3'$	θ_{12}	$\lambda\beta_{12}\theta_{23}$
y_2	$\beta_{21}\delta_{11}$	$\beta_{21}\delta_{1e}$	$\beta_{21}\underline{\alpha}_1'$	0	0	0	θ_{23}
y_3	$\beta_{31}\delta_{11}+\theta_{31}$	$\beta_{31}\delta_{1e}$	$\beta_{31}\underline{\alpha}_1'$	0	$\beta_{33}\underline{\alpha}_3'$	θ_{32}	0
y_4	$\delta_{11}(\lambda\beta_{42}\beta_{21}+\beta_{41})+\beta_{42}\delta_{21}+\theta_{41}$ $(\equiv a_4)$	$\delta_{1e}(\lambda\beta_{42}\beta_{21}+\beta_{41})+\beta_{42}\delta_{2e}$ $(\equiv b_4)$	$(\lambda\beta_{42}\beta_{21}+\beta_{41})\underline{\alpha}_1'$ $(\equiv c_4)$	$\beta_{42}\underline{\alpha}_2'$	$\beta_{42}\underline{\alpha}_3'$	θ_{42}	$\lambda\beta_{42}\theta_{23}$
y_5	$\gamma_{54}a_4$	$\gamma_{54}b_4$	$\gamma_{54}c_4\underline{\alpha}_1'$	$\gamma_{54}\beta_{42}\underline{\alpha}_2'$	$\gamma_{54}\beta_{43}\underline{\alpha}_3'$	$\gamma_{54}\theta_{42}+\gamma_{52}$	$\gamma_{54}\lambda\beta_{42}\theta_{23}$
y_6	$\delta_{11}(\lambda\beta_{62}\beta_{21}+\gamma_{63}\beta_{31})+\beta_{62}\delta_{21}$ $+\gamma_{63}\theta_{31}$ $(\equiv a_6)$	$\delta_{1e}(\lambda\beta_{62}\beta_{21}+\gamma_{63}\beta_{31})$ $+\beta_{62}\delta_{2e}$ $(\equiv b_6)$	$(\lambda\beta_{62}\beta_{21}+\gamma_{63}\beta_{31})\underline{\alpha}_1'$ $(\equiv c_6)$	$\beta_{62}\underline{\alpha}_2'$	$(\beta_{63}+\gamma_{63}\beta_{33})\underline{\alpha}_3'$	$\gamma_{63}\theta_{32}+\theta_{62}$	$\lambda\beta_{62}\theta_{23}$
y_7	$\beta_{74}(\eta\gamma_{54}a_4+\beta_{21}\delta_{11}+\theta_{21})$ $+\gamma_{76}a_6+\theta_{71}$	$\beta_{74}(\eta\gamma_{54}b_4+\beta_{21}\delta_{1e})$ $+\gamma_{76}b_6+\theta_{72}$	$\beta_{74}(\eta\gamma_{54}c_4+c_2)\underline{\alpha}_1'$ $+\gamma_{76}c_6\underline{\alpha}_1'$	$\beta_{74}(\eta\gamma_{54}\beta_{42}+1)\underline{\alpha}_2'$ $+\gamma_{76}\beta_{62}\underline{\alpha}_2'$	$\beta_{74}\eta\gamma_{54}\beta_{43}\underline{\alpha}_3'$ $+\gamma_{76}(\beta_{63}+\gamma_{63}\beta_{33})\underline{\alpha}_3'$	$\beta_{74}(\eta(\gamma_{54}\theta_{42}+\theta_{52})$ $+\gamma_{76}(\gamma_{63}\theta_{32}+\theta_{62})+\theta_{72})$	$\beta_{74}(\eta\gamma_{54}\lambda\beta_{42}\theta_{23}+\lambda\theta_{23})$ $+\gamma_{76}\lambda\beta_{62}\theta_{23}$
y_8	$\beta_{81}\delta_{11}+\theta_{81}$	$\beta_{81}\delta_{1e}$	$\beta_{81}\underline{\alpha}_1'$	0	$\beta_{83}\underline{\alpha}_3'$	θ_{82}	0
y_9	$\gamma_{93}(\beta_{31}\delta_{11}+\theta_{31})$ $+\gamma_{98}(\beta_{81}\delta_{11}+\theta_{81})+\theta_{91}$	$\gamma_{93}\beta_{31}\delta_{1e}+\gamma_{98}\beta_{81}\delta_{1e}$	$(\gamma_{93}\beta_{31}+\gamma_{98}\beta_{81})\underline{\alpha}_1'$	0	$(\gamma_{93}\beta_{33}+\gamma_{98}\beta_{83})\underline{\alpha}_3'$	$\gamma_{93}\theta_{32}+\gamma_{98}\theta_{82}+\theta_{92}$	0

TABLE 3-2 Reduced-Form Disturbances in the Illustrative Structural Model

Indicator	Coefficients of:				
	ε_1	ε_2	ε_3	ε_4	$\underline{u}$
y_1	$(\lambda\beta_{12}\beta_{21}+\beta_{11})$	β_{12}	β_{13}	0	$u_1+\lambda\beta_{12}u_2$
y_2	β_{21}	0	0	0	u_2
y_3	β_{31}	0	β_{33}	0	u_3
y_4	$(\lambda\beta_{42}\beta_{21}+\beta_{41})$	β_{42}	β_{43}	0	$\lambda\beta_{42}u_2+u_4$
y_5	$\gamma_{54}(\lambda\beta_{42}\beta_{21}+\beta_{41})$	$\gamma_{54}\beta_{42}$	$\gamma_{54}\beta_{43}$	0	$\gamma_{54}(\lambda\beta_{42}u_2+u_4)+u_5$
y_6	$\lambda\beta_{62}\beta_{21}+\gamma_{63}\beta_{31}$	β_{62}	$(\beta_{63}+\gamma_{63}\beta_{33})$	0	$\lambda\beta_{62}u_2+\gamma_{63}u_3+u_6$
y_7	$\beta_{74}\eta\gamma_{54}(\lambda\beta_{42}\beta_{21}+\beta_{41})$ $+\lambda\beta_{21}+\gamma_{76}(\lambda\beta_{62}\beta_{21}+\gamma_{63}\beta_{31})$	$\beta_{74}\eta\gamma_{54}\beta_{42}+\gamma_{76}\beta_{62}+\beta_{74}$	$\beta_{74}\eta\gamma_{54}\beta_{43}+\gamma_{76}(\beta_{63}+\gamma_{63}\beta_{33})$	β_{74}	$\beta_{74}\eta(\gamma_{54}(\lambda\beta_{42}u_2+u_4)+u_5)+\lambda u_2$ $+\gamma_{76}(\lambda\beta_{62}u_2+\gamma_{63}u_3+u_6)+u_7$
y_8	β_{81}	0	β_{83}	0	u_8
y_9	$\gamma_{93}\beta_{31}+\gamma_{98}\beta_{81}$	0	$\gamma_{93}\beta_{33}+\gamma_{98}\beta_{83}$	0	$\gamma_{93}u_3+\gamma_{98}u_8+u_9$

assumptions are introduced. First, it is assumed that z is uncorrelated with v_1, v_2, and v_3. This is analogous to the reduced form of our illustrative structural model in that the observable variables of the reduced form are uncorrelated with the reduced-form disturbances. Second, it is assumed that the unobservable disturbances are composed of a common factor x^* and equation-specific factors u_1, u_2, and u_3 with variances ω_1, ω_2, and ω_3 respectively:

$$v_1 = \beta_1 x^* + u_1 , \tag{18a}$$
$$v_2 = \beta_2 x^* + u_2 , \text{ and} \tag{18b}$$
$$v_3 = \beta_3 x^* + u_3 . \tag{18c}$$

The variable x^* (whose variance is normalized to one) is assumed to be the sole common factor leading to correlations among v_1, v_2, and v_3. Accordingly, it is assumed that x^*, u_1, u_2, and u_3 are mutually uncorrelated. This is a simplified version of the structure of the reduced-form disturbances of our illustrative model. It captures the essential features of the reduced-form disturbances in our structural model.[28]

The principal value of this simple model is that it allows us to demonstrate fairly simply the way identification was verified for our more complicated structural model (and the way identification can generally be verified in structural equation models). The model contains 10 parameters: θ_1, θ_2, θ_3, β_1, β_2, β_3, ω_1, ω_2, ω_3, and $V(z)$. Data on the four observable variables (y_1, y_2, y_3, and z) can be used to compute 10 sample moments (i.e., four variances and six covariances). In the population these moments are related to the parameters of interest by[29]

$$V(y_1) = \theta_1^2 V(z) + \beta_1^2 + \omega_1 , \tag{19a}$$
$$V(y_2) = \theta_2^2 V(z) + \beta_2^2 + \omega_2 , \tag{19b}$$
$$V(y_3) = \theta_3^2 V(z) + \beta_3^2 + \omega_3 , \tag{19c}$$
$$C(y_1,y_2) = \theta_1 \theta_2 V(z) + \beta_1 \beta_2 , \tag{19d}$$
$$C(y_1,y_3) = \theta_1 \theta_3 V(z) + \beta_1 \beta_3 , \tag{19e}$$
$$C(y_2,y_3) = \theta_2 \theta_3 V(z) + \beta_2 \beta_3 , \tag{19f}$$
$$C(y_1,z) = \theta_1 V(z) , \tag{19g}$$
$$C(y_2,z) = \theta_2 V(z) , \tag{19h}$$
$$C(y_3,z) = \theta_3 V(z) , \text{ and} \tag{19i}$$
$$V(z) = V(z) .^{30} \tag{19j}$$

These 10 equations can be solved simultaneously for the parameters, θ_1, θ_2, θ_3, β_1, β_2, β_3, ω_1, ω_2, and ω_3. For example, the effect of x* on y_1 can be written[31] as

$$\beta_1 = (\{C(y_1,y_2) - [C(y_1,z)C(y_2,z)/V(z)]\}$$
$$\times \{C(y_1,y_3) - [C(y_1,z)C(y_3,z)/V(z)]\}$$
$$\div \{C(y_2,y_3) - [C(y_2,z)C(y_3,z)/V(z)]\})^{1/2} \quad (20)$$

An estimator of β_1 formed by substituting corresponding sample moments for the population moments on the right side of equation (20) is consistent for β_1. The fact that a similar procedure can be used to derive estimators for the other parameters of the model establishes that all of the parameters are identified.

In essence, it is possible to estimate effects of unobservable variables appearing in multiple structural equations because common movements of the indicators reflect in part the effects of movements in the common unobserved factors. This is illustrated by the expressions in equation (19), which relate moments of observable variables to the β's, the coefficients of the unobservable variables. In an identified model such expressions can be solved for the structural parameters. Verification of the identification status of our illustrative structural model is a straightforward if tedious application of this principle.[32]

HOW THE ILLUSTRATIVE STRUCTURAL MODEL ALLOWS DISENTANGLING THE VARIOUS SOURCES OF RACE-OUTCOME CORRELATIONS: A HEURISTIC DISCUSSION

The fundamental difficulty in empirical examinations of racial discrimination in the criminal justice system is the fact that correlations between race and case outcomes are likely to reflect both discriminatory and nondis-criminatory factors at distinct stages of the criminal justice process. Distinguishing empirically among these various sources of correlation appears to be the appropriate focus of future empirical studies. Regression analysis and other standard multiple correlation techniques seem ill-equipped for this objective: It seems quite implausible that the primary determinants of case disposition can be measured well enough to allow confident interpretation of partial correlations between race and case outcomes. In the previous two sections we presented a structural model of case dispositions and reported that the parameters of interest are in principle estimable. In this section we attempt to indicate essentially how this model allows disentangling of the parameters involving race.

The structural equations presented above can be represented most generally as

$$\Gamma \underline{y} = B\underline{x}^* + \theta \underline{z} + \underline{u} , \qquad (21)$$
$$H\underline{x}^* = A\underline{x} + \Lambda \underline{y} + \varepsilon , \qquad (22)$$

where:

Γ = a 9 x 9 nonsingular matrix[33] of structural coefficients of the indicators,

$\underline{y} \equiv (y_1, y_2, \ldots, y_9)'$

B = a 9 x 4 matrix of structural coefficients of the unobserved exogenous variables,

$\underline{x}^* \equiv (x_1^*, x_2^*, x_3^*, x_4^*)'$,

θ = a 9 x 3 matrix of structural coefficients of the observed exogenous variables directly affecting the indicators,

$\underline{z} \equiv (z_1, z_2, z_3)'$,

$\underline{u} \equiv (u_1, u_2, \ldots, u_9)'$,

H = a 4 x 4 nonsingular matrix of structural coefficients,

A = a 4 x $(K_1 + K_2 + K_3)$ matrix of structural coefficients,

$\underline{x} \equiv (\underline{x}_1', \underline{x}_2', \underline{x}_3')'$,

Λ = a 4 x 9 matrix of structural coefficients, and

$\varepsilon \equiv (\varepsilon_1, \varepsilon_2, \varepsilon_3, \varepsilon_4)$.

We have placed numerous a priori restrictions on the matrices Γ, B, θ, H, A, and Λ, the covariance matrices of $\underline{u}$ and $\underline{\varepsilon}$, and other covariances. Without restrictions, the parameters of the model described by equations (21) and (22) would not be identified. Thus, a priori restrictions are the source of identification in structural equation models. Restrictions that are inappropriate, however, introduce biases. Thus it seems especially useful to consider the nature of the restrictions of the model presented above that allow disentangling of the various possible sources of correlation between race and case outcomes.

The first column of Table 3-1 displays the elements of π_1. They are the coefficients of the race variable z_1 in the nine reduced-form equations. The structural coefficients of race are δ_{11}, δ_{21}, θ_{11}, θ_{31}, θ_{41}, θ_{71}, θ_{81}, and θ_{91}. Inspection of Tables 3-1 and 3-2 reveals that these parameters appear in no other reduced-form coefficients, nor do they appear in the variances and covariances of the reduced-form disturbances. Thus even if all the other structural parameters in π_1 were known, only these mixtures of structural parameters can be helpful in identifying δ_{11}, δ_{21}, θ_{11}, θ_{31}, θ_{41}, θ_{71}, θ_{81}, and θ_{91}. Note that the reduced-form coefficient of z_1 in the y_5 equation is merely γ_{54} times the reduced-form coefficient of y_4. Thus, if we know γ_{54}, one of these reduced-form coefficients is redundant. Accordingly, we have eight equations (corresponding to the eight linearly independent elements of π_1) that can be used to solve for the eight structural parameters that appear in π_1 but do not appear elsewhere: δ_{11}, δ_{21}, θ_{11}, θ_{31}, θ_{41}, θ_{71}, θ_{81}, and θ_{91}. Clearly, if these eight equations were to involve more than eight unknown parameters, then at least some of these parameters would not be identified.

It would appear, then, that the restrictions that z_1 does not play a role in determining y_2 (victim cooperation) nor y_5 (whether bail is made) are essential in separating the various sources of correlation between race and case disposition. The exclusion of z_1 from equation (4) seems quite warranted once it is recognized that many victims of residential thefts are of the same race as the people we fear are the victims of discrimination in the criminal justice system. It seems entirely reasonable to assume that if people discriminate on the basis of race they do not systematically discriminate against people of their own race. The other crucial restriction that allows identification is the exclusion of z_1 from the accused's decision to post bail. Such a restriction seems quite reasonable on the basis that people of the disadvantaged group do not discriminate against themselves. In fact, decisions made by the accused appear to provide extremely valuable information.

This discussion seems to provide useful guidance for construction of other models of the criminal justice process. If one is directly concerned about disentangling the various sources of correlation between race and case outcomes, especially useful are indicators

from whose structural equations the race variable may be
legitimately excluded. The literature has raised the
specter that all agents of the state (i.e., police,
prosecutors, juries, and judges) use their discretion to
discriminate against disadvantaged groups. Thus it
appears that excluding race from equations representing
decisions of agents of the state will always be
controversial. Decisions made by the accused that depend
on (at least some of) the primary determinants thus seem
to provide the most useful information in identifying the
structural parameters of racial variables.

We close this section by suggesting indicators not
represented in our illustrative model that might be
especially useful. Perhaps the most promising is whether
the accused testifies at trial. This decision should
depend on at least some of the x*'s but not directly on
race.[34] Another potentially powerful indicator is
whether the accused accepts a plea bargain. Klepper et
al. (in this volume) provide a model of the plea
bargaining process that would be helpful in structuring a
plea bargaining equation (this is discussed in greater
length below). A number of other decisions made by the
accused might also warrant more explicit consideration.
These include the choice between a bench and a jury
trial, whether the accused volunteers restitution,
whether the accused enters a drug or alcohol rehabilitation program, and more detailed information
concerning the extent of the defense effort.

IDENTIFICATION IN LATENT VARIABLE MODELS
WITH SAMPLE SELECTION

Sample selection is a natural feature of the criminal
justice system. Cases are screened from the system at a
number of junctures. In our illustrative model, some
cases are dropped from the system because of dismissals
and acquittals. The model implies that these sample
selections cannot be considered to be random. Klepper et
al. (in this volume) emphasize that this type of
nonrandom sample selection may introduce substantial
biases into statistical analyses of case disposition.
The purpose of this section is to analyze the implications of sample selection for the identification status
of our model.

It appears that sample selection does not alter the
identification status of our illustrative model (subject

to an important qualification discussed below). The basis for this claim is demonstrated in the context of the simple unobservable variable model composed of equation (18). We introduce sample selection by assuming that we observe a random sample on y_1, but y_2 and y_3 are observed only if $y_1 > 0$ (e.g., a presentence report and a sentence are observed only if the accused is convicted). In order to compute the variances and covariances of the observables in the selected sample, we augment the assumptions of the simple model by assuming that x^*, z, u_1, u_2, and u_3 are normally distributed.[35] Then the moments of the observables in the selected sample can be written as[36]

$$V(y_1|y_1 > 0) = 1 - ab^2 \tag{23a}$$

$$V(y_2|y_1 > 0) = V(y_2) - d(\beta_1\beta_2 + \theta_1\theta_2)^2 \tag{23b}$$

$$V(y_3|y_1 > 0) = V(y_3) - d(\beta_1\beta_3 + \theta_1\theta_3)^2 \tag{23c}$$

$$C(y_1,y_2|y_1 > 0) = (a^{-1} - b^2)a^{-1}(\beta_1\beta_2 + \theta_1\theta_2) \tag{23d}$$

$$C(y_1,y_3|y_1 > 0) = (a^{-1} - b^2)a^{-1}(\beta_1\beta_3 + \theta_1\theta_3) \tag{23e}$$

$$C(y_2,y_3|y_1 > 0) = C(y_2,y_3) - d(\beta_1\beta_2 + \theta_1\theta_2)$$
$$\times (\beta_1\beta_3 + \theta_1\theta_3) \tag{23f}$$

$$C(y_1,z|y_1 > 0) = (a^{-1} - b^2)a^{-1}\theta_1 V(z) \tag{23g}$$

$$C(y_2,z|y_1 > 0) = C(y_2,z) - d(\beta_1\beta_2 + \theta_1\theta_2)\theta_1 V(z) \tag{23h}$$

$$C(y_3,z|y_1 > 0) = C(y_3,z) - d(\beta_1\beta_3 + \theta_1\theta_3)\theta_1 V(z) \tag{23i}$$

$$V(z|y_1 > 0) = V(z) - d(\theta_1^2 V(z)^2) , \tag{23j}$$

where $V(y_1|y_1 > 0)$ denotes the variance of y_1 given that y_1 is positive, etc.,

$$a \equiv \beta_1^2 + \theta_1^2 V(z) + \omega_1 ,$$
$$b \equiv \phi(0)/(1 - \Phi(0)) ,$$
$$d \equiv a^{-1} - a^{-2} + b^2 ,$$

and $\phi(\cdot)$ and $\Phi(\cdot)$ are respectively the standard normal density and the cumulative distribution functions.

The expressions in equation (23) are more complicated than their counterparts in equation (19), but in fact yield solutions for all of the structural parameters.[37] Sample selection does not introduce any additional parameters to be estimated and does not reduce the number

of moments[38] of observable variables. Thus the
presence of sample selection does not appear to alter the
identification status of an otherwise identified
structural model involving latent variables.

This somewhat surprising result is attributable to the
fact that we observe multiple indicators after sample
selection occurs. To see this, consider the complications introduced by sample selection in Heckman's
(1979) model. Heckman considers a two-equation system in
which the dependent variable in the second equation is
observed only if the dependent variable in the first
equation exceeds a threshold. To make this concrete,
consider the two equations of our structural model
corresponding to the dismissal and charge decisions
(i.e., equations (3) and (5)). Suppose that the
prosecutor discriminates against lower-SES defendants in
the dismissal decision. Equation (3) implies that the
greater the three primary determinants, the greater the
probability of dismissal. Consequently, cases that are
not dismissed will tend to be above average on an index
that combines these three factors (i.e., $\beta_{11}x_1^* + \beta_{12}x_2^*$
$+ \beta_{13}x_3^*$ in equation (3)). If there is discrimination
against lower-SES defendants, then higher-SES defendants
whose cases are not dismissed will tend to have a higher
value for each of the three primary determinants than
lower-SES defendants whose cases are not dismissed.

Now consider the charge decision, which is also
affected by the seriousness of the offense and prior
record. The above argument implies that higher-SES
individuals whose cases are not dismissed will tend to be
above average on seriousness and prior record. If either
of these factors is not adequately controlled for,
estimates will suggest reverse discrimination at the
charging stage when in fact no discrimination is
present. More generally, sample selection will tend to
introduce biases understating the extent of
discrimination at all stages following the dismissal
decision when discrimination occurs at the dismissal
stage.

This problem does not appear to affect the estimability of structural equation models precisely because
they control completely for the effects of unobservable
variables. In the context of the present application
this conclusion must be qualified in one important
respect. In our simple model, we assumed that y_1 is
observable. This enabled us to estimate the covariances of y_1 with y_2, y_3, and z that would apply to

the selected sample. The unconditional covariances of y_1 with y_2, y_3, and z were then computed by adjusting the covariances calculated from the observations that were not screened from the sample. The first step in the process--the estimation of the population covariances for the selected population of cases--is essential.

Because of the presence of limited dependent variables, however, we may not observe the value of y_1 when y_2 and y_3 are observed. Instead, the variable y_1 may be qualitative and be constant for all observations that remain in the sample after selection. For example, consider the dismissal equation (3) in our illustrative model. The dependent variable in this model is an index of the strength of the case for purposes of prosecution. Generally, we cannot observe this index, but only whether a case is dismissed. In this instance, we learn nothing about the value of y_1 except that it is above or below some threshold. For cases that are not dismissed, we may observe no variation in y_1. This will preclude estimation of the covariances involving y_1 using the selected observations, implying that the approach to identification described here breaks down.

This suggests that if some information can be observed for the indicator that determines selection when cases are not dropped from the system, then it will be possible to control for the effects of selection. This may be quite possible for one of the two selection points in our model: the dismissal decision. In some instances, prosecutors must justify in writing their reasons for dropping a case. The final decision to drop a case is often made only after a number of reviews of the same case by different attorneys in the prosecutor's office (for example, see Frase's (1978) detailed analysis of the dismissal decision for federal cases). Such reviews may provide the basis for measuring the strength of the case for purposes of prosecution. Moreover, in some instances a qualitative ranking of the strength of all cases may be assigned before a final prosecution decision is made. Such information would certainly provide a means of distinguishing the strength of the case for purposes of prosecution for cases that are not dismissed.

The other selection point occurs at the trial stage. It is unlikely that any information would be available to construct an index of the strength of the evidence against the defendant for cases that result in conviction. This is not problematic, however, because this selection does not alter the distribution of any of the unobservable variables affecting the decisions that follow conviction. This is because the conviction decision is assumed to depend only on the quality of the evidence and not seriousness and prior record. Only the latter two unobservables enter later decisions.

If it is not possible to observe information about the strength of the prosecution case in cases that are not dismissed, then it may still be possible to deal with selection. An alternative approach to the selection problem is provided by Heckman (1979) and Olsen (1980). It requires restrictions on the coefficients of observable variables in the selection and later equations. Such an approach appears to be feasible and natural in our model. It is discussed in a more general context in Klepper et al. (in this volume).

ADDITIONAL SPECIFICATION ISSUES

In this section we discuss briefly three types of specification issues. First we consider some potentially worthwhile simplifications of our illustrative structural model. We then consider some interesting and (in principle) desirable extensions of the illustrative model. Finally, we discuss issues relating to the fact that often only qualitative rather than continuous data concerning various outcomes of the criminal justice system are available.

Data limitations might dictate that some of the equations of our illustrative model cannot be estimated. In fact, the equations for two indicators for which data are costly to obtain--bail amount and the forcefulness of the presentence report--could be eliminated[39] without sacrificing all of the benefits of the structural approach. Neither of these equations involves restrictions that seem crucial to sort out the roles of race in affecting the other seven indicators. The major cost of failing to observe the bail amount would be an inability to examine directly whether estimated effects of race on the probability of making bail are due to effects of race on the level of bail. The major drawback of failing to measure the forcefulness of the presentence report is similar. In such a case we would be unable to distinguish between discrimination in presentence reports and discrimination in sentencing.

Less complicated structural models would also result from further a priori restrictions on the illustrative model. Two particular restrictions seem quite reasonable and useful in terms of simplifying the analysis.[40] The first involves the assumption that all of the relevant factors affecting prior record are observed.[41] Since this would reduce the number of latent variables, we would then need fewer observable indicators (and hence structural equations) to identify the structural parameters of a model simplified in this way.[42]

Another plausible restriction that would simplify the analysis is the assumption that case quality is uncorrelated with race. As discussed above, the reasons and evidence supporting such a correlation are somewhat less compelling than the reasons and evidence supporting a correlation between race and seriousness. Such a simplication would mean that δ_{21} in equation (13) would equal zero; then, following the discussion above, we would need only a single structural equation omitting race to identify the structural coefficients of the race variable. One equation, such as the victim cooperation equation, could then be deleted without losing the ability to sort out the sources of correlations between race and the other indicators. Moreover, in some contexts it might be appropriate to assume that case quality is uncorrelated with all of the other exogenous variables in the model. Such an assumption would also reduce the number of indicators (and hence structural equations) necessary for identification.

Another possibility is to eliminate restrictions from the model even if this compromises the identification of some of the parameters. It may still be possible to extract useful information about underidentified parameters. For example, one might be willing to estimate some structural parameters conditional on imposed values of other structural parameters. Another approach involves estimating upper and lower bounds on structural parameters from the fact that the variance-covariance matrix of the true variables must be nonnegative definite (see Klepper, 1980). Finally, Bayesian analysis explicitly incorporating subjective prior information about the structural parameters may also contribute to our knowledge concerning the role of extralegal factors in affecting criminal case disposition.

There are important reasons to begin with consideration of parsimonious models. Despite this fact, it seems worthwhile to mention a few apparently useful extensions of the illustrative structural model. First, it might be particularly valuable to incorporate a plea bargain decision into the model because most convictions result from guilty pleas. Using the plea bargain theory in Klepper et al. (in this volume), an additional unobservable variable representing culpability might be introduced into the model.

Another desirable extension of the illustrative structural model would involve use of an explicit theory to structure the suspected correlations between race and seriousness and case quality. In the present formulation, for example, a positive estimate of δ_{11} would indicate the existence of a correlation between race and seriousness but would provide no information concerning the source of such a correlation. Recall from the discussion that the literature contains at least three reasons to expect race and seriousness to be correlated. If the source of the correlation is labeling, as emphasized by Lizotte, then we might interpret this as legislative discrimination. If the economic basis to expect a correlation is operative, we might interpret δ_{11} as reflecting discrimination in the labor market. Distinguishing among such possibilities would seem to be quite desirable for policy purposes.

Finally, we might not be able to observe directly anything about the financial capabilities of defendants. If so, wealth could be modeled as an unobservable. Then variables such as the average income in the census tract containing the residence of the accused might be regarded as a classical proxy and hence an indicator of the wealth of the defendant. When other indicators of wealth are observable (e.g., level of bail, release on bail, choice of attorney) models treating wealth as an unobservable are likely to be identified.

Finally, we briefly mention specification issues relating to the fact that some of the indicators we have defined may not be directly observable. In some instances such variables are modeled as direct causes of other indicators or latent variables. An interesting specification issue is whether such variables should be viewed identically in their roles as both indicators and causes. For example, consider y_2, which was defined as an index determining the probability that the victim cooperates with the prosecution. This variable also appears in equation (13) as a factor contributing to case quality. One might interpret y_2 in equation (13) as a dichotomous outcome determined by the continuous-index version of y_2. But victim cooperation might be more plausibly viewed as a continuous variable representing the enthusiasm with which the victim cooperates. Similar remarks apply to y_6 (i.e., attorney choice), which appears as an indicator in equation (8) and a cause of the trial outcome in equation (9). It seems clear, however, that y_3 (i.e., charge) and y_5 (i.e., release on bail) are most plausibly viewed as qualitative outcomes of the indexes defined in equations (5) and (7) when they appear as observable causes in equations (8) (i.e., choice of attorney) and (15) (i.e., the case quality at trial), respectively. A useful paper in this regard is Heckman (1978), which presents an estimation scheme for situations involving endogenous qualitative regressors.

Finally, the fact that we observe only partial information about various indicators raises estimation issues, even if these variables do not also appear as causes of other variables. Estimation would require explicit modeling of the links between the observed data and the indicators of the illustrative model. For example, Muthen (1979) discusses latent variable models with qualitative indicators. Maximum-likelihood techniques, while somewhat complex in this context, are likely to provide a feasible approach to estimation.

CONCLUDING REMARKS

In our view, the empirical literature on the criminal justice system has evolved in a natural and appropriate way. Total correlations between case disposition and race and SES suggest an alarming degree of discrimination. Studies aimed at probing the source of these correlations have attempted to control for the effects of legally relevant variables using crude, albeit the best available, proxies for such factors. The studies we reviewed are of this variety. For the most part, they still find evidence of discrimination, although less than is suggested by the total correlations between case disposition and race and SES.

The fact that inclusion of legally relevant variables reduces the correlations between case outcomes and variables such as race and SES provides empirical support for theories that predict correlations between legal factors and personal characteristics of defendants. Under such circumstances, failure to control fully for the effects of legally relevant factors implies that inferences about the extent of discrimination are likely to be erroneous. For this reason the techniques currently being used offer little hope of providing a reliable basis for policy reform. The approach proposed here seems like a logical next step.

Satisfactory resolution of the role of extralegal factors in determining criminal case disposition will be difficult. Structural equation modeling should help, but it is not a panacea. The restrictions in any identified structural model are likely to be controversial. The possibility of compatible indications emerging from a broad range of structural models raises the hope of developing a consensus.

NOTES

1. By case disposition we mean the outcome of a case following arrest and/or indictment. The alternative outcomes include acquittal, dismissal, and various types of sentences (given conviction). Case disposition is generally measured by an index that (arbitrarily) is commensurate to the different types of outcomes.

2. Klepper et al. (in this volume) argue that among the nine studies, these two are the most sensitive to statistical biases due to sample selection. Consequently, the extent of discrimination may be particularly underestimated in these two studies because of the specially selected nature of their samples.

3. Other factors such as prior record and extralegal characteristics of the defendant are also cited (for example, Swigert and Farrell, 1977:25; Farrell and Swigert, 1978:447), but it seems these factors are expected to operate through bail amount (only Lizotte holds constant the effect of bail amount).

4. Although Lizotte (1977) used a strange ordering for the quality of different types of legal representation.

5. For convenience, throughout this paper all random variables are expressed as deviations from their means.

6. An estimator is unbiased for a parameter if its mathematical expectation is equal to that parameter. An estimator is consistent if in the limit as the sample size goes to infinity, the estimates are arbitrarily close to the parameter of interest. Strictly speaking,

consistency of least squares requires additional (but in this context uninteresting) assumptions concerning the sampling process on x* and z.

7. When δ equals one and ε is independent of x*, z, and u, x is called a classical measurement of x*. The results discussed here are straightforward extensions of results discussed by Garber and Klepper (1980) for the case of classical measurements.

8. Formally, $f = V(\varepsilon)/V(x|z)$.

9. This result is due independently to McCallum (1972) and Wickens (1972). For cases in which more than one variable is measured with error, this result does not generalize straightforwardly (see Garber and Klepper, 1980).

10. These conditions follow from

$$f\alpha\beta/\theta = f\rho_{x,z}[\rho_{y,x*|z}V(y|x*)/\rho_{y,z|x*}V(y|z)] \ ,$$

where $\rho_{y,x*|z}$ and $\rho_{y,z|x*}$ are respectively the correlation coefficients of y and x* given z and y and z given x* and $\rho_{x,z}$ is the correlation coefficient of x and z. This result can be derived by exploiting the relationship between regression coefficients and the second moments of the respective conditional distributions.

11. An especially valuable collection of theoretical and empirical studies is Goldberger and Duncan (1973). Our discussion borrows from Goldberger (1973), the introductory essay in this volume.

12. We consider residential thefts to include the crimes of breaking and entering, petit larceny, grand larceny, second-degree burglary, first-degree burglary, etc.

We avoid the plea bargain issue, despite its importance, because of the apparent lack of any widely held views concerning the determinants of the plea bargain decision. Incorporation of especially controversial relationships in the illustrative model could seriously compromise our objectives.

13. In the Washington, D.C., superior court about 50 percent of all arrests are rejected at the initial

screening or subsequently nolled by the prosecutor (Forst et al., 1977).

14. We use β's throughout for coefficients of unobservable variables and θ's for coefficients of observable variables. The first subscript of each coefficient refers to the indicator and the second to the respective unobservable or observable exogenous variable.

15. Discrimination is presumed to be on the basis of race and wealth. The two variables together can be interpreted as the primary components of the SES of the defendant. Alternatively, we might have introduced another observable variable to represent the SES of the defendant. The additon of an accurate measure of SES would not alter the model in any fundamental way. We assume discrimination on the basis of race and wealth alone only to simplify the exposition.

16. Typically, the bail is paid by a bail-bonding agency. The accused pays a nonrefundable fee based on the amount of the bail. Equation (7) can be interpreted as describing the decision to pay this fee.

17. Recall that we model only those cases of residential theft disposed by a dismissal or trial verdict.

18. As will become clear with the introduction of equation (15) below, we distinguish between case quality before and at trial to examine the claim that release on bail is an important determinant of the quality of the defense.

19. As will be more clear when equation (13) and the stochastic assumptions pertaining to ε_1 are introduced, we attempt to use observable variables to control entirely for correlation between x_1^* and x_2^*. Education is viewed as an important correlate of each of these variables.

20. In the section on additional specification issues, we consider treating prior record, or more precisely all the determinants of prior record, as known and observable.

21. Since x_1^*, x_2^*, x_3^*, and x_4^* are never observed, the scales on which these variables are measured are arbitrary. Until these scales are specified, the

magnitudes of their coefficients are trivially indeterminate. In order to remove such indeterminacies it is necessary to "normalize" these coefficients by directly or indirectly specifying the units of measurement of each of the unobservable variables. Specific normalizations are chosen for analytic convenience. The coefficient of x_2^* in equation (15) is chosen as one to specify the scale on x_4^*, given the normalization (presented below), which defines the scale of x_2^*.

22. Note that y_5 was specified as an index variable in equation (7) but as a dichotomous outcome in the present equation. The complications associated with this type of specification issue are discussed in a later section.

23. Inspection of equations (3) through (15) reveals that ω_{77} and $V(\varepsilon_4)$ are not identified. This is obvious since both x_4^* and u_7 appear only in equation (9). Thus in this model randomness in convictions (represented by u_7) cannot be distinguished empirically from random influences on the quality of the evidence at trial (represented by ε_4). This lack of identifiability is of minimal concern since neither ω_{77} nor $V(\varepsilon_4)$ is of direct interest.

24. The second step involves solving for the structural parameters as functions of the reduced-form parameters (this is illustrated by equation (7)). Use of Slutsky's Theorem (see Goldberger, 1964:118-119) establishes that these solutions provide a basis for consistent estimation of the structural parameters.

25. This follows from the fact that the reduced-form disturbances are uncorrelated with the independent variables of the reduced form.

26. These population variances and covariances can be computed quite simply from Table 3-2 since the u_i ($i = 1, 2, \ldots, 9$) and ε_j ($j = 1, 2, 3, 4$) are mutually uncorrelated.

27. Various symbols (such as y_1, v_1, etc.) are redefined here in order to emphasize the analogies between the simplified model employed here and our illustrative model of the criminal justice process.

28. These features are the ones that enable us to estimate the various mixtures of structural parameters appearing in the reduced-form disturbances of our model.

29. To see how these expressions are computed, consider for example equation (19d). Since all variables are assumed to have zero means, the covariance of y_1 and y_2 can be computed as

$$E(y_1, y_2) = E(\theta_1 z + \beta_1 x^* + u_1)(\theta_2 z + \beta_2 x^* + u_2) .$$

Equation (19d) then follows from the assumptions that z, x^*, u_1, and u_2 are independent and $V(x^*) = 1$.

30. The apparently trivial nature of equation (19j) merely reflects the fact that since z is observable its variance can be estimated directly.

31. This expression for β_1 results from the use of equations (19d), (19e), (19f), (19g), (19h), (19i), and (19j). It can be verified straightforwardly by substitution of these equations into equation (20).

32. For example, consider how we checked that γ_{54} is identified. Table 3-1 indicates that the coefficients of z_3 in the reduced-form equations for y_5 and y_4 are respectively $\gamma_{54}\lambda\beta_{42}\theta_{23}$ and $\lambda\beta_{42}\theta_{23}$. Division of the former coefficient by the latter provides a solution for γ_{54} and thus a basis for consistently estimating γ_{54}.

33. The assumption that Γ^{-1} exists says merely that values of the x^* and z variables and the values of the structural disturbances uniquely determine the values of the indicators.

34. It might be argued that race would enter into this decision: Perhaps anticipation of racial discrimination would affect the accused's decision concerning testifying. If that is the case, however, this indicator would still be quite valuable. Suppose that defendants anticipate discrimination in the way described by the other structural equations. In that case race will affect the testimony decision through its effect on expected sentence. This would provide other restrictions that would be useful in disentangling the various structural parameters associated with race.

35. Dealing with sample selection requires the use of a specific distribution because the observed sample is viewed as a random sample from a truncated distribution. Assuming normality per se is not required.

36. The expressions in equation (23) correspond to those in equation (19) and are derived using results reported in Johnson and Kotz (1970:81-83; 1972:70).

37. Perhaps the easiest way to verify this is to solve the expressions in equation (23) for the unconditional moments given by the expressions in equation (19). As reported above, knowledge of these moments is sufficient to identify all of the structural parameters. A particularly helpful fact in checking identification here is that $a = V(y_1)$ can be consistently estimated by the sample variance of y_1 computed from all of the observations on y_1.

38. Although it does complicate the form of these moments.

39. Formally, they can be eliminated by substitution of y_4 from equation (6) into equation (7) and substitution of y_8 from equation (10) into equation (11).

40. We did not invoke these restrictions in the illustrative model because incorporation of controversial assumptions would compromise the major purpose of this paper.

41. Formally, this involves assuming that the variance of ε_3 (see equation (14)) is zero. The attractiveness of such an assumption certainly depends on the extensiveness of the available information concerning prior record.

42. Note, however, that one would not want to delete equations representing decisions resulting in sample selections because it is precisely the structure provided by these equations that allows us to correct the sample selection bias.

181

REFERENCES

Arkin, S. D.
1980   Discrimination and arbitrariness in capital
        punishment: an analysis of post-Furman murder
        cases in Dade County, Florida, 1973-1976.
        Stanford Law Review 33(November):75-101.
Chiricos, T. G., and Waldo, G. P.
1975   Socioeconomic status and criminal sentencing:
        an empirical assessment of a conflict
        proposition. American Sociological Review
        40(December):753-772.
Clarke, S. H., and Koch, G. G.
1976   The influence of income and other factors on
        whether criminal defendants go to prison. Law &
        Society Review 11(Fall):59-92.
Farrell, R. A., and Swigert, V. L.
1978   Prior offense record as a self-fulfilling
        prophecy. Law and Society 12(Spring):437-453.
Forst, B., Lucianovic, J., and Cox, S. J.
1977   What Happens After Arrest? A Court Perspective
        of Police Operations in the District of
        Columbia. Washington, D.C.: Institute for Law
        and Social Research.
Frase, R. S.
1980   The decision to prosecute federal criminal
        charges: a quantitative study of prosecutorial
        discretion. University of Chicago Law Review
        47:246-330.
Garber, S., and Klepper, S.
1980   Extending the classical normal errors-in-
        variables model. Econometrica
        48(September):1541-1546.
Gibson, J. L.
1978   Race as a determinant of criminal sentences: a
        methodological critique and a case study. Law
        and Society 12(Spring):455-478.
Goldberger, A. S.
1964   Econometric Theory. New York: Wiley.
1973   Structural equation models: an overview. Pp.
        1-18 in A. S. Goldberger and O. D. Duncan, eds.,
        Structural Equation Models in the Social
        Sciences. New York: Seminar Press.

Goldberger, A. S., and Duncan, O. D., eds.
  1973 Structural Equation Models in the Social
        Sciences. New York: Seminar Press.
Hagan, J.
  1974 Extra-legal attributes and criminal sentencing:
        an assessment of a sociological viewpoint. Law
        and Society Review 8(Spring):357-383.
  1975 Parameters of criminal prosecution: an
        application of path analysis to a problem of
        criminal justice. Journal of Criminal Law &
        Criminology 65(4):536-544.
Heckman, J. J.
  1978 Dummy endogenous variables in a simultaneous
        equation system. Econometrica 46(July):931-959.
  1979 Sample selection bias as a specification error.
        Econometrica 47(1):153-161.
Johnson, N. L., and Kotz, S.
  1970 Distributions in Statistics: Continuous
        Distributions-1. New York: Wiley.
  1972 Distributions in Statistics: Continuous
        Multivariate Distributions. New York: Wiley.
Klepper, S.
  1980 Summarizing the Data for the Classical Normal
        Errors-in-Variables Model. Unpublished
        manuscript. Department of Social Science,
        Carnegie-Mellon University.
LaFree, G. D.
  1980a The effect of sexual stratification by race on
        official reactions to rape. American
        Sociological Review 45(October):842-854.
  1980b Variables affecting guilty pleas and convictions
        in rape cases: toward a social theory of rape
        processing. Social Forces 58(March):833-850.
Lizotte, A. J.
  1977 Extra-legal factors in Chicago's criminal
        courts: testing the conflict model of criminal
        justice. Social Problems 25(5):564-580.
McCallum, B. T.
  1972 Relative asymptotic bias from errors of omission
        and measurement. Econometrica 40(July):757-758.
Muthen, B.
  1979 A structural probit model with latent
        variables. Journal of the American Statistical
        Association 74(December):807-811.

Olsen, R.
   1980   A least squares correction for selectivity
          bias. <u>Econometrica</u> 48(November):1815-1820.
Swigert, V. L., and Farrell, R. A.
   1977   Normal homicides and the law. <u>American
          Sociological Review</u> 42(February):16-32.
Tiffany, L. P., Avichai, Y., and Peters, G. W.
   1975   A statistical analysis of sentencing in federal
          courts: defendants convicted after trial,
          1967-1968. <u>The Journal of Legal Studies</u>
          4:397-417.
Wickens, M. R.
   1972   A note on the use of proxy variables.
          <u>Econometrica</u> 40(July):759-761.

4

Empirically Based Sentencing Guidelines and Ethical Considerations

Franklin M. Fisher and Joseph B. Kadane

INTRODUCTION

The U.S. Parole Board initiated the study of empirically based guidelines to describe the decision rules it had been using implicitly. The board's purpose was to inform itself about the pattern of its own decisions. As a purely descriptive device, such a study has no ethical implications. Later the research emphasis shifted from parole to sentencing and to a more normative focus on what decisions should be. Nonetheless, the technology involved in developing empirically based guidelines still bears a strong resemblance to the analysis of parole decisions. Ethical considerations in particular are avoided in these analyses.

This paper examines the philosophy of empirically based sentencing guidelines. The strong basic philosophy we pursue is to follow an empirically based mode as far as we can, not because we are particularly attracted to the conservatism inherent in this line (whatever was done in the past must have been just, even if we cannot explain it), but because we find that surprisingly quickly our thoughts lead us to require new ethical judgments. Thus, in particular, we find that even when empirically based guidelines are expected to do no more than reduce sentence disparity, some ethical judgment is required. If past decisions may have involved ethically irrelevant factors such as race, the purging of those factors, while possible, requires more than the judgment

184

that they should be purged. Further ethical judgments are necessarily involved.

THE SIMPLEST CASE:
NO ETHICALLY IRRELEVANT VARIABLES

Consider first the simplest case, in which sentences have in the past depended on a set of independent variables, all of which are believed to be ethically appropriate. Thus, for example, variables such as those describing seriousness of offense are appropriate in sentencing; variables such as race are not. We can represent this situation by the following equation:

$$S = \delta + R\alpha + \varepsilon , \qquad (1)$$

where S is sentence length; R is a set of ethically relevant variables; α is a set of unknown slope parameters; δ is an unknown constant term; and ε is a random disturbance. (For ease of exposition, we deal for the present with the linear case only and restrict attention to sentence length as the variable to be determined.[1])

In this situation, if we suppose that the decisions of the past were ethically acceptable on the average, the justification for guidelines becomes the presence of the random disturbance, ε. That disturbance may involve factors affecting particular judges on particular days, or it may involve the factors peculiar to individual cases that lead judges to sentence differently.

There is an apparent tension here as to whether it is desirable that equation (1) fit the data well or badly. If the equation fits badly, then apparently it will provide only an uncertain guide as to what past practice actually was. If the equation fits well, then the influence of the random term, ε, will be small and there will be little disparity to reduce.

In fact this apparent tension is not real, because there is a difference between how well the model fits and how closely the parameters δ and α are estimated. With large enough sample sizes or enough variation in the underlying data, it is quite possible to estimate α and δ with considerable precision while still having a large unexplained variance. In that case we could estimate average past behavior quite accurately but there would be considerable disparity in the sense of scatter around such average behavior. Note that this makes it particularly important not to use overall measures of goodness-of-fit such as R^2 as the sole or principal measures with which to assess the model. What really matters are the standard errors of the estimated parameters.[2]

If the parameters and thus past average behavior can be reliably estimated but there is considerable variation around that behavior, it may appear desirable to reduce that variation. This is the basic rationale for empirically derived guidelines. It rests on the view that judges were correct in the past on the average but that judges themselves or society would wish to reduce the extent of individual variation around those averages. If the model has been correctly specified so that all the important variables affecting the sentencing decision have been included, and if all these variables are ethically relevant ones, this may be an appealing view, provided disparity is high. While some room for individual factors and individual judgment will always be necessary, it may seem reasonable to require judges explicitly to justify any large departures from the systematic collective wisdom.

In the context of this model, this is easy to do in principle. The process of estimating equation (1) will also estimate σ^2, the variance of ε. We denote that estimate by $\sigma*^2$. Now choose a constant, k. Judges will be required to write an explicit justification of their actions whenever their sentence does not lie within $k\sigma*$ of the estimated average sentence for the particular value of R present in the case decided. The predicted sentence is

$$S* = \delta* + R\alpha* ,$$

where asterisks denote estimates.

How should k be chosen? Given the distribution of ε (which can be approximated from the data), a choice of k is equivalent in the above procedure to requiring that judges write explicit justifications for cases that fall farther away from the average sentence than some stated fraction (e.g., 90 percent) of cases would have done in the past. What fraction should be chosen depends on the extent to which one wishes to reduce disparity in this way. While such a choice depends in part on what one sees as the source of past disparity, it is also an ethical choice.

"This is perhaps seen most easily by considering the following. There is no intrinsic reason why upward departures from average sentencing behavior (harsh sentences) and downward departures (lenient sentences) should be treated identically. One might, depending on one's ethical views, choose different values of k, say k_1 and k_2, for the two different types of departures, using a smaller value when departures are considered worse. Plainly, the choice of such values depends on ethical considerations; those considerations cannot be avoided by restricting the choice to $k_1 = k_2$ and treating both kinds of departures symmetrically.

Before moving into more complicated cases, one point is worth making. Using models in this way requires that the model be either correct or a close approximation. (It also requires that it be estimated using the best available practice.) If, in particular, variables are wrongly omitted from equation (1) that are correlated with those included, the estimated effects will be wrong and the guidelines misleading. This will be particularly important if the omitted variables are ethically irrelevant.

To take a leading example, suppose that the true model is not equation (1) but rather

$$S = \delta + R\alpha + I\beta + \epsilon , \qquad (2)$$

where I is a single ethically irrelevant variable that, for purposes of focusing discussion, we will take to be a dichotomous variable indicating race (with $I = 0$ for blacks and $I = 1$ for whites). Suppose also that among the variables in R are one or more that are correlated with race. To fix ideas, suppose the variable in question is a measure of prior record. Then mistaken estimation of equation (1) instead of equation (2) when race has actually mattered directly in the past will lead to erroneous estimation of α. Furthermore, the derived guidelines will build in the ethically irrelevant effect of race by giving (in the simplest case) an inappropriate coefficient to prior record (among other things). In other words, such misspecification will lead to those with longer prior records being given long sentences not simply because of the effect of prior record in judicial decisions but also because those with longer prior records tend to be black. Past racism will be incorporated in the guidelines and the resulting coefficients will be biased in more than one sense.

Other misspecifications will lead to a number of less dramatic results. In the limiting case in which the omitted variables are not correlated with any of the included ones, such omission will not lead to biased estimates of the parameters that describe average behavior. It will, however, lead to inefficient estimates of those parameters. In addition, the effects of such omitted variables will be attributed to disparity, whereas they may represent not random occurrences but precisely those explicable case-by-case variations that one would not wish to reduce.

Plainly, correct specification is very important. Whether we know enough to achieve it is a separate question.

THE PRESENCE OF A SINGLE ETHICALLY IRRELEVANT VARIABLE: THE LINEAR CASE

We now face directly the question of what to do in the situation of equation (2), in which an ethically irrelevant variable such as race has influenced past decisions. (For ease of exposition we begin with the case of only one such variable, treating the more complex case below.) We have already seen how not to treat such a case—one must not delete the ethically irrelevant variable from the equation being estimated. A positive prescription is now required.

The problem can be posed as follows. The justification for empirically based guidelines lies in the view that the collective decisions of the past represent, on average, an ethically desirable standard. In the present case, however, that is manifestly untrue; such decisions, by assumption, were contaminated by the use of an ethically irrelevant criterion, race, to affect sentence length. Is it possible to purge past decisions of that contaminating effect and to use the purged estimates to inform future decisions through the construction of guidelines?

The answer is yes but the accomplishment of this task necessarily involves another ethical choice. Begin by estimating equation (2) (in the simplest case by multiple regression). This yields estimates of δ, α, and β which we denote by asterisks. Note that $\alpha*$, in particular, is an estimate of the effect of the ethically relevant variables, R, <u>with</u> <u>the</u> <u>effect</u> <u>of</u> <u>race</u> <u>held</u> <u>constant</u>. In terms of the example used above, this procedure estimates the effect of longer prior record given race—an effect uncontaminated by the fact that blacks tend to have longer records than do whites. This is useful information, for it tells us (in this linear model) what the average difference in sentence was between offenders with good and those with bad records independent of race.[3] If we can decide on the base level of sentence in the guidelines for one case, then we can use the estimates to derive levels for others.

This can be described in an equivalent but perhaps more revealing way. Suppose that we estimate equation (2) as described. We can then go on to use the estimated equation as determining the average sentence to be used in the guidelines and purge it of the racial effects by choosing a value for I, say I', to be used for all future cases of whatever race. The average sentence used in the guidelines for cases with characteristics represented by R will then be

$$S* = \delta* + R\alpha* + I'\beta* \ . \tag{3}$$

The effect of changes in R will then be measured by $\alpha*$ so that the choice of I' is equivalent to the choice of a base level as above.

How should that choice be made? This is an inescapable ethical decision. To see this, consider what different choices of I' imply. To choose any value of I' is to treat all offenders in a racially neutral way but the particular choice determines how they should be treated. Thus, to choose I' = 0 for guideline construction is to treat later offenders on average as blacks were treated previously. To choose I' = 1 is to treat them as whites were treated previously. To choose I' = 1/2 is to treat them as getting exactly the average of previous black and white treatment. This is an essentially ethical choice that cannot be made simply by referring to the average of past experience.[4]

However I' is chosen, note that the choice of k as in the simplest case will make judges explicitly justify departures that cannot be accounted for by random variation in more than a corresponding fraction of the cases. This will force any judges who still use race in an important way to make explicit justification.

NONLINEARITIES AND MORE THAN ONE
ETHICALLY IRRELEVANT VARIABLE

This same analysis readily extends to the case in which
the relationship to be estimated is nonlinear. Suppose
that equation (2) is replaced by

$$S = F(R, I, \epsilon) , \qquad (4)$$

where $F (. . . , 1)$ is some function, and we continue
with a single dichotomous ethically irrelevant variable,
I, for the moment (and continue the race example to fix
ideas).

Noting that I still takes on the values of either
zero or one, we can represent this equivalency in a
different way. Define

$$F^0(R, \epsilon) \equiv F(R, 0, \epsilon) ; \quad F^1(R, \epsilon) \equiv F(R, 1, \epsilon) . \qquad (5)$$

Then for either for the two possible values of I,

$$F(R, I, \epsilon) = (1 - I)F^0(R, \epsilon) + IF^1(R, \epsilon) . \qquad (6)$$

This corresponds to the general case in which the
sentencing behavior of judges is allowed to be completely
different for blacks from that for whites--complete
interaction; the linear case considered above is a
special case of this.

In this circumstance we once again estimate the full
descriptive model of sentencing behavior, equation (6).
This is then purged of racial effects by applying the
model for a given choice of I, say I', to all future
cases. The form of (6) now makes it apparent that the
choice of I' is equivalent to the necessarily ethical
choice of what average between former black and former
white cases is to be used. A choice of I' = 0 treats all
offenders as if they were black; a choice of I' = 1
treats them as if they were white; a choice between zero
and one determines an average.[5]

Note that this interpretation depends on the dichotomous nature of I. If I were a continuous variable we
would estimate (4) directly. A choice of I' to use in
the estimated version of (4) would then still be an
ethical choice but, except in special cases, it would not
correspond to a simple averaging of sentences previously
given for various values of I.

If more than one ethically irrelevant variable has
mattered in the past, more than one ethical choice (in
addition to the choice of k above) must be made. Thus
consider the case of two such variables that we take to
be dichotomous. Suppose that I_1 now represents race as
above and I_2 represents whether there was a guilty plea
(assuming this to be ethically irrelevant) with $I_2 = 0$
denoting no such plea and $I_2 = 1$ denoting such a plea.
Rewrite (4) as

$$S = F(R, I_1, I_2, \varepsilon) . \tag{7}$$

Define

$$F^{00}(R, \varepsilon) \equiv F(R, 0, 0, \varepsilon) ;$$
$$F^{01}(R, \varepsilon) \equiv F(R, 0, 1, \varepsilon) ;$$
$$F^{10}(R, \varepsilon) \equiv F(R, 1, 0, \varepsilon) ;$$
$$F^{11}(R, \varepsilon) \equiv F(R, 1, 1, \varepsilon) . \tag{8}$$

Then, similar to the construction in (6), for the
possible values of I_1 and I_2 we can write

$$
\begin{aligned}
F(R, I_1, I_2, \varepsilon) = {} & (1 - I_1)(1 - I_2)F^{00}(R, \varepsilon) \\
& + (1 - I_1)I_2 F^{01}(R, \varepsilon) \\
& + I_1(1 - I_2)F^{10}(R, \varepsilon) \\
& + I_1 I_2 F^{11}(R, \varepsilon) .
\end{aligned}
\tag{9}
$$

That is, there are separate relationships allowed for
blacks not pleading guilty, blacks pleading guilty,
whites not pleading guilty, and whites pleading guilty.

The construction of empirically based guidelines now
proceeds by estimating (9) and choosing two values, I'_1
and I'_2, to be used in the estimated equation that
results. These choices, necessarily ethical, determine
the weights to be used in averaging the previous average
sentences of the four groups in guidelines to be used for
all future offenders.

Note, however, that there are only two choices to be
made, not more than two, despite the fact that four
groups are to be averaged. This corresponds to the fact
that the weights used to average the guilty plea and
not-guilty plea groups must be the same for blacks as for
whites if race is to play no role in the use of the
guidelines. Equivalently, the weights used to average
the black and white groups must be the same for those
pleading guilty as for those not pleading guilty if the

presence or absence of a guilty plea is to play no role in the use of the guidelines.

Where n ethically irrelevant variables are involved, n ethical choices must be made. If n is large, even though only n such choices must be made, the view that guidelines can or should be based on past behavior rather than constructed directly from ethical or societal considerations loses much of its force, although the estimated α coefficients may still help to inform decisions.

CONCLUSION

We are uncomfortable with the whole enterprise of empirically based sentencing guidelines, for several reasons. First, they are by their nature unthoughtfully conservative. What is past may be prologue, but it is surely not unswervingly just. We prefer guidelines that arise from ethical principles, deducing the shape of the guidelines from those principles, as was done in Minnesota.

Second, taking empirically based guidelines on their own terms leads us to require ethical judgments: For example, shall we treat blacks as we used to treat whites, or conversely, or use an average? We anticipate that ethical experts might say "neither" and propose a different punishment schedule entirely, but this would lead back to a Minnesota-type approach.

Finally, there is the matter of implementation. These procedures assume that the model is correctly specified. Incorrect specification can lead to reintroduction of racial bias and other kinds of substantial injustice. We should add that correct specification is very difficult to achieve.

In conclusion, empirically based sentencing guidelines strike us as a species of computer-driven conservatism. They do not avoid hard ethical questions, and they mislead those who would construct guidelines by substituting statistical sophistication, which is useful but not essential, for ethical sophistication, which is critical.

NOTES

1. For convenience of notation we have not written out terms such as $R\alpha$. The reader is free to think of R as a

single variable. The more general case would have

$$R\alpha = \alpha_1 R_1 + \alpha_2 R_2 + \ldots + \alpha_k R_k .$$

2. For a discussion of this and similar issues see Franklin M. Fisher (1980) Multiple regression in legal proceedings. Columbia Law Review 80(2):702-736.

3. Although prior record is itself a composite of several variables, we ignore this for simplicity of exposition.

4. Note in particular a choice of I' to generate the same average sentence length for all cases in the sample as actually occurred builds in a judgment that such an average was "right" despite the fact that it was influenced by the racial mix of cases in the sample. To attempt to set I' empirically by estimating I' together with α and δ to give the best fit in the sample is even worse. It can be shown to be equivalent to leaving race out of the estimated equation altogether (by absorbing I'β into δ, the constant term), the case of misspecification considered above.

  There may be other ways to correct for the effects of race. For example, in a rather extreme form of affirmative action, one might wish to take account of the fact that blacks are discriminated against elsewhere. Such discrimination can mean that blacks have a worse prior record or are more likely to be unemployed than whites. One can imagine correcting variables such as prior record or unemployment by regressing them on race, then giving those variables in equation (3) the values they would have on the average if the offender were white, or the values they would have if the offender were black, or some other common value. This would involve a correction for race more extreme than simply a uniform value for I' and would be likely to lead to wholesale reliance on regression rather than to analysis of individual offender characteristics.

5. Note that the choices outside the range of (0, 1) are also possible. This would mean treating all offenders better than whites were treated in the past or all offenders worse than blacks were treated in the past (assuming discrimination to have been against blacks). To do so is to depart fairly sharply from the notion that past judgments are ethically acceptable, however--the view that lies behind empirically based guidelines.

5

The Construction of Sentencing Guidelines: A Methodological Critique

Richard F. Sparks

INTRODUCTION

The purpose of this paper is to discuss critically a
number of conceptual and methodological problems associated with the construction of empirically based
sentencing guidelines.[1] Guidelines of the type with
which this paper is concerned are the most recently
proposed technique for attempting to deal with a problem
which has been a subject of concern for at least a
century: controlling the discretion of individual
decision makers in the criminal justice system.[2]
Sentencing guidelines differ in a number of interesting
and important ways from other techniques for controlling
discretion in sentencing, such as sentencing codes
(Ferri, 1921; Glueck, 1928), mandatory sentences, or
"presumptive" sentences. For this reason, sentencing
guidelines solve some of the problems associated with
these other techniques, while simply bypassing others.
Empirically based guidelines do raise a number of
problems of their own; these are the problems of most
concern in this paper.

My focus is primarily on the construction of sentencing guidelines. I do not discuss any theoretical or
empirical issues relating to the implementation of
guidelines in different types of jurisdictions; nor, a
fortiori, do I deal with assessing the impacts (in any
sense of that term) of guidelines on sentencing practice,
e.g., with the complex problem of estimating "compliance"

with guidelines after they have been introduced. Nor, indeed, do I address all the problems that might reasonably be said to be associated with constructing sentencing guidelines. A political scientist, for instance, would no doubt find it interesting to explore the relationships between different types of legal systems and judiciaries and the acceptance of judicially supported guidelines as a means of controlling discretion in sentencing; legal theorists and sociologists of organizations could similarly find grist for their respective mills. My concern is with what might be called the technology of developing sentencing guidelines, as that technology has been represented in a number of different American jurisdictions over the past decade or so.

In discussing some of the problems of this technology, I refer to the decision-making guidelines that have been developed and/or implemented in a few American jurisdictions in recent years. My primary purpose in doing this will be illustrative rather than evaluative. Much of the empirical research done by those who have been involved in developing guidelines in recent years has been severely flawed in methodological terms; as a result, that research has often yielded descriptions of antecedent sentencing practices that were both inaccurate and misleading. In one sense this may not have mattered much, since (in at least some jurisdictions) the findings of the empirical research carried out as a preliminary to the formulation of guidelines were substantially modified in the light of considerations of legal or social policy. I shall also argue, however, that much of this empirical work has rested on a faulty conception of the proper role of research in relation to the development of guidelines. There are indeed a number of ways in which empirical research--if it is correctly done--can be useful to those planning to introduce sentencing guidelines (or other techniques for controlling discretion). Much research to date in this area, however, appears to have serious technical shortcomings, which in some cases may have obscured important questions of policy and in others may lead to highly undesirable consequences-- including some consequences that guidelines are supposed to avoid.

The construction of empirically based sentencing guidelines has been said to involve three distinct steps (Zimmerman and Blumstein, 1979; Gottfredson et al., 1978; Kress, 1980). The first of these is the collection of data on past sentencing practice. The second is the

analysis of those data aimed at producing a model of past
sentencing practice; such models usually take the form of
statistical equations purporting to show the relationships between such things as seriousness of offense and
prior record to past sentencing outcomes. The third is
the translation of the model thus obtained into a
prescriptive instrument—that is, the guidelines themselves. In later sections of this paper, these three
steps are discussed in some detail; each has distinctive
problems associated with it, and as we shall see the
three-step account itself has certain flaws. But as a
preliminary, it may be useful to look briefly at the
guidelines that are meant to be the end-product of this
three-step exercise. If the objective of the collection
and statistical analysis of data on sentencing is the
construction of an instrument to guide future sentences—
rather than, say, the testing of conflict or Marxist
theories about the criminal justice system (e.g., Hagan,
1975; Lizotte, 1978)—then this has important implications for the kinds of data collection and analysis that
are reasonable to do.

THE CONCEPT OF DECISION-MAKING GUIDELINES[3]

Empirically based decision-making guidelines were first
proposed in the field of criminal justice by Don M.
Gottfredson and Leslie T. Wilkins, for use in connection
with the decisions of parole boards to release offenders
from prison. The U.S. Parole Commission has used various
versions of the Gottfredson-Wilkins guidelines since 1972
(see Gottfredson et al., 1975; Gottfredson et al.,
1978). A feasibility study of the application of
guidelines to sentencing was begun by Gottfredson and
Wilkins in 1974; while not all of the guidelines subsequently develped in various American jurisdictions have
followed what may be called the Gottfredson-Wilkins
model, the great majority have done so.

The basic concept of the Gottfredson-Wilkins model of
guidelines is as follows. Decision makers in the
criminal justice system—for example, judges or parole
board members—are given information about the patterns
of decision making in their jurisdictions in the past;
they then use this information to guide their decisions
in the future. In the case of parole decision making
(which is of course concerned only with offenders who are
already incarcerated) the information typically consists

of a range of months or years served in prison before
release on parole. The parole board may release prisoners after they have served terms falling within that
range without any further justification. Alternatively,
the board may depart from the guidelines--setting a term
of incarceration that falls outside the suggested
range--if there are special factors that appear to make
this appropriate, although the board must state its
reasons for any such departure.

The typical form of such guidelines is a two-
dimensional matrix or table, in which the rows correspond
to different types of current offense (usually although
not necessarily ordered by seriousness), and the columns
correspond to an offender score, which is usually largely
a function of prior criminal record but may also include
other personal attributes (e.g., a presumed measure of
social stability, such as employment status, education,
or the absence of drug use). Each of the cells of the
resulting matrix contains the normal range of months or
years of incarceration for offenders with the particular
combination of offense type and offender score defining
the cell. Table 5-1--which is based on the U.S. Parole
Commission's current guidelines--is an example of such a
matrix. This table shows that, for example, an offender
who has been imprisoned for an offense of "low moderate"
seriousness (examples, in the U.S. Parole Commission's

TABLE 5-1 Customary Total Times to be Served in Prison
Before Release, in Months, Under U.S. Parole Commission
Guidelines

Severity of Offense	Parole Prognosis (Salient Factor Score)			
	Very Good	Good	Fair	Poor
Low	6-10	8-12	10-14	12-16
Low Moderate	8-12	12-16	16-20	20-25
Moderate	12-16	16-20	20-24	24-30
High	16-20	20-26	26-32	32-38
Very High	26-36	36-45	45-55	55-65

SOURCE: Adapted from data in Gottfredson et al.
(1978:24-26).

matrix, include fraud involving less than $1,000 and the simple possession of marijuana) and who has a good prognosis (as measured by the commission's "salient factor" score) should normally serve between 12 and 16 months in prison before release on parole.

Evidently, a very similar kind of matrix could be used by judges in deciding what sentences to impose on convicted offenders, although there are some important differences between sentencing and parole guidelines, which follow from differences in the decisions they are meant to regulate. Before turning to those matters, however, let us consider what is distinctive about the Gottfredson-Wilkins concept of guidelines, compared with other techniques that have been proposed for regulating, controlling, or structuring discretionary decisions. Two things appear to be important:

(1) <u>Ranges rather than points</u>. The parole guidelines originally proposed by Gottfredson and Wilkins provided for a range of months or years to be served before release from prison; in this respect their guidelines differ from most forms of presumptive sentencing (e.g., California's Uniform Determinate Sentencing Law of 1976), under which the term to be imposed in the normal case is defined in terms of a single point or period of time, such as two years.[4]

(2) <u>Nonmandatory ranges</u>. It is essential to the Gottfredson-Wilkins concept of guidelines that judges or parole board members are not legally required to impose a sentence or fix a term within the range stipulated by the guidelines matrix. They may of course do this; if they do, then no further justification of that sentence or term is required. They may decide that it is appropriate to depart from the guidelines, if there are special features of a case that seem to justify a higher or lower term than the normal range of the matrix cell provides. They should state their reasons for doing so, citing the features of the case that in their opinion make a higher or lower sentence appropriate.

It is perhaps these two features--a range of permitted variation and the option of departure from that range in explicitly justified circumstances--that have led Gottfredson and Wilkins to describe sentencing and parole guidelines as a means of structuring decision makers' discretion, rather than limiting or eliminating it (Gottfredson et al., 1978:8). Providing a normal range

of prison or jail time within which no special justification is needed does two things. First, it recognizes
that for any combination of factors, such as offense type
and offender score (however those are defined), there
will probably still be some differences between cases--
for example, in the amount of property stolen or damaged,
the amount of injury inflicted, or the vulnerability of
the victim--that may justify some variation in sentences
imposed. A normal range also accepts the view that
people may reasonably disagree about the appropriate
penalty, given the facts of a particular case. Guidelines aim to set limits on that kind of difference of
opinion, by providing that sentences outside the
stipulated range must be specially justified.

It may be noted in passing that there are a number of
other features that such a system of sentencing guidelines may have, which although not intrinsic to the
process of constructing guidelines may nonetheless have
some implications for the analysis of past sentencing
practice. (Some of these features were suggested by
Gottfredson and Wilkins; others were not, but are
exemplified by guidelines now in existence.) First,
there may be rules that limit the grounds on which
sentences outside the normal guideline range may be
justified, so that departure is permissible only if one
or more of an explicit list of aggravating or mitigating
factors is present. The Minnesota guidelines, for
example, are accompanied by a list of four mitigating
factors and four aggravating factors that may justify
departure from the prescribed range; there is also an
explicit list of 11 factors that may not be used as
grounds for departure.[5] Second, there may be limits
placed on the length or type of sentence that can be
imposed by judges if they do go outside the normal range;
the first set of proposed Pennsylvania guidelines, for
example, limited aggravated and mitigated sentences to
adjacent cells of the matrix.[6]

Third, the reasons given for departing from the
guideline range may be incorporated into the process of
appellate review of sentences, if there is such a process
in the jurisdiction.[7] Alternatively or additionally,
information on the use of the guidelines (including
departures and the reasons given for them) may be made
available to the judiciary or the sentencing commission,
who may then decide whether the guidelines should be
modified in some respect. This kind of feedback process,
involving continuous monitoring of the guidelines after

their implementation, was in fact regarded by both
Gottfredson and Wilkins as central to the concept of
guidelines; it is what they meant by "making policy
explicit" and by the "evolutionary model" they proposed
(Gottfredson et al., 1975; Gottfredson et al., 1978;
Gottfredson and Gottfredson, 1980). This process is a
feature of the U.S. Parole Commission's current procedures and appears to have led to modifications of the
commission's guidelines from time to time; it is also
envisaged by the Minnesota Sentencing Guidelines Commission, although that state's guidelines have not been in
operation long enough to see how it will work in practice.

What about the empirical basis of sentencing guidelines? There is certainly an impression conveyed by the
literature on this subject that an analysis of past
sentencing practice is intrinsic to the concept of
sentencing guidelines. All the guidelines developed to
date have taken as their starting point a statistical
analysis of past practice, the purpose of which was
ostensibly to identify those factors most strongly
associated with sentencing variation in the past.
Gottfredson and Wilkins have both said on numerous
occasions that guidelines are "descriptive" rather than
"prescriptive" (see, for example, Wilkins et al.,
1976:31-32; Gottfredson et al., 1978; compare Kress,
1980:11-12). Similarly, the New Jersey guidelines state
that "it should be emphasized that the purpose of
sentencing guidelines is not to persuade judges regarding
what is the 'right' sentence or the 'best' sentence"
(McCarthy, 1978:6) and elsewhere repeat the "descriptive,
not prescriptive" idea. Given this rhetoric and its
associated history, it may seem natural to assume that
sentencing guidelines must be based on an analysis of
past sentencing practice.[8]

It takes only a moment's reflection, however, to see
that this is not necessarily so; and that the much-touted
empirical basis of guidelines is by no means intrinsic to
the construction of an instrument for controlling
decision makers' discretion.[9] On the contrary, a
matrix like that in Table 5-1 could obviously be made
up—by a legislature, a sentencing commission, or a
parole board—without any reference whatever to past
decision-making practice. This is in fact precisely what
happened with the Oregon parole guidelines, which were
first developed in 1975 and given statutory authority in
1977. No analyses of past decision-making practices were
carried out before these guidelines were formulated;

instead, the board, under the chairmanship of Ira
Blalock, simply made up the appropriate ranges of time to
be served by different types of offenders. It is in fact
unclear how far Blalock and his colleagues were trying,
in creating their guidelines and the associated defini-
tional rules, to reflect past paroling practice in the
state.[10] What is clear is that they did not carry out
any detailed analysis of those past practices, and of
course they did not need to do so. They simply
prescribed.

That said, it may be agreed that "obtaining an
empirical description of current sentencing behavior is a
reasonable first step in the process of sentencing
guideline development" (Zimmerman and Blumstein,
1979:2). There are several reasons why this may be the
case. First, most advocates of guidelines have been
animated by a belief that these will somehow help to
reduce disparity in sentencing; given this animus, it may
be thought prudent to show that there has in fact been
such disparity in the past.[11] Second, there may be a
genuine feeling that what was done in the past was by and
large right (and so ought to be incorporated into
anything aiming to prescribe what should be done in the
future); I suspect that this view has fairly widespread
support, especially among the judiciary, although it is
difficult to get anyone to say so in public. It may
indeed be agreed that past sentencing practice has been
correct on the average, but that there has been too much
variation around that average; disparity in this sense of
excessive variation need not entail, of course, that
sentences in the past were based on morally iniquitous
factors such as race or social class. If it is felt that
the judiciary's collective wisdom has in the past been
generally on target, then research may give a clearer
picture of what the targets in question have been; this
may help judges to sentence in a more consistent
fashion. Finally, and perhaps more cynically, it may be
thought that it will be comforting, especially to the
judiciary, to claim that sentences in the future will not
be too different from what they were in the past; a bit
of preliminary number-crunching may make this politically
expedient claim more plausible.[12] In any event, one
must start somewhere, when implementing sentencing
reform; and it plainly seems better to begin with good
empirical evidence than with unsupported speculation.[13]
After all, many people--including many judges and
legislators--do not know that an offender given an

"indeterminate" sentence of 5 to 15 years in prison is likely to be back out on the street in perhaps 24 months; research may help to convince them of this fact, if indeed it is a fact.[14]

It should not be forgotten, however, that it is perfectly possible to construct sentencing or parole guidelines in the back-of-an-old-envelope fashion followed by the Oregon parole board; these might be called guidelines by fiat. I shall have little to say about such guidelines in this paper, which is mainly concerned with the problems of carrying out empirical research on past sentencing practice. It is important to keep in mind the possibility of such guidelines, however, when considering the construction of empirically based ones. To do so may serve to remind us that there is no necessary connection between descriptions of current practice and guidelines as a prescriptive instrument.

THE DESCRIPTION OF PAST SENTENCING PRACTICE

I begin by distinguishing, definitionally, between a sentencing policy and sentencing practice. I use the term policy to refer to a description of the various things that enter consciously into the decisions of judges (or parole boards). It includes not only their (probably rather mixed) views about the proper goals of their decisions but also their (sometimes not fully articulated) views as to what they should do in a particular type of case to accomplish those goals, the features of the case that justify their doing one thing rather than another, and so on. A judge's sentencing policy, by this definition, would be described by a sincere answer to the question, "What do you generally do with cases of type X, and why?" In all probability, the answers to a number of supplementary questions would also be relevant. Such an account of sentencing policy assumes that it basically involves the application to particular cases of some rules or recipes of the form, "If the case is of type X, then do Y"; it also implies at least minimal self-consistency on the part of individual judges over time.

The term sentencing practice, by contrast, is used to refer to what may be called an external description of judges' sentencing behavior; it does not incorporate any reference to what the judge(s) in question thought, believed, intended, etc. when imposing the sentences in

question. Sentencing practices are what are described by
statements like "Court A imprisoned 75 percent of its
convicted burglars, whereas Court B put 95 percent of its
convicted burglars on probation"--statements than can in
principle be verified or falsified by summary statistics,
observation, etc., which entail no reference to the
conscious plans of action on the part of judges leading
up to the sentences in question. The importance of this
distinction is that there is, generally speaking, only
one correct description of the sentencing policy followed
by a judge at a particular time and place, whereas there
is an infinity of correct descriptions of the judge's
practice, consisting of the sentences imposed at that
time and place.[15]

It is clear that many if not most of those who have
done research on sentencing with a view to creating
guidelines have wanted to influence sentencing policies.
Gottfredson and Wilkins, for example, claim that their
early work with the U.S. Parole Board was "making
paroling policy explicit." Similarly, the sentencing
guidelines developed in Minnesota and Pennsylvania were
very explicit statements of policy: They were intended,
one might say, as "recipes for sentencing" that judges
were to follow in the future. Given that aim, it seems
reasonable to suppose that the empirical research that
has been carried out, as a preliminary to formulating
guidelines, should have been research on previous
sentencing policies. It is important to note, however,
that this has almost never been the case. In almost
every instance, the research on past decision making with
which we are concerned has been of a kind that (at best)
could only have produced an external description of past
practice. The earliest research of Gottfredson and
Wilkins is a sort of exception. Gottfredson and Wilkins
first obtained from parole board members their subjective
ratings of a number of variables, such as seriousness of
offense, risk of recidivism, institutional behavior,
etc., for a number of cases. They then analyzed these
(using the statistical procedure known as multiple
regression) and showed that seriousness of offense and
length of prior record were the two variables most
strongly related to the lengths of time served to parole
in the cases studied. They then categorized and cross-
classified these two variables to obtain a matrix like
the one shown in Table 5-1 above, calculated median times
to parole in each of the cells of that table, judgmen-
tally "smoothed" those medians, then bracketed them with

more or less arbitrarily chosen ranges to produce the guidelines. That was the extent of their empiricism.

To say that this method made explicit a policy of the U.S. Parole Commission that had been in effect all along was a pretty safe claim. Seriousness of current offense and length of prior record have been said to be the most important, morally appropriate determinants of sentences in an enormous number of jurisdictions; any study of sentencing practice that does not find these things to be most strongly associated with severity of sentences (at least for adults) has probably measured something incorrectly. The inferential leap that Gottfredson and Wilkins made from practice to policy was thus not a very great one—especially since those two variables were defined in terms of the assessments of parole board members rather than in some more objective fashion.

Any more ambitious inferences, however, are perilous. For one thing, even with the two obviously relevant variables just mentioned, an accurate assessment of sentencing policy requires that we know just what judges mean by saying that, for example, an offense is serious or a prior record minor; concepts of that kind may in practice be quite complex and variable, and (perhaps surprisingly) these particular concepts are still imperfectly understood.[16] To be sure, most of us have some fairly crude commonsense notions about what makes a crime serious or a prior criminal record trivial, but these notions clearly do not take us very far.

Moreover, there is not at the present time anything that could be called a theory about how judges (or parole boards or analogous decision makers) actually decide what sentences or prison terms to impose. We know next to nothing, for example, about the ways in which attributes of the current offense(s) and facts about the offender's prior criminality tend to be combined, in practice, so as to influence the judge's choice of sentence. Furthermore, we know little about what other kinds of things (prospects for rehabilitation, for example) may be considered by judges or parole boards in certain cases. As is well known, the philosophy of sentencing is now in some considerable turmoil, in the United States and elsewhere; what Allen (1964) called the "rehabilitative ideal" is fast losing what little credibility it ever had, in most jurisdictions, and "just deserts" (von Hirsch, 1975) are being served up in its place. This makes it extremely difficult to infer anything about the

sentencing policies of judges from objective data on
cases dealt with in the past--not least because a
reasonably concrete attribute like number of prior felony
convictions may have one kind of effect if rehabilitation
is the judge's goal, and quite another if the aim is what
used to be called retribution.

Very well, it may be said; in order to construct
guidelines, let us forget past policies and instead
produce a description of past practices. We can obtain
empirically a picture of what judges in fact did in
certain types of cases in the past and use that as the
basis of some rules prescribing what they should do in
the future. There is something right about this; but not
much. The definition of policy that I gave at the
beginning of this section refers to the things that are
consciously used by judges. But it plainly cannot be
assumed that the only things that influence the outcomes
of sentencing decisions are things of which the judge is
aware; just because there are reasons that judges can
give (and, we assume, sincerely give) for sentences, it
does not follow that those sentences are not influenced
by things of which they are not aware. For example: a
judge may sincerely and deeply believe that he or she is
not racially prejudiced; yet he or she may be ("uncons-
ciously") disposed to give heavier sentences to blacks
than to whites, ceteris paribus.[17] There is a story,
probably apocryphal, that it is regarded as more serious
to shoot a cow in eastern Oregon than to shoot your wife
in western Oregon. Judges from the two ends of the state
might agree on the definition of seriousness, while being
unaware of the regional difference (if there is one) in
the application of that definition in different parts of
the state.

Research on sentencing in the past, if intended as a
preliminary to guidelines prescribing sentencing in the
future, must thus examine both policy and practice. The
trouble is that, at present, we have virtually no theory
about either policy or practice, once we get beyond a
small number of commonsense ideas. This in turn is
important, since without some kind of theory, however
humble, we cannot possibly decide what information we
should obtain about sentencing practice in the past.
Consider these two statements:

(1) Court A imprisoned 75 percent of its convicted
burglars, whereas Court B put 95 percent of its burglars
on probation.

(2) Court A imprisoned 75 percent of its convicted, one-eyed, green-haired sodomites, whereas Court B put 95 percent of such convicted offenders on probation.

Suppose that both of these statements are true for some pair of jurisdictions. Which do we accept as a description of sentencing practice? The answer is that, as matters now stand, we have precious little ground for choosing between them. Of course, we may rule out statement (2) on commonsense grounds; or we may actually go out and ask judges, in an artful fashion, whether or not being monocular or green-haired is something that they ever take into account. Or we might try to get a handle on this experimentaly, e.g., by systematically varying one-eyedness and green hair among burglars, robbers, con men, etc. as well as those convicted of sex offenses (perhaps there are several green-haired judges in Court B, whereas judges in Court A have an unconscious aversion to one-eyed persons, and these two peculiar attributes are correlated). My point is that both statements could be true, for some sample of offenders; without something that can reasonably be called a theory, we have no ground for preferring one to the other.

It follows that without some sort of theory, we can have no real idea what sort of information to collect in order to give a useful description of past sentencing practice. It would probably not occur to researchers in this field to collect data on green hair and monocularity (or at least I hope it would not); if it did, they would probably not succeed, since these two attributes are not, so far as I am aware, regarded as important by the probation officers and other social workers who currently write presentence reports in most American jurisdictions.[18] By now the reader is probably thoroughly tired of these two far-fetched examples of possible correlates with sentencing outcomes. They are, of course, deliberately far-fetched; but that is not the point. What is true for them--namely, that we need some kind of theory, even if only a rather vulgar one, to make sense of their correlations with severity of sentences-- is equally true of what are, on their face, much more plausible candidates for inclusion in a useful description of sentencing practice.

I give two examples, drawn from the research that my colleagues and I recently carried out in an evaluation of statewide sentencing guidelines (Sparks et al., 1982). There are some data suggesting that the recommendations made by probation officers, as part of the pretrial or presentence reports that they prepare for judges, may exert an important influence on the judges' decisions to place convicted offenders on probation rather than incarcerating them. In field research that we carried out in Massachusetts, before that state's judicially sponsored guidelines were developed, however, we discovered that the recommendations of probation officers there cut very little ice. We also discovered, through interviews and observation, that the recommendations of prosecutors and defense counsel were important determinants of the sentences finally imposed on offenders—though in complex ways that varied considerably among judges and among the four counties in which our field research was done.[19] Had we been carrying out research on past sentencing policy—or even, more humbly, on past sentencing practice—in Massachusetts, we could properly have ignored probation officers' recommendations, but we should certainly have collected data on defense counsel's recommendations. Those who carried out the research on which the Massachusetts guidelines are based did just the opposite: They recorded the irrelevant recommendations of probation officers (when these were available from records), and failed to record those of defense counsel.[20]

With a view to prescribing sentencing policy for the future through guidelines, research has been done on sentencing in the past in several American jurisdictions. Most of this research has not, however, investigated past sentencing policies; at best, it has produced descriptions of past practice, which have not been guided by any kind of theories about how judges actually decide what sentences should be imposed, because there are no such theories at the present time.

It is vital to see, however, that some well-founded beliefs about the way in which judges actually make sentencing decisions must be thought out (and, preferably, tested by observing and interviewing judges and others involved in the sentencing process) before research on past sentencing practice is begun. Such a set of beliefs—even if they do not amount to a theory—will largely influence the kinds of information on past practice that it is reasonable to collect. As Zimmerman and Blumstein (1979:9) have pointed out, one should ideally try to obtain information only on variables that seem theoretically reasonable or are believed (perhaps from previous research) to be empirically correlated with

sentencing practice; there is no point in going to the
often-considerable expense of collecting data on variables that are irrelevant will not be used in later
statistical analyses.

Lacking any kind of theory, many if not most of those
who have done research on sentencing with a view to
formulating guidelines have, it seems, simply set out to
collect as much data of any kind whatever as they could
find in existing records and afford to have keypunched
for computer analysis. The most extreme example seems to
have taken place in New Jersey, where the guidelines
project staff "decided that every bit of data could
possibly affect sentences, and that therefore no assumptions should be made at the outset to dismiss any data"
(McCarthy, 1978:10).[21] For example, the New Jersey
project attempted to collect information from presentence
reports on "education of offender's parents/guardian."
As it turned out, however, data on this variable were
recorded (whether or not accurately) in only 7 percent of
their cases (McCarthy, 1978:16n.). This is likely to
happen with many such recondite variables, especially if
the data in question are decided upon and collected after
the fact, e.g., from presentence reports. A more
important question, however, is what would one do with
data on education of offender's parents/guardian if they
were recorded in, say, 93 percent of all cases instead of
7. There is plainly no reason to think that this item of
information should figure in judges' sentencing decisions
in any important way.[22] What reason is there to think
that it does figure--even in the handful of cases in
which the judge is aware of it?

What data on past sentencing practice should be
collected? Perhaps the best answer is that data should
be obtained on all variables that might reasonably be
supposed to have been associated with sentencing in the
past in a nontrivial proportion of the cases intended for
statistical analyses. At a minimum, as Gelman et al.
(1979) have suggested, such analyses should at least
consider the information base available to the judge at
the time when the sentencing decision was made; and if
there is doubt, it is clearly better to be inclusive at
the first stage of data collection, given that items that
subsequently prove to be clearly irrelevant can be
discarded later. Basing analyses of past practice on the
information that judges had before them conveniently
skirts one of the problems of validity commonly encountered in social research, since it does not really matter

whether that information was <u>correct</u>, so long as the
judges believed it was.[23] However, there are may be
problems in identifying the judges' information base,
especially if (as has been the case in all guidelines
research projects to date) the data on past practice are
collected from presentence reports or other records,
after the offender has been sentenced. Presentence
reports, typically compiled by probation officers,
usually give no information about the offender's demeanor
in court, the issues that may be found (either during a
trial or at the time of a plea) to justify mitigation or
aggravation of sentence, the behavior of counsel, and
many other matters that may influence the sentence
finally imposed.

As just noted, however, it is also important to
collect data on things that might have affected sentencing decisions in the past, even though this was undesired
and unintentional. A few obvious candidates, in commonsense terms, are the race and ethnicity of the offender
(and victim), the region within a state or similar
jurisdiction in which the case was dealt with, the sex,
occupation, and social status of the offender (and the
victim), and the identities of judge, prosecutor, and
defense counsel involved in the case.[24] These things
will not, presumably, be used in prescriptive guidelines,
but they may be important in analyses of past practice,
if the notion of empirically based guidelines is to have
any meaning.

A special problem is posed by the dependent or outcome
variables typically used in studies of sentencing
practice. As the next section of this paper discusses,
it is necessary to keep separate at least two outcomes of
the sentencing decision: (1) the in-out decision and (2)
the "how long?" decision for those who are incarcerated.
In most jurisdictions, determining the value of the first
of these variables--i.e., whether the offender was
incarcerated and if so where--seems unlikely to pose many
problems. But the second variable--duration of
incarceration--is more difficult. The problem is that,
in most American jurisdictions, the time to be served by
incarcerated offenders is finally determined, not by the
sentencing judge but by the parole board. Although there
are differences from state to state, in many if not most
states the judge will pronounce either a maximum term, or
a maximum and a minimum term, with the amount of time
actually served by the offender to be determined within
the judicially imposed limits.[25] In some jurisdic-

tions, indeed, the sentence imposed by the judge--usually a maximum term--may be very much a pro forma pronouncement.

If one wishes to model antecedent sentencing practice in such jurisdictions, then data on judicially imposed (maximum) terms may be of little relevance. What will matter to the length of time a prisoner stays "inside" is not what the judge says but what the parole board later decides. It appears that it was for this reason that the Minnesota guidelines researchers drew two separate samples of offenders on which they based their analyses. The decision to incarcerate was based on a sample of 2,399 persons convicted of felonies in fiscal 1978; this sample was drawn from court records. The study of sentence duration, however, was based on all 847 of the prisoners released from state correctional institutions in 1978, either on parole or at the expiration of the sentence(s) that led to their commitment (see Minnesota Sentencing Guidelines Commission, 1980:4). This was no doubt the only feasible approach, but it raises some problems of inference.[26] In general, data on a sample of parolees can provide only minimal information about judicial views as to lengths of prison terms. In very "indeterminate" jurisdictions, of course, judges may in effect have no views of their own on appropriate lengths of terms; more precisely, though they may have some views, these may not be reflected in the terms eventually served by the offenders whom they sentence, which will be fixed later by the parole board. To the extent that this is the case, the empirical analysis on which guidelines are ultimately based will not be an analysis solely of judicial behavior; instead, it will involve some composite of judicial and paroling behavior. (The matter is further complicated by the fact that judges may have effective control over the lengths of jail terms, if these are counted as "in" sentences--in the Minnesota guidelines, which are concerned solely with state prison sentences, they are not.)

Different situations may arise in other jurisdictions. In Massachusetts, for example, judges may sentence some offenders either to the state prison at Walpole or to the reformatory at Concord (or to a local jail). For those sent to Walpole, minimum parole eligibility is either one-third or two-thirds of the judicially imposed sentence, depending on type of offense. For those sent to Concord, however, the usual rule is that the offender stays inside for 6 months for each 5 years of term imposed; thus an offender sentenced to 15 years in Concord would normally be released after 18 months in the institution. Now, discussions with Massachusetts judges--by the Massachusetts guideline project staff as well as by my colleagues and me during our periods of field work in that state[27]--strongly suggested that the judges were well aware of the times that offenders would normally serve (unless penalized for institutional misconduct) in the two different institutions and that they consciously tailored the sentences they imposed, in order to try to ensure that the offender was "off the streets" for what they regarded as an appropriate period of time.[28] Data from the Massachusetts Department of Corrections, moreover, show that the state's judges were generally correct in assuming that the majority of offenders were in fact released on parole at the minimum times provided by law for the various institutions in the state. Given these facts, the Massachusetts guidelines researchers took as their "length of incarceration" variable the proportion of the total sentence to Walpole or Concorde prescribed by law as the minimum to parole eligibility given the institution and type of offender in question.

Such an approach seems to me entirely reasonable; but the same conditions may well not obtain in other juris- dictions. In Michigan, for example, there is an indeter- minate sentencing system of a fairly conventional kind. In felony cases, judges have discretion either to grant probation or to impose a jail term or a minimum state prison sentence, which by law may not be more than two-thirds the maximum (People v. Tanner, 387 Mich. 683, 199 N.W.2d 202 (1972); see Zalman et al., 1979). Release from prison, at any time between the minimum (less good time) and the maximum, is at the discretion of the parole board. The researchers involved in developing Michigan's sentencing guidelines took as their measure of length of prison sentences the minimum terms imposed, on the ground that these reflected the only meaningful use of discretion by judges (Zalman et al., 1979:172). This may be so, but the minimum terms may obviously give only an imperfect indication of the terms that prisoners eventually served.

A further practical problem concerns the numbers and kinds of cases selected for study. The sentencing guidelines research done to date displays considerable variation in this respect. At one extreme, data were collected in New Jersey on all persons convicted of

crimes in the year beginning December 1976; this yielded
a total of about 16,000 cases. This solution, apparently
adopted on political grounds,[29] has some distinct
advantages from a researcher's point of view,[30] but it
is plainly very expensive and is unlikely to be followed
in many other jurisdictions. In the other states in
which guidelines research has been done to date, the
analyses of past sentencing practice have been based on
samples of cases dealt with in, say, a year's time. In
Michigan, for example, the sample consisted of 5,909
cases of a total of 26,116 cases sentenced in calendar
year 1977 (Zalman et al., 1979). In Pennsylvania, the
sample contained about 2,900 cases; in Minnesota, about
2,400; in Massachusetts, about 1,500.[31] Although these
sample sizes might be thought adequate for many kinds of
social research, it seems from project reports that they
imposed some constraints on the analyses conducted in
most if not all of these guideline projects, not only
because of the problems of missing data inherent in
court-based records in most jurisdictions but also
because of the relative rarity of some kinds of cases
that may be of interest. For example, in most states it
will be difficult to obtain sufficient cases for analysis
in small or rural counties, and, given the usual sex
ratios among convicted offenders, it may be difficult to
get data on enough convicted females to permit more than
the most cursory analysis.

Different strategies--none of them entirely
satisfactory--have been adopted by different researchers
to cope with this problem. In Massachusetts, for
example, a few of the smaller counties in the state were
simply excluded from the sampling frame;[32] in
Minnesota, by contrast, several rural counties, including
a number with large Native American populations, were
oversampled in order to provide enough cases for
statistical analysis. In addition, in Minnesota, all of
the convicted female felons were included in the sample,
but only 42 percent of the convicted males (see Minnesota
Sentencing Guidelines Commission, 1980:4). Disproportionate sampling of this kind can cause some statistical
problems, although in practice these need not be too
serious.[33] It cannot be intelligently done, however,
unless one has some notion of the kinds of cases that are
likely to be of sufficient theoretical or practical
importance to require oversampling; and as I have already
noted, most guidelines researchers to date seem to have
had only the most rudimentary ideas about this. For

example, common sense might lead one to suppose that
sentencing practice would be different for cases disposed
of by trial and cases disposed of by a plea of guilty
(whether or not that plea was negotiated). This was in
fact found to be the case in Massachusetts, and the
guidelines eventually developed in that state were
primarily to be used in tried cases.[34] Yet no special
effort was made by the Massachusetts researchers to
oversample these cases (which account for less than a
tenth of the total); the result was that the guidelines
were based on a small number of cases, which may have
provided an unreliable or even misleading description of
past practice.[35]

A final problem of sample size concerns the fact that
any statistical model or description of sentencing
practice should ideally be validated: that is, it should
be tested on a fresh sample from the same population, to
see how well it holds up. The reason for this is
that--especially if one's research is not guided by any
kind of theory--the results from the analysis of the
first sample may be due in part to some idiosyncracies of
that sample, which reflect nothing more than chance
variation. A variety of techniques for this kind of
statistical validation exists (see, for a discussion,
Mosteller and Tukey, 1977:36-40, 133-63; Larntz, 1980).
The problem is that all of these require substantial
numbers of cases to be selected in the first place.[36]
(In this respect, one must envy the New Jersey
researchers; political pressures that apparently required
them to collect data on all cases sentenced in the year
they studied also provided them with the funds to do
this.)

In fact, few of those who have so far done research on
sentencing with a view to developing guidelines have paid
any attention to this important issue of validation;[37]
as the next section discusses, this may account for some
of the counterintuitive findings of their analyses, and
it certainly leaves room for considerable doubt about the
stability of even their apparently reasonable findings.
In some cases (e.g. in Minnesota, and probably also
Pennsylvania) this may have been due to the fact that
research on past sentencing practice was never intended
to play an important role in shaping future sentencing
policy. But in other cases, guidelines have been said
(at least by way of advertisement) to have an empirical
basis; even so, no attempt at statistical validation was
made. Yet this could easily have been done in New

Jersey, where there were over 11,000 cases in hand;[38] it could also have been done (though probably not quite so easily) in Michigan, where the initially selected sample contained nearly 6,000 cases. It probably could not have been satisfactorily done in Massachusetts, with a total of only 1,400 cases,[39] but that means that the Massachusetts sample was probably too small--suggesting that the issue of validation was not thought of by the Massachusetts research team before they began their work. (Although, to be fair, the decision to select only a sample of this size may well have been dictated by budgetary considerations. This does not seem to me to be an excuse; those who fund research of this sort ought to be told that they need to spend enough that the research can be done right, and that they should otherwise save their money. Few of us in the business of social research seem prepared to take this hard line, alas.)

PROBLEMS OF MODEL DEVELOPMENT

Having collected data on past sentencing practice, the next step is to analyze those data so as to come up with a model that satisfactorily describes that past practice, which can in turn serve as the basis of sentencing guidelines. This step can involve a number of technical--mostly statistical--problems, some of them of a quite formidable kind. It is not my purpose to deal with these problems, since they are dealt with at length elsewhere in this volume. But it is perhaps worth expatiating a bit at this point on what a model is, in this context, since to do so may help us to see more clearly where most of the research aimed at providing an empirical basis for sentencing guidelines has fallen short of its goal.

By a model in this context is meant a description that shows the ways in which such things as seriousness of offense, vulnerability of the victim, race of the offender, etc., are related to sentences. Such a description, especially if it is the outcome of a statistical analysis, is often presented in the form of an equation (though it is important to note that such equations always can, at least in principle, be translated into words). In an ideal world, as I noted, this kind of model building would be based on some theory or theories about decision making, which would have entailed descriptions about the relationships between independent

variables (such as prior record) and sentence outcomes.
As should by now be apparent, the world of sentencing
guidelines is far from an ideal one. Even so, something
can be done to summarize the data in a parsimonious and
possibly informative way, to show what variables are
associated with variation in sentencing (and thus to show
what things are not), and--more important--to say
something about the relative strength of the association
of each variable, holding constant the effects of the
others in the model. The aim is to find the model that
accounts for the greatest proportion of variation in the
dependent variable (e.g., length of prison sentence) and
that includes no variables whose effect is, on average,
irrelevant or trivial.

   Suppose, for example, that we had some data on
sentencing in the past in some jurisdiction and that
these data included an offense seriousness score of some
kind, which ranged from zero (for spitting in the street)
to 100 (for multiple rape murders).[40] Suppose further
that we analyzed these data and found that the best
prediction we could make of the sentences actually
imposed could be obtained by multiplying the seriousness
score by 5.5, so that

(predicted prison term in case i) = 5.5* (seriousness
score in case i).

(By the "best" prediction I mean the one that was nearest
to being correct, on the average, in a sense to be
discussed further below.) Suppose further that including
other variables in the prediction equation did not
improve its accuracy--perhaps because we had failed to
measure the things that are really important determinants
of sentence length. This is the kind of result one might
obtain by using the statistical technique known as
regression analysis; in general terms, the equation
representing this result is conventionally written

$$y_i = a + bx_i + e \tag{1}$$

where y stands for the dependent variable (in this case,
predicted prison term, say in months; x stands for the
independent variable (in this case, the seriousness
score); a is a constant term that can be thought of as
the prison term given to cases with a seriousness score
of zero; e is an error term that shows, for case i, how
far the prediction "missed" in that case; and, finally, b

is a regression coefficient, which shows how much the seriousness score must be weighted in order to yield our "best on average" prediction of prison terms (in the example, the value of this coefficient is 5.5). Graphically the situation is represented in Figure 5-1.

Without going into technical detail,[41] a few important points may be noted here. For one thing, the relationship between offense seriousness and prison terms depicted here is a straight-line relationship; the score is assumed to have the same effect on prison terms throughout its range (which we have assumed to be between 0 and 100). Second, as might be expected, very few of the cases plotted in Figure 5-1 lie exactly on the straight line that represents the regression equation; in some cases the sentence actually imposed was higher than the equation predicted; in some cases, lower. Thus for cases whose actual terms are above the regression line, the error term e would be positive; for those below the line, e would be negative. Third, the mathematics of regression as a statistical technique are such that they yield the coefficients a and b, which will produce the

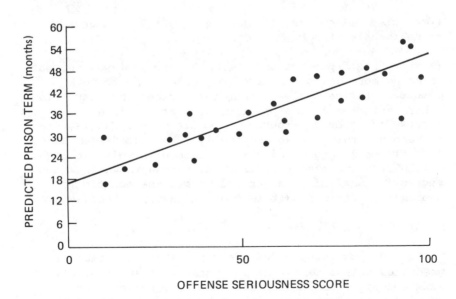

FIGURE 5-1 Illustration of a Hypothetical Relationship Between an Offense Seriousness Score and Jail or Prison Terms Imposed

straight line that is "closest" to the observed data points, in the sense that the line minimizes the sum of the squared deviations (roughly speaking, the e's) that represent the extent to which the "best on average" prediction misses its targets. I return to this last point in a moment.

Of course, in actuality it would be unreasonable to try to predict sentencing outcomes using only one other variable--even one so reasonable as our seriousness score. In all likelihood, the "best" prediction of sentences might make use of the information from, say, three or four variables--including, say, prior criminal record, race of offender, vulnerability of victim, etc. In this case, the equation whose coefficients would be estimated statistically would take the form

$$y = a + b_1x_1 + b_2x_2 + b_3x_3 + b_4x_4 + \ldots b_nx_n + e . \quad (2)$$

(In this equation I have omitted the subscript i for the sake of simplicity.) With a number of independent variables rather than just one, the mathematics get more complicated (and the computing bill increases); in general, however, the principles are the same as in the one-predictor case. One important difference is that, with more than one independent variable, each regression coefficient represents the effect of its associated variable, holding constant the effects of the other variables included in the equation. That is, coefficient b_1, represents the weight to be given to variable x_1, controlling for the effects of variables x_2, x_3, etc.; and the same for the other b's.

Again, for purposes of this paper I neglect a good many technical issues. One, however, must be emphasized. Statistical procedures like multiple regression can tell you what things may safely be left out of an equation (or model),[42] but they cannot by themselves tell you what variables or sets of variables should be put into such an equation, to be tested against the data, in the first place. Of course, a researcher may try all possible combinations of the variables in the data, say, three or four at a time; again, however, it would be utterly unreasonable to do this with, say, the 874 variables in the New Jersey sentencing data.[43] Plainly the researcher must make some choices; here again, it would be helpful to have some kind of theory to guide those choices.

How have those who have done research on sentencing with a view to developing guidelines handled these matters? Their statistical analyses have not always been as clearly or completely described as one might like, but most of them seem to have proceeded in more or less the way outlined below.

Step (1) Carry out univariate analyses of all variables for which data have been obtained, omitting those that turn out to have high proportions of missing data,[44] and also excluding those with highly skewed distributions, which make them unsuitable for further analysis. For example, dichotomous categorical variables that are split more extremely than 70:30 are likely to give unreliable statistical results (J. Davis, 1971). Interval-level variables that are badly skewed—numbers of prior arrests or convictions, for example—may be transformed by taking logarithms or square roots, so as to make their distributions more nearly normal and thus statistically more tractable.[45]

Step (2) Test all bivariate relationships among those candidate independent or explanatory variables that survive Step (1) and between those variables and the dependent or outcome variables (e.g., incarceration or not; length of prison term), again omitting all those that show no association with the outcomes one hopes to predict. One is then left with a subset of the original candidate explanatory variables, each member of which has been shown to be associated by itself, more strongly than one might expect by chance,[46] with some sentencing outcome or outcomes.

Step (3) Attempt to combine the survivors from Step (2) in some kind of multivariate analysis (compare Zimmerman and Blumstein, 1979:10) to find the combinations of variables that best predict the outcome variables in which one is interested. This is, of course, the model building process I discussed earlier, aimed at producing something like equation (2) above.

This three-step process is by no means unusual in nonexperimental social research; but it can lead to highly misleading results, especially if it is not done with some care and sophistication—qualities that are unfortunately missing from many of the analyses of past sentencing done by guidelines researchers. To begin with, the models used by all those researchers, so far as I am aware, have been of the simplest possible kind; they have, in fact, been linear additive ones like that described by equation (2) above. They assume that the

effects of the various independent variables simply add
to one another to produce (in effect) a straight-line
increase in, say, lengths of sentences. Such simplicity
is both pleasing and useful in many contexts. Yet there
is surely no reason to believe that judges' sentencing
practice is really like that; indeed, there are plenty of
reasons to doubt this. For example, such a model has as
a consequence the fact that the weight (the b coefficient, estimated from the data) will be the same for all
cases, so that, for example, each prior conviction is
supposed to have the same average effect on, say, prison
terms. It is at least as plausible to suggest that after
a certain number, prior convictions have successively
less influence on sentences, and that after a certain
point--the upper threshold of badness--they cease to have
any further effect at all.

Moreover, the models used by most sentencing
researchers have assumed that the variables used in them
have independent effects only; each one exerts its own
separate push on sentencing outcomes. It may well be
that there are in fact interactions between some variables, so that, for example, if two are present in a
particular case they have a greater effect than the sum
of what each would have separately. (If, for example, an
offender uses a weapon and inflicts severe injury, this
may lead to a heavier sentence than the separate effect
of either factor would suggest.[47]) There are statistical techniques for detecting this if it happens, but
those techniques seem not to have been used by any
guidelines researchers, in part because their use
requires at least some hunches, if not theory, about the
kinds of interactions that are reasonable to look for.
Moreover, having thrown out a number of variables at
steps (1) and (2) of their model building, they could not
have considered some of their interactions. It could be
the case that a variable has no correlation with the
dependent variable when considered by itself yet will be
seen to have an effect if some other variable's effect is
held constant; again, however, hunches or theory are
required to sort this out.[48]

Finally, the crudely empirical procedures used by many
researchers in this field can lead to apparently nonsensical results, especially if (as has generally been the
case) no statistical validation is carried out to see if
the results obtained may just be the result of chance
variation. An example is found in the research done by
Zalman et al. (1979) in Michigan as a preliminary to

developing that state's guidelines. Zalman and his colleagues assumed that sentences were a function of three kinds of variables: some relating to offenses, some relating to offenders, and another category including such things as race, region of the state, and social status. They left the third category aside for most of their analyses, on the ground that these were not explicitly considered by the judges (a point to which I return below). They carried out regression analyses for each of 10 major categories of offenses, in which sentences were predicted using whatever offense and offender variables had survived Step (2) of their work. Table 5-2, which is based on data from Zalman et al. (1979:95), summarizes the results they obtained in analyzing the in-out decision for their category of sex

TABLE 5-2 Statistically Significant Variables in the In-Out Regression Equation for Sex Crimes in Michigan Sentencing Research

	b	beta	F
Offense variables			
Seriousness (stat. max.)	.0009	.186	49.1
Extent of mental trauma	.1390	.086	12.0
Bodily beatings	-.0720	-.080	9.8
Offender variables			
Number of incarcerations	.093	.198	56.5
Relation to criminal justice system	.093	.189	55.4
"Good moves" since arrest	.204	.218	69.8
Type of work	-.085	-.130	25.7
Reason for leaving school	.108	.108	18.1
Drug use status	.093	.079	9.6
Alcohol use	.045	.084	10.7
Number juvenile violent felonies	-.318	-.087	12.2
Residential stability	.042	.077	8.8
Detainers outstanding	.133	.071	7.7

Adjusted R^2 = .31

SOURCE: Zalman et al. (1979:95).

crimes. The coefficients shown in this table were all statistically highly significant,[49] yet it is clear that some of them are counterintuitive if not downright nonsensical. For example, the coefficient for "bodily beatings" of the victim is negative, meaning that such beatings had the effect of reducing sentences; similarly, the negative coefficient for "number of juvenile violent felonies" suggests that the more such crimes the offender had committed, the shorter the sentence received. There is no reason to believe that either of those things is true. These results could have been due to a statistical fluke (since no separate validation was performed); they may have been due to the effects of measurement error or to correlations between the suspect variables and some other things; Zalman et al. seem, however, to have accepted them as being what the data show.

The Michigan researchers found that their models did not explain very much of the variation in sentences in their data; indeed, when predicting in-out sentences for sex crimes, they were wrong more often than right (see Zalman et al., 1979:97). They then concluded, at several places in their report, that there was a lot of "disparity" or unjustified variation displayed by sentencing in Michigan (see, e.g., pp. 170, 270-72, 277-78). This sweeping conclusion is not justified by their analyses; that the data did not fit their models may merely have shown that their models were wrong. (The counterintuitive coefficients they found certainly suggest this.) Such findings may furnish a handy stick with which to beat the judiciary, if one is intent on developing guidelines; judges are, after all, typically unschooled in multivariate statistics. But Zalman and his colleagues certainly did not demonstrate the existence of excessive or inexplicable variation in sentences in Michigan; more probably, they simply should have rejected their model.

How Many Models?

How many models of the kind we are considering need to be developed, in an analysis of sentencing practice that is aimed at the construction of sentencing guidelines for the future? This is a somewhat complex question.[50] Reculer pour mieux sauter: The object of the exercise is to identify (without benefit of theory, or of clergy either) those factors that appear to have been important determinants of past sentencing practice so that some of those factors can be incorporated into prescriptive instruments that, if followed, will result in sentences in the future that are more or less like those in the past. This does not mean that the description of past practice needs to be very detailed; indeed, as I noted earlier, it is one of the strengths of the Gottfredson-Wilkins concept of guidelines that it makes do with a relatively small number of offense and offender variables, leaving room within the prescribed ranges for judges to make minor adjustments and allowing them to go outside those ranges in appropriate cases. What is important is that the model(s) on which the guidelines rest should be accurate; that is, they should not omit things that were important determinants of past sentences, nor should they include things that were not. Furthermore, the statistical analyses of past sentencing should yield weights that reflect, at least approximately the relative strengths of the "effects" on sentencing outcomes associated with included factors. These weights do not need to be terribly precise, since they will almost certainly be simplified (e.g., rounded to one decimal place) in the guidelines themselves and may be explicitly modified on grounds of social policy.[51] They should not, however, be wrong.

Unfortunately, a good many of the analyses done by guidelines developers to date do seem likely to have yielded results that were wrong in important respects. I have already noted that most of the statistical "models" used by these researchers were of the simplest possible (linear, additive) kind. That apart, it seems to have been thought by many of those working in this field that a single "model" of past sentencing practice will suffice; but there are reasons for thinking that this is probably not the case.

To begin with, sentencing involves at least two different kinds of decisions, both of which guidelines may purport to regulate. On one hand, there is the decision whether to incarcerate; on the other, there is the decision, for those to be incarcerated, as to the length of incarceration.[52] The two decisions are not psychologically distinct;[53] the problem is that they apply to two different sets of offenders, the first--referred to as the "in-out" decision--being asked for all sentenced offenders, the second arising only for that subset of sentenced offenders who are incarcerated. The first decision thus essentially involves a dichotomous

outcome;[54] the second, an outcome in numbers of months
or years.

The optimal statistical machinery for predicting or
describing these two kinds of outcomes is different.
Ordinary least-squares multiple regression can be used
with a dichotomous-outcome variable (such as "in" or
"out"); if this is done, then the dependent variable (y,
in equation (2) above) is interpreted as a probability of
incarceration. Each individual's score on this variable
is 1 if he or she is incarcerated, and 0 if not. The
regression weights (the b's in the equation) then reflect
changes in that probability, for unit changes in each
independent variable (e.g. number of prior convictions).
There are some theoretical objections to this procedure,
which can be overcome by using some alternative statistical techniques, most of which are less well known, more
complicated, and more expensive computationally, than
conventional regression; in practice the use of these
more sophisticated methods does not seem to yield very
different results.[55]

A more important reason for considering these two
sentencing decisions separately is that they may well be
governed by quite different factors. Once a judge has
decided to incarcerate an offender, he or she may well
consider a further set of facts about the case in
deciding how long a sentence should be imposed. Even if
both decisions are to an important extent influenced by
the same factors (e.g., seriousness of offense, however
defined), the weights given to those factors--to be
estimated by regression equations--may be different; this
is especially likely since, as noted earlier, the
length-of-sentence decision should be estimated from data
only on those offenders incarcerated, and not on all of
those sentenced.

This point has been neglected by many guidelines
researchers. Thus, for example, despite having called
attention to the supposedly bifurcated nature of the
sentencing decision, Wilkins et al. (1976) in fact fitted
models to "the sentencing decision . . . treated as an
interval variable" (1976:84, emphasis added). All prison
sentences in their sample were given scores equal to the
number of months of incarceration involved, whereas
nonincarceration sentences were given a value of zero;
the same thing, it appears, was done by the Massachusetts
researchers.[56] Of course it may be that in some
jurisdictions, the same factors--with the same weights--
apply to both the decision to incarcerate and the "how

long?" decision. But this, if true, can only be discovered by analyzing the two decisions separately in the
first place.

Similarly, the variables that predict sentences in
cases disposed of by pleas of guilty may be different
from--or have different weights than--those that predict
sentences in cases that go to trial. This seems to have
been the case in Massachusetts, where guidelines to be
used on tried cases were in fact based on analyses of all
cases, including the much more numerous cases disposed of
by guilty pleas.[57]

Another aspect of the "how many models?" question
concerns the choice between developing a single guidelines instrument (like the matrix reproduced as Table 5-1
above) and developing separate offense-specific prescriptions for separate categories of offenses. The former
strategy is exemplified by the Massachusetts, Pennsylvania, and Minnesota guidelines; the latter strategy was
employed in New Jersey (McCarthy, 1978) and is currently
being tested in Michigan (Zalman et al., 1980). The
latter approach has a number of advantages. For one
thing, on the assumption that the severity of the
prescribed sentence will be some function of the seriousness of the current offense, this seriousness in turn
will be a function of things that are not, or are not
necessarily, the same across all categories of offenses.
To take an obvious example, the relative seriousness of
offenses against the person, such as assault, rape or
robbery, may be a function of the degree of physical
injury intended or inflicted, and the physical vulnerability of the victim(s); these would not be relevant to
most offenses classified and dealt with by the courts as
burglary, theft, or fraud. In the latter offenses,
however, the value of property stolen or damaged might
well be a factor taken into account by the courts,
although this would not normally be relevant to crimes
against the person.

In the Michigan guidelines, for example, matrices are
presented for 11 different categories of offenses (each
of which is in turn the result of a grouping of several
similar offenses as defined by statutes). For each
category of offenses, the matrix is defined by a number
of rows headed "offense severity," which are in turn
defined by the presence or absence of factors relevant to
that category of offenses; the columns are defined by
categories of "prior record." But the "severity" (row)
variables are based on somewhat different factors,

depending on the category of offense concerned. In the case of sex crimes, for instance, the "offense severity" variable depends on (1) the presence, type, and use of a weapon; (2) physical attack and/or injury; (3) whether the victim was carried away or held captive; (4) the total number of victims; (5) the vulnerability of the victim; (6) the total number of offenders; and (7) the degree of injury to the victim. These factors are given scores, which are said to be based on the results of the earlier analysis by Zalman et al. (1979) of felony sentencing in Michigan--although, as we shall see, there is in fact little correspondance.

In the Michigan guidelines, the prior record variable (which defines the columns of the various matrices) is calculated in the same way across all offense groups. This is obviously a defensible approach to the question, as it can be argued that the number of an offender's prior arrests or convictions is likely to have the same weight in determining the sentence, regardless of the type of the latest offense. However, it might well be that in some cases courts looked not only at the numbers of prior arrests or convictions, but also at the types of those offenses--and regarded repeated convictions for offenses of the same kind (e.g., violence against the person) as more serious than they would an equally lengthy "mixed" record. If so, this should be detected by an offense-specific approach to modeling like that done in Michigan. In the New Jersey guidelines, the "offender" variables included vary for different categories of offenses; even when variables are called the same thing in two or more different cases, the definitions of the factors concerned often differ. Here, however, it seems likely that these variations--which purport to be purely descriptive of previous sentencing practice in New Jersey--would not stand up to closer statistical scrutiny (in particular, validation in the statistical sense explained earlier). An analysis that Bridget Stecher and I carried out some time ago showed that the different offender variables used for different offense categories in the New Jersey guidelines did not distinguish patterns of incarceration different from what would have been obtained if the same offender variables had been used in all cases (see Sparks and Stecher, 1979).

The offense-specific approach to developing guidelines permits finer discriminations than may be possible with analyses in which all types of offenses are lumped together. Guidelines based on statistical analyses done

separately for rape, robbery, burglary, etc. may thus
better reflect the prior sentencing practice they are
supposed to perpetuate. They have the obvious practical
disadvantage that many more cases will be needed for
statistical analysis; even with their relatively large
sample (about 6,000 cases), Zalman et al. (1979) seem
occasionally to have felt the pinch of small numbers,
which would have been more painful had they carried out
the statistical validation that they should have done.

A further advantage of the offense-specific approach
is that it makes it unnecessary to develop a measure of
offense seriousness that cuts across different categories
of crime, e.g. burglary and robbery. If all previously
sentenced cases are analyzed together in the model-
building exercise, then some measure of seriousness will
be needed to discriminate between, e.g., rape and
overtime parking--especially since this concept is so
widely used, by judges, parole boards, and the public, to
justify the severity of sentences. In this case, how
might such a measure be devised? There are several
possibilities, exemplified by the guidelines so far
developed:

(1) A score supposed to reflect offense seriousness
may be devised by the researcher. This will probably
reflect an ordering of a commonsense kind of different
categories of crimes, possibly influenced somewhat by
statutory maximum penalties. This appears to be what was
done in Massachusetts, for example, by Wilkins et al.
(1976), and by the Michigan researchers.[58]

(2) Some more empirically derived measure of perceived
seriousness of various offenses may be used, for example,
like those derived from survey data by Sellin and
Wolfgang (1964), Rossi et al. (1974), or Sparks et al.
(1977). However, apart from doubts as to the extent to
which such perceptual rating reflect real differences in
offense seriousness or sanction severity, and further
doubts as to whether they really provide interval-level
measures (as some have claimed) rather than mere rank
orderings, it is far from clear that there is much
consensus in the population--even in a particular
jurisdiction or at a certain time and place--as far as
such assessments are concerned. If there is not, whose
views should prevail?[59]

(3) The most purely descriptive method of estimating
relative seriousness is to create what are called dummy
variables for the various offense types, which in effect

make it possible to distinguish rape, robbery, etc. from
all other offense types, to see how much those categories
affect such outcomes as lengths of prison terms. Thus
the dummy variable for robbery will have one weight
associated with it; that for rape, another, and so on.
This procedure, though it has more complications than
this description suggests, can work pretty well; it has
not, however, been used (so far as I know) by any
guidelines researchers.

The analysis of prior record poses similar though much
less difficult problems, in part because most variables
of this kind (e.g., number of prior arrests or felony
convictions) come naturally in the form of an interval-
level variable. But there may be problems of deciding
what to count--do we treat prior arrests, prior convictions, or prior incarcerations as the "best" measure of
prior criminality? The answer to this is almost certainly not to throw all three of these things into the
same regression equation. Rather, it is better to find
the variable or combination of variables that provides
the most robust and strongest explanatory power; whether
this variable or combination of variables is later
included in the guidelines is another matter.

What Variables Should be Included?

Another question to be asked at the model-building stage
concerns the candidate explanatory variables that should
be allowed to enter into analyses of past sentencing
practice, if the construction of decision-making guidelines is the ultimate object of the exercise. Should
one--following the example of Zimmerman and Blumstein
(1979) and other researchers--exclude variables such as
sex and race from all modeling efforts, on the ground
that such variables are (to put it mildly) unlikely to be
regarded as acceptable for inclusion in the guidelines
that are meant to be the final product of the analysis?
It seems to me that the answer to this question is no,
for several reasons.

To begin with, if the analysis of past sentencing
behavior is to have any point at all in this context, it
must surely reflect some degree of fidelity to the data
on antecedent sentencing practices; otherwise, why do
it? To see this clearly, let us consider a situation in
which an unacceptable variable (from a guidelines

constructor's point of view) has in fact been influential in sentencing decisions in the past: Race is probably a good example. Suppose that in jurisdiction X data on past sentencing practice are collected and analyzed, and it is found that blacks or other racial minorities were given markedly heavier sentences than whites--controlling for everything else that might be relevant. Surely this is something that morally sensitive guidelines developers ought to be eager to show, in order to promote the case for their brand of sentencing reform? The concept of sentencing guidelines has not infrequently been attacked, on the ground that it will lead to the institutionalization of injustices (like racism) that have characterized sentencing practice in the past. This criticism loses its force if the distinction between description of (past) sentencing practice and prescription of (future) sentencing practice is recognized and clearly maintained.

Moreover, the exclusion of a generally influential variable--even a morally iniquitous one like race--from a multivariate analysis of past sentencing practice may lead to incorrect estimates of the effects of other variables included in the model; any guidelines constructed on the basis of such a model will thus do precisely what is not intended: they will institutionalize the effects of race. Thus, to take a simple example, suppose that we fit a linear additive model to the data and find that expected terms of incarceration $y*$ are given by

$$y* = 5 * (Offense\ Score) + 2 * (Prior\ Arrests)$$
$$- 3 * (Race,\ 1 = white) . \qquad (3)$$

This says approximately that, on the average, given comparable offenses and prior records, white offenders receive lighter sentences. Evening up this injustice when constructing guidelines would involve setting the regression coefficient for race to zero, so that whites and nonwhites would get the same expected terms, given their offense scores and prior records. Suppose, however, that race were associated with both offense score and prior record, e.g., that blacks tended to commit less serious crimes but to have more prior convictions than whites. If this is the case, then an equation that does not include race as an independent variable will yield different coefficients for offense score and prior record, from those obtained from an equation in which race is included. This difference is

precisely that due to the effect of race on prior
sentencing practice. (In the situation just hypothesized, a model that excluded race would underestimate the
effect of offense score and overestimate the effect of
prior record, which should obtain if race were ignored.
Translation of those effects into guidelines would thus
build in an effect of race.)

The main objective of this modeling stage, then,
should be to try to obtain estimates of the relative
effects of the various variables which, in the past, have
had an appreciable effect on sentencing decisions. Some
of these may be included in the guidelines that will
later be developed; some (e.g., race) will not, but care
must be taken to exclude the indirect effects of these
when it comes time to make up the guidelines themselves.
Overall, the statistical models developed at this stage
may not account for an overwhelming amount of the total
variation in previous sentences, even if the statistical
work has been better done than that of many guidelines
researchers. This may indeed be because there was not
much consistency in previous sentencing practice; but it
may also in part be because the models themselves, which
deliberately incorporate only a few of the most important
determinants of previous practice, can yield only a
broad-brush picture of the ways in which sentencing was
done in the past.

Given the fact that sentencing guidelines (of the
Gottfredson-Wilkins type) themselves will have a relatively simple structure, containing enough flexibility to
permit judges to make finer discriminations on their own,
this should not matter. There is, however, a final and
important point, which (so far as I can determine) has
received no attention in research aimed at developing
guidelines but needs careful attention at the model
building stage. This concerns the ways in which
empirically derived models of past practice have failed
to describe it. Suppose, for example, that statistical
models have been fitted to length-of-term decisions in
some jurisdiction, and the best-fitting model is able to
account for 60 percent of the variance in lengths of
terms. That means that 40 percent is still unaccounted
for; where is it? To answer this question, it is useful
to look at the "residuals" (observed sentence minus that
predicted by the model), which is often best done by
plotting these against the predicted values themselves
(compare Mosteller and Tukey, 1977:Ch.16). How does the
model miss?

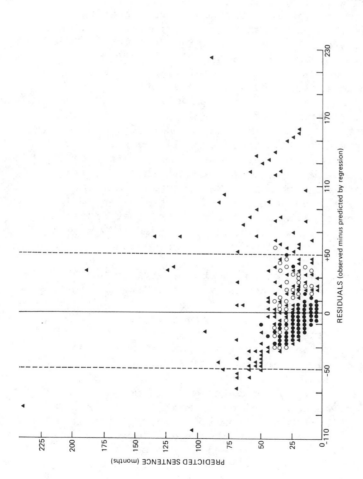

FIGURE 5-2 Plot of Residuals (i.e., Observed Sentence in
Massachusetts Guideline Construction Data Minus Sentence "Predicted"
by Guidelines Formula)

SOURCE: Sparks et al. (1982:369).

In our reanalysis of the Massachusetts guidelines construction data, Bridget Stecher and I carried out a number of analysis of this kind; the results of one such analysis are illustrated in Figure 5-2. This scatterplot shows, first, that the sentences "predicted" by the Massachusetts guidelines were not all that close to the sentences actually imposed, even in the construction data; most of these residuals are not that near to the zero line. Also apparent from Figure 5-2 is the fact that in a small number of cases--about 40 of over 1,400--the length of term actually imposed was wildly different from that "predicted" by the guidelines model. In other words, there were evidently a few cases in which the sentences actually imposed were very different from what one would predict from the "best" account that could be given of sentencing practice over the sample as a whole. Such extremely deviant cases obviously make an inordinate contribution to unexplained variance.

It is very important to ask: What are these cases like? Why do they differ so markedly from the mine-run of cases dealt with? Our approach to answering this question consisted of listing all the salient factors we could think of for each of the cases in question, and eyeballing the data to see if any plausible reasons appeared for such gross departures from the norms applicable to the rest of the sample. In a few cases, we found factors that seemed to supply such reasons; for example, one of the extreme outliers had had no fewer than 19 previous prison sentences. But such satisfying reasons could not be found, at least in the data available to us, for all of the cases in question.

The general point here, I believe, is that in estimating a model that will satisfactorily describe and/or explain past sentencing practice, it is important to exclude any egregious cases in which the imposed sentence is grossly different from what would be expected, given the general pattern of antecedent sentencing. It seems to me that this is so, whether or not a plausible explanation for those deviant cases can be found in the available data. It would no doubt be comforting to find such a plausible explanation; but in the nature of things, such factors as "judge temporarily insane," "judge had indigestion," "prosecutor new to the job," etc. are unlikely to be recorded in the data available for analysis. Despite this, it seems reasonable to regard such gross departures--if any are found--as abnormal in some respect, and therefore to exclude them from an attempt to model the majority of normal cases. A failure to exclude such grossly deviant cases may well result in misleading estimates of the general effect of explanatory variables (such as seriousness of offense and prior record) on the bulk of cases.[60]

It should be noted that no analysis of residuals--or, analogously, of mistaken classifications along the "in-out" dimension--has been presented by any of those who have so far carried out empirical research on sentencing with a view to developing guidelines.[61]

FROM MODELS TO GUIDELINES

After an analytical model has been found that reasonably characterizes past sentencing practice, the next step (according to the original Gottfredson-Wilkins concept of guidelines) is the construction of a prescriptive instrument that can be used to guide sentencing in the future. The various guidelines developed to date illustrate a number of ways in which this has been done; in all of these, however, the results of the empirical analyses have been heavily overlaid with policy considerations. Thus, for example, in the Denver demonstration model (Wilkins et al., 1976:41) six independent variables--number of offenses of which the offender was convicted, number of prior incarcerations, seriousness of the offense (as defined by research staff), weapon usage, legal status of the offender at time of conviction, and employment history--were found to be significantly associated with the sentencing decision. The guidelines themselves contained a matrix or grid for each of eight groups of felonies and misdemeanors; within each group, offenses were further classified by estimated seriousness, based on rankings by research staff; to this seriousness rating was added a "harm/loss modifier" ranging in value from zero for a victimless crime to five for death, though injury to victim was not significantly associated with sentence in the regression analysis. The offender score that defined the columns of the matrix was based on prior adult incarcerations, parole or probation revocations, legal status at time of offense, prior convictions, and employment history. The second and fourth of these were not significantly related to sentence in the regression analysis, and the weights assigned to each seem to have been purely judgmental.[62]

The Michigan felony sentencing project (Zalman et al., 1979) produced "empirical sentencing matrices" that tolerably well reflected the regression analyses that had previously been carried out (ignoring, for the moment, the methodological defects of those analyses discussed earlier). These empirical matrices were then used to construct guidelines. In this case, however, the guidelines differ in so many respects--size and shape of the matrices, variables included, weights assigned to them--that the empirical basis is hard to find; so hard, in fact, that a judge or legislator who had been sold such guidelines in part on the strength of their empirical basis might well feel that he or she had bought a pig in a poke instead. For example: an offender convicted of violent rape, who had two prior convictions of which one was also a sex crime, would (on certain not unreasonable assumptions) have fallen into a cell in the appropriate empirical matrix with a median of 53 months and a range of 6 to 180 months; the same offender would have fallen into a cell in the guidelines that had a median prescribed term of about 108 months, with a "normal" range of 96 to 120 months. [63]

Other states' guidelines, though yielding less bizarre results, also show substantial departures from the results of empirical analyses, on what are avowedly grounds of policy. Thus, for example, the Minnesota sentencing guidelines were developed after analyses that showed seriousness of current offense (as ranked by the commission) and prior record to be the most important determinants of sentence severity; employment status-- which was "marginally associated" with the decision to incarcerate in the construction data--was deliberately excluded from the offender score used in the guidelines. As noted earlier, the Massachusetts guidelines do not take a matrix form, but consist rather of a fairly straightforward transformation of (unstandardized) regression coefficients into weights that permit calculation of an "expected" sentence. Table 5-3 shows that the weights finally adopted in the guidelines are, with the exception of the one for weapon use, fairly close to the coefficients obtained by regressing sentences in months on those variables, counting (incorrectly) all "out" cases as zero. However, the variables included in the guidelines themselves and the scoring of the "offense seriousness" variable were not purely empirically derived; instead, they were based on policy decisions by the project's judicial steering committee.

TABLE 5-3 Unstandardized Regression Coefficients From
Analysis of Massachusetts Guideline Construction Data and
Weights Given to the Same Factors in the April 1980
Version of the Massachusetts Guidelines

Factor	Unstandardized b Coefficient	Weight in Massachusetts Guidelines (April 1980)
Current offense seriousness	1.26	2.1
Use of dangerous weapon	2.13*	9.0
Degree of injury to victim	9.54	9.0
Seriousness of prior record	1.34	1.6
(Intercept)	-1.18	--

* p = .118; all other coefficients significant below .05.

I am certainly not suggesting that it is in some sense
wrong for considerations of social policy, morality, or
whatever to enter into the formulation of guidelines--
even if empirical models of past practice are the primary
determinants of the sentences the guidelines prescribe
(which is, of course, itself a policy decision). Even
supposing that the modeling of past practice has been
carefully and correctly done, there is bound to be a fair
amount of "smoothing" of the results of that modeling
exercise involved in the translation of those results
into workable guidelines. In particular, with guidelines
presented in matrix form (Table 5-1 above), the rows and
columns will typically have to be defined by grouped
offense and offender scores, so that even quite substantial alterations in scoring may have little effect on the
classification of cases within the matrix. Technical
matters of this kind need not involve explicit alteration
of the results of the empirical analyses--like that
involved in, say, eliminating the effects of racial
discrimination or excessive regional variation that may
have characterized sentencing in the past.

There are, however, two very fundamental respects in
which guidelines--even if they purport to be empirically
based in a very strict sense--are necessarily shaped by
judgmental or policy considerations. These concern the

in-out decision and the width of the prescribed normal
range of jail or prison sentences.

The Decision to Incarcerate

In most if not all of the analyses reported to date, the
probability of incarceration increases directly, and in a
fairly orderly fashion, with seriousness of the current
offense and prior record (see, for example, Zalman et
al., 1979; Wilkins et al., 1976; Parent, 1979 [personal
communication]; Zimmerman and Blumstein, 1979). But a
probability of imprisonment is of very little use, when
guidelines are concerned. Suppose that a statistical
analysis of past sentencing practice showed that 70
percent of all cases falling within a given cell in a
guidelines matrix had in the past been given "out"
sentences such as probation or a fine. How can judges be
instructed to comply with this finding in sentencing in
the future? They cannot send 30 percent of the offender
to prison--at least unless more elegant forms of "split
sentence" can be invented than now exist in most jurisdictions. Nor can they easily comply with a prescription
to the effect that only 30 percent of the group of
offenders falling into that cell in future should be
incarcerated. It may be that some further criteria
(beyond those used to construct the matrix) can be found
that will distinguish the 70 percent of "out" cases in
the cell from the 30 percent going "in." This is by no
means guaranteed, since the 70-30 split may reflect,
e.g., random variation among judges. The only purely
statistical way of complying with the empirical findings
would be to toss a biased coin--designed to come up heads
7 times out of 10, on average--when dealing with cases in
that cell; such a procedure is unlikely to commend itself
to anyone. The only alternative, however, is to declare
that cases falling into this cell shall presumptively be
treated as "out" cases.

It is possible to do this, and still provide a range
of months or years to be served if the presumption is
overridden; both Minnesota's and Pennsylvania's guidelines, for example, do this. The need to rely on a
presumptive "in" or "out" decision, however, does away
with the flexibility inherent in the concept of a normal
range, which was said earlier to be a distinctive feature
of the Gottfredson-Wilkins concept of guidelines (and
which of course remains intact in the case of parole

decision making, in which the concept was originally developed). Moreover, the choice of which cells of the matrix to treat as "in" and which to treat as "out" is obviously a matter of judgment, not something capable of being settled empirically. (In Zimmerman and Blumstein's (1979) reanalysis of the Denver data, cells containing 51 percent of cases incarcerated were arbitrarily classified as "in" cells in order to test the predictive accuracy of their model; it is unlikely that this cutting point would be accepted in practice.) Finally, even if an analysis of antecedent practice revealed a fairly sharp split between "in" and "out" cases (70-30, say, or even 65-35) it may be difficult to declare that cases receiving the less common outcome after implementation of the guide- lines are departures from the guidelines--unless the grounds for departure are quite strictly specified (as they are, for example, in Minnesota and Pennsylvania).

It may be thought that the presumptive character of the "in-out" decision can be avoided by designating "out" sentences as being of zero months and including them in prescribed guidelines ranges; as Table 5-4(a) shows, this is done in the current Michigan guidelines. Similarly, under the Massachusetts guidelines it is possible to have an expected sentence of zero; it (i.e., nonincarceration) is the lower range limit for cases with a guideline score or expected sentence of between one and five months. But the difficulty with this approach is that it gives virtually no guidance on a crucial question, Should this offender be incarcerated or not? A guidelines matrix containing a range of 0-18 constrains only the upper end of that range; an "out" sentence is by definition not a departure from the prescribed range, but neither is any sentence of incarceration of 18 months or less. Even the New Jersey guidelines, which show the proportions of offenders (in the construction data) who were not incarcerated, do a better job of structuring discretion than this.

In summary, the problem is that empirical analysis of past sentencing can yield only probabilities of imprisonment, conditional on various offense and offender attributes; it is difficult to turn these probabilities into effective prescriptions for future sentencing, since it is not easy to follow a rule that says something like "Do such-and-such 35 percent of the time." It may well be, as Zimmerman and Blumstein (1979) have suggested, that one can identify three groups of cases: a group with very high rates of incarceration (presumptively "in"

TABLE 5-4 Michigan Sentencing Guidelines for Burglary and Residuals from an Additive Model

Offense severity	Prior record					
	A	B	C	D	E	F
	0	1-2	3-4	5-6	7-8	9+

(a) Michigan sentencing guidelines for burglary offenses with statutory maximum terms of 180 months; figures in table indicate minimum sentences, in months[a]

	A	B	C	D	E	F
Low (0-3)	0-12	0-18	0-18	6-24	12-30	18- 36
Medium (4-6)	0-18	0-18	6-24	12-30	24-42	36- 48
High	12-30	24-48	36-60	48-60	48-60	60-120

(b) Midpoints of ranges in (a)

	A	B	C	D	E	F
Low	6	9	9	15	20	26
Medium	9	9	15	20	32	42
High	20	36	48	54	54	90

(c) Residuals (in months) from fitting additive model to data in (b), and row and column effects in months

	A	B	C	D	E	F	Row Effects	
Low	2.5	5.5	0	0	0	-10.5	12	-5.5
Medium	0	0	0.5	-0.5	6.5	0	17.5	0
High	-20.0	-4.0	2.5	2.5	-2.5	17.0	48.5	31.0
Column effects	-8.5	-8.5	-3.0	3.0	8.0	24.5	--	17.5

[a]Zalman et al. (1980).

in the guidelines); a group with very low rates (presumptively to be "out"); and a middle group with rates of incarceration around 40-60 percent (in which no presumption would be made). The difficulty remains, however, that designating some cases as presumptively "in" or "out" is likely to lead to changes in sentencing practice. Consider a cell in which 80 percent of preguidelines cases were imprisoned. If this cell is designated presumptively as "in," the proportion of cases imprisoned in this cell after the guidelines are implemented seems likely to rise, unless it should happen that judges will

find grounds to rebut the presumption in just 20 percent
of the cases; it is not easy to see how they can be given
guidance of a kind that is likely to bring this about.

Widths of Prescribed "Normal" Ranges

There also seems no way to answer the question "How wide
should 'normal' ranges be?" merely by an analysis of past
sentencing practice. Guidelines developed to date
display wide variations in this respect. Those in
Minnesota and Pennsylvania, at one extreme, average plus
or minus 5 percent or so around midranges; in Massachusetts, by contrast, the range of permitted variation is
plus or minus 50 percent around the calculated guidelines
sentences. Simple inspection of the frequency distributions of lengths of terms in particular cells may show
that these cluster within a reasonably narrow range in
most cells; and an examination of cases falling outside
that range may show that they have features that would
justify their being treated as "departures." But it may
also turn out that this is not the case; if it is not,
then decisions as to the widths of "normal" cell ranges
will necessarily be made purely on grounds of policy,
unless they are completely arbitrary.

In summary, most of the supposedly empirically based
guidelines that have been developed to date appear to
have modified the results of their empirical analyses, to
a greater or lesser degree, in terms of the choice of
modeled variables to be included in the guidelines, and
the weights used to calculate offense seriousness ratings
and prior record scores. It is impossible to say just
how different the resulting guidelines are from those
that would have emerged from a stricter transformation of
empirical models. While seriousness of current offense
and length of prior record are the major dimensions of
most guidelines developed to date, the definitions of
these factors, and the scoring methods used to classify
cases into guidelines matrix cells, seem in most cases to
have been suggested rather than dictated by the analyses
of antecedent sentencing practice earlier carried out.
Of course, this is not necessarily a bad thing; careful
empirical research on past sentencing can provide
valuable guidance to policy makers in a variety of ways,
even if the resulting guidelines are shaped by explicit
considerations of policy--as was the case, for example,

with the in-out lines in the Minnesota and Pennsylvania
guidelines, which were largely determined by a notion of
just deserts and a desire to limit incapacitation. But
this kind of guidance suggests a very different role for
research from that described by some of those who have
advocated empirically based guidelines (e.g., Gelman et
al., 1977); it also suggests a need for different kinds
of research from what has been done for most guidelines
that have so far been developed.

ASSESSING THE STRUCTURE AND IMPACT OF GUIDELINES

Evaluating the impact of sentencing guidelines may mean
many things. Perhaps the most obvious of these concerns
the question: "Do guidelines make any difference?" That
is, if sentencing or parole guidelines have been introduced in a particular jurisdiction, do patterns of
decision making in that jurisdiction subsequently change
in ways desired by those who implemented the guidelines?
What other consequences do guidelines have, e.g., on case
flow, prosecutorial decision making, police practices, or
other phases of the criminal justice system? These are
questions of the "wait and see" variety; they entail
before-and-after comparisons, of a kind with which this
paper is not concerned. There are other evaluative
questions, however, which are not of this kind: questions that make no assumptions, or only the simplest
assumptions, about the changes in behavior that may not
take place after the guidelines are introduced; for
example, they may rest on the assumption that the
guidelines are strictly and rigorously complied with.
Even if this assumption is made, there is still plenty of
room for a question of the form, "So what?"

In other words, suppose we neglect, for the moment,
the variety of techniques discussed earlier in this
paper, for constructing guidelines; suppose, moreover,
that we assume that the guidelines--whatever form they
may happen to take--are rigidly complied with, after
their introduction. What can we say now--before the
guidelines take effect--as to their likely consequences,
under those assumptions? There are in fact several
things which may be said relevant to the guidelines as
constructed, rather than to the guidelines as they may
(or may not) be consistently applied in practice. This
section discusses some of these issues and some analytical methods that can be used to deal with them.

To begin with, how may one assess the structure of a
set of sentencing guidelines? Typically, guidelines have
taken the form of a matrix with rows and columns, defined
by offense and offender scores of some kind, and cells
containing "normal" ranges in which incarceration is
prescribed. Do these ranges "step up" in a reasonably
orderly fashion? Are the effects of offense and offender
score reasonably consistent across the matrix--or are
there some cells that--for whatever reason--contain
ranges that are markedly different from what one would
expect? Does the offender score, which is usually
largely a function of prior record, have the same effect
on prescribed sentences for the less serious offenses as
it does for the more serious ones--or is it (for example)
having more of an effect when the offense is less
serious? It may be that those involved in constructing
guidelines will decide, upon reflection, that what seemed
like anomalies were in fact justifiable. For instance,
it may be that there are some offense-offender combinations for which a very much heavier (or lighter) sentence
than would be suggested by the general pattern of the
matrix is reasonable. But they will not be able to reach
this conclusion, unless the apparent anomaly is pointed
out to them. And it may not be obvious from simple
inspection of the matrix itself.

A set of techniques recently developed by Tukey (1977)
and his colleagues can be used to address some of these
questions. Suppose we represent the ranges stipulated in
guideline matrices by their midpoints, on the assumption
(which is explicit in the Minnesota guidelines, and not
unreasonable in others) that, all other things being
equal, cases falling into a particular cell should
normally expect to be given a term in the middle of the
stipulated range. On this assumption, each cell in the
matrix is represented by a single number (the midrange);
and we can seek the relations between these midranges, as
we move across and up or down the grid. Briefly, Tukey's
method involves computing "effects" associated with each
row and column of the matrix, and subtracting these from
the cell midranges themselves to leave "residuals," which
are the (positive or negative) amounts in each cell
midrange that cannot be accounted for by the row and
column effects. Table 5-4, which is based on the matrix
in the Michigan guidelines for burglary offenses with a
120-month statutory maximum, illustrates this procedure.
Table 5-4(a) gives the guidelines ranges themselves;
Table 5-4(b), the midranges. In Table 5-4(c), the row

and column effects are displayed outside the grid; the cells of the grid themselves contain the residuals that are left after these two effects--which, in this case, relate to offense seriousness and prior record--are removed.

In essence, the model fitted here is an additive one, in which the midrange for any particular cell can be represented by a row (offense) effect, plus a column (prior record) effect, plus or minus a residual that cannot be accounted for by the simple sum of those effects.[64] If this model fits the data given by the midranges of the matrix, then the residuals ought to be more or less zero; and as Table 5-4(c) shows, this is by and large the case. Thus we might say that the Michigan guidelines for this group of burglaries prescribe midrange terms of about 17.5 months, plus or minus an effect depending on the seriousness of the particular offense, plus or minus an effect reflecting the offender's prior record, with generally small residuals. For example, for the least serious offenses of this kind, and for offenders with prior records in the "C" category, the middle of the prescribed range is 12 months, minus three months; equivalently, it can be thought of as 17.5 months (the middle term across the whole of the matrix), minus 5.5 months for being in the least serious offense category, minus another three months for being in the "C" prior-record category--in each case, there is no residual, so that the overall effects reproduce the cell midrange perfectly.

Analyses of this kind are useful in several ways. For one thing, simple additive models may not adequately reproduce the structure of the cell midranges; instead, the offense and offender effects may be related multiplicatively rather than additively.[65] For another, it may be that in some cells the residuals--that is, the difference between guidelines midranges and what would be expected given the general structure of the table--may be large rather than negligible or small. Inspection of Table 5-4(c) shows that this is the case for the cell for high offense severity and "A" prior record, for which the observed midrange is 20 months less than an overall additive structure for the matrix predicts; similarly, in the cell for high offense severity and "F" prior record, the observed midrange is some 17 months greater than the overall additive model predicts. An analysis like that of Table 5-4(c) readily displays such anomalies, and enables us to ask why they occur and if they are defensible.[66] Parallel analyses can be carried out for other aspects of a guidelines matrix structure, e.g., the ratios of cell ranges to midranges, when these are or purport to be derived empirically rather than being laid down by fiat (as in Minnesota).[67]

The impact of a set of sentencing guidelines on the overall pattern of dispositions in a jurisdiction--even assuming that the guidelines are strictly adhered to--will in part be a function of the structure of the guidelines, e.g., the ranges and midranges prescribed by various cells; in part, however, it will be determined by the numbers of cases falling into the various cells. Thus, for example, Table 5-4(c) suggests that for the Michigan burglary guidelines, the lower righthand cell (high offense severity, prior record category "F") prescribes terms that on average are almost a year and a half heavier than the overall structure of the matrix would suggest. As I have noted elsewhere (Sparks, 1981) this tendency to produce guidelines structures that promise to thump the worst cases appears in several different jurisdictions; it may be explained by the fact that cases falling in those cells really are much more serious (or at least that they were in construction data); it may, however, reflect nothing more than a guidelines developer's wish to appear suitably ferocious in dealing with arch-criminals. Either way, the fact that that cell prescribes heavier-than-average terms will make no difference, if no cases of that kind are ever dealt with after the guidelines are implemented.

The importance of this can be seen by considering the distribution of cases (in the construction data) in the cells of the Minnesota matrix (Minnesota Sentencing Guidelines Commission, 1979). No less than 60 percent of those cases fell into the lowest criminal history category; only 8 percent of those offenders were imprisoned. Similarly, 78 percent of the cases (sentenced in 1978) had been convicted of crimes falling into seriousness levels 1 through 4--that is, the least serious crimes covered by the matrix. In fact, the 4-by-2 submatrix in the upper lefthand corner of the Minnesota matrix contained almost two-thirds of the felons sentenced in Minnesota in 1978. For these cells, and several of their neighbors, the matrix prescribes a presumptive "out" sentence. Elsewhere in the matrix, heavy presumptive terms are prescribed; for example, those convicted of second-degree murder with a criminal history score of six (the worst possible) are presumptively to be sentenced to 27 years in prison. But such cases are very rare; and that cell will thus have only a slight impact on the overall pattern of sentencing in Minnesota under the guidelines. This fact was well appreciated by the Minnesota commission, whose legislative mandate directed it to have regard to institutional overcrowding in devising the guidelines. A computer program for projecting not only the size but also the composition of the Minnesota prison population was developed by the commission's research staff and was used to illustrate the consequences of different policy choices concerning the "in-out" line and lengths of presumptive prison terms (see Minnesota Sentencing Guidelines Commission, 1980); it was thus possible for the commission to choose from the several options available to it and to design guidelines that were consistent with the aim of keeping the prison population at an appropriate level.[68]

CONCLUSIONS

It has not been the intention of this paper to criticize the research that has been done to date by those who have been involved in constructing guidelines; there is little profit, and even less fun, in doing that. It seems more important to ask what the future role of empirical research might be, not only in constructing guidelines but also in sentencing reform generally.

It should be remembered that, as originally conceived of by Gottfredson and Wilkins, the notion of decision-making guidelines was a very simple one: all that they wanted to do was to "make explicit" a policy that the U.S. Parole Board had in fact (despite its denials) been following: The "policy" consisted of according relatively great weight to offense seriousness and prior record in parole decisions. It does not take very elaborate research to show that. The question is, is it worth doing more elaborate modeling of sentencing behavior if the object is merely to develop guidelines and (perhaps) to focus public and judicial attention on questions of policy and principle that may not emerge from data analysis but may be deliberately adopted because they are believed to be just, efficacious, or both?

The answer to this question is not clear to me, but the question does seem to have consequences. If it is agreed that such modeling should be done, then clearly the best available research methods and analytical techniques should be employed. This would mean (for example) the prospective collection of data rather than reliance on case records; the use of estimation procedures other than ordinary least squares when modeling dichotomous outcomes; and the careful development of some theory about judicial decision making as a preliminary to these and other things.

If it is decided that highly rigorous modeling is not necessary, then this does not mean that empirical research has no role at all in assisting sentencing reform. I suspect, however, that different tasks and different techniques will be relevant. For example, more attention may be paid to the residuals from models than to estimation of the parameters of those models; there may be more concern with exploratory data analysis than with statistical inference; and an interest taken in research on the impact of guidelines on the rest of the system--illustrated, for example, by the Minnesota research on projecting institutional populations.

The political role of the research that has been done to date, and the importance of providing a seemingly empirical basis for sentencing guidelines, should not be overlooked. It may well be that, without an analysis of past practice as a starting point, the use of guidelines as a technique for structuring discretion would not have achieved even its present measure of judicial and public acceptance. Whether that justifies the research that was done--as distinct from that which could have been done-- is not an easy question to answer.

NOTES

1. For convenience, I refer for the most part to sentencing guidelines throughout this paper. But as will be seen, guidelines very similar in concept may be and indeed are used for many other decision points in the criminal justice system, e.g. bail and institutional classification; for a detailed discussion, see Gottfredson and Gottfredson (1980).

2. An overview of the history of concern about the control of discretion and "disparity" (often defined in rather different ways) is contained in Chapter 2 of the Final Report of the Evaluation of Statewide Sentencing

Guidelines Project (henceforth cited as Sparks et al., 1982).

3. Portions of this section are adapted from Sparks (1983).

4. The structure of the California law is in fact somewhat more complicated than this brief description suggests; there are three base terms from which the sentencing court may choose, the middle one being the presumptive term subject to rules promulgated by the state's judicial council. In addition, it is possible in certain circumstances to enhance a sentence (i.e., aggravate the chosen base term by adding on extra years of imprisonment), although there are no parallel provisions for reducing sentences below the lower base term if the court decides to imprison at all.

5. The list of mitigating and aggravating factors (which is said to be nonexclusive, which may mean nonexhaustive) actually includes four grounds for mitigation and four grounds for aggravation; however, the last of the aggravating factors (which refers to "major economic offenses") requires two of a list of five further conditions to be met. Initially the commission had proposed to specify only the five grounds on which departure would not be permissible; this position was changed early in 1980 (letter from Dale Parent to Andrew von Hirsch dated 24 September 1979).

6. According to s.303.4(e)(1) of the Pennsylvania rules, the departure range for aggravation is limited to one cell in the righthand (heavier) direction, unless the guideline cell is the rightmost in its row; then the movement is one cell above, which is also in a heavier direction. The rules for mitigation are the mirror image of this. So far as I am aware, Pennsylvania's guidelines rules are the only ones that provide for such a limitation; in the absence of this kind of provision, of course, a court that decided to depart from the stipulated guideline range might impose literally any legal sentence.

7. See Minnesota Laws (1978:Ch.723, s. 244.10). In Massachusetts, appellate review of sentences to Walpole State Prison also exists; at the time of this writing it is not known how these appeals will be affected by that

state's guidelines. For a discussion of the Massachusetts and Connecticut appeal procedures in relation to
sentences, see Zeisel and Diamond (1976).

8. There may be other reasons for this belief. For
example, both Gottfredson and Wilkins had previously made
distinguished contributions to the literature on criminological prediction, and the model building analyses that
preceded their formulations of guidelines (and those of
others) have many affinities with prediction problems in
the field of criminology.

9. Part of the reason for a belief to the contrary may
lie in a bogus distinction between description and
prescription. If I say "The stuff in this bottle is
poison" or "There is a mad bull in this field" (or even
put up a sign saying "Bull") I am making a descriptive
statement that has a truth value, etc., but I may thereby
intend to warn others; warning is a species of prescription (see Sparks, 1979; for a general discussion of the
linguistic point see Austin, 1962). The prescriptive
nature of guidelines is briefly discussed in Gottfredson
et al. (1978:141,159).

10. In interviews with me in 1979, Blalock asserted that
there had not been a deliberate attempt to mirror past
practice, on the grounds that there had not been a
consistent practice prior to the guidelines. He then
explained that the matrix had been constructed in part by
reference to the maximum time that an offender would have
to serve, given full "good time," and the board's desire
to make the longest terms (i.e., those in the lower
righthand corner of the matrix) sufficiently shorter to
induce prisoners to leave the institution on parole
rather than "maxing out" without parole supervision.

11. Thus, for example, Zalman et al. (1979), in their
study of sentencing in Michigan, came to the conclusion
that "there is not much predictability in sentencing,
since similar cases are being treated very differently"
(1979:142). As we shall see below, there is good reason
to doubt that Zalman and his colleagues did in fact find
this; their claim to have done so, however, undoubtedly
helped them to argue for guidelines as the best alternative to what they described as "the current sentencing
morass" in Michigan (p. 17).

12.   This may have seemed especially important to
Gottfredson and Wilkins when they were conducting their
initial feasibility study; as each has pointed out to me
in a personal communication, there was at that time
little prospect of legislative mandate for change (of the
kind subsequently to emerge in Minnesota), and self-
regulation by the judiciary seemed the best bet—quite
apart from the concept (which they considered important
on the basis of their work with parole guidelines) of
making policy explicit.   For a similar statement of the
importance of involving judges, see Kress (1980).

13.   It may be for this reason that the Minnesota
legislature directed that state's sentencing commission
to ". . . take into substantial consideration current
sentencing and release practices . . ." in devising its
guidelines (Minn. Laws 1978, cg. 723; Minn. Stat. ch. 244
et seq.; see Minnesota Sentencing Guidelines Commission,
1980:1).   It appears that no similar injunction was
contained in the Pennsylvania Sentencing Commission's
legislative mandate.

14.   In at least one state, however (namely Pennsylvania), the dissemination of this information appears to
have been counter-productive politically: see the
discussion in Martin (in this volume).

15.   For good discussions of the many ways in which this
variety of descriptions may be true, see, e.g., Austin
(1961), D'Arcy (1963), Anscombe (1961), Wisdom (1959).
Lawyers are well aware of this: See the discussion in
Hart and Honore (1959).

16.   Both concepts, of course, have clear-cut examples,
but both have a large and vaguely bounded middle ground
in which there is a lot of room for dispute, not only
among lawyers but also among others.   For example, does
being drunk while you commit a crime mitigate (on the
ground of lessened self-control) or aggravate (on the
ground that you shouldn't have let yourself get into that
state)?   Should hitherto blameless characters receive
less censure for a first lapse—or more, on the ground
that they should be held to the higher standards they
have previously shown themselves to have been capable of
meeting?   Examples of the English courts' different
approaches to these and kindred questions are found in
Thomas (1972).

17.   This issue is discussed at greater length in Stecher and Sparks (1982).

18.   On the relations between information in presentence reports (and probation officers' preconceptions as well), and the sentences imposed by judges, see, e.g., Emerson (1968), Davis (1971), Cicourel (1968), Carter and Wilkins (1967).   Cicourel's work makes clear the advantage to most offenders that they are the primary sources of information about themselves that is likely to play any part in their fates.   They, at least, never learned to "interpret" their behavior in the way that many social workers can, and they are sometimes fairly skilled at lying about it.

19.   The complexities in question would no doubt be even greater in most states, in which a small group of judges hear cases in a single county or similar jurisdiction only.   In Massachusetts, by contrast, there remains something of the circuit system still in use in England and formerly found in many American states.   Our observation was that this system was a bit rigid, even in Massachusetts; and of course even judges who travel throughout the state may have modified their sentencing policies in response to what they see as local community attitudes.   (The same may be true for public defenders, who in Massachusetts are organized and paid by a state organization; prosecutors, however, are elected at county level.)   This may seem to be too microscopic to bother with.   I believe it is not, however: Attention to such details might enable us to sort out the consequences of judicial role behavior from those attributed (as too many probably are) to personal idiosyncracy.

20.   For a further discussion of the bargaining processes, which in Massachusetts often led to both prosecutor and defense counsel making recommendations as to sentence, see Sparks et al. (1982:Ch.6).

21.   This conclusion was said to be based on inspection of an initial sample of 500 presentence reports and on consultation with probation officers involved in the preparation of those reports (McCarthy, 1978:10-11).   This surely illustrates vividly the caution needed in dealing with this information source.

22.   A New Jersey judge of my acquaintance once confided that he often decided whether or not to incarcerate a

convicted offender by looking at the man's wife or girlfriend. A beatific air usually led to probation, a slatternly look to the jail; this curious rule was based on a theory of sorts about what a "good woman" can do for a man, etc. Stranger theories have been espoused by judges—in books yet (see, for example, Alexander and Staub, 1956).

23. There may, however, be problems of validity surrounding the available data on judges' and others' beliefs. There may also be problems concerning the consistency with which such data are recorded. A comprehensive discussion is found in Belson (1963) and Hood (1964); again, Cicourel (1968) has informative illustrations.

24. Analyses of variations in sentencing between judges are reported by Rich et al. (1980) and Zalman et al. (1979); this method of identifying "disparity" in sentencing was also the focus of the earliest studies in this field, e.g., Gaudet et al. (1933). Studies that have claimed to find substantial variation of this kind have done little to explain why it occurs. For example, do the judges in question differ in their perceptions of certain sorts of cases, in what they believe to be appropriate objectives for those cases, or in their beliefs concerning the sanctions best suited to accomplish those objectives? Interesting discussions of this problem are found in Hogarth (1971) and, concerning juvenile court judges, Wheeler et al. (1968).

25. In addition, of course, in some jurisdictions the minimum term to parole eligibility is determined by the minimum sentence imposed by the judge (with or without allowance for "good time"). Even so, it may be necessary to take into account judges' beliefs about paroling practices in deciding on the appropriate definition of length of term.

26. The extent to which estimates of time served will vary according to whether admission or release samples are used is not easy to predict. There may not be much difference if paroling rates and term-setting policies remain reasonably constant over time. However, since the stock of prisoners available to be paroled depends in part on the numbers and types of prisoners admitted in preceding years, and since these are unlikely to remain constant in most jurisdictions, the times served by those

released in any year may still differ from the expected
times to be served by those admitted in the same year--
which is presumably what is to be reflected in the
sentencing guidelines. Even worse problems of inference
will arise if a sample of the prison population is used
to estimate lengths of terms; long-term prisoners are
even more heavily overrepresented (see Sparks, 1971, for
a discussion). There are some demographic methods (e.g.,
life tables, demographic input-output) that are useful in
tackling some aspects of this problem (see, for example,
Stone, 1972; Keyfitz, 1977), but these do not seem to me
to be of much help in dealing with the issue involved
here.

27. These field studies were carried out in June-August
1979 and July-August 1980 (see Sparks et al., 1982).

28. The judicially imposed sentence to Walpole or
Concord did not in fact mean that the offender spent time
in the designated institution; this was in the end
determined by the Department of Corrections. As an
example, we observed a case in which a slightly built
white youth was convicted of apparently irrational
aggravated assaults with a hammer on a number of
persons. Prosecution and defense counsel had agreed on a
recommendation of 15 years in Concord, which would have
meant that the offender was eligible for parole in about
18 months; the judge sentenced the offender to 15 years
in Walpole, which would have meant parole eligibility
after 10 years. In an interview after the sentencing
hearing the judge stated that he had passed a "Walpole
sentence" precisely because of the difference in parole
eligibility rules; he was confident that the defendant
would not be kept by the Department of Corrections in
Walpole State Prison, where (as it seemed to all concerned) he might have been subjected to sexual attack,
etc.

29. This assertion is based on personal communication
with the New Jersey guidelines project director, John P.
McCarthy, Esq., at the very beginning of the project; it
was thought necessary to base the guidelines on all cases
sentenced in the year, rather than on a sample, if the
resulting guidelines were to be credible to the state's
judges.

30. Especially since it is extremely important when
carrying out statistical modeling to validate one's

findings in the technical sense of seeing whether they
hold up in a fresh sample from the same population; there
is always a nonzero probability (which tests of statistical significance minimize but do not eliminate) that a
model--especially if it is based on little or no theory--
merely reflects some idiosyncracies of the first sample
from which it was derived. Moreover, the larger the
sample, the greater the chance that rare events (e.g.,
multiple rapes, in this context) will be represented in
it.

31. In less-than-statewide studies, much smaller samples
have been used: e.g., in the Denver study (Wilkins et
al., 1976) the analysis was ostensibly based on about 200
cases, though because of missing data the number actually
used seems to have been between 50 and 80 (compare Rich
et al., 1980; Hewitt and Little, 1981).

32. A sampling frame is technically the list of units
from which the sample is chosen; for example, a roster of
organizational members, a list of census tracts, or a set
of registers containing court convictions. Excluding
some blocks of units at random from the frame will not
necessarily introduce bias into one's results; doing so
in a systematic way (e.g., excluding the small counties
in Massachusetts) may well do so, and it is safest to
conclude that the findings simply do not apply to the
excluded blocks (in this case, the small counties).
Since these may well differ in important respects, they
ought to be included, and oversampled (as the Minnesota
and Michigan researchers in effect did), rather than
thrown out.

33. It requires weighting the cases finally selected in
such a way that they will represent, numerically, the
actual population. A careful example is Zalman et al.
(1979).

34. For a further discussion see Sparks et al.
(1982:Ch.7-8). As noted earlier, guilty pleas often had
negotiated (and sometimes agreed) recommendations for
sentence by prosecution and defense. In addition, we
were told by a number of judges, during our Massachusetts
field work, that they paid little or no attention to
information in presentence reports in cases in which
there had been a trial, since they felt that by the end
of the trial they usually knew what sort of person the
defendant was.

35. The results of an analysis based on trial and plea
cases lumped together will be--as might be expected--an
amalgam; in this case, one dominated by the much more
numerous cases disposed of by guilty pleas. In Massachusetts, the differences between the two types of cases
were not insignificant (see Sparks et al., 1982:Ch.8).

36. See Gelman et al. (1979), in which precisely the
wrong account of this matter is given; the authors
confuse statistical validation (which requires a sample
from the original population) with checking to see
whether things have changed since the first sample.

37. Although it is an issue on which both Gottfredson
and Wilkins insisted (see, e.g., Gottfredson et al.,
1978; Gottfredson and Gottfredson, 1980; Mannheim and
Wilkins, 1955).

38. The figure of approximately 11,000 refers to the
main categories of offenses for which the New Jersey
guidelines were developed; the remaining 5,000 or so
cases were a miscellany, including (if I remember
correctly) three cases of "setting fire to paramour's
bed."

39. The exact total, and the ways in which these cases
were selected, are unclear from the Massachusetts
projects's reports and the information they provided to
us. The figure of 1,400 excludes cases sentenced to
"life without parole" and a few others unusable for
analysis (see Sparks et al., 1982).

40. Technically, we also need to suppose that this scale
is a genuinely "interval-level" one, with properties like
those of the natural number system. This assumption is
of course often violated (or, as economists tend to say,
"relaxed") in practice.

41. Clear and concise discussions of regression techniques include Blalock (1972), Cohen and Cohen (1975),
and Walker and Lev (1953); a more advanced treatment will
be found in Mosteller and Tukey (1977).

42. That is, variables whose coefficients are no larger
than might have been expected purely by chance (and thus
are not statistically significant) thus make no contribu-

tion to the prediction when other things are held
constant.

43. If all of those variables made sense and had sufficient nonmissing values (which, as we have seen, is far
from the case), there would be 381,501 different pairs of
variables--candidate x's--to be tried; triplets, four-
somes, etc., would make matters even worse. There are
some sensible techniques for carrying out what Mosteller
and Tukey (1977:Ch.15) have called guided regression in
situations of this kind, in which one knows literally
nothing about what variables ought to be considered. But
it is better not to get oneself into such a situation in
the first place.

44. Such data should not, of course, have been collected
to begin with. The question of what is a missing value
can get a little complicated. In the nature of things,
there are some stigmata--certain sexual deviations, for
example, and gross physical peculiarities--that are apt
to be mentioned if present, but whose absence would be
pedantic to record. Thus the safe coding of a questionnaire item such as "defendant into frottage" or "defendant is a Siamese twin" is almost certainly "no" rather
than "not known," if explicit mention is not made. Yet,
vagueness aside, what is normal is very much conditioned
by the preconceptions of the beholder. Probation officers and other social workers, whose professional train-
ing typically contains a healthy if diluted dollop of
Freudianism, seem able to see peculiarities that humbler
folk do not; conversely, they often display a capacity to
explain to their own satisfaction (and thus to treat as
normal, at least sometimes) many things on which others
would be inclined to comment. An illuminating study of
institutional records on this point is Belson (1963); see
also Cicourel (1968).

45. See, for a discussion, Mosteller and Tukey
(1977:Ch.4-6). In some cases, a logarithmic transformation may be theoretically reasonable--it may be reasonable to assume, for example, that prior arrests or convictions have a diminishing effect, perhaps after a
threshold has been reached. This is one reason why the
grouping of such things as prior arrests (which is often
accomplished in constructing offender scores used in
guidelines) may introduce relatively little error into
the calculation of expected sentences. This kind of

transformation is to be distinguished from that which is involved if it is assumed that relations between outcome and explanatory variables are multiplicative rather than simply additive (as is the case, for instance, with some kinds of "interactions"--see below).

46. This refers, again, to the issue of statistical significance. It cannot be too often repeated that this kind of significance does not license any conclusions about meaningfulness (see the discussion below of the analyses done by Zalman et al., 1979).

47. Unfortunately, the term interaction is sometimes used by statisticians to refer to other things, in particular the situation in which a set of relationships (e.g., between offense and offender variables and sentences) differs between subpopulations (e.g., whites and nonwhites). A situation of this kind, and the example given in the text, are by no means necessarily equivalent.

48. In such a case, the other variable is sometimes called a suppressor (see, for example, Rosenberg, 1968; J. Davis, 1971). But it makes no sense to test all pairs of variables that seem to display no association with each other, to see if this kind of suppression is taking place--not least because it may look that way, purely by chance, if enough candidate suppressors are tested.

49. Almost all of the "significant" relationships reported by Zalman et al. had a probability of occurring purely by chance (according to statistical theory) of less than 1 in 1,000. A more common level of this kind of significance uses a probability of chance occurrence of less than 1 in 20 as a criterion. Neither is proof against nonsense, however. If one looks at 500 bivariate associations, for example, the latter criterion means that one should expect, on average, 25 associations of the requisite strength, just by chance. If one ends up with 26 such associations, which is not just a fluke?

50. This question should be distinguished from the question of the number of alternative but equally suitable models that one should seek for the same decision, e.g., lengths of terms given to those imprisoned after a trial and conviction. Statistical analyses may (and crudely empirical ones almost certainly will) yield several such models of about equal explanatory power (see Gelman et al., 1979).

51. Quite commonly, for example, offense and offender variables that emerge from regression models will be combined into what are sometimes called Burgess scales (in honor of their use in the first parole prediction study by Burgess et al. (1931)): that is, each included factor will simply be given a score of +1 rather than a weight estimated by regression or some other procedure. The scale scores thus derived may further be grouped into categories (e.g., 0-2, 3-5, etc.) in guidelines. Such scores are quite robust in the sense that they tend to hold up on cross-validation (for a discussion, see Wainer, 1976, 1978). They obviously permit only crude categorizations of offenders into matrix cells; but, as I noted earlier, the concept of guidelines has enough flexibility that this does not much matter. Such smoothing or rounding techniques need to be distinguished, however, from modifications of the results of analyses of past practice that are explicitly based on considerations of policy, e.g., removing the effects of racial discrimination or regional variation.

52. Strictly speaking, guidelines may also prescribe the place of incarceration, e.g., jail or prison. The New Jersey guidelines do in fact give a hint to judges about this, although no more (see Sparks et al., 1982).

53. Wilkins seems to believe that they are (see, for example, Wilkins et al., 1976:2-3; contrast, however, Gottfredson et al., 1978:Ch.5). At any rate, neither he nor anyone else to my knowledge has presented psychological evidence in support of this view.

54. Further guidelines may be developed to deal with each category defined by the first decision: Thus guidelines that aim to regulate the decision to incarcerate can coexist with durational guidelines, which may be used by another agency, e.g., a parole board (for a further discussion see Sparks et al., 1982:Ch.2,3,11).

55. For descriptions of some of these methods--LOGIT and PROBIT models, and logistic regression--see Fienberg (1977); Bishop et al. (1975); Cox (1970). Applications to criminal justice problems include Solomon (1976); Larntz (1980); Zimmerman and Blumstein (1979); Gottfredson and Gottfredson (1980). The finding--e.g., by Zalman et al. (1979) and Gottfredson and Gottfredson (1980) that the results of using such procedures do not differ substantially from those of simpler and better-

known techniques--may be largely due to the crudeness with which many criminal justice data are measured (contrast Rhodes, 1981, who takes a different view).

56. It is important to note that this scoring of nonincarceration sentences as zero, at the modeling stage of guidelines development, is quite a separate matter from the use (or the misuse) of zero to represent such sentences in the guidelines themselves. This problem is discussed below.

57. See above, notes 34 and 35. In fact, the Massachusetts guidelines are (or initially were) "advisory" in cases in which there was not an agreed recommendation following a plea of guilty. Cases of this type, which would seem to have a sort of intermediate status in the adversary process, might themselves be modeled separately, since the determinants of sentences in such cases could well be different from both those operating in those cases that went to trial and those for which there were agreed guilty pleas. This matter is currently being studied by Bridget Stecher and me, using the Massachusetts data.

58. In the Michigan study (Zalman et al., 1979) offenses were grouped into broad categories of similar sorts of behavior (e.g., sex crimes); within each of these categories, the various offenses were given a seriousness score that was the maximum sentence provided by statute, in months.

59. Marvin Wolfgang and his colleagues at the University of Pennsylvania have recently completed a survey of perceived crime severity using a large national probability sample (drawn from respondents in the National Crime Surveys); preliminary results from this study, as yet unpublished, suggest that there is in fact considerable variation in the numerical scores assigned to offense descriptions among subgroups of the population. For the view that such differences may reflect variations in the use of the natural number scale as well as the sparseness of the descriptions typically used in this kind of research, see Shelly and Sparks (1980).

60. The situation seems exactly analogous to that of von Bortkewitsch, who showed that the Poisson distribution fitted the observed distribution of deaths from horse-

kicks in 10 corps in the Prussian army over 20 years.
There were in fact 14 corps, but von Bortkewitsch
excluded four that had abnormally large numbers of
deaths, thus sparing himself the necessity of fitting
negative binomials or something similar instead of the
Poisson (see Coleman, 1964:291). No doubt it is nice to
have reasons—if not theories—to justify such exclu-
sions; the point is that such abnormal cases should be
excluded, whether or not an apparent reason for their
abnormality is present. The basis for deciding that a
case is abnormal is, of course, somewhat subjective if no
such theory is available.

61. See, however, the discussions of "in-out" predictions by Zimmerman and Blumstein (1979), Rich et al.
(1980), and Zalman et al. (1979), and criticism of their
techniques by Sparks et al. (1982:Ch.11). For several
reasons, a cutoff of exactly 50 percent is too peremptory
a measure of "in" versus "out."

62. They were agreed after discussion with the project's
Steering and Policy Committee, which consisted mostly of
judges. No pun is intended.

63. Further details of this analysis are reported in
Sparks et al. (1982:Ch.9). It may well be, of course,
that such changes in outcome are precisely what is
wanted, on grounds of social policy. However, it seems
to me important to try to estimate (at a minimum) what
the aggregate consequences of such a change in sentencing
practice would mean, e.g., for prison populations; as I
note below, only the Minnesota researchers have so far
considered this issue.

64. The midranges are thus treated as a "response" or
dependent variable, which is assumed to be determined by
the variables that define the rows and columns; the
effect of the technique is thus rather like that of the
analysis of variance. See also Mosteller and Tukey
(1977); McNeil and Tukey (1975); Fairley (1978); and for
applications of this method to parole guidelines matrices
see Perline and Wainer (1980); Sparks (1983).

65. A multiplicative model of this kind involves the
same techniques applied to the logarithms of the midranges rather than to the midranges themselves (see
Tukey, 1977). The value of such a model is that the

effect of, say, prior record, differs according to the
level of seriousness of the offense one is considering.
Both the Minnesota and Pennsylvania sentencing guidelines
display such a structure (see Sparks et al., 1982:Ch.9).

66. I am not suggesting that such anomalies must be
indefensible; perhaps there really is a case for a very
much heavier or lighter prescribed term in this or that
cell, than what the best-fitting overall structure would
dictate. But if so, why? The point of the techniques
discussed here is that they may help to make perspicuous
matters that may otherwise remain unnoticed. To the
extent that they succeed in doing this, they surely
contribute to what Gottfredson and Wilkins primarily had
in mind when they sought to make paroling policy
"explicit," which is not the same thing as "making
paroling policy."

67. It is open to argument whether range widths within
cells should be evaluated in terms of absolute numbers of
months (in which case the heavier midranges will usually
seem to have the wider ranges), or in terms of cell
ranges standardized by their midranges, i.e., in "plus or
minus" percentages around the midrange (in which case the
greatest latitude will often be elsewhere in the matrix,
probably in those cells prescribing on average the
lightest terms). For example, in a cell with a prescribed range of 12-18 months, an offender getting the
maximum "normal" term will serve half again as long as
one receiving the minimum; in other words, around the
midrange this is equivalent to a plus-or-minus permissible variation of 20 percent. Compare the situation in
a cell prescribing a range of 96-120 months (plus or
minus about 11 percent, around a midrange of 108
months). In which case is there more variability?

68. At present, however, this computer program (which
takes initial inputs, e.g., conviction patterns, as
relatively static) looks forward only five years;
longer-term projections are needed for many purposes,
including planning for prison capacity. The program is,
however easily modifiable to permit this. (Minnesota
Sentencing Guidelines Commission, 1981, gives details and
a program listing; the commission's research director,
Kay Knapp, should be contacted for further information.)

259

REFERENCES

Alexander, Franz, and Hugo Staub
  1956 The Criminal, the Judge and the Public. Revised
        edition. Glencoe, Ill.: Free Press.
Allen, F. A.
  1964 The Borderland of Justice. Chicago: University
        of Chicago Press.
Anscombe, G. E. M.
  1961 Intention. Oxford, England: Basil Blackwell.
Austin, J. L.
  1961 Philosophical Papers. Edited by J.O. Urmson and
        G.J. Warnock. Oxford, England: Oxford
        University Press.
  1962 How to Do Things with Words. Oxford, England:
        Oxford University Press.
Belson, William
  1963 The Development of Stealing in Adolescent Boys.
        Unpublished paper. London School of Economics.
Bishop, Yvonne M. M., Stephen E. Fienberg, and Paul W.
Holland
  1975 Discrete Multivariate Analysis: Theory and
        Practice. Cambridge, Mass.: M.I.T. Press.
Blalock, Hubert M.
  1972 Social Statistics. 2nd edition. New York:
        McGraw-Hill.
Burgess, Ernest W., Andrew A. Bruce, Albert J. Harno, and
John Landesco
  1928 Parole and the Indeterminate Sentence. Spring-
        field, Ill.: Illinois State Board of Parole.
Carter, Robert M., and Leslie T. Wilkins
  1967 Some factors in sentencing policy. Journal of
        Criminal Law, Criminology and Police Science
        58(4):503-514.
Cicourel, Aaron
  1968 The Social Organization of Juvenile Justice.
        New York: John Wiley.
Cohen, Jacob, and Patricia Cohen
  1975 Applied Multiple Regression/Correlation Analysis
        for the Behavioral Sciences. New York: John
        Wiley.
Coleman, James
  1964 Introduction to Mathematical Sociology. New
        York: Free Press.
Cox, D. R.
  1970 The Analysis of Binary Data. London: Methuen.
D'Arcy, Eric
  1963 Human Action. London: Routledge and Kegan Paul.

Davis, James
   1971 Elementary Survey Analysis. Englewood Cliffs,
         N.J.: Prentice-Hall.
Emerson, Robert M.
   1968 Judging Delinquents: Context and Process in the
         Juvenile Court. Chicago: Aldine.
Fairley, William B.
   1978 Accidents on Route 2: two-way structures for
         data. In William B. Fairley and Frederick
         Mosteller, eds., Statistics and Public Policy.
         Reading, Mass.: Addison-Wesley.
Ferri, Enrico
   1921 Report and Preliminary Project for an Italian
         Penal Code. Translated by Edgar Betts.
         London: His Majesty's Stationery Office.
Fienberg, Stephen
   1977 The Analysis of Cross-Classified Categorical
         Data. Cambridge, Mass.: M.I.T. Press.
Gaudet, F. J., G. S. Harris, and C. W. St. John
   1933 Individual differences in the sentencing
         tendencies of judges. Journal of Criminal Law,
         Criminology and Police Science 23(5):811-817.
Gelman, A. M., Jack Kress, and Joseph Calpin
   1979 Developing Sentencing Guidelines. Washington,
         D.C.: U.S. Department of Justice.
Glueck, Sheldon
   1928 Principles of a rational penal code. Harvard
         Law Review 41(4):453-482.
Gottfredson, D. M., P. B. Hoffman, M. H. Sigler, and L.
T. Wilkins
   1975 Making paroling policy explicit. Crime &
         Delinquency 21:34-44.
Gottfredson, Don M., Leslie T. Wilkins, and Peter B.
Hoffman
   1978 Guidelines for Parole and Sentencing: A Policy
         Control Method. Lexington, Mass.: Lexington
         Books.
Gottfredson, Michael R., and Don M. Gottfredson
   1980 Decision-Making in Criminal Justice: Toward the
         Rational Exercise of Discretion. Cambridge,
         Mass.: Ballinger.
Hagan, J.
   1975 Extra-legal attributes and criminal sentencing:
         an assessment of a sociological viewpoint. Law
         & Society Review 8:357-383.
Hart, H. L. A., and A.M. Honore
   1959 Causation in the Law. Oxford, England: Oxford
         University Press.

Hewitt, J. D., and B. Little
  1981 Examining the research underlying the sentencing
        guidelines concept in Denver, Colorado: a
        partial replication of a reform effort. Journal
        of Criminal Justice 9:51-62.
Hogarth, John
  1971 Sentencing as a Human Process. Toronto, Ont.:
        University of Toronto Press.
Hood, Roger
  1964 Sentencing in Magistrates' Courts. London:
        Sweet and Maxwell.
Keyfitz, Nathan
  1977 Introduction to Population Mathematics.
        Reading, Mass.: Addison-Wesley.
Kress, Jack M.
  1980 Prescription for Justice: The Theory and
        Practice of Sentencing Guidelines. Cambridge,
        Mass.: Ballinger.
Larntz, Kinley
  1980 Linear logistic models for the parole decision-
        making problem. In S. E. Fienberg and A. J.
        Reiss, Jr., eds., Indicators of Crime and Crimi-
        nal Justice: Quantitative Studies. Washington,
        D.C.: U.S. Government Printing Office.
Lizotte, Alan
  1978 Extra-legal factors in Chicago's criminal
        courts: testing the conflict model of criminal
        justice. Social Problems 5:564-580.
Mannheim, Herman, and Leslie T. Wilkins
  1955 Prediction Methods in Relation to Borstal Train-
        ing. London: Her Majesty's Stationery Office.
McCarthy, John P.
  1978 Report of the Sentencing Guidelines Project to
        the Administrative Director of the Courts. Ad-
        ministrative Office of the Courts, Trenton, N.J.
McNeil, D. R., and J. W. Tukey
  1975 Higher-order diagnosis of two-way tables,
        illustrated on two sets of demographic empirical
        distributions. Biometrika 31:487-510.
Minnesota Sentencing Guidelines Commission
  1979 Summary Report: Preliminary Analysis of Sen-
        tencing and Releasing Data. St. Paul, Minn.:
        Minnesota Sentencing Guidelines Commission.
  1980 Report to the Legislature. St. Paul, Minn.:
        Minnesota Sentencing Guidelines Commission.
Mosteller, Frederick, and John W. Tukey
  1977 Data Analysis and Regression: A Second Course
        in Statistics. Reading, Mass.: Addison-Wesley.

Perline, Richard, and Howard Wainer
    1980 Quantitative approaches to the study of parole.
          In S. E. Fienberg and A. J. Reiss, Jr., eds.,
          Indicators of Crime and Criminal Justice. Wash-
          ington, D.C.: U.S. Government Printing Office.
Rhodes, William
    1981 Comments on the Methodology Used in the
          Construction of Sentencing Guidelines.
          Unpublished paper prepared for the Panel on
          Sentencing Research, National Research Council.
Rich, William D., L. Paul Sutton, Todd Clear, and Michael
J. Saks
    1980 Sentencing Guidelines: Their Operation and
          Impact on the Courts. National Center for State
          Courts, Williamsburg, Va.
Rosenberg, Morris
    1968 The Logic of Survey Analysis. New York: Basic
          Books.
Rossi, Peter H., E. Watie, C. Rose, and R. E. Berk
    1974 Seriousness of crimes: normative structure and
          individual differences. American Sociological
          Review 39:224-237.
Sellin, Thorsten, and Marvin E. Wolfgang
    1964 The Measurement of Delinquency. New York: John
          Wiley.
Shelly, Peggy L., and Richard F. Sparks
    1980 Crime and Punishment. Paper presented at the
          annual meetings of the American Society of
          Criminology, San Francisco.
Solomon, Herbert
    1976 Parole outcome: a multidimensional contingency
          table analysis. Journal of Research in Crime
          and Delinquency 13:107-126.
Sparks, Richard F.
    1971 Local Prisons and the Crisis in the English
          Penal System. London: Heinemann Educational
          Books.
Sparks, Richard F.
    1979 Prediction and Guidelines. Paper presented at
          the annual meetings of the Academy of Criminal
          Justice Sciences, Cincinnati, Ohio.
    1981 The structure of the Oregon parole guidelines.
          Chapter 9 in Sheldon Messinger, Richard F.
          Sparks, and Andrew von Hirsch, eds., Final Re-
          port on the Strategies for Determinate Sentenc-
          ing Project. National Institute of Justice,
          Washington, D.C.

1983 Sentencing guidelines. In Encyclopedia of Crime and Justice. New York: Free Press.

Sparks, Richard F., and Bridget A. Stecher
1979 The New Jersey Sentencing Guidelines: An Unauthorized Analysis. Paper presented at the annual meetings of the American Society of Criminology, Philadelphia.

Sparks, Richard F., Hazel G. Genn, and David J. Dodd
1977 Surveying Victims. London: John Wiley.

Sparks, Richard F., Bridget A. Stecher, Jay S. Albanese, and Peggy L. Shelly
1982 Stumbling Toward Justice: Some Overlooked Research and Policy Questions Concerning Statewide Sentencing Guidelines. School of Criminal Justice, Rutgers University.

Stecher, Bridget A., and Richard F. Sparks
1982 Removing the effects of discrimination in sentencing guidelines. In Martin Forst, ed., Sentencing Disparity. Beverly Hills, Calif.: Sage.

Stone, Richard
1972 Mathematics and the Social Sciences. London: Chapman and Hall.

Thomas, David A.
1972 Principles of Sentencing. 2nd edition. London: Heinemann Educational Books.

Tukey, John
1977 Exploratory Data Analysis. Reading, Mass.: Addison-Wesley.

von Hirsch, Andrew
1975 Doing Justice: The Choice of Punishments. New York: Hill and Wang.

Walker, H. M., and J. Lev
1953 Statistical Inference. New York: Holt.

Wainer, Howard
1976 Estimating coefficients in linear models: it don't make no nevermind. Psychological Bulletin 83:213-217.

Wheeler, Stanton, et al.
1968 Agents of delinquency control; a comparative analysis. In S. Wheeler, ed., Controlling Delinquents. New York: Wiley.

Wilkins, Leslie T., Jack M. Kress, Don M. Gottfredson, and Joseph Calpin
1976 Sentencing Guidelines: Structuring Judicial Discretion. Final report of the feasibility study. Albany, N.Y.: Criminal Justice Research Center.

Wisdom, John
  1959 Philosophy and Psychoanalysis. Oxford: Basil
         Blackwell.
Zalman, Marvin, C. W. Ostrom, Jr., P. Guilliams, and G.
Peaslee
  1979 Sentencing in Michigan: Final Report of the
         Michigan Felony Sentencing Project. Lansing,
         Mich.: Michigan Office of Criminal Justice.
Zeisel, Hans, and Shari Diamond
  1976 The search for sentencing equity: sentence
         review in Massachusetts and Connecticut.
         American Bar Foundation Research Journal 881-940.
Zimmerman, Sherwood E., and Alfred Blumstein
  1979 The Construction of Sentencing Guidelines.
         Paper presented at the annual meetings of the
         Academy of Criminal Justice Sciences,
         Cincinnati, Ohio.

6

The Politics of
Sentencing Reform:
Sentencing Guidelines in
Pennsylvania and Minnesota

Susan E. Martin

The 1970s were characterized by a variety of reforms
designed to increase determinacy in criminal sentences.
Among these reforms was the legislative creation of state
sentencing commissions to develop and implement guidelines to structure sentencing decisions. In 1978 two
states, Minnesota and Pennsylvania, adopted this route to
change.[1] The Minnesota commission's guidelines were
accepted and have been in effect since May 1980. The
Pennsylvania legislature passed a resolution in April
1981 rejecting its commission's guidelines as submitted
and asking for revisions within six months; revised
guidelines were submitted in January 1982 and became
effective in July 1982.

This paper is an examination of the social, political,
and organizational factors that influenced these events
in Minnesota and Pennsylvania.[2] Two limitations should
be noted. First, the findings are preliminary; no data
on implementation or on the impact of the guidelines in
either state are examined. Second, generalizing the
experience of these two states to other jurisdictions is
highly conjectural given the diversity of social histories, sentencing structures, and political cultures.
Examining the Pennsylvania and Minnesota experiences
seems worthwhile nonetheless. At the very least it can
provide a preliminary interpretation of the forces that
shaped an ongoing institutional change. Such an interpretation may serve to indicate that the complexities of
developing sentencing guidelines involve not only the

technical issues related to development of statistical models of past sentencing practices and projections of future prison populations, but also the political aspects of the policy-making process.

The first section of this paper examines the central issues in sentencing reform. The second section reviews particular state and local issues: the legislative maneuvering and the resulting statute that created the sentencing guidelines commissions and their mandates. The third section describes the two statutes and the mandates of the Pennsylvania and Minnesota commissions. Section four examines the internal dynamics of each commission in interpreting its mandate, defining its tasks, and organizing its work; the guidelines each commission produced; and the key elements shaping the creation of guidelines in each state. The final section considers the role and effectiveness of interest groups and the activities of the commissions that shaped the reaction to the guidelines that each legislature received.

DISPARITY, SEVERITY, AND THE DISTRIBUTION OF AUTHORITY: CENTRAL ISSUES IN SENTENCING REFORM

Discontent with the goal of rehabilitation and the disparity resulting from indeterminate sentences led to a debate in many jurisdictions over three overlapping sets of questions. First, what is the proper goal of punishment? How should the competing goals of deterrence, incapacitation, rehabilitation, and retribution be ordered or balanced? Second, what should the criteria be for applying different types of sanctions--incarceration, community supervision, fines, or a combination of these? How severe a sanction is necessary to achieve the goal of the sentencer? Third, who should have authority to establish sentencing standards and to make individual sentencing decisions?

Under indeterminate schemes legislatures established very broad policies--generally through statements of purpose, establishment of maximum sentences, and authorization of general sentencing procedures--and left vast discretion in the hands of sentencing judges and parole boards to decide on the type and amount of punishment appropriate in individual cases. In such a system the goal of protecting society through the rehabilitation of criminal offenders and their incapacitation until they are rehabilitated are the principal considerations in

deciding whether to incarcerate and the length of
imprisonment. The severity of the punishment depends
more on the individual characteristics of the criminal
than on the nature of the crime. It is expected that two
offenders who have committed similar offenses might serve
quite different prison terms, since release is contingent
on evidence of reform. Disparity, or variation in
sentences, is an accepted part of a system of indivi-
dualized treatment for offenders.

Such a system for a long time satisfied a wide
spectrum of opinion. Liberals liked the purported
rejection of the notion of retribution and the possibility of speedy release of offenders amenable to
rehabilitation. Judges enjoyed wide authority but were
relieved of responsibility for actual release decisions.
Prison administrators had flexibility in controlling
hostile inmates. Politicians could act irresponsibly in
raising statutory penalties to appease public passion
without affecting actual time served.

In the early 1970s support for the prevailing system
of indeterminate sentencing crumbled under a variety of
criticisms. Civil libertarian and prisoners' rights
groups initiated the attack, charging that the system
gave unchecked discretion to paroling authorities, was
based on inadequate assumptions about the predictability
of human behavior, resulted in long and arbitrary
sentences, and led to prisoner unrest and frustration.
In addition, a widely publicized research review (Lipton
et al., 1975) reporting that rehabilitation programs are
ineffective undermined the rationale on which indeter-
minacy rested. And rising crime rates led to demands for
surer and stiffer sanctions against criminals to prevent
crime. These criticisms led legislators and the legal
and professional communities to seek to replace the
indeterminate system with one that established explicit
standards for the amount of punishment to be imposed
under normal circumstances on persons convicted of
different types of crimes. But establishment of explicit
sentencing standards that control or structure discretion
and reduce disparity opened the door to disagreement over
the aims of punishment, who should establish the specific
standards to be applied (the legislature, parole board,
or another administrative body), how narrow and binding
these standards should be, and how discretion to make
individual sentencing decisions should be distributed
among the judiciary, prison officials, and parole
authorities.

In considering the goals, some writers (e.g., Wilson, 1975) have suggested that sentencing standards can improve the effectiveness of the criminal justice system in preventing crime through general deterrence and the incapacitation of offenders. Others (e.g., von Hirsch, 1976) view the principal aim of determinacy as making penalties more just, i.e., more closely apportioned to the blameworthiness of criminal conduct, by scaling punishments to the seriousness of crimes.

These goals point toward different philosophical and practical concerns. The goals of deterrence and incapacitation suggest standards that emphasize certainty, celerity, and (in some cases) greater severity of punishment. Disparity is objectionable because it undermines certainty. Von Hirsch's "just deserts" approach seeking to make punishment commensurate with offenses is not concerned with random variation per se but with the establishment of norms, the elimination of unexplained variation from the norm, and the provision of reasons for variation that occurs.

Any state's efforts to reconsider sentencing goals, redistribute discretionary authority, and determine the appropriate level of sanction are strongly affected by the distribution of discretion, the extent and nature of sentencing disparity, and the political influence of interest groups with a stake in the debate. These factors shape the legislative definition of the sentencing problem and affect the outcome of reform efforts.

LEGISLATIVE POLITICS AND SENTENCING REFORM

Both the Minnesota and Pennsylvania legislatures struggled for four years over the question of distributing discretionary authority in establishing sentencing policy. And although in 1978 both states created sentencing guidelines commissions, existing institutional arrangements and thus the reasons for the resulting legislation differed.

Minnesota

Prior to 1978 Minnesota had an indeterminate sentencing law that divided decision-making authority between the courts and the parole board. The courts decided between probation and imprisonment and set the conditions of

probation, including a jail sentence, for offenders not
sent to prison. The parole board had authority to
release inmates on parole at any time prior to the
completion of long maximum terms. Actual prison terms
were relatively short, but parole decision making was
capricious and arbitrary, particularly prior to the
adoption of parole guidelines in 1976. Despite this
reform effort, parole decision making became the primary
target of sentencing reformers in a bitter three-way
struggle among proponents of legislatively set flat-time
sentences, presumptive guidelines to be established by a
sentencing commission composed of judges, and continuation of the existing parole board control over the
release decision.

Throughout the struggle the senate leader was William
McCutcheon, who introduced a flat-time sentencing bill in
1975. His initial proposal was not seriously considered
but led to hearings and a flat-time sentencing bill that
handily passed the Senate in 1976. The 1976 McCutcheon
bill was seen as "tough on crime" (largely because
McCutcheon was a deputy police chief in St. Paul and
because his initial proposal had been quite harsh),
although it was designed to maintain the average time
currently being served and the current level of prison
populations. It would have eliminated the parole board
but would not have affected judicial discretion over the
probation decision. The McCutcheon bill was opposed in
the house by Donald Moe, chairman of the committee to
which it was referred, and brought to the house floor
only through a parliamentary maneuver. After heated
debate the house voted to defer the bill's effective date
to permit "technical revisions," then passed it. The
senate adopted the amended measure the next day; the
governor vetoed it, however, citing "serious technical
inadequacies."[3] Observers speculated that Moe and
corrections officials had convinced the governor to use
the technical defect as a politically expedient reason
for his veto.

When the new legislature convened in 1977 the
McCutcheon bill again sailed through the senate and was
sent to the house. But momentum had shifted.
McCutcheon's energies were directed elsewhere, and the
opponents of flat-time sentencing had turned to Representative Arnold Kempe, a conservative former supporter of
the McCutcheon bill, to support an effort to develop
sentencing guidelines. Kempe had read of the development
of sentencing guidelines and drafted a bill to establish

a sentencing guidelines commission composed entirely of judges. The guideline sentence was to be the presumptive sentence, although a judge could depart from it by providing written reasons for doing so. He introduced the idea to Moe, who realized that he could accept this approach to determinate sentencing if he could shape the final bill to permit the parole board to determine sentence length.

Another parliamentary maneuver permitted the Kempe and McCutcheon bills to move forward in the house as a single bill. When the house passed the Kempe version and the Senate rejected it, the matter was sent to a joint conference committee. The conference committee had to resolve three principal issues: whether the legislature or a commission would set sentencing policy; whether there would be a single or dual sentencing authority; and whether the single commission would be composed of judges or be a mixed group (see Table 6-1). Senate conferees, led by McCutcheon, supported abolition of the parole board as well as legislatively set flat-time sentences that left the dispositional decision in the hands of judges, shifting discretion from the correctional bureaucracy to the courts. The house conferees, however, were divided. Moe, fearful that legislative term-setting would ultimately increase sentence severity, advocated a dual concept with dispositional guidelines to be established by a sentencing commission and durational guidelines established by the parole authority. Kempe supported a single guidelines commission made up of judges that would design presumptive guidelines for both sentence disposition and duration. The compromise bill that emerged from committee established a single, legislatively authorized guidelines commission with a

TABLE 6-1   Issues and Positions of Leaders in the Minnesota Legislative Struggle

Legislator	Discretion Over Duration	Role of Parole	Structure of Commission	Severity	Client Constituency
McCutcheon	Legislature	Abolish	--	No Increase	Police and Prosecutors (Judiciary)
Kempe	Judiciary	Abolish	Single	--	
Moe	Administrative Body	Retain	Dual	No Increase	Corrections Bureaucracy

diverse membership. This commission was to determine
sentence dispositions and durations, both of which would
be presumptive.

The guidelines alternative appeared to offer a rare
acceptable compromise between fiscal conservatives and
corrections liberals. It promised the most important
changes or provisions that several key interest groups
had sought, met other goals of those interest groups, or
offered them a share in decision making. The compromise
revolved around the allocation of decision-making
authority within the criminal justice system, since once
it was agreed that prison sentences would be of fixed
duration, the key question became who would determine
these durations. There was little explicit debate over
the goals of punishment or what is an "appropriate"
sentence because there was agreement that the overall
level of severity would not be increased. Police and
prosecutors had sought and won greater influence in
shaping the sentencing decision and more predictable
sentences for the "worst" offenders. The judiciary got
structured discretion over sentence lengths rather than
no discretion over them. To the corrections bureaucracy
and the defense bar, less concerned with discretionary
authority than with warding off increased severity, the
guidelines seemed to offer a better prospect than
legislatively set flat-time sentences. Even the parole
board had won something--temporary survival and a seat on
the sentencing commission.

Pennsylvania

In Pennsylvania the establishment of a sentencing
guidelines commission was also a compromise, but it
stemmed from a different set of pressures emanating from
a different distribution of discretion. Pennsylvania
judges set both maximum and minimum prison terms, the
minimum permitted to be no more than half the maximum
within wide statutory limits. The court also may
determine whether to send offenders serving a maximum of
2-5 years (usually with a minimum of 1-2 1/2 years) to a
local jail or state prison. The parole board has the
authority to release offenders at any time after they
have completed their minimum terms, and in fact had been
releasing about 80 percent of state prisoners on
completion of their minimum terms. Thus judges have
authority over both the dispositional and sentence length

decisions while the parole board exercises limited discretion. This arrangement permits symbolically tough maximum sentences and relatively short minimums and has resulted in wide interdistrict disparity, as minimum sentences for urban offenders are more lenient than those given out in suburban and rural areas. This pattern of wide regional variation in the sentences and thus the actual minimum terms served by offenders across the state stems in large part from Pennsylvania's heterogeneity and strong traditions of local autonomy. It proved to be a major stumbling block in the development of statewide sentencing guidelines.

Pressure for sentencing reform came from several sources, focused on efforts to reduce judicial discretion and increase sentence severity, and centered on proposals for a mandatory minimum sentencing law that had wide symbolic appeal by looking tough on crime but affected the sentences of only the most serious repeat felons. In 1976 the senate passed a mandatory minimum sentencing bill that was then rejected by the house of representatives on the last vote of the session. Opposition in the house came from both the Democratic chairman of the judiciary committee, Norman Berson, and the Republican leader on criminal justice matters, Anthony Scirica, both of whom opposed mandatory minimum sentences as too rigid and the senate bill as too severe and costly to implement.

In the next session, having staved off the mandatory minimum bill by a slim margin and a parliamentary maneuver, Berson and Scirica adopted sentencing guidelines as an alternative approach to sentencing reform. As in Minnesota, the impasse between the two legislative chambers was broken when the house attached the guidelines bill to one already approved by the senate, resulting in conference committee negotiations. A final compromise, approved in the fall of 1978, established a sentencing commission to design guidelines for sentencing both felony and misdemeanor offenders.

The proposed mandatory minimum sentencing legislation would have substantially increased prison populations and corrections system costs. The liberals' alternative, sentencing guidelines, promised reduction in judicial discretion without immediate costs, while obscuring the severity issue, an outcome that was a satisfactory compromise for all parties. Rural legislators and district attorneys were satisfied with greater certainty in sentencing as well as an opportunity to look tough on crime at little cost. The Philadelphia district attorney (a rising political figure in the state) gained the promise of greater severity and certainty of incarceration via guidelines as well as the inclusion of an interim sentencing guideline (to avoid the term <u>mandatory sentencing provision</u>) for repeat person offenses and the right of the state to appeal a sentence. Prison officials avoided the prospect of vast overcrowding posed by the mandatory minimum bill. Liberals had sought and won an opportunity to reduce the vast disparity and judicial abuses through a more comprehensive and flexible sentencing reform than mandatory minimum sentences. The judiciary went along, viewing some change as imminent and guidelines as more flexible and less threatening than mandatory minimums. In the interim, the issue of severity was set aside as conservatives assumed that the guidelines would increase the severity of sentences; liberals viewed the legislation as a victory for structuring discretion without across-the-board increases in severity.

THE STATUTES AND THE MANDATES OF THE COMMISSIONS

The mandate of the Minnesota Sentencing Guidelines Commission (MSGC) was both more limited and more specific than that of the Pennsylvania Commission on Sentencing (PCS), making the task of the Minnesota commission more feasible. The MSGC was to determine the circumstances under which imprisonment is proper and to establish a presumptive fixed sentence for such cases based on "reasonable" offense and offender characteristics. In establishing the presumptive sentence, the commission was directed to "take into substantial consideration current sentencing and releasing practices and correctional resources including but not limited to the capacities of local and state correctional facilities." The commission was permitted to establish a range of up to 15 percent within which the presumptive sentence could vary. For sentences deviating from the applicable guideline sentence, the court was directed to make a written statement of the reasons for the departure. Only felons may go to prison in Minnesota so only felony sentences were to be addressed, although the commission was permitted but not required to design guidelines for nonimprisonment felony sentences. In the sentencing of misdemeanants and felons who would not go to state prison, the existing judicial discretion to determine the conditions of probation (including a jail term) might remain unaffected. Other provisions included the right of both the state and defendant to appeal sentences that are either stayed or imposed; the elimination of the parole board's authority to establish release dates for those imprisoned after May 1, 1980, the effective date of the guidelines unless they were rejected by the legislature;[4] establishment of good time earned at the rate of one day for every two days of good behavior in the institution; and provision for a separate sentencing hearing for convicted offenders.

The commission's mandate was shaped in large part by the desire of reformers to eliminate the parole board's authority rather than reshape the entire sentencing system. Only those sentence durations formerly determined by the parole board were to be set by the guidelines (i.e., sentence duration for executed sentences). Once the conference committee had agreed that there was to be no increase in the net amount of imprisonment, a framework for resolving other issues of severity existed, and the provision directing the commission to consider prison capacity and past practice could be included in the statute at the prodding of the commissioner of corrections with little opposition or notice.

The Pennsylvania commission's broad and ambitious mandate made the commission responsible for creating guideline sentences for both felony and misdemeanor offenses but left intact the parole board's authority. The object of reform was the judiciary's vast discretionary authority. Supporters of mandatory minimum sentences had attempted to deal with the problem by rigidly fettering judges' dispositional authority in sentencing a limited but politically visible fraction of the offender population. But their solution, the 1976 bill as drafted, was so severe and inclusive that it could not feasibly be implemented. It was also viewed by liberals as inflexible and too narrow an approach to reducing disparity. These problems plus the existence of the option of imprisonment for misdemeanor I and II offenses led to the more inclusive mandate of the commission. This in turn put it in the position of attacking the discretion of the judiciary, a more powerful group than the parole authority, over the entire range of judicial authority. The legislature's concession to the judiciary was to make the guidelines advisory

rather than presumptive, leaving the actual degree to
which they would be binding to resolution by the commission and the appellate courts. This compromise thwarted
the desire of the police and prosecutors for certainty
and hampered reliable projection of the guidelines'
impact on prison populations. The legislation made no
mention of considering corrections facilities or costs,
leaving the issue of severity effectively unresolved.
The guidelines were to specify a "range of sentences applicable to crimes" of a certain degree of seriousness,
the range of sentences of increased severity for defendants previously convicted of felonies or of crimes
involving a deadly weapon, and deviations from the range
of applicable sentences due to the presence of aggravating or mitigating circumstances. Sentences outside the
guidelines required the judge to provide a written statement of the reasons for the deviation.

Draft guidelines were to be published in the Pennsylvania Bulletin, followed by public hearings between 30
and 60 days later. The final (revised) guidelines were
to be simultaneously published in the Pennsylvania
Bulletin and submitted to the legislature; they would go
into effect 90 days (subsequently amended to 180 days)
after submission unless rejected in their entirety by a
concurrent resolution of the general assembly. In brief,
the Pennsylvania commission was expected to create guidelines covering a broader range of offenses with less
guidance than the Minnesota commission. And the Pennsylvania mandate passed on to the commission dilemmas that
the divided legislature had been unable to resolve.

INTERPRETING THE MANDATES AND CREATING GUIDELINES

Each commission's guidelines were conditioned by the
existing state traditions and political culture,[5] the
criminal justice system, the interest groups, and the
mandate given by the statute itself. The viability and
integrity of the guidelines and their acceptance by their
legislatures were largely dependent on the effectiveness
of each commission's membership, leadership, and staff in
interpreting and carrying out its mandate, addressing
policy choices, resolving differences, establishing and
carrying out a strategy for achieving its tasks, and
responding to the concerns of groups affected by the
guidelines.

Membership, Leadership, and Staff

The Minnesota Sentencing Guidelines Commission was to
consist of the chief justice of the state supreme court
or his designee and two judges appointed by the chief
justice, two citizen members, a prosecutor and a public
defender appointed by the governor, the state commissioner of corrections, and the chairman of the state
parole board.[6] No legislators were included on the
commission because the legislature had resolved the issue
of the distribution of discretionary authority to
establish sentencing policy, after an exhausting four-
year battle, by creating the commission. The exclusion
of legislators might have been politically disastrous,
but several members had sufficiently strong personal ties
to legislative leaders and experience in lobbying the
legislature to avoid problems. Minnesota has traditionally included private citizens representing the public
interest on policy-making bodies. Furthermore, the
citizen chair appointed by the governor proved to be
structurally freer to aggressively promote acceptance of
the guidelines than a commission member representing a
specific interest group would be. Membership for the
commissioner of corrections and the chairman of the
parole board was a concession to the agencies whose
activities were to be most directly affected by the
guidelines. The membership of the former had the largely
unintended virtues of ensuring the presence of a member
of the governor's cabinet on the commission, providing
access to the state house, and increasing the governor's
stake in the commission's product. This proved important
when the Republicans took over the governorship from the
Democrats prior to submission of the guidelines to the
legislature.

The Pennsylvania Commission on Sentencing was to
consist of four legislators; four judges appointed by the
chief justice; and a prosecutor, a public defender, and a
criminologist or law professor appointed by the
governor.[7] The exclusion of private citizens and
inclusion of legislators was in keeping with Pennsylvania's political tradition of limited citizen participation and of policy making as the province of professional
politicians. The exclusion of the commissioner of
corrections and chairman of the parole board (neither of
whom had actively pressed for membership) subsequently
limited the articulation of corrections system concerns
and commission access to the governor. This limited

access was particularly unfortunate, since the commission's three gubernatorial appointments had been made in the waning days of a Democratic administration that was succeeded by a new Republican governor.

The leadership, internal dynamics, and staff affected decision making in each commission and contributed to the content of and reaction to the guidelines. Minnesota's chair, Jan Smaby, a citizen member with strong political ties and experience as a lobbyist, acted as an advocate of the guidelines. She met with numerous groups around the state and with the press to explain and sell the guidelines idea. Her consultative leadership style, political skills, and willingness to make the guidelines a personal crusade contributed to their acceptance. She and other commission members viewed the task of designing guidelines as an exercise in public policy development requiring the active involvement of groups to be affected by that policy. Although the commission was not without internal tensions, it functioned harmoniously for the most part and permitted itself to be guided by its staff. The MSGC staff was able to articulate clearly the complexity of the issues the commission faced, to focus the commission's attention on the policy choices, to provide a bridge between the language and concepts of social science and law as it made research findings accessible to nonsocial scientist commission members, and to press the commission to make decisions.

In Pennsylvania the chair, Judge Richard Conaboy, was less involved than his Minnesota counterpart in the guideline development process and far more restrained in advocating their acceptance by interest groups and the legislature. His leadership style was probably affected by the combination of the pressure of other responsibilities when he was appointed to the federal bench in the middle of the guidelines development, his conception of the chairman's task as carrying out the legislature's mandate without "huckstering," and a sense of judicial propriety that restricted active advocacy on behalf of the guidelines. He did not treat the guidelines development as a political process, perhaps because his perspective was shaped by judicial experience of independent decision making without challenge or compromise rather than legislative experience of constant consultation with interest groups and frequent compromise. The commission's work was hindered by internal dissension, high absenteeism at meetings, weak leadership, personal animosities among members and toward staff, and resistance of members to reliance on data on past practice or on data projections indicating the implications of various policies for prison and jail populations as a guide to decision making. The staff had difficulty focusing commission discussion, articulating policy choices, presenting technical issues to members, and pressing the commission to make prompt decisions.

The Guidelines:
Construction Process and Their Content

In both states the construction of the guidelines proceeded in several overlapping steps. The commissions initially spent several months reading, discussing, and collecting data on existing sentencing practices in the state. Each commission adopted a single-guideline, grid-type format.

In each state ranking the severity of offenses was the first step in the actual construction process. Both commissions decided not to rely on existing statutory maximums and spent considerable time debating how offenses (felonies in Minnesota; all offenses in Pennsylvania) should be ranked. Minnesota divided all felonies into six generic groups for ranking within groups, then undertook an overall ranking. In Pennsylvania after initial difficulty the commission adopted a set of principles to guide the ranking exercise. In subsequent versions of the guidelines, the original ranks of many offenses were changed, but the ranking structure remained the same. Both commissions then divided the ranked crimes into 10 severity levels. The offense severity levels constituted one dimension of the grid.

The second step was creation of a criminal history index, which was the other dimension of the grid. The MSGC quickly agreed to include prior felonies and the offender's custody status at the time of the current offense. It agreed to exclude explicitly all social status factors (e.g., education, marital status, and employment) in sentencing felony offenders (although judges continue to be free to consider these factors in establishing nonimprisonment sentences). Two other aspects were matters of considerable debate in Minnesota: the treatment of juvenile record, and of prior misdemeanors and gross misdemeanors. After a public hearing on juvenile record, the commission compromised by allowing limited use of juvenile offenses in the criminal history index. Although the commission's research indicated that misdemeanors were not an explanatory factor in felony sentencing, the commission was uncomfortable with their exclusion from the index. It adopted a weighted system permitting these offenses limited influence in the criminal history score.

In the initial Pennsylvania guidelines the commission adopted a criminal history index in which prior offenses were weighted by seriousness.[8] This index included juvenile record but only for offenses with a seriousness score of 6 or above. These offenses were then scored like adult felonies. There was recurrent debate about treatment of social status factors, an important element in judicial decision making in Pennsylvania. The commission's original guidelines after several divided votes excluded social status factors from both the criminal history score and a list of aggravating and mitigating circumstances for which departures from the guidelines were justified, but the commission made no statement in the guidelines with respect to this exclusion. The third guidelines explicitly permit their consideration.

The third and fourth steps for the two commissions were drawing a disposition line and establishing sentence durations. When past practice failed to provide a clear pattern on which to base a disposition line with which commission members were comfortable, the MSGC staff began exploring the implications of using various philosophical models as guides. They drew four disposition lines, labeled "just deserts," "modified just deserts," "incapacitation," and "modified incapacitation,"[9] and tested the implications of each line with respect to prison capacity. The labeling clarified the choices and facilitated decision making. The commission rejected the just deserts line because it would have overcrowded prisons and the two incapacitation lines on philosophical grounds. It readily adopted the modified just deserts approach, emphasizing the current offense seriousness but giving some weight to the offender's prior record (which was more influential in existing sentencing decisions) as the basis for dispositions; in establishing sentence durations assigned to each cell of the guidelines grid the commission adopted a modified incapacitation model. When the commission subsequently tested its grid with respect to projected prison population, they found that the modified just deserts disposition line and sentence durations together would result in average annual prison

populations at capacity with no margin for fluctuation;
the MSGC reluctantly agreed to a 10 percent decrease in
all sentence durations rather than modify the disposition
line to keep policy within the constraints of existing
prison resources.

Pennsylvania, too, designed its disposition line and
sentence durations on a modified just deserts model. In
that state, however, such a policy continued rather than
altered prevailing practice. In constructing its grid,
which included felonies and misdemeanors, the PCS adopted
two disposition lines. One, the prison line, separated
offenders recommended for prison sentences from others.
The other, the jail line, separated recommended jail
sentences from recommended nonincarcerative sentences.

In dealing with sentences that deviate from the
guidelines, the MSGC adopted a nonexclusive (but relatively limited) list of aggravating and mitigating
circumstances, established a high legal standard for
invoking these circumstances ("substantial and compelling
reasons"), and left the judge free to determine the
extent of deviation when departing from the presumptive
sentence in the appropriate guideline grid cell.

In Pennsylvania the commission's first and second
guidelines included exclusive lists of aggravating and
mitigating circumstances and permitted judges to invoke
them without being considered outside the guidelines. In
determining such a sentence, the judge was to move one
cell to the right or left of the applicable guideline
sentence cell (or one cell up or down at the far right or
left of the grid). In essence this allowed an increase
or decrease of a sentence by up to 6 months if an
aggravating or mitigating circumstance warranted it.
Judges could also go outside the guidelines if an
additional "compelling reason" were found for doing so.
In the third set of guidelines the list of aggravating
and mitigating circumstances was eliminated, permitting
judges to consider social status factors in sentencing.
Sentencing ranges for offenses with aggravating and
mitigating circumstances were widened, and these ranges
were built into the guidelines chart for each offense
seriousness and offender history combination. In
addition, departures from the guidelines were allowed,
unfettered by any specified legal standard, although
judges were still required to state in writing the
reasons for departure.

As a final step in designing the guidelines, each
commission considered related policy questions. These

included handling convictions for attempted crimes,
consecutive and concurrent sentences, appeals of sentences, and plea negotiations. Each commission recognized that the effect of punishment standards depends
crucially on the actions of system officials, particularly prosecutors, and that the guidelines would increase
the prosecutors' discretion through control of charging
and plea negotiation decisions. But both commissions
decided not to attempt to limit prosecutorial discretion
or to structure plea negotiation until the guidelines had
been implemented and the behavior of prosecutors could be
studied. The MSGC explicitly considered and rejected
"real offense" sentencing and explicit sentence discounts
for guilty pleas; the Pennsylvania Commission considered
the effect of plea bargaining more generally and concluded that there was little the commission could do to
limit it.

Key Elements in Designing the Guidelines

Minnesota

In interpreting the legislative mandate and developing
guidelines, three interlocking elements were the keys to
the outcome of the Minnesota commission's work: interpretation of the law as imposing an absolute limit on
prison populations; research and its uses in policy
development; and a strategy of public involvement. The
commission was convinced early by staff arguments
charting an overall strategy that the guidelines should
represent both a change from the past sentencing policy
and a new approach to the way guidelines were developed.
The Minnesota commission rejected the notion that its
task was simply to model and systematize past practice
and abandoned the Albany descriptive guidelines approach
used in the development of the Minnesota parole guidelines.[10] It adopted instead a more actively policy-
oriented approach.[11]

The interpretation of the legislative mandate to
"consider . . . correctional resources" as an absolute
limit was central to the commission's work for several
reasons. First, it facilitated the development of a
viable research methodology which, once adopted, reinforced the need to consider the population constraint.
If the guidelines were to link sentencing policy with
future prison population by maintaining that population

at the current capacity level or below it, data on
existing practice had to be used to project the consequences for prison populations of different sentencing
policies, and those outcomes had to be predictable. The
need for predictability reinforced the necessity of
designing presumptive guidelines with a sharply limited
range of variation within each cell of the grid. Second,
the interpretation of the legislative mandate as an
absolute limit on prison population imposed self-
discipline on the commission. Its task became the
allocation of limited prison space among the universe of
potential occupants. Third, this interpretation forced
principled, responsible decisions within the bounds of
discourse established by the commission and put interest
groups lobbying the commission in the position of having
to argue on the commission's terms, namely, which types
of offenders most merited imprisonment rather than simply
calling for the imprisonment of more offenders. Several
commission members were initially uncomfortable with what
they viewed as a pragmatic approach to establishing
policy, but they gradually embraced the population
limit. When the prosecutor and conservative commissioner
of corrections both publicly supported the population
constraint (which the commission members did not hesitate
to point out grew from the language of the statute), the
interest group representatives were forced to argue
according to the commission's rules and to realize the
need for compromise.

The MSGC's allocation policy was only feasible,
however, if it was accompanied by accurate estimates of
the effects on the prison population of various policies
and the support of the interest groups that would be
affected by the guidelines.

The MSGC's projection of prison populations required
research consisting of three components: a dispositional
study, a durational study, and a simulation or population
projection model to predict the impact of various
potential policy options under consideration on state and
local corrections facilities. Data from the dispositional and durational studies indicated that the most
significant factors in judges' decisions regarding
imprisonment were the seriousness of the current offense
and the offender's criminal history. The most influential criminal history items were the number of prior
felony convictions, followed by whether the offender was
on probation or parole at the time of the current
offense, and the extent and severity of the juvenile

record. Seriousness of the current offense and criminal
history were also strongly associated with parole board
decisions on duration of prison terms. Consideration of
other factors contributing to sentence variation indicated the presence of modest regional differences (but
not the substantial difference in urban and rural
sentencing severity that had been anticipated), the
absence of systematic bias by race and gender, and the
association of employment but of no other social status
factors with sentencing in Minnesota. These data were
then used in an innovative way. Rather than merely
building a model of sentencing behavior that mirrored the
past, the commission developed a population projection
model that, using case data from the durational and
dispositional studies, could simulate the 5-year population effects of various sentencing policies and commission decisions. Policies that would lead to prison
overcrowding were rejected; those that were feasible were
considered, and choices were made on the basis of both
past practice and the values of commission members and
the interest groups they represented.

The third essential element was a broad and successful
campaign of constituency building. The commission sought
to develop interest group participation as a way of
gaining support and accommodating potential opponents.
The commission held a series of initial regional public
meetings to build interest in the guidelines. The staff
and members made numerous presentations, established
liaison with groups and agencies regarded as important,
and established good relations with the press, ensuring
favorable publicity. Members kept in frequent contact
with the constituent groups they "represented" on the
commission, including judges, prosecutors, the defense
bar, the corrections bureaucracy, and public interest
groups (blacks, Indians, and women in particular). By
the time the guidelines were developed, no group could
realistically protest that it had not had an opportunity
to make an input and had not won some concessions.

This strategy succeeded because it was conducted
effectively and because the preconditions for success
were present. First, Minnesota's opinion leaders
generally agreed that the goal was to establish determinate sentences while maintaining existing prison
population levels. Commission members shared this goal.
This permitted discussion to revolve around the means to
achieve that end. Second, the members and particularly
the chair were willing to take the time to attend

countless meetings and make clear and convincing presentations. Third, the criminal justice community was small enough to be reached and induced to participate in the process on a sustained basis. Whereas such a participatory process might have highlighted irresolvable differences had they existed, in Minnesota it made clear the necessity of compromises in allocating prison space once the commission's ground rules were established and contributed to open negotiation among commission members at commission meetings that were attended by interest group representatives. In the end all groups made a contribution and gained some concessions. The guidelines became their product, too. Although some were unenthusiastic, each agreed not to be the first group to upset the edifice that had been delicately constructed.

Pennsylvania

The Pennsylvania commission had a nearly impossible political task--creating guidelines that would simultaneously hold prison population constant, reduce disparity, and limit judicial discretion--given its mandate and the existing sentencing system, regional disparity, and extensive judicial discretion. In considering the prison population/severity level question, the Pennsylvania commission had to face the dilemma that the legislature had failed to resolve. Commission members did not want to create guidelines that would overcrowd prisons or be impossible to implement; at the same time, many supporters of the statute expected the guidelines to increase sentence severity, the certainty of punishment, and, by implication, the prison population. Without a legislative mandate to consider prison capacity, and concerned about the political consequences of adopting a policy of limited, selective increases in sentence severity, the commission assumed a "principled" stance in determining "appropriate sentences." They rejected a formal limit on the number of offenders to be incarcerated based on prison capacity. Instead they agreed to remain publicly silent but to informally consider prison capacity in designing the guidelines. The first guidelines would have resulted in a slight decrease in prison populations but an increase of 16.3 percent in the number of months to be served by incarcerated inmates according to the PSC's projections.[12] The absence of a clear policy limiting prison populations

to existing capacity, however, left the commission
vulnerable to the terrific pressure to increase sentence
severity, to which it ultimately succumbed in the second
and third guidelines. According to the commission's
projections the second guidelines would have increased by
61.3 percent the number of months of incarceration to be
served and also would have increased the proportion of
offenders to be incarcerated. Yet these guidelines
failed to be severe enough. And since these guidelines
could not have been implemented given existing prison
space and resources, moderates also opposed them. The
severity/population dilemma was resolved by a legislative
resolution calling on the commission to revise the
guidelines, by further increasing sentence severity and
widening the ranges of judicial discretion. This meant
that the likely effect of the guidelines would be much
more limited. By the time the third guidelines were
formulated, their function had become largely symbolic:
to affirm the desirability of statewide policy limiting
judicial discretion, to serve as a common starting point
in determining minimum sentences, and to provide the
basis for the appellate review of sentences, from which
narrower standards may gradually develop. In the third
round of guidelines development, several commission
members continued to express concern about the impact of
the guidelines on the prison population. But these
members were overruled by those who viewed their primary
goal as the creation of guidelines acceptable to the
legislature, regardless of their effect on the prison
system.

An important part of the political dilemma, as the
commission's research on past practice made painfully
clear, grew from extensive regional disparity. The PCS
collected and analyzed data on sentencing dispositions
and durations pronounced by judges based on a sample of
cases disposed of in 1977.[13] Ultimately the study
proved to be a two-edged sword. It indicated the extent
of disparity across the state and highlighted the
difficulty to be encountered in significantly reducing
it. One finding overshadowed all others: the extent of
regional disparity. Statewide, 38.9 percent of all
offenders in 1977 were incarcerated. But in Philadelphia
and Allegheny (Pittsburgh) Counties, which have the
highest crime rates and the highest proportion of violent
crimes, only 28.5 and 23.8 percent of the convicted
offenders, respectively, were incarcerated. The suburban
incarceration rate was 44.1 percent, that in small

cities/urban counties was 47.4, and in rural areas 53.9 percent. Sentences in Philadelphia and Pittsburgh were also shorter for similar offenses, particularly misdemeanors.

Although the PCS developed a projection methodology, it was less accurate than that of the MSGC. First, the wide ranges in the PCS guidelines and the unpredictable compliance rates in jurisdictions with varied sentencing practices meant that projections rested on uncertain assumptions. Second, the projection model produced estimates of changes in incarceration rates and sentence lengths resulting from various sentencing policies that were being considered but did not provide for a simulation of changes in the prison population over several years. The PCS projection technology could not provide quick feedback on the likely consequences of the policies that were being considered during a commission meeting, but such data were not viewed as necessary by commission members, since the policy to be embodied in the guidelines was not closely linked to or limited by prison capacity. The absence of data on actual sentence durations and indications of changes in sentencing patterns between 1977 and 1980 also undermined confidence in the accuracy of projections.

The projections of the impact of the guidelines on prisoner populations based on the 1977 data made by the PCS provided ammunition for opponents of the guidelines. As indicated in Table 6-2, according to the commission's calculations the first set of guidelines would have decreased the total percentage of offenders to be incarcerated from 38.6 to 36 percent, assuming 100 percent compliance and the use of probation in cells with a range of 0-2 months in Philadelphia and Allegheny Counties. But the proportion of offenders that would be incarcerated varied widely by region; the proportion of Philadelphia and Pittsburgh offenders to be incarcerated would increase substantially, and the proportion to be incarcerated from elsewhere in the state would fall.

When judges and prosecutors around the state vehemently protested the leniency of guidelines that would have reduced sentence severity in their jurisdictions, the commission revised the guidelines prior to submitting them to the legislature in January 1981. Even the second guidelines, however, would have caused a substantial shift in prison populations. Many more offenders from Philadelphia and Pittsburgh would be incarcerated and, as indicated in Table 6-3, would serve substantially longer

TABLE 6-2   Estimated Changes in Incarceration Rates, 1977
Data Compared With October 1980 Guidelines (assumes 100
percent compliance with guidelines and no aggravating or
mitigating circumstances)

	Percent "In"[a] Less than 12 Months		Percent "In" 12 Months or More		Total Percent "In"	
	1977 Data	Proposed Guidelines	1977 Data	Proposed Guidelines	1977 Data	Proposed Guidelines
Philadelphia County	13.5	22.2	15.0	22.5	28.5	44.7
Allegheny County	10.9	18.6	12.9	11.5	23.8	30.1
Suburban	29.0	26.8	15.1	8.3	44.1	35.1
Small cities/ urban counties	28.6	26.0	18.8	6.6	47.4	32.6
Rural	32.7	24.4	21.3	4.7	54.0	29.1
Total	22.2	23.8	16.7	12.2	38.9	36.0

[a]Assumes an alternative to incarceration sentence when the guidelines
sentence allows either incarceration of alternative in Philadelphia and
Allegheny Counties; all others give incarceration.

SOURCE: Unpublished data, Pennsylvania Commission on Sentencing.

terms, while fewer offenders from rural areas and
somewhat fewer from small cities and suburban areas would
be incarcerated, and the terms of small city and rural
offenders would be shortened. These guidelines were
therefore unacceptable. It was simply not politically
tolerable to reduce disparity by leveling sentences to
the mean; only guidelines that proposed bringing all
jurisdictions up to the level of the most severe could
pass political muster.

Such guidelines emerged from the commission in October
1981 and were submitted to the legislature in January
1982. According to the commission's calculations, based
on a new study of sentencing in Pennsylvania in 1980
(which indicated an increase in sentence severity between
1977 and 1980), the guidelines would increase sentence
severity for felony convictions across the state, by
about the same amount as a pending mandatory minimum
sentencing bill that was subsequently adopted (see Table
6-4).

Pennsylvania, unlike Minnesota, initially had no
strategy of public involvement in guidelines development.
Legislators, divided and ambivalent about the level of
severity and how much to limit judicial discretion, had
passed the problem to the commission. Commission members

TABLE 6-3 Estimated Percentage Changes in Inmate Months, 1977 Compared with First (October 1980) and Second (January 1981) Guidelines

	Percentage Change Less than 12 Months		Percentage Change 12 Months or More		Percentage Change Total Inmate Months	
	October 1980 Guidelines[a]	January 1981 Guidelines[b]	October 1980 Guidelines	January 1981 Guidelines	October 1980 Guidelines	January 1981 Guidelines
Philadelphia County	+57.2	+111.9	+115.3	+215.2	+102.4	+204.9
Allegheny County	+73.1	+158.6	+17.1	+98.7	+29.3	+117.5
Suburban	+17.9	+16.6	-4.9	+18.3	+2.9	+17.7
Small cities/ urban counties	-7.6	-5.0	-35.6	-22.5	-27.1	-17.2
Rural	-26.1	-8.2	-54.2	-44.1	-46.2	-33.8
Total	+14.4	+37.8	+17.0	+68.8	+16.3	+61.1

[a]Assumes Philadelphia and Allegheny Counties comply with minimum of range, others with maximum, and no aggravating or mitigating circumstances. If minimum guideline sentence is an incarceration range beginning with zero, then for Philadelphia and Allegheny Counties incarceration length assigned is 1 month.

[b]When the guidelines authorize either incarceration or an alternative to incarceration, only those cases that received incarceration sentences are assumed to receive incarceration sentences under the guidelines. In these cases the minimum of the guidelines range is assumed to be 1 month.

SOURCE: Unpublished data, Pennsylvania Commission on Sentencing.

TABLE 6-4 Projected Percentage Changes in Total Months of Confinement Sentenced, Third Guidelines (October 1981) and Proposed Mandatory Minimum Sentencing Bill Compared with 1980 Sentences)

Sentencing Option	Philadelphia County[a]	Allegheny County[b]	Others[c]
Mandatory bill only	+109	+156	+39
Guidelines only (12 months for deadly weapon)	+95	+102	+28
Guidelines only (24 months for deadly weapon)	+128	+155	+50
Mandatory plus guidelines (12 months for deadly weapon)	+169	+216	+60
Mandatory plus guidelines (24 months for deadly weapon)	+188	+241	+73

[a]All aggravated assault (felony II and misdemeanor I), burglary, murder III, rape, robbery (felony I, II, and III), voluntary manslaughter.

[b]All aggravated assault (felony II and misdemeanor I), burglary, rape, robbery (felony I, II, and III), and firearms (misdemeanor I).

[c]All felonies (except theft and drug offenses), weapon misdemeanors, and misdemeanor Is against the person. The counties in this sample are: Beaver, Berks, Blair, Cambria, Centre, Crawford, Cumberland, Dauphin, Delaware, Indiana, Lawrence, Lehigh, Luzerne, Lycoming, Montgomery, Northampton, Perry, Schuylkill, Warren, and Washington.

SOURCE: Unpublished data, Pennsylvania Commission on Sentencing.

gradually hammered out a set of compromises in developing the draft guidelines without public input. They informally agreed that the guidelines would provide presumptive sentences within relatively narrow ranges, that the severity of the punishment for some offenses against persons would increase but that punishment for most offenses would be close to the statewide mean, and that prison populations would not substantially increase. The chair did not view constituency building as necessary; several members lacked the time or interest in making the effort that would have been required. Involving interest groups, which themselves were often divided by regional differences, in the development process would have required an enormous effort in such a populous state with several urban centers. Moreover, the interest groups had conflicting goals. The more presumptive the guidelines, the more they satisfied prosecutors and alienated judges. An explicit statewide policy increasing both the proportion of person offenders to be incarcerated and their sentence lengths while holding the prison population constant meant a radical increase in the number of offenders from Philadelphia and Pittsburgh in state prisons and a "bumping" of property offenders from suburban and rural counties into the already overcrowded urban jails. Given regional jealousies and the substantial increase in the costs to some counties that such a change implied,[14] it is doubtful that even an aggressive campaign to develop support and openly discuss these issues would have resulted in compromise or agreement on meaningful sentencing guidelines. But the absence of involvement of many groups prior to the presentation of the guidelines at the October 1980 public hearings contributed to the predictable reaction they provoked: opposition from all quarters. The changes incorporated in the January 1981 guidelines--removal of language implying that the guidelines were presumptive, increases in offense severity scoring for crimes involving a firearm, alteration in offender history scoring, and increases in the range and overall severity of guideline sentences in many cells-- also failed to satisfy critics.

As a result, the commission's legislative strategy backfired. It attempted to lie low, anticipating that the guidelines would be overlooked by a uninterested public and legislature, and relied on the legislative members of the commission to prevent a resolution of rejection from emerging from the judiciary committees onto the floor for a vote. When a moderate house member announced plans to submit a resolution to reject the guidelines, the house leadership pressed it through committee and onto the floor with uncharacteristic speed to prevent the guidelines from going into effect after 90 days. There simply was no time for discussion and education of legislators. Furthermore, commission members put little pressure on legislative leaders to prevent rejection, while there was a strong negative reaction to the guidelines from legislators who reported opposition from their constituents. The commission salvaged what could be saved: the guidelines concept. Representative Hagarty was persuaded to phrase the resolution so that it rejected the specific guidelines before the legislature, retained the commission, and called on it to revise and resubmit the guidelines in 6 months.

When the third guidelines came before the legislature
they aroused little opposition because their meaning and
probable impact had changed. First, a mandatory minimum
law, supported by both the Republican governor and his
most visible Democratic challengers, had been adopted by
the legislature. Guidelines were no longer viewed by
many legislators as the less desirable alternative to
mandatory minimums; they could be regarded as a supplementary crime-fighting measure. Second, the commission had addressed specific objections to the earlier
guidelines. Prosecutors could no longer credibly
complain of their leniency, nor judges of being fet-
tered. Technical ambiguities and criticisms that the
guidelines were unintelligible and complex had been dealt
with. The previously vocal opponents could only oppose
the guidelines on principle, and the legislators who
voted for the majority resolution were on record as
having supported them in principle. Criticisms from city
and county government officials, faced with likely
increases in jail overcrowding and costs, might have
surfaced, but the law-and-order atmosphere in Pennsylvania made it politically too dangerous for public
officials to suggest that the guidelines were too severe
and costly. In addition, the commission, during both the
redrafting and legislative consideration period, adopted
a much more energetic constituency-building strategy.
The new chair, Anthony Scirica, and a new district
attorney appointed to the commission established close
contact with the trial judges' and district attorneys'
organizations. Scirica, an experienced and respected
former legislator, also contacted and won the support of
legislative leaders and of many individual legislators
formerly opposed to the guidelines. Although there was
little enthusiasm for the guidelines, their apparent
acceptance by the legislative leadership led isolated
opponents to conserve their political capital and avoid a
losing battle over a measure likely to have limited
impact.

THE POLITICS OF GUIDELINE DEVELOPMENT:
THE ROLE OF INTEREST GROUPS

Both the Minnesota and the Pennsylvania guidelines
proposed changes in existing policies and practices. The
MSGC's guidelines were accepted because the changes they
introduced were principled and limited in scope, because

they left important areas of discretion untouched, and because they gave more than they took from virtually all interest groups affected by them. They altered existing practice by reducing the number of chronic property offenders who would be imprisoned and replaced them with more person offenders, including first time offenders. This represented a shift from an incapacitation policy to a just deserts policy, caused a small decrease in the number of rural offenders who would go to state prison, and changed the type but not the number of offenders from the Twin Cities. The commission highlighted the change in principle underlying imprisonment, downplayed the regional redistribution of prisoners, and added a number of concessions that had both popular appeal and, more important, won the support of the primary interest groups.

The county attorneys went along with the guidelines, convinced that they had won concessions, including the right of the state to appeal a sentence, the inclusion of consideration of the juvenile record and the elimination of social status factors (often used to mitigate sentences) from consideration in sentencing, and greater certainty of imprisonment of those offenders the county attorneys most wanted to imprison. The public defenders came around when they were convinced that they had limited the effects of prior misdemeanors and juvenile adjudications on criminal history scores and that their clients would gain by a policy of holding prison populations constant. The judges were divided, and so were neutralized as an important potential source of opposition. While occasional protests surfaced that judges would become robots, the guidelines shifted rather than diminished judicial discretion by limiting it with respect to dispositions while giving the judges structured authority to determine the actual duration of prison terms, which formerly had been set by the parole board. Community Corrections Act counties were given a financial incentive to support the guidelines because the guidelines eliminated the rationale for the charge to the county for the imprisonment of any offender sentenced according to the guidelines.[15] The reaction of corrections personnel was mixed. Probation officers were concerned about being made responsible for providing accurate criminal history information, but leaders in the Department of Corrections were pleased with a policy that ensured a limited and predictable prison population and increased their leverage over prisoners by a provision that increased good time. Indian and black groups, while

suspicious of the guidelines, felt they gained by the
elimination of social status factors from consideration.
Feminist groups were pleased with the increased severity
of the recommended sentences for sexual offenders. When
the guidelines were submitted to the legislature, all
organized opposition had been neutralized and key
legislators went along with what otherwise was likely to
have been a controversial policy.

In Pennsylvania the initial guidelines would have
reduced disparity; held prison populations near current
levels; increased the likelihood of imprisonment for
those convicted of offenses against persons; reduced the
number of offenders from small cities, suburban, and
rural areas to be incarcerated; and forced judges to
deviate from the guidelines to jail chronic minor
offenders. Such a proposal, while arguably equitable and
ostensibly responsive to the legislative mandate, was
politically unpalatable. The guidelines made mandatory
minimum sentences look less inhibiting to judges, more
certain to prosecutors, more reasoned to corrections
administrators, and less costly to county government
officials. When the implications of the guideline
changes to reduce regional disparity became apparent,
discussion of disparity virtually disappeared; each
county's unique problems gained attention, and sentencing
uniformity became a pejorative term.

In what proved to be a futile attempt to meet mounting
criticism, the commission modified the initial guidelines. The second guidelines, however, would have
increased prison populations but reduced sentence
severity for rural, suburban, and small-town property
offenders; continued to restrict judicial discretion; and
failed to satisfy the Philadelphia district attorney's
demand for certainty or severity in treating offenders
convicted of violent offenses. The changes undermined
the integrity of the guidelines and proposed an irrespon-
sible policy to the legislature but salvaged the guidelines concept through legislative deferral and revision.
The third guidelines made no pretense of trying to
resolve the disparity, discretion, and severity dilemma
that the legislature had passed to the commission. These
guidelines are designed to increase sentence severity
across the state but substantially widen the sentencing
ranges within the guidelines, so that judicial discretion
is hardly affected. For example, for an offender with
one prior felony conviction for burglary who is convicted
of robbery threatening serious bodily injury, the range

within the guidelines extends from 12 months, when a mitigated sentence is recommended, to 42 months, when there is an aggravating circumstance, to 66 months when a 24-month "enhancement" for use of a deadly weapon is proved. Furthermore, if several offenses are charged and proved the court has wide discretion in determining whether to impose consecutive or concurrent sentences, widening the possible range of time to be served. In contrast, conviction for a similar robbery with one prior burglary conviction in Minnesota results in a guideline sentence of 30-34 months; any aggravating or mitigating circumstance permits the judge to deviate from the guidelines only if there are "substantial and compelling reasons" for doing so.

The likely consequence of the Pennsylvania guidelines is a shift from sentence to charge bargaining, limited change in current sentencing practices, some increase in the length of prison terms, and little reduction in the vast regional disparity. Philadelphia and Pittsburgh judges are likely to find mitigating circumstances in a substantial number of cases, and the district attorneys offices are likely to adopt charge bargaining practices in which substantial discounts for guilty pleas circumvent the guidelines to avoid trials and move cases through the courts. In the rest of the state, symbolically severe sentences will be given in the few notorious serious offenses, and sentencing will probably continue much as before. Even a modest level of compliance with the normal guidelines sentences, however, would result in increased prison and jail populations. Although the legislature has approved a new bond issue to increase prison capacity, short-term increases in prison populations are likely to necessitate more case dismissals, charge reductions, and sentences in the mitigated range or below the guidelines—or the adoption of an emergency early release mechanism to reduce prison overcrowding.

CONCLUSION

Each commission met the real expectations of the legislature that created it. In Minnesota there was a consensus favoring presumptive sentences for felonies, elimination of the parole board, and reduction of existing disparities through greater certainty of punishment of certain offender types without overall increases in severity or in prison populations. The commission had a limited mandate, which it fulfilled by providing guidelines with a principled and feasible policy; interest groups that participated in creating the guidelines gained more than they lost in accepting them. In Pennsylvania the commission failed initially to create politically acceptable guildelines and failed, too, to maintain its principled stance on prison populations. But the guidelines commission may have achieved a latent goal of the Pennsylvania legislature. The commission bought time and subsequently heightened awareness of the dilemmas and policy choices involved in simultaneously seeking to reduce disparity, increase severity, and hold down prison populations and costs. When the choice was finally clear, the legislature made a symbolic gesture toward disparity reduction by adopting guidelines with broad ranges and made a real commitment to increased severity and the associated costs of an expansion in prison capacity. Rather than adopting either guidelines or mandatory minimums, it chose both.

The contrasting outcomes in the development of sentencing guidelines in the two states caution against generalizing from the experience of a single state. Other jurisdictions considering adopting a guidelines approach cannot simply attempt to duplicate the Minnesota commission's experience. Its success rests on that state's small and homogeneous population, its political traditions of moderation in punishment and a relatively centralized authority, the legislature's consensus not to increase severity in introducing sentencing reform, the commission's willingness to design a system and to convince interest groups that the constraints imposed by such a system would not be disruptive, the avoidance of politicization of sentencing issues, and the redistribution of authority such that the only group that clearly lost was the parole board, which had limited political clout. In contrast, the Pennsylvania commission gave way under the pressure of law-and-order politics, traditions of localism, a lack of legislative agreement on goals and the means to achieve them, and vested interests in preserving the existing distribution of authority in the criminal justice system. In the face of this organized opposition the Pennsylvania commission repudiated the principled initial guidelines, replacing them with guidelines proposals that were progressively more severe and less likely to effect changes in either the exercise of discretion or the resulting disparity in sentencing across the state.

The outcome of efforts to alter sentencing practices are likely to depend on the unique combination of forces, factors, and existing practices present in a jurisdiction. But the experiences of the two states in this study also suggest that the principal factors shaping the outcome of efforts to change the sentencing system in any jurisdiction are similar. These include the political climate; the existing distribution of authority; the level of consensus in the legislature about the nature of the desired change and the expression of this consensus in a legislative mandate; the goals and influence of interest groups in bringing about change; and, in the case of sentencing guidelines, the skills of the commission both in creating a rational, coherent, feasible, and equitable system and in enlisting the support of the most powerful interest groups affected by the change.

This study also raises questions about the magnitude, impact, permanence, and broader implications of the changes that have been adopted with sentencing guidelines. The Pennsylvania statute creating the guidelines commission did not alter sentencing practices in any important ways. The statute retained judicially determined minimum and maximum sentences as well as release decisions determined by the parole authority. The guidelines do not go very far in structuring the sentencing decisions to be made by court and parole officials: They leave enormous judicial discretion and increase without seeking to restrain the authority of the prosecutor. While the guidelines are based on a just deserts philosophy, the legislature did not explicitly alter the goals of punishment, nor were these goals an important factor in the commission's deliberations. Thus determinacy has not come to Pennsylvania either in theory or practice, and the guidelines are likely to have limited impact on either case processing or sentence outcomes.

Minnesota appears to have adopted a real change. From a system resting on indeterminate sentences and on rehabilitative and utilitarian goals, it moved to one in which punishments of determinate length are announced at the time of sentencing and are based on a just deserts model. Several caveats are still necessary. First, there are several avenues for reintroducing utilitarian considerations in sentencing and altering sentence lengths. The retention of a good-time provision permits corrections officials to increase time to be served by up to one-half. The new system greatly increases the influence of prosecutors, whose discretion is not regulated by the guidelines. How prosecutors will affect sentencing outcomes by their charging and plea negotiation practices, the effectiveness of the commission's effort to eliminate consideration of offender characteristics, and the extent to which similar offenders will actually receive like sanctions--particularly the 80 percent of the felons who are not imprisoned--are empirical questions remaining to be answered. In Minnesota the reforms were shaped so as to be consistent with the perspectives and interests of the central criminal justice agencies and strengthen statewide control of the criminal justice system.

Second, determinate systems are unstable. Indeterminate sentencing systems permit legislative increases in punitiveness by raising maximum sentences in response to public pressure without altering the sentences actually given out. But under a policy of determinacy the legislature can, and the California experience indicates that the legislature will, under public pressure, increase sentence severity without providing safety valves for increased prison populations. Guidelines represent an uneasy intermediate position. As the Pennsylvania experience demonstrates, the sentencing guideline commission is also vulnerable to public pressures it may not be able to withstand. In Minnesota the guidelines now face pressures from four sources that potentially threaten their survival: the legislature; the judiciary; the governor; and the commission itself. The legislature may pass mandatory minimum sentencing bills or other legislation that undermines the balance between prison capacity and population. Thus far it has not done so, and bipartisan legislative support for the guidelines appears to have grown. The judiciary may deviate consistently in the direction of greater severity, increasing population pressure on the prisons or, alternatively, sentence at or below the guidelines in several cases that lead to public outcry over leniency that threatens the existing system. Departures have thus far been limited and publicly explained when they have occurred. The governor may alter the commission by appointing new members not committed to the current guidelines to replace members whose terms have expired. All members' terms had expired in May 1982, and the governor had five appointments to make, including the chair.[16] How the commission will function with a new chair and four new members is not clear. And the commission may alter the guidelines, may not resist pressure from groups demanding increased severity for particular types of offenders, and may fail to maintain its legislative support.

Finally, the development of sentencing guidelines must be considered in light of the current movement to change sentencing structures and the questions surrounding it. These include the relative contributions of ideology and of group interests in changing criminal justice system policies and practices; the relationship of recent sentencing reform efforts across the United States to broader political, social, and economic changes occurring in this nation; and an explanation of the movement toward determinacy at this time. Such a perspective on the sentencing reform movement and its outcomes, however, requires ". . . a theory about the forces moving persons to change the institutions that govern them" (Messinger and Johnson 1978:57) that remains to be developed.

NOTES

1. In April 1981 Washington became the third state to pass a statute creating a sentencing commission. Its guidelines were to be submitted to the legislature by September 1, 1982.

2. The data for this study come from a review of written materials produced by each commission, public documents related to the guidelines, and from unstructured interviews with participants in the legislative and guidelines construction processes and representatives of various concerned interest groups. Written materials include sentencing reform bills submitted to the Minnesota and Pennsylvania legislatures and the statutes creating the commissions in each state ((1978, Nov. 26 P.L. 1316 No. 319 Sec. 3) and (18 Pa.C.S.A. Sec. 1381)); minutes of all meetings of both commissions up to submission of the guidelines that subsequently went into effect to each legislature; staff concept papers and other materials prepared for presentation at commission meetings; written testimony presented at public hearings of the Pennsylvania Commission on Sentencing on December 2, 1980, in Scranton, December 8, 1980, in Pittsburgh, December 10, 1980, in Harrisburg, December 11-12, 1980, in Philadelphia, November 16, 1981, in Harrisburg, November 18, 1981, in Pittsburgh, and November 20, 1981, in Philadelphia; and the Pennsylvania commission's draft

and final guidelines published on October 25, 1980 (10
PA. ADMIN. BULL. 4181 (1980)), January 24, 1981 (11 PA.
ADMIN. BULL. 463 (1981)), October 17, 1981 (11 PA. ADMIN.
BULL. 3597 (1981)), and January 23, 1982 (12 PA. ADMIN.
BULL. 431 (1982)); the Minnesota Sentencing Guidelines
Commission's Report to the Legislature of January 1, 1980
[hereinafter cited as Minnesota Guidelines Report]; and
the Minnesota sentencing guidelines and commentary (rev.
ed. 1981).

Interviews were conducted in Minneapolis and Saint
Paul on March 6-7 and May 11-13, 1981, with legislative
leaders and former staff, and with Chairperson Jan Smaby,
members and former members, and Dale Parent, Director,
and Kay Knapp, Research Director, of the Minnesota
Sentencing Guidelines Commission. Interviews were
conducted in Pennsylvania between March and May 1981 with
all members of the original commission except Robert
Colville, with several legislators and staff members,
with representatives of the Pennsylvania Prison Society,
Women Against Rape, the District Attorneys' Association,
with the commissioner of corrections, and with John
Kramer, Executive Director, and Robin Lubitz, Research
Director, of the Pennsylvania Commission on Sentencing.
In March 1982 additional interviews were conducted with
the new chairman, Anthony Scirica, commission members
Terrence McVerry and Frank Hazel, and John Kramer.
Interviews were unstructured and ranged from half an hour
to several hours in length.

3. In drafting a major clause had inadvertently been
omitted from the bill. It is unclear whether this clause
could have been included as a technical revision by the
house. This omission was the justification for the veto.

4. A decision regarding the continued existence of the
parole board was deferred. The legislature subsequently
voted to abolish the parole board as of July 1, 1982.

5. Minnesota and Pennsylvania have distinctive and
contrasting political cultures and traditions, shaped by
different historical circumstances. A political culture
is defined as "the particular orientation to political
action in which each political system is embedded"
(Elazar, 1972:85). In analyzing the political cultures
of states in terms of the behavior permitted and expected
of public officials, the kinds of people involved in
government and politics, and the manner in which govern-

ment is practiced, Elazar identifies three ideal types of political cultures: the individualistic, the moralistic, and the traditionalistic. Minnesota typifies the moralistic political culture and Pennsylvania the individualistic.

The moralistic political culture is characterized by a view of government as a means of achieving the good community through positive political action; the belief that politics is a responsibility of citizens; a strong merit system that keeps politics "clean"; and political parties that are weak, open, issue-oriented, and dominated by middle-class activitists who view participation as public service. Internal cohesion often rests on an ethnically homogeneous population. In the individualistic political culture, government is viewed principally as a means of responding to the competing demands of the interest groups and individuals it serves; the civil service is viewed with suspicion because it limits political patronage, which greases the wheels of government; politics is regarded as the business of professionals, and public participation is limited; parties operate like businesses, demanding strong loyalty and cohesiveness and distributing the tangible rewards of power to members; elections are rarely issue-oriented; and elected officials tend to act as brokers for private interests in an ethnically and regionally diverse society with a tradition of local government.

6. The judicial members included George Scott, associate justice of the supreme court; Douglas Amdahl, chief judge of the district court (Hennepin County, including Minneapolis), who is now chief justice of the supreme court; and Russell Olson, of the third district. The governor's appointments included Jan Smaby, a Comunity Corrections Act administrator for Hennepin County; Barbara Andrus, a black community activist; Steve Rathke, a young prosecutor from Crow Wing County and a political activist with experience as a senate staff member; and William Falvey, the public defender of Ramsey County (St. Paul). The commissioner of corrections, Ken Schoen, and the chairman of the parole board, Richard Mulcrone, both of whom had taken an active role in shaping the legislation, both left their positions on the commission by the end of 1978. They were replaced by Jack Young and Les Green, respectively.

7. The four judicial members of the Pennsylvania commission included Richard Conaboy of Lackawanna County (Scranton), who had been an active supporter of the guidelines approach as president of the Pennsylvania Joint Council on the Criminal Justice System; John O'Brien of the Allegheny County (Pittsburgh) court of common pleas; Merna Marshall and Curtis Carson (the only black member), from the Philadelphia bench. Legislative members included Senator George Gekas, senior Republican on the judiciary committee; James Kelley, a Democratic senator; Norman Berson and Anthony Scirica, from the house judiciary committee. The gubernatorial appointments included Robert Colville, district attorney of Allegheny County; Michael Minney, an attorney in private practice in Lancaster County; and Albert Pelaez, of Duquesne University Law School in Pittsburgh. Judge Marshall died in December 1979; her vacancy was subsequently filled by Anthony Scirica, who had been elected to the bench. Judge Scirica, in turn, was replaced by Representative Terry McVerry of Allegheny County. Following the legislative rejection of the guidelines in April 1981, since the terms of all members had expired, the governor appointed three new members: Frank Hazel, district attorney of Delaware County; Charles Scarlata, an attorney from Allegheny County; and David Jones, a law professor at the University of Pittsburgh. The legislative members were reappointed and three of the four judges were reappointed by a new chief justice. Conaboy, who had moved to the federal bench, was not reappointed; he was replaced by Lynn Abraham of Philadelphia. Judge Scirica was elected chair. While the major urban and suburban counties were well represented, the rural counties were not represented at all, even though their representatives make up a substantial proportion of the Pennsylvania house of representatives.

8. The initial guidelines were those created by the commission and published in the Pennsylvania Bulletin in October 1980; following the public hearing, the initial guidelines were modified. The second guidelines were presented to the legislature in January and rejected in April 1981. Following legislative rejection and the appointment of several new members, the commission produced a third set of guidelines. Reference to the third guidelines includes both those published in the Pennsylvania Bulletin in October 1981 and the slightly

modified version presented to the legislature in January 1982 and now in effect.

The weighted scoring system for seriousness provided that two or three misdemeanors were assigned 1 point; four or more prior misdemeanors were given 2 points; one felony was assigned 1 point; two or three prior felonies were assigned 2 points; and four or more prior felony convictions were assigned 3 points, with a maximum possible score of 4 points based on prior offense convictions. The scoring system permitted the addition of 1 point for prior convictions for offenses ranked 6 or 7 in seriousness and 2 points for those ranked 8. In the second set of guidelines the scoring was changed to allow 1 point for one or two misdemeanors and 2 points for three or more misdemeanors, in order to permit incarceration sentences for chronic misdemeanants. The third set of guidelines reverted to the first scoring weights.

9. The two just-deserts lines place great weight on the current offense and little weight on previous criminal history, seeking to make punishment proportional to the gravity of the offense. Incapacitation-oriented sentencing schemes are concerned with the effects of punishment, seeking to remove from society those offenders viewed as likely to commit further crimes on the basis of those offenders' prior criminal history, which weighs heavily in the sentencing decision.

10. See Wilkins (1981), Wilkins et al. (1978), and Sparks (Volume 2) for a fuller discussion of this approach.

11. See the staff concept paper by Parent and Knapp (1978) outlining the issues and strategy options that were available to the commission.

12. These projections were based on sentencing data for 1977. Estimates of the impact of the guidelines suggested a decrease from 38.9 percent to 36 percent in the proportion of offenders to be incarcerated. Subsequently, data gathered on sentencing in 1980 indicated that sentence severity had increased between 1977 and 1980. Thus the earlier projection figures, by underestimating actual sentence severity, had underestimated the decline in the proportion of offenders that would be imprisoned and overestimated the increase in sentence length that would result from the guidelines.

13. The study almost was not conducted because the chair and several members did not understand the value of information on existing practices as a departure point for shaping the guidelines and feared "making decisions based on a computer."

14. The costs of housing prisoners in state prisons come from the state's budget; maintenance of offenders in jail facilities is a county expense. Thus decreased use of prisons and increased jail populations had fiscal consequences for many counties.

15. Under the Community Corrections Act, counties were expected to keep felons sentenced to less than 5 years in local facilities. To encourage local treatment counties were given a subsidy to develop local programs from which were deducted the per diem expenses of those "chargeable" felons with terms of less than 5 years that were sent to state prison. Realizing that under the guidelines some chargeable offenders would be sent to state prison, the commission recommended passage of legislation providing that counties not be charged for any offender sentenced according to the guidelines.

16. In August 1982 Governor Quie reappointed William Falvey (public defender), Stephen Rathke (county attorney), and Barbara Andrus (citizen) to the commission. He appointed Daniel Cain to replace Jan Smaby (citizen) and Sheriff James Trudeau to the new law enforcement seat created by the legislature to replace the seat formerly held by the chair of the parole board. He named Rathke chair. Chief Justice Amdahl named Justice Glen Kelley to serve in his own place and reappointed judges Russell Olson and David Marsden. In October Orv Pung became commissioner of corrections and thus a member of the MSGC.

REFERENCES

Elazar, D.J.
    1972 American Federalism: A View from the States.
          2nd edition. New York: Thomas Y. Crowell.
Lipton, D., R. Martinson, and J. Wilks
    1975 The Effectiveness of Correctional Treatment:
          A Review and Agenda for Research. Report
          #R-2497-CRB. Santa Monica, Calif.: Rand
          Corporation.

Messinger, S.L., and P.E. Johnson
    1978 California's determinate sentencing statute:
          history and issues. Pp. 13-58 in Determinate
          Sentencing: Reform or Regression? Washington,
          D.C.: U.S. Department of Justice.
Parent, D., and K.A. Knapp
    1978 Concept Paper on Guideline Development.
          Minnesota Sentencing Guidelines Commission, St.
          Paul, Minn.
von Hirsch, Andrew
    1976 Doing Justice: The Choice of Punishments. New
          York: Hill and Wang.
Wilkins, L.T.
    1981 The Principles of Guidelines for Sentencing:
          Methodological Issues in Their Development.
          Washington, D.C.: U.S. Department of Justice.
Wilkins, L., J. Kress, D. Gottfredson, J. Calpin, and
A. Gelman
    1978 Sentencing Guidelines: Structuring Judicial
          Discretion--Report on the Feasibility Study.
          Washington, D.C.: U.S. Department of Justice.
Wilson, James Q.
    1975 Thinking About Crime. New York: Basic Books.

7

Sentencing Reforms and Their Impacts

Jacqueline Cohen and Michael H. Tonry

INTRODUCTION

The sentencing reform movement has forced us to look at the sentencing process whole. Until recently the word <u>sentencing</u> usually evoked images of defendants in the dock, berobed judges, and high-ceilinged courtrooms. The roles of police, prosecutors, and parole and prison professionals in sentence outcomes were little attended to. Now, after a decade of ferment, most discussions of sentencing reform address not only the discretion of judges, but also that of prosecutors, parole boards, and sometimes other officials. Sentencing is no longer commonly perceived as simply what the judge does, but rather as a complex process in which various people make decisions that influence the quality and quantum of punishment a defendant receives.

Most sentencing reforms have focused on only one part of the process. Maine, for example, abolished parole but addressed no other punishment power; the abolition of parole without development of criteria and constraints for judges, however, gave little reason to expect that sentences imposed by judges would also change in some desired way. California "abolished" parole and set detailed statutory criteria for judges imposing prison sentences on convicted offenders, raising the possibility that much of the power in determining sentence outcomes would thereby be shifted to prosecutors through the charging and plea negotiation processes. Illinois abolished parole, set only loose statutory sentencing criteria, and established "day-for-day" good time. Prisoners, however, have no vested entitlement to accrued good-time credits, leaving corrections authorities with the power to increase a prisoner's nominal sentence by as much as 100 percent by withdrawing good-time credits to penalize prisoner misconduct.

In view of this complexity, evaluations of the impact of sentencing reforms should not be limited to the domain in which these schemes are implemented. To see the impact of parole guidelines, one must consider not only the actions of the parole board, but also those of judges, lawyers, and prison officials. To see the impact of sentencing guidelines, one must consider their implications for plea bargaining, parole release decisions, and so on.

This paper reviews the scanty evaluation literature on the impact of various sentencing reforms. We begin with the abolition of plea bargaining. The next section deals with mandatory-minimum sentencing laws and is followed by one on California's determinate sentencing scheme. The next section is concerned with the impact of sentencing guidelines: both the descriptive variety first developed in Denver and their prescriptive cousins promulgated by the Minnesota Sentencing Guidelines Commission. The final section discusses the abolition of parole and parole guidelines.

Impacts Considered

We use the term _impact evaluation_ as if it were a term of art in this context. In fact, _evaluation_ may be, but _impact_ certainly is not. In order to assess the impact of anything sensibly, one must have some sense of what to look for. In considering the impact of a sentencing reform scheme, one might look at any of the following:

(1) The realization of proponents' purposes or goals. One would be interested to identify in legislation or the legislative history (or their analogues in an administrative or judicial innovation) precisely what various architects of reform wanted, then to consider the extent to which those wants were satisfied.
(2) Mechanical or literal compliance with the statute (or rule or guideline, etc.). One might assume

that the purpose of the reform scheme was that all cases covered by the literal terms of the rule be handled in a manner consistent with the rule.

(3) The effect on crime rates. The extent to which crime and criminality are affected, particularly any reduction or redirection, as a result of deterrence, incapacitation, or rehabilitation.

(4) Work group behavioral and attitudinal reactions. What precisely did judges, lawyers, and defendants do under the new scheme that was different from their behavior under the preexisting law; what are their reactions to the new scheme; what changes, if any, do they believe have resulted; do they approve or disapprove of the new regime and why.

(5) Sanctioning rates and distributions. What effect has the new scheme had on the distribution of sanctions--did more people go to prison for shorter or longer terms, did different people go to prison, etc.

(6) Case flow. Was the flow of cases through the system changed; did guilty plea rates, trial rates, dismissal rates, charging rates, and indictment rates change, in what directions, and for what categories of offenders and charged offenses.

(7) Public attitudes/opinions/morale. Did public attitudes about the legitimacy or effectiveness of the punishment process specifically, or the criminal process generally, change, and if so in what ways.

We are here primarily concerned with the effectiveness of sentencing reforms as means to reduce disparities, to increase or decrease sentence severity, and to systematize decision making by reducing discretion. Our analysis thus concentrates on how innovations have affected what happens to defendants and how judges and lawyers have changed their behavior. These concerns relate primarily to the impact criteria listed as numbers 2, 4, 5, and 6 above. The literature on crime rate impact through deterrence and incapacitation as well as rehabilitative effects has been reviewed elsewhere (e.g., Blumstein et al., 1978 and Sechrest et al., 1979). Relatively little effort has been made in impact evaluations to measure the congruence between proponents' goals and system effects (but see Casper et al., 1981). Similarly, we are aware of no useful body of literature that assesses the impacts of sentencing innovations on public attitudes or opinions.

Innovations Considered

The broadest continuum of decisions that affect criminal punishment begins at one pole with the victim or witness who elects whether to report an apparent crime to the police and terminates at its opposite pole with officials who decide whether to revoke the parole status of an uncooperative parolee. Recent reform efforts attend to a shorter continuum ranging from prosecutorial charging and bargaining decisions through initial parole release. From a civil liberties perspective this narrower focus may not be too unfortunate. "Wrong" decisions not to report, record, or charge are a windfall to the suspect, who certainly has no basis for complaint. "Wrong" decisions to complain or initiate charges are unfortunate, but they are reviewed by prosecutors and judges. The reform movement's failure to address parole revocation procedures and standards may be more troublesome: Those proceedings afford parolees only rudimentary procedural safeguards, are of low visibility, and are not subject to judicial review on their substantive merits.

This review is thus concerned with reforms and evaluations of reforms directed at the actions and decisions of prosecutors, judges, and parole authorities. Often one reform scheme affects more than one actor and causal relationships are difficult to isolate. For organizational purposes only, this review somewhat artifically isolates reform efforts, beginning with the prosecutor and ending with parole.

ABOLITION OF PLEA BARGAINING

Plea bargaining has long been subject to criticism. Calls for its abolition have been frequent. For many years, it was a dirty secret and required that defendants be thespians who would affirm in court, before lawyers and judges who knew better, that guilty pleas were wholly voluntary, the consequence of contrition, and not induced by assurances of leniency.

Plea bargaining has now been legitimated by the Supreme Court and has become overt. The Supreme Court

has established that the defendant is entitled to the
bargain that has induced a plea and that the judge must
accept the arrangement or permit the defendant to
reconsider whether to plead guilty (Santobello v. New
York, 404 U.S. 25 7 [1971]). The Supreme Court has also
held that the prosecutor's charging and threat tactics
before and during plea bargaining are not subject to
review by the courts; virtually anything goes
(Bordenkircher v. Hayes, 434 U.S. 357 [1978]). These
developments and the advent of sentencing schemes that
specify criteria for sentencing give the prosecutor
immense influence over the applicable sentence through
charging and dismissal decisions; the courts can do
little about it.

General antipathy for plea bargaining and the
realization that prosecutors can manipulate determinate
sentencing laws have led to a number of efforts to
"abolish" plea bargaining in full or in part. Some of
these efforts are directed principally at plea
bargaining. The attorney general of Alaska in 1975
forbade plea bargaining (Rubinstein et al., 1980). The
prosecutor of one county in Michigan abolished charge
bargaining in drug trafficking cases (Iowa Law Review,
1975; Church, 1976). Other plea bargaining bans have
been associated with other major reforms. The Wayne
County (Detroit) prosecutor, for example, forbade
bargaining over firearms charges carrying a mandatory
two-year sentence (Heumann and Loftin, 1979).
Restrictions were also placed on negotiated charge
reductions in New York's mandatory sentencing law for
drug offenses (Joint Committee, 1977).
Only the first three of these plea bargaining bans have
been studied in any detail; these impact evaluations are
reviewed in this section.

The broadest generalization that derives from these
evaluations is that plea bargaining can be substantially
controlled when the chief prosecutor wishes to do so and
establishes internal reviews and management systems that
effectively monitor the behavior of assistant
prosecutors. Conversely, if controls are not
established, there is a strong tendency for judges and
lawyers to establish alternative bargaining systems.
Subsidiary generalizations supported by the studies
reviewed are that increased numbers of defendants are
diverted from the system at screening or by dismissal,
that assistant prosecutors generally prefer working in a
system having little or reduced plea bargaining, and that
defense lawyers generally dislike the new systems.

Plea Bargaining Ban in Alaska

Alaska is the only state to attempt to eliminate plea bargaining statewide in all its variant forms. On July 3, effective August 15, 1975, the attorney general of Alaska ordered Alaskan prosecutors to desist from plea bargaining and sentence recommendations. There was early ambiguity about the legitimacy of charge bargaining, but the policy was soon clarified: Charge dismissals or reductions as inducements to guilty pleas were forbidden; unilateral charge dismissals for good faith professional reasons were permitted.

The Alaska Judicial Council evaluated the impact of the abolition in Anchorage, Fairbanks, and Juneau (Rubinstein et al., 1980). The evaluation involved statistical analyses of case processing for the 12-month periods preceding and following implementation of the ban and a series of structured and open-ended interviews with police, lawyers, and judges. The statistical analyses included tabular presentations of disposition data and a multiple regression analysis to investigate factors influencing outcomes. Nearly every judge, prosecutor, assistant public defender, and active private defense lawyer in the three cities was interviewed, many of them several times.

There were, in the mid-1970s, stark differences in legal culture in the three cities. Prosecutors and defense lawyers were highly adversarial in Fairbanks, and judges were "relatively tough and unsentimental." Counsel in Juneau prided themselves on their harmonious relations, and judges had reputations for leniency. Styles in Anchorage were more varied and fell somewhere in between (Rubinstein et al., 1980:45). The interviews indicated that local legal culture affected implementation of the ban. Plea bargaining was greatly diminished in all three cities, but it appears that there were greater flexibility and accommodation in collegial Juneau than in legalistic Fairbanks.

Because the Alaska plea bargaining ban is the most ambitious effort of its type, and because the evaluation appears to be the most comprehensive, we describe it in considerable detail below.

Many observers expected either widespread circumvention of the ban or, if plea bargains were truly eliminated, a slowdown in case processing with resulting backlogs, many more trial demands, and longer disposition times. None of these occurred. The Rubinstein et al.

(1980) evaluation concluded that during the first 12
months after the ban took effect:

(1) Plea bargaining was effectively curtailed and was
    not replaced by covert or implicit substitutes;
(2) Defendants continued to plead guilty at about the
    same rates as before;
(3) The trial rate increased, but the absolute number
    of trials remained small;
(4) Sentence severity generally did not increase,
    except for drug offenses and less serious offenses
    committed by offenders with modest criminal
    records; and
(5) Conviction rates changed little.

These conclusions, however, must be viewed in the
light of several methodological shortcomings. First and
foremost, we are skeptical in the extreme about the
credibility of the statistical analyses and conclusions
deriving from them. For reasons not made clear, the unit
of analysis in the statistical analyses of case
processing is separate charges. These are referred to as
"cases," defined as "a single charge against a single
defendant" (Rubinstein et al., 1980:135). Using this
approach, multiple charges against a single defendant
appear as several cases in the data.

These "cases" may be seriously misleading. Table 7-1
shows the breakdown of "cases" and defendants, by year
when possible. The only information provided about
defendants is that there were 2,283 defendants in the
2-year period, of whom 56 percent (1,278) were charged
with only one felony charge (Rubinstein et al.,
1980:134). Apparently screening eliminated 137
single-charge defendants (Table V-4), leaving a total of
1,141 single-charge defendants. It is impossible to
determine how many multiple-charge defendants were
screened out of the system or how many defendants were
charged with specific offenses, either in specific years
or in specific cities.

All the statistical analyses of screening,
dispositions, and sanctions are based on cases (i.e.,
charges), not defendants. This approach seems to us
unsatisfactory. If it is true that sentence bargaining
was prevalent before the ban took effect (Rubinstein et
al., 1980:1-11), the number of separate charges, that is,
"cases," would usually have been irrelevant. The central
issue is the sentence for the defendant; whether, for

TABLE 7-1 Description of Data Available for "Cases" and
Defendants in Evaluation of Alaska Plea-Bargaining Ban

A. Number of "Cases" and Defendants

Years	Number of "Cases"	Number of Defendants
Both Years	3,586	2,283
Arrests	3,483	N/A
Information/Indictments	103	N/A
Year 1	1,815	N/A
Arrests	1,776	N/A
Information/Indictments	39	N/A
Year 2	1,771	N/A
Arrests	1,707	N/A
Information/Indictments	64	N/A

B. Defendants by Number of Charges

Years	One Charge	More Than One Charge	Total Defendants
Both Years	1,278	1,005 (2,308 charges)	2,283
Screened Out	137	N/A	137+
Prosecuted	1,141	N/A	Fewer than 2,146
Year 1	N/A	N/A	N/A
Year 2	N/A	N/A	N/A

NOTE: Breakdowns by offense and by city were not
available.

example, a three-year sentence was for one charge, with two others dismissed, or one year for each of three charges served consecutively, or three years for each of three charges served concurrently would often have been immaterial. These alternative configurations would nevertheless appear to be quite different when outcomes on the separate charges were examined. There is thus every reason to suspect that the "case" is not a meaningful unit for characterizing case processing before the ban. If sentence and charge bargaining did substantially disappear after the ban, the judges' sentencing decisions would appear no more inherently related to the number of charges, or cases, than before.

Many of the findings based on comparison of dispositions in different cities, years, and offense types may be artifactual. If "cases" are not a meaningful operational unit, analyses based on comparison of "cases" are likely to reveal case-processing patterns, although they may not accurately reflect processing of defendants. Many of the "case" analyses show substantial dispositional stability over time. Why that should be, we cannot say. Prosecutors' charging patterns and judicial sentencing patterns for defendants might remain relatively consistent or change during the two years, and the "case" analyses could remain consistent.[1] Whatever the reason for the "case" approach, we believe it substantially diminishes the integrity and credibility of the resulting statistical analyses.

There are other problems as well. First, the study considered developments only in the years immediately before and after August 15, 1975; apparent changes during those two years may reflect long-term trends that the research design fails to identify.

Second, offenses are divided into six ad hoc vertical classes (murder and kidnapping; other violent felonies; burglary, larceny, and receiving; fradulent property offenses; drug felonies; and "morals" felonies). Primary reliance on those classes for year-to-year comparisons may mask changing patterns within a class. Crimes charged as aggravated assaults in year one, for example, may be charged as simple assaults in year two. The maximum authorized sentences would be affected and judges might react differently to the different offense labels. The classification scheme is insensitive to changes of that type.

Third, the study looks only at felony prosecutions in either year. If the ban caused prosecutors to file misdemeanor charges in year two when they would have filed felony charges in year one (or vice versa), the study design will miss that change. There are other, lesser limitations to the design that we mention below as they become pertinent.

Because of these methodological problems, the statistical analyses should be regarded with skepticism, if they are not disregarded altogether. Fortunately, most of the study's major conclusions derive from extensive interviews. In our discussion we draw heavily on the interview data and use the statistical data as supplementary information.

Prosecutorial Involvement in Sentence Bargaining

Although sentence bargaining was routinely practiced before the ban took effect, the study concluded that "plea bargaining as an institution was clearly curtailed" (Rubinstein et al., 1980:31, emphasis in original). Sentence bargaining and prosecutorial sentence recommendations declined abruptly in all three cities, with the greatest drop in Fairbanks.

Table 7-2 shows the patterns of sentence recommendations in guilty plea cases before and after August 15, 1975. Here and elsewhere, periods 1 and 2 refer to the two six-month periods preceding the ban and periods 3 and 4 refer to the two six-month periods immediately after the ban. Before the ban, Anchorage prosecutors made sentence recommendations in half the guilty plea "cases" (i.e., charges); afterward in about 16 percent. In Fairbanks, sentence recommendations declined from a third of guilty plea charges to 6 percent. In Juneau sentence recommendations declined the least, from over half of guilty plea charges before the ban to 25 percent afterward.[2] Interview respondents "agreed with the statistical finding that sentence bargaining had been essentially terminated" (Rubinstein et al., 1980:93). The report contains numerous references to statements by judges, prosecutors, and defense counsel who believed that the ban was observed and, often, especially among defense counsel and in Juneau, that substantive justice had suffered as a result.

TABLE 7-2   Sentence Recommendations in Alaska Guilty Plea
Cases Before and After the Ban on Plea Bargaining

Jurisdiction and Time	Percentage of No Recommendations	Percentage of Specific Sentence Length	Percentage of Other Recommendations	N
Anchorage				
Period 1	49.0	25.2	25.7	210
Period 2	53.9	21.2	24.9	193
Period 3	87.4	6.3	6.3	175
Period 4	78.8	8.9	12.3	146
Fairbanks				
Period 1	66.3	15.1	18.6	86
Period 2	72.7	20.7	6.6	121
Period 3	94.9	4.3	0.9	117
Period 4	93.0	2.0	5.0	100
Juneau				
Period 1	21.4	28.6	50.0	14
Period 2	51.2	31.7	17.1	41
Period 3	79.2	4.2	16.7	24
Period 4	68.8	12.5	18.8	16

NOTE: Periods 1 and 2 refer to the two six-month periods
prior to the plea bargaining ban; periods 3 and 4 are the
two six-month periods immediately following the ban.

SOURCE: Rubinstein et al. (1980:Table II-1).

Charge Bargaining and Other Circumvention

Lawyers and judges have personal and bureaucratic
interests that may be served by the expeditious
disposition of cases. Private defense lawyers often
operate high-volume practices in which fees per case are
low. Public defenders often have large case loads.
Negotiated pleas involve less work for everyone.

Prosecutors are often concerned about keeping conviction rates high and backlogs low. Judges also typically want to keep backlogs low. In the face of an effective sentence bargain ban, one might expect to see overt or covert charge bargaining or implicit sentence bargaining.

An early evaluation of a charge bargaining ban in Michigan found that court participants quickly shifted to a system of sentence bargaining (Iowa Law Review, 1975; Church, 1976). In Alaska, sentence bargaining was the predominant method of disposition before the ban. Since the attorney general's directive was ambiguous in its references to charge bargaining,[3] and it is difficult to distinguish unilateral charge dismissals from bargained dismissals, one might have expected the reverse shift in Alaska, from sentence bargaining to charge bargaining. There was interview evidence that charge bargaining was "rampant" in Fairbanks, "to fill the gap" left by the prohibition of sentence bargaining. This continued for eight months after the ban took effect, until the Fairbanks district attorney himself prohibited it (Rubinstein et al., 1980:235). The statistical evidence on this episode is mixed: There was a temporary increase in the percentage of guilty pleas to substantially reduced charges (Table V-1), but there was no surge in the number of charges originally filed per defendant. There was no statistical basis for believing that charge bargaining increased, and the study concluded that overall charge bargaining did not replace sentence bargaining (pp. 233-36).

Consequences of the Ban on Case Processing

The conventional wisdom about plea bargaining and the processing of criminal cases is that negotiated guilty plea "discounts" are imperative if the flow of cases is to be maintained, if backlogs are not to accumulate, and if the courts are not be be overwhelmed by trials. The commonsense premise is that defendants will not give up tactically valuable trial rights for nothing. If the premise is correct, one might expect a successful plea bargaining ban to decrease guilty plea rates and to increase case-processing time and the incidence of trials. Finally, one might expect to see a tendency for earlier disposition of cases other than on the merits. In order to reduce case pressure and to avoid harsh sentences for defendants for whom lenient sentence bargains would have been arranged, prosecutors might reject more arrests at screening or effect postscreening dismissals, or acquiesce in judicial dismissals.[4]

Case processing changed very little. There was a slight tendency to screen out more cases. A slight tendency was also found toward earlier dismissal of cases, but dismissal rates overall were unchanged. Sentencing severity seemed little changed except for cases involving minor offenses by inexperienced offenders (they received harsher treatment than before the ban). Guilty plea rates changed little. Trial rates increased, but the absolute number of trials remained low. The average case-processing time declined.

Screening Table 7-3 shows screening rates expressed as percentages of felony arrests during the 12 months before and the 12 months after August 15, 1975, in criminal courts in Anchorage, Fairbanks, and Juneau. Because the plea bargaining ban made disposition of minor cases more difficult, one might have expected that more cases would be screened out at the very beginning of the process. Indeed, the attorney general emphasized tighter screening as an integral part of the policy against plea bargaining (Rubinstein et al., 1980:73). As the first section of Table 7-3 indicates, the percentage of cases screened out in the year after August 15, 1975, increased to 12.9 percent from the 10.0 percent screening rate of the preceding year. The increase was relatively small in Anchorage but more substantial in Fairbanks and Juneau.

The screening rejection percentages are low in both periods, probably because court rules predispose prosecutors to pro forma screening decisions. Alaska court rules required that defendants' first court appearances take place no later than 24 hours after they are taken into custody; otherwise, the judge or magistrate must discharge the defendant immediately. Assistant prosecutors thus had only a few hours within which to make charging decisions and had generally to base them on the police report alone. As cases can always be dismissed later, these timing and information constraints probably created a conservative screening policy.

Rubinstein et al. (1980) conducted a statistical analysis of factors associated with changes in screening outcome by offense class and various case and processing factors. The only striking changes found were that

TABLE 7-3 Case Screening by Prosecutor and Dismissals in Court in Alaska Before and After the Ban on Plea Bargaining

	Combined Cities		Anchorage		Fairbanks		Juneau	
	Year 1	Year 2	Year 1	Year 2	Year 1	Year 2	Year 1	Year 2
"Cases" dismissed by prosecutor at screening as percentage of felony arrests[a]	10.0	12.9	13.1	14.7	3.7	8.9	8.9	13.9
District court dismissals as percentage of "cases" disposed after screening[b]	21.9	24.8	18.8	27.8	27.1	18.7	25.2	28.7
Superior court dismissals as percentage of "cases" disposed after screening[b]	30.4	27.9	37.6	31.5	17.8	31.5	25.2	25.5
All court dismissals as percentage of "cases" disposed after screening[b]	52.3	52.7	56.4	59.3	44.9	40.7	50.4	54.2

[a]Murder and kidnapping charges are omitted. Data are from Rubinstein et al. (1980:Table IV-1).

[b]Data are from Rubinstein et al. (1980:Table V-1).

screening rejections of drug felonies increased in all
cities and that there was a substantial increase in
screening out "morals" felonies in Anchorage--from 6.5
percent to 40.9 percent (pp. 140-146). The report
concludes (p. 146):

> On balance, then, the increases in screening that did
> occur suggest that rather than an increase in the
> systematic evaluation of evidence and aggravating
> factors in preparation for trial, there was a
> deliberate prosecutorial decision that some kinds of
> cases were expendable.

There is one other form of early case diversion that
the report does not discuss: felony arrests that were
prosecuted as felonies before the ban and as misdemeanors
afterward. Prosecutors who do not want to expose a
defendant to the risk of a prison sentence could approve
a misdemeanor charge. The report discusses only
screening and disposition of felony charges. Whether
screening "rejections" included cases processed as
misdemeanors is not stated, but, if not, a charging drift
for some kinds of cases from felonies before the ban to
misdemeanors after might evidence greater screening than
the report indicates. The annual number of felony
arrests declined after the ban, as the figures below
indicate:

City	Number of Felony Arrests Subject to Screening	
	Year 1	Year 2
Anchorage	1,124	1,080 (- 4%)
Fairbanks	517	526 (+ 2%)
Juneau	135	101 (-25%)
Total	1,776	1,707 (- 4%)

Assuming that the 4 percent decline in arrests represents
misdemeanors formerly prosecuted as felonies, the extent
of "diversion" caused by the ban may be greater than the
screening rejection figures indicate. The decline in
felony prosecutions over all three jurisdictions would
then be 6.4 percent--a shift whose composition would be
worth knowing.[5]

Dismissals of Cases Concern was expressed by defense
counsel and, to a lesser extent, prosecutors that minor
cases were treated more severely after the abolition than
before (Rubinstein et al., 1980:32-34, 50). If cases
were not being diverted at screening, one might have
expected a significant increase in outright dismissals as
a means to avoid severe sentences for minor offenses.
Once the formal complaint is filed, there is ample time
for the prosecutor to assess facts and entertain appeals
from defense counsel, and, if appropriate, dismiss
charges. Most charge dismissals in both years were at
the initiative of the prosecutor. As Table 7-3
indicates, once a case reached court there was some
shifting of dismissals between courts, but the overall
dismissal rate in court was essentially unchanged (from
52.3 percent to 52.7 percent). The differences in
individual cities were only slightly greater.

Method of Disposition The interviews did not evidence
any general belief among court participants that sentence
bargaining was replaced by charge bargaining.
Statistical analyses confirmed that conclusion. Table
7-4 sets out year-to-year comparisons of felony charge
dispositions among those arrests that survived
screening. The percentage of guilty pleas to reduced
charges declined from 17.4 percent to 15.2 percent. (If
the interviews in the evaluation are to be believed, most
of this residual consisted of cases in which the
prosecutor independently reduced charges.) There was a
slight contrary tendency in Fairbanks, which was
consistent with the interview data indicating that
Fairbanks experienced a flurry of charge bargaining after
the ban took effect (Rubinstein et al., 1980:235).
Guilty pleas without charge reductions also declined only
slightly. Acquittals at trial were essentially
unchanged, while trial convictions increased by 69
percent from 4.2 percent of disposed cases before the ban
to 7.1 percent after the ban. Thus, those defendants who
refused to plead guilty and waive trial rights without
inducements to do so appear to have been convicted at
trial.

Despite an abolition of plea bargaining that
prosecutors appear substantially to have honored and
despite the increase in trials, "guilty pleas continued
to flow in at nearly undiminished rates (and) most
defendants pled guilty even when the state offered them

TABLE 7-4   Percentage Disposition of Cases on the Merits
in Alaska

Disposition	Combined Cities Year 1	Year 2	Anchorage Year 1	Year 2	Fairbanks Year 1	Year 2	Juneau Year 1	Year 2
Guilty Plea/ Reduced Charge[a]	17.4	15.2	17.6	12.6	16.6	19.1	18.9	18.1
Guilty Plea/ No Reduction	23.6	22.5	23.0	21.9	24.4	22.9	24.4	24.5
Trial Acquittal	2.5	2.5	1.1	1.7	4.5	4.2	5.5	1.1
Trial Conviction	4.2	7.1	1.8	4.4	9.6	13.0	0.8	1.1

NOTE: The sum of dispositions does not total 100 percent. Dismissals in
court are not included here; they are reported in Table 7-3.

[a]A guilty plea to a charge different from that originally charged was
considered meaningfully reduced only if the statutory maximum sentence
for the conviction charge was less than 75 percent of the statutory
maximum sentence for the original charge.

SOURCE: Rubinstein et al. (1980:Table V-1).

nothing in exchange for their cooperation" (Rubinstein et
al., 1980:80). Why would defendants plead guilty who
were offered no inducement to do so? Rubinstein et al.
suggest several reasons. The first is that "human nature
does not want to engage in fruitless acts" (p. 81). In
many cases the defendant's role in the criminal act is
incontrovertible. The authors observe: "whether there
was a plea or a trial depended more on the nature of the
case and on the client than on whether plea bargaining
was permitted" (p. 83). A second reason is that "no
lawyer likes to make a fool of himself in public" (p.
87). Several of the interview respondents expressed the
view that an unwinnable case is an unwinnable case and
little benefit would accrue to the defendant or to the
lawyer who had to argue it (pp. 87-89). Third, while the
patterns varied between offense types, defendants may
have responded to "a large trial/plea sentencing
differential" (pp. 88-90). Whatever the reasons, the
guilty plea rate changed very little when plea bargaining
substantially disappeared.

This conclusion, however, must be viewed cautiously.
The "cases" used in the analyses were limited to "cases"
initiated in the 12 months before or 12 months after the
plea bargaining ban went into effect (from August 1974 to

August 1976) and finally disposed in court by the end of
1977. Of the cases initiated in the 24-month period 81
were excluded from the analysis: Files were unavailable
for 47 cases that were the subjects of appeals, and 34
cases had not been finally resolved at the trial court
level. Since trials take more time to dispose than
guilty pleas and the follow-up period was shorter for the
postban sample, the excluded cases are more likely to be
trial cases initiated after the plea bargaining ban.
These additional cases would increase even further the
postban trial rate. Unfortunately, no information is
provided on the sample year, jurisdiction, or disposition
type for the excluded cases in order to assess the extent
of that impact.[6]

Sanctions Policies Sentencing outcomes apparently
changed little. Because of our skepticism about the
credibility of inferences drawn from charge-based as
opposed to offender-based analyses, we do not examine the
disposition data closely. Table 7-5 shows sentencing

TABLE 7-5 Sentence Severity--All Cities

Offense Type	Percentage of All Original Felony "Cases" Resulting in Conviction and Sentence of 30 days or more		Mean Active Sentence, in Months	
	Year 1	Year 2	Year 1	Year 2
Murder and Kidnapping	50.0 (24)	52.6 (19)	171.2	238.8
Other Violent Felonies	21.9 (547)	22.3 (497)	24.8	22.7
Burglary, Larceny Receiving	12.9 (534)	18.1 (497)	6.8	4.3
Fraud, Forgery, Embezzlement, Bad Checks	16.8 (298)	14.3 (252)	9.5	6.2
Drug Felonies	14.8 (352)	16.7 (360)	8.0	25.4
"Morals" Felonies	16.7 (60)	20.0 (45)	25.5	16.6
All offenses	17.2 (1,815)	18.9 (1,771)	Not available	

SOURCE: Rubinstein et al. (1980:Tables VI-1, VII-1).

patterns by offense class. The measures of sentencing severity used were the likelihood of conviction and imprisonment for at least 30 days and mean active prison sentence. There were few marked changes in sentence severity. Closer analyses, not shown on Table 7-5, led the evaluators to conclude that there were some important changes in sanction severity. Sentences did not become more severe if the original charge was a violent felony, "high risk" larceny, or receiving stolen property ("high risk" and "low risk" characterizations were based on indicators of persistent criminality). Drug cases, however, experienced the greatest increase in sentence severity (Rubinstein et al., 1980:113). The other conspicuous change was a substantial increase in sentence severity in "low risk" burglary, larceny, and receiving stolen property cases (p. 113):

> Thus where the prosecutor's power to recommend sentences was sharply curtailed by the plea bargaining ban, defendants in nonviolent, low-risk cases tended to lose the advantage they had formerly enjoyed, and received more severe sentences.

Disposition Time   Given the conventional view that plea bargaining lubricates the machinery of justice and keeps it operating efficiently, one might have expected a widespread refusal by defendants to plead guilty with resulting processing delays. Rubinstein et al. conclude that this did not happen. As Table 7-6 indicates, the evaluation reported a dramatic decrease in case-processing time after the ban took effect. They conclude that "the curtailment of plea bargaining did not in any way impede court efficiency—and it may have had the reverse effect" (Rubinstein et al., 1980:103). The qualified conclusion was necessary because administrative changes taking place in Anchorage are partly responsible for the reduction in processing time. The court switched to a master calendar system under the control of a presiding judge, and at the same time a new presiding judge was appointed who was reputed to be a "tough administrator"; he made a special effort to control and discourage continuance motions. However, while those changes may have affected case disposition times in Anchorage, they do not explain the decreases in the other two cities. The plea bargaining ban was most strictly enforced in Fairbanks and the trial rate there rose

TABLE 7-6 Mean Court Disposition Times for All Felonies
that Went to Court (in days)

	Year 1		Year 2	
	Period 1 (8/15/74- 2/14/75)	Period 2 (2/15/75- 8/14/75)	Period 2 (8/15/75- 2/14/76)	Period 2 (2/15/76- 8/14/76)
Anchorage	192.1	153.8	125.3	39.5
Fairbanks	164.6	129.9	134.1	120.4
Juneau	105.7	102.5	92.1	85.1

SOURCE: Rubinstein et al. (1980:Table II-2).

substantially (see Table 7-4), yet disposition times in
the Fairbanks sample also decreased substantially.

This decrease in disposition times reported in the
evaluation is overstated. All cases in the evaluation
sample, regardless of when they were initiated, had to be
disposed by the end of 1977 in order to enter the
sample. The 34 cases not disposed of in court by that
time, and the 47 cases on appeal for which case files
were unavailable were eliminated from the data. If data
were available on the 34 cases not disposed, average
case-processing times would increase. By definition
these cases were pending for considerable periods. Since
most of these cases were probably initiated in periods 3
and 4, data on them would increase disposition time for
those periods and reduce the apparent decline in
disposition times. We lack adequate data to calculate
whether the effect of including these cases would reduce,
eliminate, or reverse the apparent decline in case
processing times.

Conclusion

What should be made of all this? The writers of the
Alaska evaluation are ambivalent. They were surprised
that the system adapted so readily to so dramatic a
change. Three interrelated questions seem to us to
require discussion. First, what did the courtroom
participants think of the change? Second, was the ban a

good thing? Third, what are the implications of the
Alaska evaluation for thinking about the prospects for
plea bargaining abolition in other jurisdictions?

Participants' Reactions Many prosecutors liked the new
system, and many defense lawyers did not. Under the new
system, prosecutors "could achieve the same results . . .
but with less time spent on routine cases, and with less
responsibility for the outcome" (Rubinstein et al.,
1980:221). Some prosecutors had valued their prior
freedom to make specific sentence recommendations in order to individualize justice; these people chafed under
the ban, although it appears that they approved the ban
for the majority of cases. Other prosecutors appear to
have accepted the attorney general's proposition that
sentencing is a judicial function. Some prosecutors appear to have enjoyed their work more under the new regime, even though they sometimes had to work harder at
case preparation. One, represented to be typical,
observed (p. 46):

> I find practice to be preferable . . . much less time
> is spent haggling . . . bargaining is probably inher-
> ently inconsistent with the job . . . I was spending
> one-third of my time arguing with defense attorneys
> . . . I am a trial attorney and that's what I am sup-
> posed to do. The haggling . . . [had] much to do with
> sentencing--what I thought a person should get. The
> judge should do that.

The ban had differential impact on public defenders,
private counsel paid through a union legal services program, and the rest of the defense bar. The public defenders felt disadvantaged because they were unlikely to
receive favorable dispositions in isolated cases; previously, prosecutors were presumed to be loath to act in
a way that could be used as precedent against them in
later cases by other defenders. Public defenders felt
obliged to prepare seriously to defend persons charged
with serious crimes or who were likely to receive long
sentences; resources spread only so far and the low-
severity, minor-record defendant may have suffered in
consequence. Before the ban, such cases could be
resolved expeditiously by means of a sentence bargain to
a nonincarcerative sentence. After the ban, public
defenders simply lacked the resources to defend minor
offenders vigorously (Rubinstein et al., 1980:36-37).

The private defense bar also suffered from the disappearance of routine sentence bargains that required little effort. Lawyers could no longer easily demonstrate to clients that their efforts had produced a benefit; yet the economics of private defense practice require high-volume turnover of cases and make it difficult to file motions, prepare for trial, and vigorously represent all clients in all cases (Rubinstein et al., 1980:38-40).

Lawyers paid by the union legal services program and their clients may have benefited. These lawyers, who represent 6-10 percent of defendants, are paid on an hourly basis at prevailing market rates and thus could devote as much time to a case as the case required and could gain clients some advantage from full defense (Rubinstein et al., 1980:42-44).

The evaluation does not discuss the reactions of judges to the ban in detail, merely noting that some judges complained about "unnecessary" trials (Rubinstein et al., 1980:241-42).

Was the Ban a Good Thing? The traditional arguments against plea bargaining are powerful. It creates a demeaning, street market atmosphere. It fosters the possibility, and no doubt occasionally the reality, that innocent defendants are pressured by circumstances to plead guilty. It diverts the primary focus from the questions of guilt and adjudication to the questions of pricing and sentence. It shifts the locus of sentencing power from the judge, where it is theoretically most appropriately lodged, to counsel.

Given the conclusion that the ban succeeded, one might expect the evaluators to praise its implementation. Instead they express ambivalence as to whether plea bargaining was such a bad thing after all. Under a sentence bargaining system like that of Alaska before the ban, they argue, the negotiation sessions allowed relatively full discussion of the issues and the defendant's circumstances. The need for judicial acquiescence brought an impartial third person to the process and thereby ensured that three professionals were involved in the final decision. The attorney general's new rule, however, "reduced the number of individual viewpoints informing the final disposition. . . . In this sense it impoverished the sentencing process" (Rubinstein et al., 1980:242). The evaluation concludes (p. 243):

The Attorney-General proved that it was possible to make large and significant state-wide changes in an institutionalized plea bargaining system, that this could be done rather quickly and without spending a lot of money and that the curtailment of plea bargaining would not necessarily bring about breakdown in the administration of justice. He did not prove, however, that plea bargaining was the "least just aspect of the criminal justice system" as he said it was; and it is far from clear that his successful prohibition brought about the "better kind of sentencing" that the Attorney-General was looking for.

Implications of the Alaska Experience The Alaska experience is evidence that individual prosecutors who wish to abolish plea bargaining should, under opportune circumstances, be able to do so. This conclusion, readers will note, is hedged. There are many respects in which Alaska's criminal justice system is atypical. First, public prosecution is centrally organized on a statewide basis under the attorney general; although each office has its own district attorney, each is institutionally subject to the policies and procedures of the attorney general.

Second, Alaska is thinly populated, and the volume of felony prosecutions is small. Only 2,283 defendants were charged with felonies over a 2-year period in the three main cities studied. Fewer than 800 felony charges result in convictions each year. The courts in all three cities disposed of only 1,551 cases initiated in the year after the ban took effect: Anchorage, 934; Fairbanks, 523; Juneau, 94. The report does not indicate the numbers of judges and prosecutors in the three cities, but the numbers cannot be large. Anonymity is unlikely to shelter noncompliance with rules in a jurisdiction in which the number of principals in any one city is small.

Third, the evaluation may have influenced implementation: It began soon after the rule took effect, and the presence of researchers may have made lawyers more self-aware. Fourth, the ban attracted considerable media attention, both locally and nationally. It may have appeared that the public eye was fixed on Alaska more than before.

Fifth, two other features of Alaska practice may have facilitated the abolition. Decisions of the Alaska supreme court prohibited judges from direct dealings with

defense counsel that could have permitted sentence discussions. In addition, Alaska is a leader in judicial
technology, and all presentence hearings are recorded on
videotape. The last is important because Alaska Criminal
Procedure Rule 11 requires the judge to inquire about
negotiated guilty pleas. The combined effect of these
rules and the technology may have been to heighten the
appearance of public accountability. For all these reasons, Alaska appears to have been a more congenial site
for an attempt to abolish plea bargaining than many other
jurisdictions would have been.

Having said all that, it remains the case that Alaska
accomplished what many thought was impossible: substantial abolition of plea bargaining without gross disrup-
tion of the processes of the criminal courts. If Alaska
could do it, albeit with some facilitative demographic,
governmental, and structural advantages, it should be
possible for a well-managed prosecutor's office to do
likewise. If rules are sufficiently clear, if internal
management processes are used to monitor day-to-day
decisions, and if prosecutors can withstand the complaints of defense counsel, the Alaska experience ought
to be replicable.

The "Hampton" County Charge Bargaining Ban

In January 1973, after an antidrug law and order election
campaign, a newly elected prosecutor in "Hampton" County,
Michigan,[7] instituted a strict policy forbidding bargained charge reductions in drug sale cases. Prior to
his initiative, most drug cases in the jurisdiction were
resolved by charge bargains: "In drug cases . . . a
charge of delivery of a controlled substance could nearly
always be reduced to attempted sale or possession in exchange for a guilty plea" (Church, 1976:379). At the
time the ban took effect, the prosecutor also substantially tightened the standards by which drug prosecutions
were authorized: No drug warrant would be issued unless
there had been a "controlled buy" by a police undercover
agent. This resulted in a 30 percent decline in the number of drug sale warrants issued.

Church collected information on drug sale warrants and
dispositions for the two 12-month periods before and after
January 1, 1973. The data were not subjected to sophisticated statistical analyses but were presented in tabular form. Although an effort was made to collect data on
all drug sale cases warranted in 1972 and 1973, the

numbers are small (321 warrants in 1972; 224 in 1973) and
dispositional data could be obtained in only 71 percent
of those cases. Church notes: "Several passes through
various files of the prosecutor, circuit, and district
courts, however, produced reasonably complete and (I
believe) accurate information" (p. 381). No reason is
given for that conclusion. We have no special reason to
reject it, but the fugitive nature of the missing 30
percent of cases may indicate that they are in some
systematic respects not ordinary. Church also conducted
a series of interviews with judges, defense counsel,
prosecutors, and the court administrator.

Church concludes that charge bargaining effectively
disappeared but that it was quickly replaced by sentence
bargaining involving the judge and the defense lawyers.
As Table 7-7 indicates, 81 percent of drug sale cases
warranted and disposed in 1972 (all under the previous
prosecuting attorney) involved guilty pleas to reduced
charges. By 1974, for cases warranted in 1973 (all under
the new prosecutor) there were no guilty pleas to reduced
charges. The small number of guilty pleas to reduced
charges in 1973 result, says Church, from confusion and
errors by assistant prosecutors in the early days of the
ban. Also, the trial rate increased, but the absolute
number of trials remained small.

TABLE 7-7   Trial and Plea Rates in 1972 and 1973 Drug
Sale Cases in Hampton County, Michigan

Disposition	1972 Warrants		1973 Warrants	
	1972 Disposition	1973 or Later Disposition	1973 Disposition	1974 or Later Disposition
Guilty Plea to Reduced Charge	88 (81%)	5 (10%)	5 (10%)	0
Guilty Plea to Original Charge[a]	19 (17%)	29 (62%)	39 (75%)	37 (90%)
Total Guilty Pleas	107 (98%)	34 (72%)	44 (85%)	37 (90%)
Trials	2 (2%)	13 (28%)	8 (15%)	4 (10%)
Total Dispositions[b]	109 (100%)	47 (100%)	52 (100%)	41 (100%)

[a]Includes those defendants convicted as youthful trainees (see Church,
1976:Table 2).
[b]Excludes dismissals and nolle prosses (see Church, 1976:Table 2).

SOURCE: Church (1976:Table 1).

Church found that the system adapted to the ban in ways which permitted business as usual. First, sentence bargaining filled the charge bargaining void: "Roughly half the bench would make some form of pre-plea sentence commitment in [plea-bargaining ban] policy cases--a sizable shift given former practices and strong system norms against judicial participation in plea bargaining" (Church, 1976:387). Second, there was an increase in the rate at which cases were dismissed outright. Because of the relative inflexibility of the new system, "some drug sale cases that would have been prime candidates for reduced charge convictions in 1972 found their way out of the system altogether in 1973" (p. 390).

Screening

All cases in the sample had been warranted. Consequently no information is available on changes in screening outcomes over time. Recall that heightened screening of cases reduced the number of drug sale warrants by 30 percent.

Dismissals

Table 7-8 shows the disposition of drug cases from 1972 to 1974. Nolle prosequi rates declined slightly from 15 percent before the ban to 10 percent after the ban, while judicial dismissal rates increased from 19 percent for 1972 warrants to 28 percent after the ban, as did "youthful trainee" convictions from 3 percent to 17 percent. (Youthful trainee convictions permit sentences to probation under circumstances that may result in no record of conviction.) The nolle statistics, Church claims, understate prosecutorial participation in case disposition because assistant prosecutors often tacitly assented to judicial dismissals and youthful trainee convictions.

Sanctions

Despite the reputed shift to sentence bargaining, no systematic information is provided on sentences imposed. Table 7-8 reveals a slight decline in total conviction rates in 1973 but a return to the 1972 rate in 1974.

TABLE 7-8 Disposition of 1972 and 1973 Drug Sale Cases in Hampton County, Michigan

| Disposition | 1972 Warrant | | 1973 Warrant | |
	1972 Disposition	1973 Disposition	1973 Disposition	1974 Disposition
Plea of Guilty to Original Charge	15 (10%)	25 (31%)	24 (27%)	27 (43%)
Plea of Guilty to Reduced Charge	88 (56%)	5 (6%)	5 (6%)	0
Convicted as Youthful Trainee	4 (3%)	4 (5%)	15 (17%)	10 (16%)
Convicted at Trial	2 (1%)	7 (9%)	8 (9%)	3 (5%)
Total Convictions	109 (69%)	41 (51%)	52 (59%)	40 (63%)
Dismissal (Judge)	26 (17%)	19 (24%)	30 (34%)	13 (21%)
Nolle Prosse (Prosecutor)	22 (14%)	14 (18%)	6 (7%)	9 (14%)
Acquittal (Trial)	0	6 (8%)	0	1 (2%)
Total Cases	157 (100%)	80 (101%)	88 (100%)	63 (100%)

SOURCE: Church (1976:Table 2).

Without information on prewarrant screening and subsequent sentences imposed, it is difficult to infer anything from the conviction rate changes. The decreased-to-stable conviction rates could obscure a real decline in severity. Because the more stringent "controlled buy" requirement reduced the number of drug sale warrants by 30 percent, a stable conviction rate for these presumably stronger cases should perhaps be seen as a decline in the likelihood of conviction.

On the basis of his research, Church was pessimistic about the practicality of a plea bargaining ban (Church, 1976:450):

> Given equally "resourceful" attorneys, prosecutors, and judges everywhere, it is unclear how any fundamental shift away from bargain justice could occur without even a more fundamental change in the incentive structure of the participants.

Practitioners' Reactions

While the basic conclusions of the Hampton County and Alaska evaluations are opposite--the ban apparently worked in Alaska but was circumvented in Hampton County--there are striking similarities in the ways lawyers reacted to the two reforms.

The general reaction by prosecutors was favorable: Under the new regime, prosecutors were prosecuting, not sentencing, and sentencing was placed in judicial hands, where it belongs. Furthermore, "a uniform reaction of those assistant prosecutors interviewed was that 'the policy makes my job a lot easier'" (Church, 1976:388). As in Alaska, mild resentment was expressed by several assistants that diminished flexibility for handling troublesome cases might be contributing to occasional injustices.

Defense lawyers were generally dissatisfied with the new system and, as in Alaska, the bases of dissatisfaction varied with the nature of defense practice. Most defense lawyers stressed the importance of plea bargaining as a tool for obtaining substantive justice by means of sentences tailored to fit the circumstances of individual cases. However, "when pressed, attorneys generally conceded that a fundamental source of their distaste was indeed the difficulties it caused them in dealing with clients" (Church, 1976:392). Under the new prosecutor, drug sale cases were warranted only when there was a controlled buy, the likelihood of an acquittal at trial was small, and, without charge reductions, defense lawyers had difficulty demonstrating to their clients that their representation had gained anything for the client except a legal fee. Although judges became willing participants in sentence negotiations, defense lawyers found sentence bargaining frustrating. It required that they invest considerable effort in learning about their clients and their clients' cases. Moreover "the kinds of assurances possible in sentence bargaining were usually vague, ephemeral, and dependent on unpredictable contingencies, such as the probation report" (Church, 1976:394).

The primary inconvenience to retained counsel was that plea bargaining became somewhat more ambiguous and it was more difficult to convince the defendant who was pleading guilty that he or she would receive something of value for the lawyer's fee. Court-appointed counsel had a more difficult time (Hampton County has no public defender). The fees paid to appointed counsel were small and "most attorneys agreed that economic incentives work strongly toward disposing of a case as soon as possible through a plea since little additional income could be obtained to

offset the considerable time and effort needed for a
trial" (Church, 1976:394). Appointed counsel, like that
in most jurisdictions, tended to be mistrusted by their
clients and, because sentence bargaining requires
considerable background information about the offense and
the defendant and requires both attorney effort and
client confidence, the job of the defense lawyer became
more arduous and more frustrating (Church, 1976:395).

Conclusion

The Hampton County study supports the argument that under
some circumstances criminal court practitioners will
circumvent controls on their discretion by revising their
behavior to achieve their traditional ends in new ways.
Sentence bargaining did replace charge bargaining;
however, without more information on screening outcomes
and sanctions imposed, it is unclear whether the charge
bargaining ban had significant substantive consequences.

Michigan

The third major study that involved an assessment of the
abolition of plea bargaining also involved Michigan
(Heumann and Loftin, 1979). Effective January 1, 1977,
the Michigan Felony Firearm Statute mandated a prison
sentence for any defendant who possessed a firearm while
engaging in a felony. In addition to the sentence for
the primary felony, the law required imposition of a
two-year sentence that cannot be suspended or shortened
by parole release. Although the law did not prohibit
plea bargaining, the Wayne County (Detroit) prosecutor
forbade dismissal of firearms charges pursuant to plea
bargains. Since the charge determined the incremental
mandatory sentence, prohibition of charge bargaining also
accomplished a prohibition of sentence bargaining.

Because both the plea bargaining abolition and
mandatory sentencing laws were involved, we discuss this
study here and in the next section. Here the emphasis is
mostly on adaptive reactions and some statistical data on
dispositions.

The research consisted of 23 formal interviews with
judges, prosecutors, and defense counsel (and numerous
informal discussions) and a statistical analysis of data
from the Detroit PROMIS system, the computerized court

information system, and the prosecutor's paper files
(including arrest reports). The evaluation compares case
processing in the 6-month periods before and after
January 1, 1977.

Although there were numerous opportunities for
assistant prosecutors to circumvent the plea bargaining
ban, Heumann and Loftin conclude that "the interview and
quantitative data lend qualified support to a conclusion
that in fact the Prosecutor was successful in obtaining
the compliance of his subordinates" (Heumann and Loftin,
1979:402). There were familiar objections from defense
counsel that assistant prosecutors inflexibly refused to
bargain, even in exceptional cases, and the familiar
ambivalent expressions of support from assistant
prosecutors, who approved the ban in general but would
have permitted some exceptions. Unlike the Alaska
attorney general, but like the Hampton County prosecutor,
the Wayne County prosecutor used management supervisory
methods to ensure that assistant prosecutors followed the
policy. It appears that prosecutors adhered to the rule
except possibly for warranting prosecutors who simply
failed to charge or record firearms involvement in some
cases. "Interviews, however, suggested some slippage at
this stage, though the consensus seemed to be that
exceptions were relatively infrequent and made only in
borderline cases" (p. 405).

To test the extent of underwarranting, Heumann and
Loftin examined all armed robberies, felonious assaults,
and other assaults involving firearms that were prosecuted and disposed during the first six months after the
new law took effect. The gun law charge had been made in
95 percent of those cases, suggesting that underwarranting was not widespread (Heumann and Loftin, 1979:407).

To assess the combined impact of the mandatory
sentencing law and the prohibition of plea bargaining,
Heumann and Loftin compared data on dispositions and
sentences in cases originally charged as felonious
assault, other assault, or armed robbery in which a gun
was used. The "before" sample consisted of offenses
committed any time before January 1, 1977, and disposed
of between July 1, 1976, and June 30, 1977. The "after"
sample consisted of all offenses committed and disposed
in the first six months after the law took effect on
January 1, 1977. Like the Hampton County study, the
statistical analysis consists of inferences from a
tabular presentation of information on dispositions from
pretrial dismissal through sentencing.

For a number of reasons, the data can be no more than suggestive and they will not be discussed at length here. First, although Heumann and Loftin looked at all of the cases within their categories during the time periods involved, the numbers of cases in their samples, especially the "after" samples, are small. Moreover, while they do not suggest any reason to be concerned that the different composition of cases comprising the two samples reduces their comparability (Heumann and Loftin, 1979:409), we are somewhat less sanguine about that. Table 7-9, showing sample sizes and median case-processing times, suggests that the cases constituting the before and after samples may have been significantly different. The before sample required almost three times longer for disposition and generated samples four times larger than the after samples. It is not unreasonable to speculate that the before sample is more heterogeneous than the after sample: It includes cases that required very long processing times as well as open-and-shut cases that were dispatched in a few days or weeks. The after sample contains no cases, by definition, that required more than six months for disposition and is probably heavily skewed toward easily disposed cases that may be systematically different from cases that take longer to resolve. Virtually any case that can be disposed within a few weeks that was filed

TABLE 7-9 Sample Size and Case Processing Time for Wayne County, Michigan

| | Felonious Assault | | Other Assault | | Armed Robbery | |
	Before[a]	After[b]	Before	After	Before	After
Sample Size	145	39	240	53	471	136
Median Processing Time (Days)	150	54	212	50	164	57

[a]Offense committed before January 1, 1977, and case disposed between July 1, 1976, and June 30, 1977.
[b]Offense committed and case disposed between January 1, 1977, and June 30, 1977.

SOURCE: Heumann and Loftin (1979:Table 3 and p. 409, n. 31).

TABLE 7-10 Disposition of Original Charges in Wayne County, Michigan, by Offense Type and Time Period

	N	Dismissed at/Before Pretrial (%)	Dismissed or Acquitted After Pretrial (%)	Convicted/ No Prison (%)	Some Prison (%)	Total[a] (%)
Felonious Assault						
Before[b]	145	24	31	31	14	100
After[c]	39	26	26	31	18	101
Other Assault						
Before	240	12	24	28	37	101
After	53	26	24	9	41	102
Armed Robbery						
Before	471	13	19	4	64	100
After	136	22	17	2	60	101

aThe totals do not always sum to 100 percent because of rounding.
bOffense committed before January 1, 1977, and case disposed between July 1, 1976, and June 30, 1977.
cOffense committed and case disposed between January 1, 1977, and June 30, 1977.

SOURCE: Heumann and Loftin (1979:Table 3).

within the six-month study period is included in the sample. However, if we assume that cases requiring the median disposition times of 150, 212, and 164 days continued to require comparable disposition times, few of them would be included in the after sample.

We do not know whether the two samples are so non-comparable as to make comparisons suspect. We shall accordingly, somewhat uneasily, accept Heumann and Loftin's assurances that they see no reason to doubt comparability (in fairness they do many times suggest that their findings are tentative) and report their findings.

Dispositions

Overall it did not appear that there was a substantial impact on sentences for defendants processed in court (including those dismissed and acquitted). The proportion of all defendants receiving incarcerative sentences did not increase.

Many armed robbery defendants--more than a third in each sample--avoided prison sentences altogether, primarily through dismissal or acquittal (see Table 7-10). There were, however, some increases in the severity of prison terms imposed. The proportion of armed robbery defendants who received sentences of five years or more increased from 34 to 41 percent. The proportion of defendants receiving sentences equalling or exceeding the two-year minimum increased by 50 percent or more for other assaults (from 22 to 33 percent of defendants) and felonious assaults (from 4 to 13 percent of defendants).

Taking the conventional view that sentencing concessions are required to induce guilty pleas and that their denial will result in more trials, Heumann and Loftin compared modes of disposition during the two periods. The number of trials overall is small, but their data suggested that bench trials increased for felonious and other assault cases but not for armed robberies and that jury trials increased for felonious assault cases but not for other assaults and armed robberies (see Table 7-11). They also found that trials were associated with relatively light sanctions.

Concerning the combined impact of the mandatory law and the plea bargaining abolition, Heumann and Loftin conclude overall (pp. 415-416):

TABLE 7-11 Mode of Disposition of Cases Not Dismissed At
or Before Pretrial Conference in Wayne County, Michigan,
by Offense Type and Observation Period

Offense	Observation Period	N	Percent No Trial	Percent Trial	Percent Bench Trial	Percent Jury Trial
Felonious	Before[a]	110	84	16	9	7
Assault	After[b]	29	59	41	21	21
Other	Before	212	67	33	15	18
Assault	After	39	72	28	20	8
Armed	Before	411	70	30	9	21
Robbery	After	106	76	24	8	16

[a]Offense committed before January 1, 1977, and case disposed between
July 1, 1976, and June 30, 1977.
[b]Offense committed and case disposed between January 1, 1977, and
June 30, 1977.

SOURCE: Heumann and Loftin (1979:Table 4).

In sum, the experience with cases completed during the
six months after the intervention of the gun law
indicates that there has been only a slight upward
shift in the average sentence. Clearly there has been
no massive increase in the number of cases that
receive a sentence of two years or more. Furthermore,
the only increase in the proportion of cases that go
to trial is in felonious assaults and these trials are
associated with light sentence.

Adaptive Responses

If prosecutors consistently filed gun law charges and
refused to bargain them away, why did sentence severity
not increase dramatically? Heumann and Loftin offer
several answers.

First, especially for felonious assault cases,
"waiver" trials were used to avoid the mandatory two-year
sentence. Judges and lawyers openly acknowledged that
the waiver trial was a mechanism for avoiding the impact
of the mandatory sentence law. In one form of waiver

trial judges gave explicit prior indications that they would dismiss the gun charge at trial, often with the prosecutor's acquiescence. In a second form of waiver trial there was no explicit understanding between the defense lawyer and the judge, but "these judges concede that they would consider every possible defense and require evidence of every element of the charge such as the presence of an operable firearm; but when the case is technically indisputable they feel trapped by the law and left with no option but to apply it" (Heumann and Loftin, 1979:419). One judge had managed in every case over two years to find justifiable reason to reduce the felony charge to a misdemeanor (thus making the mandatory sentence inapplicable) or to dismiss the gun charge, but he expressed apprehension that some day he would not be able to find a good faith reason to circumvent the mandatory sentence (pp. 419-420).

Finally, interviews led Heumann and Loftin to conclude that judges routinely nullified the mandatory two year add-on by reducing the sentence imposed on the primary felony by an offsetting two years (Heumann and Loftin, 1979:422):

> Essentially, the respondents agreed that the gun law would not lead to a substantial increase in the "going rates." Most respondents claimed that judges adjusted their prior going rate to take into account the two years added by the new law.

This observation is not inconsistent with the statistical data that showed an insubstantial increase in sentence severity. As in Alaska, it appears that the primary effects of the Michigan law were on marginal defendants. In cases in which it was relatively clear that some prison sentence would be imposed, prisoners who might otherwise have received a one-year sentence could not benefit from the judges' new math (Heumann and Loftin, 1979:423):

> In particular some [respondents] felt that in the "less serious of the serious" armed robberies and assaults, the Gun Law marginally increased the sentence. For example, a defendant convicted of armed robbery in Segment I could receive as little as one year from some judges, two from others. In Segment II the minimum would be three years (one year for the armed robbery, two for the Gun Law.

Heumann and Loftin's policy conclusions resemble those of Church. They endorse a static notion of the disposition process in which the courtroom community will co-opt formal changes so that things may go on as before (Heumann and Loftin, 1979:426):

> The system managed to digest the two policy innovations without a radical alteration in its disposition patterns. Court personnel suspected as much: time and again in their interviews they indicated that somehow the system would accommodate itself, that things would work themselves out without any major departures from past practice.

And later the authors conclude (p. 429): "We are therefore pessimistic about effecting radical changes in the criminal justice system."

MANDATORY SENTENCING LAWS

Polemically and politically speaking, mandatory sentencing laws have much to offer. As a means of gun control they sidestep the gun lobby. They are simple and easy to understand. They sound severe. It makes intuitive sense that crime will abate if miscreants are inexorably convicted and imprisoned. Practically speaking, the case for mandatory sentencing is more ambiguous. Prosecutors can always and everywhere elect whether to file charges bearing mandatory minimum sentences or some other charge, and whether to dismiss charges. As under any severe but rigid rule, sympathetic cases cause decision makers to seek ways to avoid the rule. Juries, judges, and lawyers have routinely evaded mandatory sentencing laws for 300 years (Hay et al., 1975:Chapter 1; Michael and Wechsler, 1940). Finally, if literally applied, mandatory sentence cases would engorge the prisons.

Numerous mandatory sentencing laws have been passed in recent years. Impact evaluations of three of them have been published and are reviewed here (Beha, 1977; Joint Committee, 1977; Heumann and Loftin, 1979; Loftin and McDowall, 1981).

First, however, a few words might usefully be devoted to considering the criteria by which the success of a mandatory sentencing law should be appraised. Mandatory laws can be seen as only political theater: The purposes are rhetorical and are achieved at the moment of passage. This is not so cynical a position as it may appear. The lawyers and legislators who preside over the enactment of such laws surely appreciate the ambivalence with which they will be administered and the financial costs and incidental injustices that would result if every person who did X received a three-year prison sentence. With this possibility in mind, we review findings of the impact of such laws on case processing and dispositions.

We note one caveat: The studies considered here were largely concerned with the deterrent effects of the laws studied. Case processing and dispositions received subsidiary attention and, accordingly, the quality of the data adduced is sometimes unsatisfying. To assess the impact of a mandatory sentence law on case processing, one needs to know about patterns of arrest, charging, indictment, dismissal, plea bargaining, conviction, and sentencing over time. Unfortunately, none of these studies provides all that information in adequate detail, and therefore much of our effort to draw conclusions from these works involves the drawing of weak inferences, commonsense speculations, and the like.

Michigan

The Michigan Felony Firearm Statute is described above in some detail. It created a new offense of possessing a firearm while engaging in a felony and mandated a two-year prison sentence that could not be suspended or shortened by release on parole and that must be served consecutively to the sentence imposed for the underlying felony. The gun possession charge had to be separately charged; its applicability thus depended on the decisions of Michigan prosecutors. The law took effect on January 1, 1977, and was supplemented by the Wayne County prosecutor's ban on charge bargaining in firearms cases.

Two evaluations of Michigan are available. The first (Heumann and Loftin, 1979) consists of a statistical analysis of case processing and dispositions for the six-month periods before and after January 1, 1977, and a series of 23 interviews with judges, lawyers, and prosecutors. The second (Loftin and McDowall, 1981), analyzed dispositions for 8,414 cases originally charged with a violent felony[8] and disposed of in court during 1976, 1977, and 1978. While the second study covers a longer time period and includes considerably more cases, no descriptive statistics on case dispositions or distributions are provided. The description of case processing that follows is drawn entirely from the more limited six-month samples in Heumann and Loftin (1979).

Arrest and Case Screening

Arrest information is not germane because the firearms charge is dependent on the underlying felony charge. The primary data for the study available from PROMIS were inadequate to examine early case screening; the data begin with cases already warranted for prosecution. Separate analysis of case files to determine whether the firearms charge was in fact warranted when supported by the facts found that "in the overwhelming majority of cases, the prosecutor did indeed charge the gun count" (Heumann and Loftin, 1979:407).

Dismissal and Conviction Rates

One conventional prediction concerning mandatory sentencing laws is that lawyers and judges will dismiss charges and acquit defendants in order to avoid imposition of sentences they believe are unduly harsh. Table 7-10 shows Heumann and Loftin's data on case dispositions for felonious assault, other assault, and armed robbery.[9] Felonious assaults typically "grow out of disputes among acquaintances or relatives and are, by conventional standards, less predatory than armed robberies (Heumann and Loftin, 1979:412). "Other assaults" were an intermediate category including a variety of "assault with intent to commit . . . " charges.

Table 7-10 reveals little change in disposition patterns for felonious assault: Just under half of the persons charged were convicted but fewer than 20 percent received a prison sentence in either period. Armed robbery processing changed little, although there was a tendency toward increased early dismissal of charges, which rose from 13 percent of persons charged to 22 percent, with slight declines at each critical juncture thereafter. "Other assault" shows a marked tendency toward increased early dismissal, rising from 12 percent to 26 percent, and an offsetting decline in the percentage of convictions, even though the likelihood of incarceration, given warranting, increased. This combination of findings is consistent with a hypothesis that efforts were made to ensure that sympathetic defendants would not be vulnerable to imprisonment. The "other assault" cases were the middle category, in which the greatest ambiguities were likely to exist, and they exhibit the greatest changes in dispositions.

Sanctioning Rates

Overall, the percentage of defendants who were incarcerated did not change markedly in Wayne County. However, the likelihood of incarceration after conviction did change significantly, from 57 to 82 percent, for offenders convicted of "other assault." This increase in imprisonment more than offset the increased number of early dismissals.

There was also an increase in the length of sentences for imprisoned offenders after the new law took effect. While the sample sizes involved are small and suggest caution in accepting the findings derived from them, there did appear to be increased sentence severity for individual offense categories. Of offenders imprisoned for felonious assault, the proportion sentenced to terms of two years or more increased from 30 to 71 percent. For imprisoned "other assault" offenders, the portion receiving at least two-year terms rose from 59 to 81 percent after the law. There was little increase in the use of the minimum two-year term for armed robbery (from 87 to 93 percent).

Loftin and McDowall (1981) report similar effects on a considerably expanded data set. Using modified multiple regression analysis,[10] they find no effect of the gun law on the expected time served for offenders charged with murder or armed robbery. The expected sentences for felonious assault and other assaults, however, did increase more for cases involving guns. Similar results were found for the probability of prison among charged offenders.

Trial Rates

Table 7-11 shows mode of disposition by offense type and time period. The only substantial change shown is the trebled rate of felonious assault cases resolved at

trial. Even this increase, from 16 to 41 percent, probably understates the shift: The after period includes
only cases initiated and resolved within the six-month
study period for a maximum follow-up of six months; the
before period, by contrast, includes cases for offenses
committed any time before January 1, 1977, but disposed
of between July 1, 1976, and June 30, 1977, for a minimum
follow-up of six months. The shorter follow-up in the
after period is likely to disproportionately exclude
unresolved trial cases for felonious assault.[11] The
large increase in the bench trial rate observed is mainly
due to judges' use of the "waiver" trial as a mechanism
to circumvent both the mandatory gun law and the prosecutor's ban on charge bargaining.

To summarize: There was a significant increase in
dismissals of "other assault" and robbery cases, effecting for "other assault" a significant decrease in the
percentage of cases convicted at trial but without imprisonment. The likelihood of imprisonment once charged
remained the same for all three categories of crime. The
likelihood of imprisonment after conviction increased for
"other assault." There was a discernible increase in
sentence severity for those imprisoned. And the trial
rate trebled for felonious assault cases but decreased
slightly for the other two offense categories.

Massachusetts

Massachusetts's Bartley-Fox Amendment required imposition
of a one-year mandatory minimum prison sentence, without
suspension, furlough, or parole, for anyone convicted of
carrying an unlicensed firearm. Unlike the Michigan law,
Bartley-Fox did not require that the defendant be charged
or convicted for another offense. The law took effect on
April 1, 1975.

To assess the law's impact on case processing and
sanctioning, Beha (1977) collected data on all prosecutions for firearms crimes in the six months after the law
took effect and for the corresponding six months of the
preceding year. All complaints relating to the illegal
use, possession, or carrying of a firearm were included
in the samples, comprising 467 cases in 1975 and 615 in
1974. Some defense lawyers were interviewed, but no
judges or prosecutors.

The Massachusetts study was designed to test a number
of specific hypotheses about police, prosecutorial, and

judicial adaptations to a law that practitioners generally disliked. We summarize some of Beha's findings below, but first want to suggest several reasons why the findings of this study are inherently more ambiguous than those of other studies discussed in this review. First, the Boston district courts that were studied serve as preliminary hearing courts for the Massachusetts superior court in Boston: Some cases are simply bound over, and any district court conviction can be appealed to the superior court for a trial de novo. Thus a conviction or sentence in the district court need not mean that the defendant will ultimately be convicted or receive that sentence. Second, prosecutors and judges were not interviewed; the analysis draws almost entirely on statistical data. It is not impossible that judges and prosecutors could explain ambiguous or perplexing statistical findings. For example, Michigan lawyers explained the threefold increase in trials for felonious assault in Michigan as a way to get around the prosecutor's plea bargaining ban. Third, unlike that of Michigan, the Massachusetts law did not require an incremental sentence, and thus firearms carrying charges were of marginal importance to prosecutions for violent crimes, for which an incarcerative sentence was likely in any event.

Arrests and Prosecutorial Screening

Illegal possession of a firearm is a misdemeanor that does not require imposition of a prison sentence. Consequently, one might expect police to substitute "possession" charges for "carrying" charges when sympathetic defendants are involved. Similarly, one might expect prosecutors to screen out carrying charges or reduce them to possession. Beha concluded that neither adaptation occurred. Firearms arrests did decline by 31 percent from the 1974 period to the 1975 period. Both carrying and possession arrests declined, as did arrests for carrying a firearm in a nongun felony (by 49 percent). These developments and others "are strong evidence for the argument that the (decline) . . . was due primarily to increased citizen compliance" with Massachusetts's gun registration law (Beha, 1977:135). Furthermore, on the basis of a case-by-case analysis of police files in firearm possession cases, Beha concludes, "Police evasion of the mandatory penalty by this route (downgrading to possession) simply did not occur" (p. 135).

Nor according to Beha was there prosecutorial circumvention. As a practical matter, police initiate complaints in the district court, and there is little plea bargaining. There is considerable plea bargaining in the superior court. Beha found only a few cases in which carrying charges were dropped to possession, and they were all plausibly explained on the basis of case circumstances: "Prosecutorial discretion . . . has been exercised in favor of the Bartley-Fox defendants in our Boston sample rarely or not at all" (Beha, 1977:137).

Dismissal and Conviction

The effects of the carrying law on the district courts were to increase the incidence of acquittals, to increase greatly the rate of appeals to the superior court, to eliminate the use of several nonadjudicative dispositions, and to increase the rate of absconding (i.e., jumping bail).

Table 7-12 shows district court dispositions for the before and after periods. The dispositions "continued for dismissal" and "guilty, filed" were equivalent to stays of judgment and were expressly forbidden by the

TABLE 7-12 Disposition of Carrying Firearms Charges in Boston District Courts by Most Serious Accompanying Charge

Disposed Cases	Percent Each Charge							
	Robbery		Assault with a Deadly Weapon		Nongun Felony		Firearms Only	
	1974 (N=16)	1975 (N=14)	1974 (N=27)	1975 (N=19)	1974 (N=36)	1975 (N=25)	1974 (N=145)	1975 (N=107)
Dismissed	19	8	36	6	3	6	12	15
Continued for Dismissal	6	0	4	0	9	0	9	0
Not Guilty	6	31	8	12	25	11	16	36
Guilty, filed	0	0	0	0	0	0	2	0
Guilty, penalty	0	8	36	24	38	6	40	1
Guilty, appeal	0	8	0	47	9	61	12	38
Bound Over	64	46	16	12	16	11	9	6
Indicted	6	0	0	0	0	6	1	3
All Dispositions[a]	101	101	100	101	100	101	101	99

[a]The totals do not always sum to 100 percent because of rounding.

SOURCE: Adapted from Beha (1977:Table II).

statute. Their use ceased. More important, there was a
general increase in acquittals, especially for defendants
also charged with robbery and those charged only with the
firearms violation. An additional one-fifth (36 percent
less 16 percent) of the defendants charged only with a
firearms offense who might have been convicted under the
former law were acquitted under the new law.

On the basis of several inquiries--including interviews with defense attorneys and comparisons of presentence reports of acquitted and nonacquitted defendants--
Beha concluded that part of the acquittal increase reflects greater efforts by attorneys because the stakes
had been raised and that part of the increase reflects
a greater receptivity by judges to technical defenses.
However, he found no evidence of wanton evasion and "as
a usual matter, judges did not change their approach to
deciding cases merely to avoid the mandatory sentence"
(Beha, 1977:143).

Beha indicates that "all defendants found guilty of
the carrying violation in the district court were
sentenced to the mandatory one year of imprisonment"
(Beha, 1977:127). Looking at the line "guilty, appeal"
in Table 7-12, the incidence of appeal to the trial de
novo in superior court tripled for firearms carrying
charges by themselves; the increase in appeals was even
greater for assault with a deadly weapon and nongun
felonies. Patently, judges were imposing the minimum
sentences and defendants did not like it. Unfortunately,
the cases were not followed into the superior court to
determine final dispositions.

The increase in appeals is more striking in Table 7-13.
Excluding robbery, the percentage of total cases that
proceeded to the superior court increased from less than
one-fifth to more than half. But as Table 7-13 shows,
the percentage of defendants absconding also increased,
especially for robbery and other nongun felonies.

Sanctions and Delay

Unfortunately, nothing can be said about either sanctions
or delay. Implicitly the appeals increase suggests that
the imposition of prison sentences increased substantially in district courts, but whether these sentences
survived superior court processing is unknown. Similarly,
the increased rate of appeals suggests that average court
processing times increased.

TABLE 7-13 Summary of Dispositions for Carrying Firearms
Charges in Boston District Courts by Most Serious
Accompanying Charge

| | Percent Each Charge | | | | | | | |
| | Robbery | | Assault with a Deadly Weapon | | Nongun Felony | | Firearms Only | |
Total Cases	1974	1975	1974	1975	1974	1975	1974	1975
Default/Pending	0	7	7	11	11	28	12	12
To Superior Court	75	50	15	53	22	56	19	42

SOURCE: Adapted from Beha (1977:Table II).

To sum up: Adaptation is evident in the substantial
increase in acquittals for defendants charged only under
the carrying statute and those also charged with robbery;
appeals to the superior court increased enormously, suggesting that the minimum sentence was being imposed at
district courts; and the absconding rate increased.

New York

The Rockefeller Drug Law took effect on September 1, 1973.
It prescribed severe and mandatory prison sentences for
narcotics offenses at all levels and included selective
statutory limits on plea bargaining. The statute divided
heroin dealers into three groups based on the quantities
sold or held for sale:

Category	Quantity	Minimum Sentence
A-I	sell 1 oz. or possess more than 2 oz.	15-25 years
A-II	sell 1/8 oz. or more; possess 1-2 oz.	6-8 1/3 years
A-III	sell less than 1/8 oz; possess less than 1 oz.	1-8 1/3 years

The law permitted plea bargaining within the A felony class but forbade bargained dismissals that would reduce the offense of conviction below Class A-III (there were exceptions for informants and for offenders ages 16-18).

The impact evaluation of the Joint Committee on New York Drug Law Evaluation was primarily interested in the deterrent effects of the new law in diminishing drug trafficking and use and in reducing drug-related crime. There was no evidence that any of these goals were accomplished, although publicity about the law may have caused a short-term suppression effect in some areas (Joint Committee, 1977:7-11).

The case processing evaluation primarily involved aggregate state-level data; less attention was paid to some data from New York City and five other counties. With the exception of two small projects intended to measure the use of a related provision that required that a prison sentence be ordered for any defendant previously convicted of a felony, the case-processing analysis depended on statistics routinely compiled by operating agencies. Case processing was not examined closely; some interviews were conducted with judges and lawyers, but they were not systematic and apparently focused on general reactions to the law and not on the details of case processing.

Unfortunately, the parts of the evaluation that deal with case processing do not shed much useful light on the questions with which we are concerned. The statewide data simply do not permit detailed analysis of why judges and lawyers did what and when. Summarizing the results from 1972 to 1976: Drug felony arrests, indictment rates, and conviction rates all declined; imprisonment rates among convictions increased steadily; and the likelihood of imprisonment given arrest for a drug felony remained the same, at approximately 11 percent.

Table 7-14 shows state-level drug felony disposition figures for the period January 1, 1972, through June 30, 1976. Some caveats may be in order about the numbers it contains. First, the data are aggregates that include all drug felony charges, including marijuana offenses and other than Class A drug felonies. Public attitudes and drug law enforcement patterns were in considerable flux during the period 1972-1976 and felonies other than Class A were subject to mandatory sentences but not to the plea bargaining abolition. Unless the data are disaggregated, only weak inferences can be drawn from them about Class A felony processing. Second, the number

TABLE 7-14   Drug Felony Processing in New York State

	1972	1973[a]	1974	1975	1976 (Jan.- June)
Arrests	19,269	15,594	17,670	15,941	8,166
Indictments	7,528	5,969	5,791	4,283	2,073
(% of Arrests)	(39.1)	(38.3)	(32.8)	(26.9)	(25.4)
Indictments disposed	6,911	5,580	3,939	3,989	2,173
Convictions	6,033	4,739	3,085	3,147	1,724
(% of dispositions)	(87.3)	(84.9)	(78.3)	(78.9)	(79.3)
Prison and jail sentences	2,039	1,555	1,074	1,369	945
(% of Convictions)	(33.8)	(32.8)	(34.8)	(43.5)	(54.8)
(% of Arrests)	(10.6)	(10.0)	(6.1)	(8.6)	(11.6)

[a]The new drug law went into effect September 1, 1973.

SOURCE: Joint Committee (1977:Tables 19, 24, 27, 29).

of drug felony arrests declined after 1972, suggesting major changes in police policies. (The evaluation indicates that New York City police did adopt a restrictive arrest policy [Joint Committee, 1977:90-91].) Third, the data are statewide aggregates. Inferences derived from them are subject to an ecological fallacy; statewide trends do not necessarily parallel local trends anywhere. Indeed, there is evidence in the report that arrest and prosecution trends varied substantially among different counties over the five-year period (pp. 123-145). Fourth, some jurisdictions implemented more stringent screening standards for drug cases, thus reducing the numbers but increasing the "convictability" of defendants arrested (pp. 123-124).

Given the smaller number of (possibly higher-quality) arrests, it is not surprising that the percentage of convictions resulting in incarceration increased (from 33.8 percent to 54.8 percent). It is initially surprising, however, that the percentage of indictments resulting in convictions declined, from 87.3 percent in 1972 to 79.3 percent in the first half of 1976. On one hand, this could reflect increased dismissals after

indictment to avoid the mandatory prison sentences. Data
for New York City showed a marked increase in the percentage of drug felony indictments resulting in dismissals: 1972--6.8 percent; 1973--6.9 percent; 1974--16.7
percent; 1975--21.3 percent (Joint Committee, 1977:Table
28). Or the decline could be the product of processing
delays resulting from implementation of the new law that
slowed final disposition for convictions. On the other
hand, the apparent decline in the conviction rate may
understate a real decline. Because drug felony case
disposition times doubled in New York City between 1973
(172 days) and the first half of 1975 (351 days), convictions in each succeeding year relate to increasing
numbers of arrests made in earlier years. The arrest
numbers in those earlier years were substantially greater
than in 1975 and 1976, and it may be that the percentages
of those earlier cases resulting in convictions are much
lower than the figures shown in Table 7-14.

No serious effort to study case processing was made,
and it is difficult for us to say much about it or about
the implications of the aggregate disposition data presented in Table 7-14. We do make several points below.

Dismissal

The numbers of arrests and indictments for drug felony
offenses in New York City declined greatly. Arrests
dropped from 26,378 in 1970 to 7,498 in 1975, while
indictments declined from 4,388 in 1972 to 2,250 in 1975.
For felony heroin cases, arrests went from 22,301 in 1970
to 3,937 in 1975 (Joint Committee, 1977:Tables 20 and 21).

Incarceration Rates

The risk of incarceration for the small numbers of
defendants who were convicted increased significantly.
However, the steady decline in the number of drug felony
convictions from 1972 to 1976 offset the increased probability of incarceration given conviction, to yield a
fairly stable probability of incarceration given arrest.
Overall and statewide, the proportion of drug felony
prisoners in the state prisons was essentially unchanged
from 1972 (10.7 percent) to 1975 (10.8 percent) (Joint
Committee, 1977:Table 17). However, in 1976 prison
commitments for drug offenses rose substantially, increasing 35 percent over the number in 1975 (Table 18).

Similar results on increased incarceration rates emerge in an analysis of the impact of a related law, requiring imposition of prison sentences on any person convicted of a felony who had a previous felony conviction. For these second felony offenders, the probability of imprisonment, given conviction, rose from 70 percent to 92 percent (Table 8).

Severity of Prison Sentences

The severity of prison terms imposed on sentenced drug offenders increased markedly. Under the old law, between 1972 and 1974 only 3 percent of sentenced drug felons received minimum sentences of more than three years. Under the new law, the use of long minimums increased to 22 percent. Between September 1973 and June 1976, an astonishing 1,777 offenders were sentenced to indeterminate lifetime prison terms, a sentence rarely imposed before the new drug law (Joint Committee, 1977:99-103).

Trial Rates

Probably because the drug law forbade plea-bargained charge dismissals below a Class A-III offense, the trial rate as a percentage of dispositions in New York City rose from 6 percent in 1972 to 17 percent in the first six months of 1976 (Joint Committee, 1977:104). During the period January 1, 1974, to June 30, 1976, 23.4 percent of all Class A dispositions involved trials; for all Class A-II dispositions the trial rate was 34.6 percent (Table 35).

Delays in Court

Presumably because of the increased trial rates (in New York City in 1974 it "took between ten and fifteen times as much court time to dispose of a case by trial as by plea" [Joint Committee, 1977:105]), average case processing times in New York City increased steadily:

Sept-Dec 1973	172 days
1974	239 days
1975	265 days
Jan-June 1976	351 days

Not surprisingly, and notwithstanding the addition of 31 new criminal courts in New York City, the drug case backlog increased by 2,205 cases from September 1, 1973, to June 30, 1976, representing 85 percent of the rise in backlog over that period (Tables 33 and 34).

The substantial delay in case processing has implications for the impact assessment. The first six months' experience in 1976--some two and one-half years after the drug law took effect--were the last observations before implementation of major amendments to the law. The experiences in the first half of 1976 reflected sharp increases in prison commitments as well as increases in both the number of disposed indictments and convictions over the previous two years' performance. This suggests that, because of the delays in case processing, it might not have been until 1976 or later that the impact of the law in generating more severe case outcomes was beginning to be fully realized. Unfortunately, from the perspective of our knowledge of the impact process, the mid-1976 changes in the law to permit expanded plea bargaining will confound any conclusions from subsequent observations.

Conclusion

For the reasons stated above, we are skeptical about the meaning of the New York dispositional data. The probability of incarceration given conviction presumably increased steadily, but whether that signifies harsher sentences in general, or simply that less serious offenders were increasingly filtered out before conviction, is unclear. It is clear that trial rates and court delays increased dramatically. Both trends contributed to the 1976 repeal of the plea bargaining restrictions.

The different reactions to radical changes in sentencing procedures in Alaska and New York may reflect no more than differences between the two states. Alaska's courts processed a total of only 2,283 defendants in two years. New York has a much higher volume of high-severity crime. The stakes are higher for more defendants, and the critical mass of high-stakes defendants, may be too large for any system to fully absorb.

DETERMINATE SENTENCING IN CALIFORNIA

The most extensively studied sentencing reform is the California Uniform Determinate Sentencing Law (DSL), which went into effect July 1, 1977. Many factors contributed to the widespread interest in the impact of this law. A primary consideration was the comprehensiveness of the change that affected sentencing to prison for all felonies. The new sentencing law also represented a substantial departure from the rehabilitative philosophy that had pervaded sentencing in California for 60 years. Determinate sentencing, with fixed prison terms set by the judge, replaced indeterminate sentencing (ISL), in which judges merely sentenced offenders to the statutory maximum with the release time being set by the Adult Authority. The California criminal justice system has also long been regarded as a preferred one for research purposes because of its integrated and automated records system and its accessibility to outside researchers.

At least seven major research projects have examined the impact of determinate sentencing in California. As summarized in Table 7-15, these studies vary considerably in the relative strengths and weaknesses of their evaluation designs. Different studies focus on different jurisdictional levels and different stages in case processing. While most are limited to statistical analyses of statewide data, three studies (Hubay, 1979; Casper et al., 1981; Utz, 1981) include greater controls for jurisdictional differences in case mix and in case processing by focusing on individual counties. Several of the studies are limited primarily to consideration of impact on sentence outcomes, particularly the proportion sentenced to prison after conviction and the length of prison terms imposed and served. Lipson and Peterson (1980) and to a much greater extent Casper et al. (1981) and Utz (1981) explicitly examine changes in charging practices and plea bargaining associated with DSL in addition to impacts on sentence outcomes. Such studies are intended to capture changes in the intervening processes leading to conviction and thus in the mix of cases actually available for sentencing as well as changes in sentences imposed.

The studies also vary in the degree of control for variations in case seriousness and for preexisting trends in case processing. With the exception of Utz (1981), the studies include minimal controls for case seriousness using legally defined crime type categories. Utz (1981), by contrast, employs elaborate controls including weapon use, use of threat or force, presence of victim, harm to victim, value of property taken, degree of criminal sophistication displayed, and whether the offender was implicated in multiple offense incidents. While the Utz study is strongest on controls for case seriousness, it is weakest on time controls, using only two points for comparisons of pre- and post-DSL changes. Two points do not permit adequate controls for preexisting trends in case processing. The other studies are better on this dimension because they involve multiple observations (at least in the preperiod) in most ISL/DSL comparisons. While the various studies are each individually flawed, combined they provide a fairly rich picture of impact at a variety of levels for determinate sentencing in California.

A procedural change as fundamental and complex as DSL has potential for widespread impact on the processing of criminal cases. In actual practice, however, we found relatively few changes that might be attributed to DSL:

- Judges largely complied with the requirements of the law when sentencing convicted defendants; the considerable discretion of the prosecutor in initial charging and later dismissal practices was not affected.
- There is no evidence of substantial changes in initial charging practices, at least for cases finally disposed of in superior court.
- Explicit bargaining over the length of prison terms was limited to those jurisdictions already engaged in extensive sentence bargaining.
- Enhancements and probation ineligibility provisions represented important bargaining chips for the prosecutor; these allegations were frequently dropped in return for defense agreements to prison terms.
- While there were no substantial changes in aggregate guilty plea rates, there is some evidence that early guilty pleas did increase after DSL.
- Prison use definitely increased after DSL; this increase was accompanied by apparent increasing imprisonment of less serious, marginal offenders. These increases in prison use, however, are best viewed as continuations of preexisting trends toward increased prison use in California and not as effects of DSL.
- Also consistent with preexisting trends, both mean and median prison terms to be served continued to decrease after DSL. There are also some indications of a decline in variation of sentences for

TABLE 7-15 Variations in Impact Evaluation Design: California Determinate Sentencing Law

Characteristics of Evaluations	Sparks (1981)	Hubay (1979)[a]	Brewer et al. (1980)	Lipson and Peterson (1980)	Ku (1980)	Casper et al. (1981)	Utz (1981)
Jurisdiction studied	State-wide	County	State-wide	State-wide	State-wide	Counties	Counties
Stages of case processing studied							
Charging		n.a.				yes	yes
Plea bargaining						yes	yes
Sentence outcomes in superior court	yes	n.a.	yes	yes	yes	yes	yes
Controls for variations in case seriousness							
Limited to control for crime types (legal categories)	yes		yes	yes	yes	yes	
Consideration of wide variety of factors, in addition to crime type, contributing to case seriousness							yes
Time frame studied							
Simple two-point pre/post design		n.a.					
Multiple observations in pre/post design	yes		yes	yes	yes	yes	yes

[a]The final report of Hubay (1979) was not available at this writing. Many of the details of the study design were therefore not available (n.a.).

the same convicted offense, although the range of
sentences observed under DSL remains broad.

- The Adult Authority exercised an important role in
controlling the size of prison populations through
their administrative releasing function; without
some similar "safety valve" release mechanism,
California's prison population can be expected to
increase dramatically as a result of increasing
prison commitments and only marginal decreases in
time served, particularly in view of legislative
increases in prison terms.

Description of the
California Uniform Determinate Sentencing Law

The original determinate sentencing law (SB42 as amended
by AB476) took effect July 1, 1977. The bill was
subsequently amended in 1978 by SB709 and SB1057 to
increase the severity of penalties for offenses committed
after January 1, 1979, especially for violent offenses.

In contrast to the indeterminate prison sentences
previously imposed by judges, under DSL judges are
charged to set a fixed term of sentence for each offender
sentenced to prison. This term is to be selected from
the set of three base terms determined by the legislature
for each offense type (e.g., for robbery the terms are 2,
3, and 5 years). The middle term is the presumptive
sentence to be imposed except in cases with mitigating or
aggravating circumstances that warrant use of the lower
or upper base terms.

In cases involving conviction for multiple charges the
judge may impose separate terms on each charge to be
served consecutively or concurrently. The law also
provides for enhancements that further increase prison
terms in cases involving weapon use, great bodily injury
to the victim, excessive property loss, or prior prison
terms. These enhancements provide an opportunity for
assessing differences in the gravity of offenses within a
conviction category. Enhancements must be formally
charged by the prosecutor and then pled or proved in
court. Once proven the judge may impose the addition to
the base sentence or stay its imposition. The legislation also includes provisions for mandatory probation
ineligibility for certain violent felonies, certain heroin
trafficking offenses, defendants convicted of specified
felonies who were twice convicted of designated felonies

in the preceding 10 years, and defendants personally
using a firearm in the commission of any of 10 enumerated
crimes. The 1978 amendments further extended mandatory
prison terms to defendants convicted of various sex
offenses or who inflicted great bodily injury during
commission of designated serious felonies.

DSL created a new Board of Prison Terms, whose main
function is to review all prison sentences imposed for
disparity and, in cases of apparently disparate
sentences, to recommend resentencing to the sentencing
judge. Under DSL all inmates are subject to parole
supervision upon release for a time in addition to their
prison term (originally for one year for most prisoners,
and later increased to three years by the 1978 amendments). The new law also provided "good-time" credits of
up to 3 months off every year of sentence for good behavior and another month off for program participation.
Good-time credits vest at the end of each eight months
and once vested they cannot be taken away. Upon implementation the sentence provisions of DSL were applied
retroactively to all persons serving indeterminate sentences, except dangerous offenders deemed eligible for
extended terms.

The statutory changes were generally expected to reduce
disparity in sentences and to increase the severity of
punishment. The reductions in disparity were expected to
follow directly from increases in uniformity in sentences.
The increases in severity of punishment through expanded
use of prison for convicted felons were expected to result
from judges' increased willingness to impose prison sentences of more certain duration and from the extended
probation ineligibility provisions.[12]

Formal Compliance With DSL

In this section we review the available evidence on
formal compliance with the procedural requirements of
DSL. These include use of the middle base term as the
presumptive sentence in most cases, charging and imposition of enhancements when warranted by the facts, and
enforcement of the probation ineligibility provisions.

Selection of Base Terms

Available evidence for 1977-1978 and 1979 indicates that
most offenders sentenced to prison in those years

received the presumptive middle base term, but that a
shift toward greater imposition of the lower base term
occurred in 1979. The shift appears to have resulted
from the 1978 amendments to DSL that increased the middle
and upper terms for many offenses.

Table 7-16 shows the distribution of base sentences,
by offense type, for prisoners received by the California
Department of Corrections in fiscal 1977-1978 and
calendar 1979. The middle base term was imposed in 61
percent of cases received in 1977-1978,[13] in 1979 the
rate declined to 54 percent. The data on 1979 receptions
indicate general changes in the distribution of base
sentences, including declines in use of middle and/or
upper terms and increases in use of lower terms across
offense types. As in 1977-1978, however, despite changes
in magnitude, upper terms remained more likely than lower
terms for most crimes against persons and lower terms
were more common for property and drug offenses.

One factor potentially contributing to this tendency
to impose the lower base terms in 1979 was implementation
in 1979 of the amendments to DSL in SB709, which
increased the length of middle and upper base terms for
certain offenses committed after January 1, 1979.[14] To
the extent that these new longer terms were regarded as
too severe by court participants, one would expect a
decrease in use of middle and upper terms. Consistent
with this expectation, the largest decreases in the use
of upper terms combined with the greatest increases in
the use of lower terms shown in Table 7-16 were found in
just those offenses directly affected by SB709. Most of
the other offenses also experienced decreases in the use
of middle terms and increases in the use of lower terms,
but in contrast to the SB709 offenses, they experienced
increases in the use of upper terms.

The Board of Prison Terms study (1981:Table VI)
directly compares cases sentenced before and after the
SB709 changes. This comparison indicates definite
decreases in the use of the longer middle and upper terms
for cases sentenced under SB709. This decrease, however,
extends well beyond the offenses directly affected by
SB709 to include offenses for which the base terms did
not change. While the overall shift to increased use of
lower terms may reflect a generalization of a direct
response to the increased sentences mandated by SB709,
these results are potentially confounded by the
possibility of seasonal variations in sentences. Cases
sentenced in the second half of the year, which includes
the Thanksgiving and Christmas holiday seasons when

TABLE 7-16   Use of Base Term Options for Offenders Received by the California Department of Corrections on a Single Count Conviction: Fiscal 1977-1978 and Calendar 1979

Offense Type	Year	% Cases with Each Base Term Option			% Single Count Convictions Among Total
		Lower	Middle	Upper	
All Offenses	1977-1978[a]	20.1	61.3	18.5	73.0
	1979[b]	27.1	54.0	18.9	69.8
Persons Offenses	1977-1978	20.5	57.2	22.3	69.1
	1979	24.8	54.3	20.9	63.4
2nd Degree Murder	1977-1978	18.4	57.9	23.7	82.6
	1979	22.8	45.5	31.7	71.1
*Voluntary Manslaughter	1977-1978	18.3	63.4	18.3	90.3[c]
	1979	21.7	53.0	25.3	89.0[c]
*Robbery	1977-1978	22.1	55.5	22.4	64.9
	1979	24.2	58.0	17.8	62.0
Assault	1977-1978	20.0	60.0	20.0	74.3
	1979	24.5	50.3	25.2	73.5
*Rape	1977-1978	17.0	53.2	29.8	54.7
	1979	33.6	50.4	16.0	33.5
*Crimes Against Children	1977-1978	12.5	37.5	50.0	61.5
	1979	22.2	42.9	34.9	67.0
*Oral Copulation	1977-1978	4.8	61.9	33.3	52.4
	1979	30.4	39.1	30.4	46.9
Property Offenses	1977-1978	18.3	67.1	14.6	76.5
	1979	27.4	55.2	17.4	74.0
*Burglary 1	1977-1978	19.7	59.1	21.0	65.3
	1979	31.1	52.3	16.4	61.1
Burglary 2	1977-1978	19.8	66.4	13.8	78.7
	1979	27.1	56.0	17.0	75.9
Grand Theft	1977-1978	19.2	70.7	10.1	82.8
	1979	29.4	53.2	17.4	80.4
Auto Theft	1977-1978	18.1	72.3	9.6	83.0
	1979	26.4	56.1	17.5	79.5
Forgery	1977-1978	12.5	70.8	16.7	61.5
	1979	30.8	47.4	21.8	53.0
Receiving Stolen Property	1977-1978	11.6	65.2	23.2	84.1
	1979	23.0	59.4	17.7	77.3
Drug Offenses	1977-1978	22.1	62.1	15.7	75.7
	1979	35.7	51.3	13.0	75.7

*Crime types with increased base terms in 1979.

[a]Derived from Brewer et al. (1980:Tables 9, 10).
[b]Derived from Board of Prison Terms (1981:Tables IV, VI).
[c]The portion of single count convictions for all manslaughter cases is reported here.

sentences might tend to be more lenient, were found predominantly among post-SB709 cases. Such a holiday effect would tend to decrease the severity of post-SB709 sentences relative to pre-SB709 sentences in this sample. A longer follow-up in both the pre and post samples, including data for comparable portions of the year, is needed to rule out a seasonal effect.

The general increase in the use of lower base terms from fiscal 1977-78 to calendar 1979 might also reflect a trend toward increased use of prison for less serious cases--an outcome anticipated by many at the time of DSL's passage. Under ISL, a judge who thought a defendant warranted a short state prison term, say two years, might hesitate to impose such a sentence because the defendant could be held by the Adult Authority for much longer. Under DSL, defendants could be sentenced to short determinate prison sentences, and it was widely expected that these marginal prison cases would then shift from local jails or probation to prison.

If expanded prison use were occurring through shifts from probation or jail to prison, the greatest changes would be expected among the less serious crime types, which are most likely to include marginal prison cases. The results in Table 7-16 are generally consistent with this hypothesis; the greatest increases in the use of lower base sentences were found in property and drug offenses. Indeed, aside from the offense types directly affected by SB709, the greatest shifts toward shorter sentences were for the less serious offenses of forgery, receiving stolen property, and drug offenses.

Despite the definite shift away from longer terms in 1979 for offenses directly affected by SB709 (Table 7-16), these offenses still experienced increases in the mean and median sentence length imposed between 1977-1978 and 1979.[15] The mean sentence for robbery, for example, increased from 51.8 to 56.9 months; for first-degree burglary the mean increased from 45.3 to 47.6 months, while the median went from 36 to 48 months. Thus, the decline in the use of upper and middle terms for these offenses was not sufficient in the aggregate to offset the increases in the length of their base terms.

Enhancements

Even when warranted by the facts of a case, enhancements tend to be used sparingly. Low charging rates combined

362

TABLE 7-17 Use of Enhancements Among Cases Received by California Department of Corrections in 1979

Enhancement and Offense Type	% Eligible Cases (Number Eligible)	% with Enhancement Charged Among Eligible Cases	% with Enhancement Pled or Proved Among Charged Cases	% with Enhancement Imposed Among Pled or Proved Cases	% with Enhancement Imposed Among Eligible Cases
Firearms					
All offenses	22.8 (n=2,365)	84.6	69.6	85.9	50.6
Burglary 1	6.7 (n=24)	83.3	60.0	83.4	41.7
Burglary 2	2.1 (n=37)	62.2	39.1	88.9	21.6
Robbery	56.4 (n=1,249)	90.1	73.7	87.0	57.8
Injury to victim	Minor / Major				
All offenses	9.1 (n=948) / 8.8 (n=917)	31.7	44.7	81.9	11.6
Burglary 1	8.9 (n=32) / 3.6 (n=13)	28.9	53.9	85.7	13.3
Burglary 2	1.8 (n=32) / 0.3 (n=6)	7.9	(1 of 3)	(1 of 1)	2.6
Robbery	14.0 (n=310) / 8.7 (n=192)	36.7	50.5	86.1	15.9
Violent prior prison terms					
All offenses	2.5 (r=262)	40.5	52.8	91.1	19.5
Burglary 1	2.8 (n=10)	50.0	40.0	(1 of 2)	10.0
Burglary 2	1.0 (n=18)	27.8	20.1	(0 of 1)	(0.0)
Robbery	2.0 (n=43)	67.4	41.4	91.8	25.6
Nonviolent prior prison terms					
All offenses	37.6 (n=3,907)	44.2	53.6	89.5	21.2
Burglary 1	37.6 (n=175)	57.8	68.0	88.5	34.8
Burglary 2	44.0 (n=786)	46.6	50.2	92.3	21.6
Robbery	33.5 (n=742)	55.4	60.2	86.2	28.8

SOURCE: Derived from Board of Prison Terms (1981:Tables VII to IX).

with substantial dismissal rates for various enhancements
indicate considerable prosecutor discretion in actively
pursuing enhancements. Some evidence suggests that
enhancements may be used selectively for just those
defendants most likely to go to prison. Once the
applicability of an enhancement is established, however,
judges routinely impose the add-on to the base term.

Both Judicial Council data on sentenced cases (Lipson
and Peterson, 1980:Table 11) and Department of
Corrections data on commitments to prison (Brewer et al.,
1980:Tables 9, 10; Board of Prison Terms, 1981:Tables
VII-IX) indicate that, statewide, the use of enhancements
tended to be limited to weapon or firearm use, especially
in robbery cases (Table 7-17). Among persons committed
to prison, victim injury and prior prison enhancements
were charged and established in court in less than
one-quarter of eligible cases.

Data are also available on the use of enhancements in
superior court cases for individual counties in Casper et
al. (1981) and Utz (1981). For burglary cases finally
disposed in superior court, Utz (1981) found weapons
allegations in 59.7 percent of cases with a weapon in the
offense in Alameda and Sacramento counties, compared with
70.5 percent charging of the firearms enhancement among
burglary cases received in prison statewide. Likewise
for robbery cases finally disposed of in superior court
in San Bernardino, San Francisco, and Santa Clara
counties, Casper et al. (1981) report that about 30
percent of all robbery cases in those counties had the
firearms enhancement alleged (without controlling for
eligibility of the cases). The corresponding figure
among statewide prison receptions for robbery was 50.8
percent charged with firearms use. In both cases
charging of enhancements was more likely among statewide
prison cases than among court cases in individual
counties.

Similarly, Utz (1981) found that for burglary cases in
Alameda and Sacramento superior courts, less than 25
percent of those charged with either weapons or injury
enhancements were pled or proved, compared with 48.8
percent proved for firearms and 50 percent proved for
injury among prison receptions statewide for burglary.
Among robbery cases in the three county superior courts,
Casper et al. (1981) found that the firearms enhancement
was struck in about 40 percent of cases, while the injury
enhancement was struck in 65-70 percent of cases.
Failure to prove these allegations was much lower

statewide among prison receptions for robbery, at 26 percent for firearms and 49 percent for injury allegations. As with charging, proving enhancements once charged was considerably higher among statewide prison receptions than among superior court cases in individual counties. While it is possible that the counties were different from the state as a whole, the evidence is also consis- tent with a selection effect by which prosecutors were more likely to pursue enhancements in cases that are more likely to end up in prison.

The generally low rates of charging and proving enhancements evident in Table 7-17 reflects the sizable discretion in initially charging and then dismissing these charges available to the prosecutor under DSL. One of the issues that could be further explored is the degree to which this is a manifestation of the plea bargaining process, in which one would expect dismissals of charged enhancements to be more prevalent in pled cases than in those that go to trial. None of the studies reviewed here provides data useful to examining this issue. In contrast to the evident wide prosecutor discretion, the rate of actually imposing sentence enhancements when the allegations are pled or proved is quite high, indicating considerable compliance by judges with the formal requirements of DSL.

Probation Ineligibility

There is relatively little separate attention in these California studies to the use of probation ineligibility provisions. When established in court these provisions provide for mandatory incarceration, effectively limiting judicial discretion in that decision. Casper et al. (1981) found that these mandatory prison provisions were invoked relatively rarely in the robbery and burglary cases they examined in three California counties (Table 7-18); only Santa Clara county made any appreciable use of these provisions.

To some degree their use was restricted by the rarity of cases that meet the charging criteria. This was especially likely to be true for the prior convictions and injury to the elderly provisions. This was less likely to be true of the firearms provision. As shown in Table 7-19, even when cases were eligible for charging, as indicated by the presence of a firearms enhancement allegation, the probation ineligibility provisions were rarely invoked, except in Santa Clara.

TABLE 7-18 Allegation and Disposition of Probation
Ineligibility Provisions

Probation Ineligibility Provision	San Bernardino	San Francisco	Santa Clara
Two Prior Convictions:			
% robbery cases in which alleged	0.0 (n=173)	1.4 (n=289)	6.9 (n=232)
% allegations struck	--	*	25.0 (n=16)
% burglary cases in which alleged	1.0 (n=300)	1.0 (n=293)	10.4 (n=346)
% allegations struck	*	*	47.3 (n=36)
Personal Use of Gun			
% robbery cases in which alleged	0.0 (n=232)	10.0 (n=289)	22.0 (n=232)
% allegations struck	--	37.9 (n=29)	35.3 (n=51)
Crime Against Elderly or Disabled			
% robbery cases in which alleged	0.0 (n=232)	2.8 (n=289)	0.0 (n=232)
% allegations struck	--	*	--

*Percent not calculated for n less than 10.

SOURCE: Casper et al. (1981:Table 7-1).

Charging

Prosecutors in the counties studied adhered to an
explicit policy of full initial charging; screening on
the merits of the case was permitted but was not to
involve consideration of possible sentences. Various
administrative procedures, typically involving supervisor
approval before dropping charges, were employed to ensure
compliance by assistant prosecutors. The observation and
interview data as well as the statistical analysis found
little evidence of any major changes in initial charging,
at least for cases finally disposed of in superior court.

TABLE 7-19 Comparison of Charging Enhancement and Probation Ineligibility in Cases Involving Firearms Use

	% Robbery Cases with Allegation		
	San Bernardino (n=173)	San Francisco (n=289)	Santa Clara (n=232)
Enhancement	31.8	27.3	30.6
Probation ineligibility	0.0	10.0	22.0

SOURCE: Casper et al. (1981:Tables 7-1 and 7-2).

Table 7-20 reports the average number of initial charges and the average seriousness of those charges under ISL and DSL. With the exception of San Francisco and to a lesser extent San Bernardino, cases disposed in superior court involved about the same number of charges of the same seriousness before and after DSL. In San Francisco and San Bernardino, the number of charges at initial filing increased, especially in robbery cases. These charging differences, however, apparently did not affect prison outcomes. Casper et al. (1981:5-19 to 5-20) reports the same changes in prison use in these counties for multiple- and single-charge defendants.

Furthermore, in a multivariate analysis of changes in initial charging for burglary cases in Alameda and Sacramento, Utz (1981) found that controlling for other attributes of the case, initial charging was not affected by DSL. In this analysis, the dependent variable combines both number and types of initial charges in a score representing the maximum possible DSL prison term for all charges, including allegations of enhancements. Using multiple regression, a difference in jurisdictions was found with "like" cases being charged less severely in Sacramento.[16] No difference was found between the two periods. The other significant variables all related to the seriousness of the offense and contributed positively to the charge score: vulnerable victim,

TABLE 7-20 Changes in Initial Offense Charging in
California: ISL versus DSL

Jurisdiction and Offense	Mean Number of Charges Filed		Average Serious Score of Initial Charges[a]	
	ISL 1976	DSL 1978	ISL 1976	DSL 1978
Alameda[b]				
Burglary	2.4	2.5	not available	
Sacramento[b]				
Burglary	2.7	2.6	not available	
San Bernardino[c]				
Robbery	2.0	2.6	33.5	36.2
Burglary	1.8	2.2	29.4	30.1
San Francisco[c]				
Robbery	2.3	3.2	33.7	40.0
Burglary	1.6	2.2	25.3	28.1
Santa Clara[c]				
Robbery	2.5	2.6	37.6	35.9
Burglary	2.6	2.3	32.8	31.7

[a]The average seriousness score is estimated from the
 inverse of the "hierarchy score" assigned to different
 offense types by the Bureau of Criminal Statistics. In
 cases with multiple charges, the scores for each charge
 are totaled.
[b]Utz (1981:216-217).
[c]Casper et al. (1981:Table 5.1).

weapon use, physical harm to victim, sophistication in
committing the offense, and defendant implicated in
multiple-offense incidents.
   Unfortunately, all the analyses of charging are
limited to cases that are finally disposed of in superior
court. No evidence is available on the way these charges
emerge. One effective way to circumvent the determinate
sentence provisions would be to charge cases initially as

misdemeanors rather than as felonies, so they do not
appear in superior court at all. Such changes would not
be evident in the data analyzed.

Plea Bargaining After DSL

In all California counties, criminal matters are handled
in municipal and superior courts. The municipal court is
the lower court handling preliminary filings and final
disposition of misdemeanor charges. After filing, the
superior court has final jurisdiction over all felony
charges.

Any formal plea bargaining held under the auspices of
the superior court usually occurred in a pretrial
conference held some time before the case was scheduled
for trial. This plea bargaining process was studied in
five separate California counties in Casper et al. (1981)
and Utz (1981). In all counties both Casper and Utz
observed heavy emphasis in bargaining discussions on the
facts of the offense and the defendant characteristics as
a basis for determining culpability and hence "case
worth" in terms of the most appropriate sentence. Both
researchers concluded that prior record is a key factor
in the decision to imprison or not (Utz, 1981:75; Casper
et al., 1981:5-19).

The character of plea bargaining varied considerably
among California jurisdictions, even though all operated
within the same statutory limits and court structure.
Only those jurisdictions already engaged in substantial
sentence bargaining before DSL incorporated explicit
agreements on the length of prison terms into their
bargaining practices after DSL. There was also almost no
change in the overall rate of guilty pleas after DSL;
although there were definite indications that early
guilty pleas (e.g., at initial court appearance) did
increase. The provisions for enhancements and probation
ineligibility allegations appeared to function as
important bargaining chips for the prosecutor, who
frequently dropped these charges in exchange for
agreements to prison sentences.

Patterns and Trends in Plea Bargaining

Table 7-21 summarizes the major distinguishing features
of plea bargaining under DSL identified in each county.

Despite the common structure and shared laws and rules of procedures governing the processing of criminal cases in all California jurisdictions, the form of bargaining varied substantially among counties. Two counties, Sacramento and San Bernardino, made only limited use of pretrial conferences. Both these counties made considerably greater use of "certifications," in which guilty pleas to felony charges were accepted in municipal court and the case was then certified to superior court for sentencing. Certifications represented about one-third of all convictions in superior court in these two counties, compared with less than one-tenth in the other three counties. The pattern in these two counties was to bargain early and to restrict bargaining primarily to consideration of charges.

By contrast, the two heavy-case load, predominantly urban counties--Alameda and San Francisco--made extensive use of pretrial conferences that were highly centralized, rarely involving more than one or two judges in each court. Pretrial conferences in both jurisdictions involved detailed bargaining over the sentence, including explicit agreements on the length of prison terms. They differed mainly in the role of the judge in the bargaining process. In San Francisco the judge took an active role in actually setting the terms of the bargain. In Alameda County the judge rarely became involved until after a bargain was struck.

Despite the opportunity for extensive bargaining over the specific details of sentence outcomes, Alameda County was plagued by inefficiency at pretrial conferences, reflected in the low rates of agreement reached at these scheduled pretrial conferences. Utz (1981) attributes this to the limited role of the judge in bargaining. Judges in the county once took a more active role, but more recently they rarely became involved until after a bargain was struck. This judicial retreat has eliminated the pressure on the parties to reach agreement in a timely fashion. Defense attorneys appeared at pretrial conferences unprepared to negotiate, seeking postponements of the case in hopes of getting a more favorable offer later (pp. 92-97).

Another equally plausible reason for the breakdown in bargaining was suggested by the frequent practice of defense attorneys of bypassing the prosecutor altogether and pleading as originally charged, with indications, and sometimes "promises," from the court about an acceptable sentence (Utz, 1981:97). This suggests a lack of

TABLE 7-21 Features of Pretrial Bargaining in California Jurisdictions After Implementation of the Uniform Determinate Sentencing Law

County	Major Use of Pretrial Conferences	Conferences Centralized	Dominant Actor	Focus of Bargain
Alameda[a]	Yes	Yes	Prosecutor	Sentence Length
Sacramento[a]	No	No	Prosecutor	Charges and Sentence Type
San Bernardino[b]	No	No	Prosecutor	Charges
San Francisco[b]	Yes	Yes	Judge	Sentence Length
Santa Clara[b]	Yes	No	Prosecutor	Sentence Type

[a]See Utz (1981) for detailed description of these counties.
[b]See Casper et al. (1981) for detailed description of these counties.

agreement between judge and prosecutor on the appropriate
sentence outcome, the prosecutor being more severe than
the judge. When faced with a rigid and unacceptable
offer from the prosecutor, the defense often rightly
perceived that a better deal could be obtained from the
judge. The breakdown in effective bargaining seems to
stem more from the judge's unwillingness to enforce the
prosecutor's offers. Rather than accept these offers,
the judge was sentencing independently.

Further supporting the crucial role of
judge-prosecutor consensus on appropriate sentences, Utz
(1981:94) reports that many more pretrial agreements were
reached in Alameda when pretrials were conducted before
judges who were less lenient and thus more likely to be
in accord with sentence offers of the prosecutor than
when judges were more lenient. These other judges also
took a more active role in the negotiations, actively
pressing the parties to reach agreement.

Santa Clara fell between the two extremes represented
by limited charge bargaining on one end and detailed
sentence bargaining on the other. Considerable sentence
bargaining occurred in Santa Clara, but it was restricted
to discussions of sentence type, especially the prison/no
prison option. Bargaining was also decentralized, with
pretrial conferences scheduled before all criminal court
judges.

Guilty Plea Rates

In Table 7-22 we see that controlling for crime type
there were no marked changes after DSL in the
already-high proportion of guilty pleas among convictions
found in all five counties and for the state as a whole.
Likewise there were only marginal increases in trial
rates (Table 7-23). There were, however, some
differences of note across counties and case
seriousness. Regardless of which law was in effect,
heavy-case load, urban courts (Alameda and San Francisco)
had the highest guilty plea rates (Table 7-22), while
lower-case load counties (Sacramento) had slightly higher
trial rates (Table 7-23). This greater inclination to go
to trial was especially pronounced for cases that were
presumably more vulnerable to long sentences, as in cases
involving more serious offenses in Alameda (Table 7-24)
and for offenders with prior criminal records in

TABLE 7-22 Changes in Guilty Plea Rates in Superior Court in California

| Jurisdiction | % Guilty Pleas Among Convictions in Superior Court | | | % Guilty Pleas Among All Dispositions in Superior Court |
	Burglary	Robbery	All Convictions	
Alameda[a]				
ISL-1976	96.1	n.a.	94.2	80.9
DSL-1978	93.6	n.a.	96.1	79.3
(1979) [b]	(99.6)	(99.1)	(98.3)	(85.5)
Sacramento[a]				
ISL-1976	90.4	n.a.	84.0	63.6
DSL-1978	91.1	n.a.	86.1	67.8
(1979)	(93.8)	(87.4)	(91.9)	(78.3)
San Bernardino[c]				
ISL-1974	93	85	91	84.3
1975	95	86	92	80.6
1976	87	75	86	74.5
DSL-1977	91	83	84	73.0
1978	89	81	87	78.0
(1979)	(94)	(88)	(87)	(81.6)
San Francisco[c]				
ISL-1974	96	90	93	83.2
1975	95	90	93	77.8
1976	90	83	86	73.6
DSL-1977	93	83	91	78.7
1978	93	84	89	72.9
(1979)	(96)	(91)	(94)	(78.0)
Santa Clara[c]				
ISL-1974	95	93	87	83.2
1975	93	91	84	82.9
1976	95	92	84	82.3
DSL-1977	n.a.	n.a.	n.a.	n.a.
1978	97	94	91	83.9
(1979)	(98)	(91)	(95)	(85.9)
Statewide[d]				
ISL-1975	n.a.	n.a.	87	72
1976	n.a.	n.a.	87	74
DSL-1977	n.a.	n.a.	n.a.	75[c]
1978	n.a.	n.a.	88	76
(1979)	(93)	(88)	(90)	(80)

n.a. Data not available

[a]Utz (1981). The results for burglary cases are derived from Tables 13A and 28. The results for all convictions and all dispositions are derived from data in Appendix F.
[b]Numbers for 1979, available from California Department of Justice (1980), are reported in parentheses throughout the table.
[c]Casper et al. (1981). The numbers reported here are taken from Figures 6-1 to 6-3 on pages 6-6 to 6-9.
[d]Lipson and Peterson (1980:Table 3).

TABLE 7-23 Trial Rates Among California Superior
Court Dispositions for Samples of Defendants
Originally Charged with Burglary (in percent)

	Alameda	Sacramento
ISL-1976	4.44	9.28
DSL-1978	6.15	10.08

SOURCE: Utz (1981:Tables 13A and 28).

TABLE 7-24 Trial Rates Among Convictions in
California Superior Courts for Samples of Defendants
Originally Charged with Burglary, Controlling for
Offense Seriousness (in percent)

	Low and Moderate Seriousness[a]	High Seriousness[a]
Alameda		
ISL	2.72	6.02
DSL	1.61	12.77
Sacramento		
ISL	10.00	8.97
DSL	9.63	7.35

[a]Offense seriousness was scored on the basis of the
attributes of the offense, including whether the
offense was burglary of a residence, whether there
was confrontation with a victim, whether threat or
force was used, whether the victim was harmed, the
value of the property taken, whether the offense
displayed special criminal sophistication, and
whether the defendant was implicated in multiple-
offense incidents.

SOURCE: Utz (1981:Tables 2, 13A, 28 and 29).

Sacramento (Table 7-25). Furthermore, in Alameda County the trial rates for the high-seriousness cases increased from ISL to DSL (Table 24). Unfortunately, the data on trial rates for offenders with prior records were not available for the DSL period, and trial rate comparisons before and under DSL could not be made.

Timing of Guilty Pleas

Under ISL the actual time to be served on a prison sentence was uncertain: There were strong incentives for the defense to delay dispositions in hopes of receiving a nonprison sentence or outright dismissal as the prosecution's case strength deteriorated. Because of the greater certainty about prison sentence outcomes under DSL, there was a widespread expectation that more defendants would be willing to plead guilty early. As indicated in Figure 7-1, without controlling for any variations in crime type mix over time, a simple two-point comparison of ISL in 1976 with DSL in 1978 shows sharp increases in the proportion of early pleas entered at initial appearance among all guilty pleas in

TABLE 7-25 Trial Rates Among Convictions in California Superior Courts for Samples of Defendants Originally Charged with Burglary, Controlling for Offender Prior Criminal Record (in percent)

| | ISL Period Only | |
	Alameda	Sacramento
Any Prior Felony Convictions	4.44	14.55
No Prior Felony Convictions	3.02	4.67
Thievery Repeaters[a]	4.62	12.38
Non-Repeaters	3.75	4.21

[a]Thievery repeaters had prior convictions (felony or misdemeanor) for burglary, robbery, or other theft-type offenses.

SOURCE: Utz (1981:Tables 4 and 6).

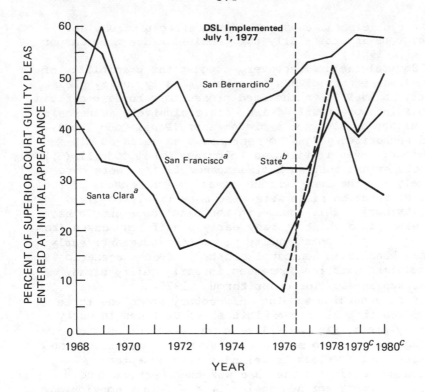

FIGURE 7-1 Trends in the Timing of Guilty Pleas in California: Percent of All Superior Court Guilty Pleas Entered at Initial Appearance

[a]Casper et al. (1981: Figure 6-7).
[b]Derived from Lipson and Peterson (1980: Table 3).
[c]The rates for 1979 and 1980 are derived from data reported in California Department of Justice (1979, 1980).

superior court. Considering a longer time period before DSL implementation, however, there was a long-term decline in the rate of early pleas from the late 1960s to 1976. The increases in the early guilty plea rate after DSL represent a return to the higher rates prevailing in the late 1960s.

Without a better sense of the factors contributing to the long-term pre-DSL decline in early guilty pleas and a longer follow-up after DSL, it is difficult to sort out whether the post-DSL increase represents a real effect of DSL on early guilty pleas or merely a random fluctuation

in a cyclic phenomenon. That the effects of DSL are
ambiguous is essentially the conclusion drawn by Casper
et al. (1981).

Several factors, however, suggest the possibility of
some real effect of DSL on rates of early guilty pleas.
First, a 1969 law authorized prosecutors to file certain
complaints previously dealt with exclusively as felonies
as either a felony or a misdemeanor (Penal Code 17b(4))
and authorized judges to sentence such cases as misdemeanors even if filed as felonies (Penal Code 17b(5)).
To the extent that such misdemeanor filings were more
likely for the less serious cases, which because of the
milder sanction risks were also more likely to plead
guilty early, this change in the penal code should have
resulted in a shift of many early plea felony cases from
among superior court guilty pleas to misdemeanor early
pleas handled in municipal court.[17] Such a scenario is
consistent with the decreases in early guilty pleas
observed in superior court through 1976.

San Bernardino was the only county among the three
compared that did not exhibit sharp declines in early
guilty pleas (Figure 7-1). It was also the only county
among the three to make extensive use of certifications
whereby guilty pleas to felonies were accepted in
municipal court and the case was then certified to
superior court for sentencing on the felony conviction.
This extensive use of certifications would account for a
more stable rate of early pleas in San Bernardino.

The combination of increased reliance on optional
misdemeanor filings and limited use of certifications
suggests that the dramatic declines in early guilty pleas
observed in San Francisco and Santa Clara between 1969
and 1976 may have been the result of real changes in
charging policies and not just random fluctuations. The
sharp increase after DSL would then more likely be a real
effect of DSL on early guilty plea rates rather than a
random fluctuation. When 1979 and 1980 data are added to
Figure 7-1, the generally higher level of early guilty
pleas found in 1978 is maintained in all cases except San
Francisco. This further supports a real change in the
early guilty plea rate after DSL.

Variations in Plea Bargaining Practices

Table 7-26 highlights the major changes in the nature of
sentence agreements in the five counties studied by Utz

TABLE 7-26 Changes in Sentence Agreements from ISL to DSL in California

Jurisdiction	Type of Sentence Agreement		
	No Promises	State Commitment or Prison	No Prison/ Jail/ Probation and Jail/ No Jail
Alameda[a] (Burglary Sample)			
ISL-1976	21.7%	11.3%	67.0%
DSL-1978	4.4%	40.7%	54.9%
Sacramento[a] (Burglary Sample)			
ISL-1976	42.6%	2.5%	54.8%
DSL-1978	39.3%	4.4%	56.3%
San Bernardino[b] DSL	Substantial "open pleas" (predominantly charge bargaining)		
San Francisco[b] DSL		Substantial (with length of term specified)	
Santa Clara[b] DSL			Many "conditional pleas" (direct discussion of sentence type)

[a]Utz (1981).
[b]Casper et al. (1981).

and Casper et al. after DSL. The two counties in which
charge bargaining was prevalent, Sacramento and San
Bernardino, showed little change in bargaining practices,
relying heavily on "open pleas" with no commitments on
sentence outcomes both before and after DSL. Where
extensive sentence bargaining occurred before DSL--in
Alameda and San Francisco--there was substantial use
after DSL of agreements not only specifying state prison
sentences but also specifying the length of prison
terms. After DSL in Alameda County, for example, 83
percent of the prison agreements had the length of term
specified. The more involved a jurisdiction was in
detailed sentence bargaining before DSL, the more likely
that jurisdiction was to move the next logical step
provided by DSL and bargain directly over prison terms.
If sentence bargaining was not the practice before DSL,
then the opportunities to negotiate directly about the
length of prison terms provided by DSL were not likely to
alter past bargaining practices.

Despite explicit prosecution policies in all five
counties of "full enforcement" of enhancement and
probation ineligibility provisions, both Casper et al.
(1981) and Utz (1981) report that the opportunities for
prosecutors to drop these allegations played a
significant part in plea negotiations. These allegations
represent important bargaining chips for the prosecution,
often being used to gain defense agreement to prison
sentences. The general view was that sufficient prison
time could usually be obtained with conviction for the
basic offense charge, and allegations were often dropped
as part of a prison plea. This is evident in the
generally low rates of proving charged allegations found
in Table 7-19.

Both Casper et al. (1981) and Utz (1981) report that
participants in jurisdictions characterized by particular
plea bargaining practices expressed surprise at, and
sometimes disapproval of, the operations of plea
bargaining in other jurisdictions. The different forms
of plea bargaining observed across counties reflect
differences in the role definitions of participants and
in the nature of incentives to bargaining. With respect
to role definitions, the main difference appears to be
whether the court participants adhered to traditional
conceptions of adversary roles. In a traditional court
the prosecution and defense viewed themselves as partisan
adversaries, each pursuing a one-sided consideration of

the issues. The judge struck the balance between the two parties, weighing the facts as presented by the opposing parties and coming to a fair resolution of the matter. These traditional roles appear to be maintained in lower-case load courts, as exemplified by Sacramento, San Bernardino, and Santa Clara, and abandoned in heavy volume courts like Alameda and San Francisco. In nontraditional courts it was the aim of all parties to achieve agreement on the facts and on an appropriate sentence, the judge often serving as a mediator in a process of arriving at consensual agreements.[18]

The differences across jurisdictions also reflect the variety of incentives to behavior. In the jurisdictions studied, the incentives to plea bargaining were highly system-dependent; what motivated agreement in one system would not necessarily result in agreement in another. Participants in San Francisco, whose experience included explicit resolution of the details of a bargain before it was concluded, found the absence of specific terms in agreements in Santa Clara totally foreign. Without explicit negotiation on terms, San Francisco participants saw no basis for reaching agreement and wondered what the incentives to plead guilty were in Santa Clara (Casper et al., 1981:56).

Participants in Santa Clara, for their part, found the explicit involvement of San Francisco judges in detailed bargaining over sentences unseemly. In Santa Clara the outcome and incentives surrounding the dispositions of criminal cases were not overt parts of the bargaining process or the agreement reached. Rather they were tacit, embodied in expectations about outcomes that were shaped and reshaped by the participants' experiences in the system and with one another.

Sacramento was a traditional court much like Santa Clara. Utz (1981:126) reports confronting one judge there with the apparent conflict between judicial resistance to overt sentence bargaining and the attorneys' need for some certainty about likely outcomes. The judge responded that sentence bargaining was not the only way to achieve such "certainty." In a small court the attorneys developed a pretty good feel for likely outcomes, relying on their knowledge of the track record of the judge and their ability to read indirect signals from the judge. In this setting most cases were routine and predictable for the parties and they reached agreement based on their expectations of likely sentence outcomes.

In view of these differences among jurisdictions, participants from one system would not be immediately interchangeable with those from another. If participants in San Francisco were to function effectively in Santa Clara or Sacramento, or vice versa, they would have to learn anew what counts as a bargain and how to go about bargaining. Attempts to model the plea bargaining process must be sensitive to these differences across systems in fundamental aspects of the process.

Impact on Prison Use

Trends in Prison Use

Prison use definitely increased after DSL, whether measured by the commitment rate to prison (commitments/population) or the likelihood of a prison sentence after conviction in superior court. This increase, however, is best viewed as a continuation of preexisting trends toward increased prison use in California and not as an effect of DSL. The increasing use of prison was accompanied by increasing imprisonment of less serious, marginal offenders; this trend is reflected in changes in the crime type mix. There was increased representation of less serious offenses among persons received in prison and increased use of prison relative to jail. Several factors are potentially important in accounting for the trend toward greater prison use in California:

(1) The changing role of probation subsidies to local jurisdictions;
(2) Increased punitiveness;
(3) The commission of increasingly more serious offenses;
(4) Increased early filtering of cases, resulting in a greater concentration of more serious cases in superior court; and
(5) Demographic shifts in the population toward increasing representation of older offenders who are more vulnerable to prison sentences.

Because of the greater certainty about lengths of prison terms, it was generally anticipated that prison use would increase as a result of DSL. Consistent with this expectation, most of the studies reviewed found a definite increase in prison use, measured both by commitments per population and by the proportion sentenced to prison among convictions in superior court.

As indicated in Table 7-27, the commitment rate for all offenses increased between 1976 and 1978 for the state as a whole and for individual jurisdictions within the state. Similar increases were generally found in Table 7-28 for the proportion sentenced to prison among convictions in superior court, both across jurisdictions and for different offense types. The principal exception

TABLE 7-27 California Adult Prison Commitment Rate (Commitments/100,000 Residents)

Jurisdiction	Commitment Rate	
	1976 Before DSL	1978 After DSL
Males Only[a]		
State total	30.0	39.3
Counties		
Southern California	25.1	37.6
Los Angeles	27.9	39.1
9 other counties	22.5	35.9
San Francisco Bay	29.3	39.4
Alameda	25.0	46.0
San Francisco	50.2	83.7
7 other counties	26.5	37.1
Rest of state	37.8	44.8
10 Sacramento Valley counties	40.9	43.3
7 San Joaquin Valley counties	37.5	51.4
22 other counties	34.3	37.1
All Adults[b]		
State Total	32.1	41.8

[a]Lipson and Peterson (1980:Table 12). The reported rates represent the number of males committed to state prisons per 100,000 total resident population (males and females).
[b]Brewer et al. (1980:Table 5). The rates are total adult commitments (male and female) to state prisons per 100,000 total resident population.

TABLE 7-28 Proportion Sentenced to Prison Among
Convictions in California Superior Courts

Jurisdiction	% to Prison Among Convictions	
	1976 Before DSL	1978 After DSL
All Offenses		
State total	17.8	23.0
Counties		
Alameda[b]	14.2	23.2
Sacramento[b]	25.4	26.9
San Bernardino[c]	29.5	38.5
San Francisco[c]	25.0	31.5
Santa Clara[c]	25.0	16.5
Burglary		
Alameda[d]	17.8	42.5
Sacramento[d]	23.0	21.3
San Bernardino[e]	29.5	38.5
San Francisco[e]	24.5	32.0
Santa Clara[e]	24.5	16.0
Robbery		
San Bernardino[e]	65.0	63.0
San Francisco[e]	44.0	49.5
Santa Clara[e]	59.5	57.0

[a]These data from the California Bureau of Criminal
Statistics are reported in Lipson and Peterson (1980)
and Brewer et al. (1980).
[b]Derived from Utz (1981:Appendix F).
[c]Casper et al. (1981:Figure 5.5).
[d]Utz (1981:Table 39).
[e]Casper et al. (1981:Figures 5-6 and 5-7).

is Santa Clara County, where the rate of prison sentences
among convictions decreased for all offenses and for
defendants charged with burglary and robbery.

When the observation period was extended to include
multiple observations, several studies concluded that the
increase in prison use after DSL was best viewed as a
continuation of a preexisting trend toward increased
prison use in California (Brewer et al., 1980; Lipson and
Peterson, 1980; Ku, 1980; Casper et al., 1981). This was
true especially for all offenses for the state as a whole
(see Figure 7-2) and in the individual counties of San
Bernardino and San Francisco (Figure 7-3). Santa Clara,
by contrast, appeared to be returning to previous low
rates of prison use after a brief period of increased use
of prison sentences for offenders convicted in superior
court. The increase in prison use also predated DSL
implementation for offenders originally charged with

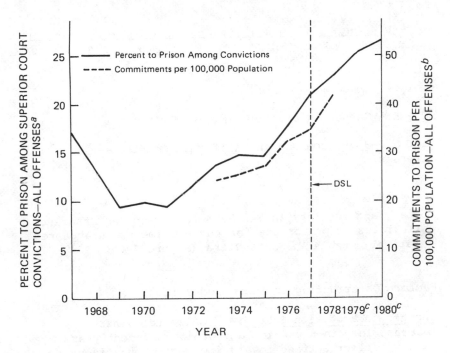

[a]Lipson and Peterson (1980:Figure 2) and Brewer et al. (1980:Table 5).
[b]Brewer et al. (1980:Table 5).
[c]California Department of Justice (1979, 1980).

FIGURE 7-2   Prison Use in California

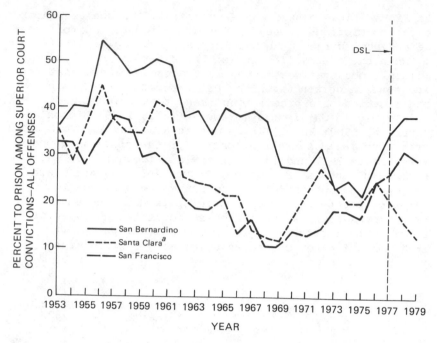

[a]No data were available in 1977 for Santa Clara.

SOURCE: Casper et al. (1981:Figure 5-5).

FIGURE 7-3   Prison Use in California Counties--All Offenses

robbery and burglary in San Bernardino and San Francisco, while rates of prison use for these crime types appeared relatively stable in Santa Clara (Figure 7-4).

Factors Contributing to Increased Prison Use

Changes in Probation Subsidies   While the general increase in prison use in California in recent years may simply reflect a trend toward increasing punitiveness, a number of other factors have been cited to account for this rise.   First, Brewer et al. (1980) note the contributing role of changes in the probation subsidy program to counties.   This program, which began in 1965, was intended to provide economic incentives for local

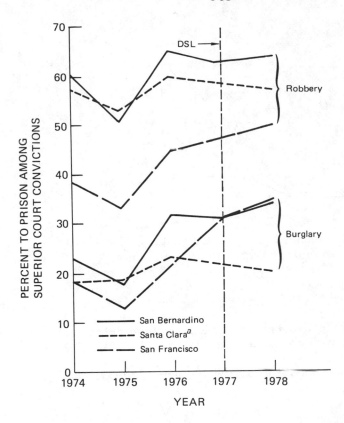

^aNo data were available for 1977 in Santa Clara.

SOURCE: Casper et al. (1981:Figures 5-6 and 5-7).

FIGURE 7-4 Prison Use in California Counties for
Burglary and Robbery Cases Disposed of in Superior Court

jurisdictions to keep offenders under local supervision
within their own communities. As is evident in Figure
7-5, the program appeared to be achieving just this end;
the use of probation increased while prison use declined
through the early 1970s. By the early 1970s, however,
because of dissatisfaction with local programs and rising
costs, prison commitments began to increase again. Under
the structure of the subsidy program, any increase in
prison commitments in a jurisdiction resulted in decreases
in probation subsidies, which served to encourage further

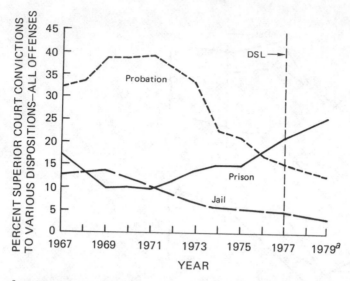

[a]Data for 1979 were obtained from California Department of Justice (1979).

SOURCE: California Bureau of Criminal Statistics as reported in Lipson and Peterson (1980:Figure 2).

FIGURE 7-5 Sentences in California Superior Courts

increases in prison commitments. This declining role of probation combined with increases in prison commitments beginning in the early 1970s is also evident in Figure 7-5.

Changes in Case Seriousness Another factor in the increased use of prison is increases in the seriousness of cases sentenced in superior court. Utz (1981) included elaborate controls for the seriousness of burglary cases disposed in superior court in Alameda and Sacramento Counties pre-DSL in 1976 and post-DSL in 1978. Based on the weight of the many variables compared, Utz (1981:22-27) concluded that ISL cases in Alameda were more serious than those in Sacramento and that case seriousness was relatively stable across the two time periods in Alameda County.

Contrary to Utz's findings, there were some indications of increasing case seriousness in Alameda

between 1976 and 1978. In particular, the proportion of
burglaries involving stranger-to-stranger altercations
increased from 60.4 to 71.4 percent of cases; cases
involving harm to victim(s) increased from 30.7 to 36.5
percent; the incidence of nighttime burglaries increased
from 48.7 to 55.3 percent; and the proportion of cases of
high seriousness disposed of in superior court increased
from 36.1 to 44.3 percent. (The indicators of high
seriousness are listed in Table 7-24.)

In Sacramento the changes in case seriousness were
more general, reflecting shifts to defendants with less
serious prior records, but to more serious offense
incidents. On the whole, DSL cases in Sacramento became
more like those in Alameda. Burglary cases under DSL
were more likely to involve a victim (30.7 versus 23.6
percent) and to result in harm to the victim (39.7 versus
23.2 percent). There were also increases in assaults
involving strangers (68.4 versus 52.0 percent) and in
weapon use (13.0 versus 5.5 percent). With only minimal
controls for case seriousness, Casper et al. (1981:5-19)
observed a slight increase in the percent of burglary and
robbery defendants who had served prior prison terms in
San Bernardino and San Francisco.

To the extent that prison use is positively correlated
with case seriousness, any increases in the seriousness
of cases convicted in superior court would result in
increases in prison use upon conviction, as was observed
in Alameda, San Bernardino, and San Francisco counties.
The principal exception to this pattern is Sacramento,
where, despite the increasing seriousness of offense
incidents, the rate of prison use among convictions was
relatively stable. In this case, however, the effect of
increases in seriousness of offense incidents may have
been offset by the simultaneous decreases in the
seriousness of defendants' prior records noted above.

Changes in Case Filtering   Related to the changes in case
seriousness are indications that the increases in prison
use among superior court convictions resulted from
changes in the pretrial filtering process affecting the
case mix in superior court. In particular, a shift of
less serious cases to municipal court for final
disposition would leave the superior courts with
increasing proportions of more serious prison-eligible
cases. In this event the increase in prison use in
superior courts would be more apparent than real, as the

cases sentenced to prison remain essentially unchanged, but many less serious cases are eliminated from the available pool of convictions. (Note: This would not explain the increases in the prison commitment rate per population.)

Figure 7-6 indicates that major changes have in fact occurred in the distribution of cases between superior and municipal courts. The proportion of total court dispositions handled in superior courts dropped dramatically, from 70.7 percent in 1968 to 30.9 percent in 1980. This decline in dispositions in superior courts followed legislative changes that permitted prosecutors to file either as felonies or misdemeanors certain complaints previously handled exclusively as felonies (California Penal Code 17b(4)). This same legislation similarly permitted judges to sentence certain cases as misdemeanors even if they were filed as felonies (California Penal Code 17b(5)).[19] In response to this legislation the representation of felonies among superior court convictions increased from 54.7 percent in 1969 to 80.4 percent in 1974, while misdemeanor prosecutions under section P.C. 17 increased from 6.4 percent of total municipal court prosecutions in 1969 to 68.1 percent in 1973.[20] With this shift of less serious cases from superior court to municipal court, superior court was left with increasing proportions of prison-eligible cases among the convictions that remain. In this situation the changes in prison rates among convictions could reflect changes in the mix of convictions available for sentencing in superior court, and not any change in sentencing policy for prison-eligible cases.

This situation highlights the vital importance of monitoring and controlling for changes in case filtering before sentencing that could affect the character of cases available for sentencing. Without these controls, changes in the ways cases are filtered, which may or may not be directly associated with a sentencing reform, could be mistakenly interpreted as changes in sentencing policy for "like" cases.

One way of controlling for the impact of changes in presentence filtering is to include data on a wide range of variables reflecting important aspects of the character of cases--i.e., attributes that identify "like" cases for sentencing purposes. These control variables increase the likelihood of distinguishing sentence changes due to differences in the character of cases

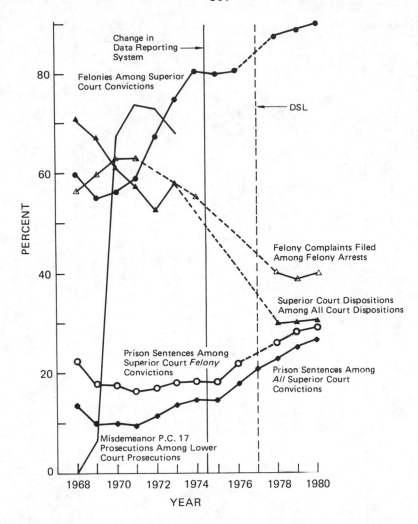

Change in
Data Reporting
System

Felonies Among Superior
Court Convictions

DSL

Felony Complaints Filed
Among Felony Arrests

Superior Court Dispositions
Among All Court Dispositions

Prison Sentences Among
Superior Court *Felony*
Convictions

Prison Sentences Among
All Superior Court
Convictions

Misdemeanor P.C. 17
Prosecutions Among Lower
Court Prosecutions

PERCENT

YEAR

SOURCE: Derived from data reported in California
Department of Justice (1980, 1981).

FIGURE 7-6 Changes in Filtering Cases Through California
Criminal Justice System

TABLE 7-29 Use of Prison Among Convictions in California Superior Courts Resulting from Burglary Charges in Alameda and Sacramento Counties

% Prison Sentences Among Superior Court Convictions

Offense Attributes	Alameda			Sacramento		
All Cases						
ISL: 1976	17.83			23.04		
DSL: 1978	42.45			21.29		
Weapon Use[a]	No Weapon	Weapon		No Weapon	Weapon	
ISL: 1976	29.50	45.80		29.20	66.00	
DSL: 1978	43.50	68.00		27.20	37.10	
Victim Harm[a]	No Harm	Harm		No Harm	Harm	
ISL: 1976	23.91	69.57		27.91	46.15	
DSL: 1978	40.82	87.50		39.02	39.13	
Aggregate Measure of Seriousness	Low	Moderate	High	Low	Moderate	High
ISL: 1976	7.50	12.15	30.12	18.92	21.36	27.27
DSL: 1978	31.25	26.74	60.64	24.32	17.35	25.37
Offender's Prior Conviction Record	Murder-Violence	Theft	Drugs or None	Murder-Violence	Theft	Drugs or None
ISL: 1976	25.00	20.77	11.25	38.89	38.46	3.16
DSL: 1978	63.64	55.75	16.88	42.86	39.73	4.63

[a]These offense attributes include other state commitments in addition to prison sentences.

SOURCE: Utz (1981:Tables 39, 40, 42, 44, 45, 48, 49).

available for sentencing from sentence changes due to
real shifts in the sentencing policy for "like" cases.

The Utz (1981) study is the only one to employ any
extensive controls for case mix changes among sentenced
cases. As indicated in Table 7-29, with no controls for
case mix, or controlling for only one case attribute at a
time, Sacramento exhibited a consistent pattern of little
change in prison use from pre-DSL to post-DSL
implementation. In Alameda, by contrast, prison use
consistently increased across all seriousness levels
compared.

When multivariate controls simultaneously controlling
a variety of case attributes were introduced in a simple
linear model of choice among sentence types, Utz found
that cases of the same level of seriousness at sentencing
were more likely to result in prison sentences in
Sacramento than in Alameda. This difference between
counties increased after DSL implementation.[21]

Based on these results, the dramatic increases in
prison use from ISL to DSL in Alameda evident in Table
7-29 were due to greater increases in the seriousness of
cases available for sentencing in Alameda than found in
Sacramento. Some indirect evidence of this shift to more
serious cases at sentencing in superior court is
available from the data in Utz (1981:Appendix F) on case
dispositions for all offenses in Alameda and Sacramento
Counties.

As indicated in Table 7-30, Alameda exhibited a
dramatic shift of both dispositions and convictions from
superior court to municipal court, while use of lower
courts decreased slightly in Sacramento. The shift of
less serious convictions out of superior court in Alameda
was associated with an increase in prison sentences among
the remaining superior court convictions. This contrasts
with relatively stable prison use in Sacramento. When
prison use was examined for all convictions regardless of
court type, however, the greater ISL to DSL increases in
prison use for Sacramento found in the multivariate
analysis become evident.

Some other differences between the counties evident in
Table 7-30 are worth noting. Sacramento made
considerably greater use of felony complaints for felony
arrests with less screening of cases at the charging
stage. This lack of early screening was compensated for
later in higher dismissal and acquittal rates, especially
in superior courts. Sacramento also had higher trial
rates in superior court than Alameda. The failure to

TABLE 7-30 Disposition of Felony Arrests Brought to California Prosecutors in Alameda and Sacramento Counties--All Offenses

| | % Each Outcome | | | |
| | Alameda | | Sacramento | |
Disposition	ISL 1976	DSL 1978	ISL 1976	DSL 1978
Of Felonies Brought to Prosecutor	(n=9,714)	(n=7,663)	(n=4,671)	(n=5,335)
DA rejects	13.47	18.60	8.84	8.58
Misdemeanor complaint filed	40.01	38.03	28.64	27.74
Felony complaint filed	46.52	43.38	62.51	63.60
Of All Felony Complaints	(n=4,519)	(n=3,324)	(n=2,920)	(n=3,397)
Lower Court Dispositions (including certifications)	59.64	72.35	72.19	65.56
Dismissals	37.74	33.64	38.95	44.50
Guilty pleas (including certifications)	59.37	65.11	60.44	55.28
Trial convictions	2.37	0.96	0.28	0.13
Upper Court Dispositions	40.36	27.65	27.81	34.44
Dismissals	12.72	16.32	21.55	18.97
Acquittals	1.26	1.09	2.83	2.22
Guilty pleas/nollo contenderes (excluding certifications)	80.92	79.33	63.55	67.78
Trial convictions	5.00	3.26	12.07	10.94
Other	0.10	--	--	--

	(n=1,602)	(n=873)	(n=916)	(n=1,271)
Convictions Among All Felony Complaints	71.50	70.64	64.86	63.44
Lower court convictions				
Among all convictions	51.50	67.67	67.58	57.26
Of Superior Court Sentences	(n=1,602)	(n=873)	(n=916)	(n=1,271)
Prison	13.85	20.16	22.49	24.78
Other state commitments	7.54	6.42	10.70	7.78
Probation	20.54	18.10	10.43	11.96
Probation and jail	55.43	50.86	49.02	50.12
Jail	2.43	4.24	7.21	4.80
Fine	0.12	0.23	0.11	0.55
Other	0.06	--	--	--
Prison Among Felony Complaints	4.91	5.29	7.05	9.27
Prison Among Conviction Any Court	6.87	7.50	10.88	14.62

SOURCE: Utz (1981:Appendix F).

screen out weak cases early and the greater use of trials are both luxuries of a relatively low-case load court. The pressures of heavy-case loads in Alameda, by contrast, encouraged more efficient allocation of limited resources.

It is also important to remember that all the results in Table 7-30 refer to all offense types disposed of in each county. Thus the differences observed might be confounded by differences in crime type mix between counties and over time within a county. In view of this, controls for case mix are essential. Minimally, they would include controls by crime type. Unfortunately, however, the Utz study does not report comparable data for burglary cases—the crime type of main interest in that study. Nevertheless, the overall consistency of the results for all offenses in Table 7-30 with those found by Utz using various levels of control for the seriousness of burglary cases suggests that differences in case mix are not a serious problem in interpreting the results in Table 7-30.

Demographic Changes Another factor potentially contributing to the recent rise of prison use in California not mentioned in any of the studies is the role of general demographic shifts in the population. Figure 7-7 compares annual prison admissions rates (admissions per 100,000 general population) in California and the United States. The pattern in California of a decline in the admission rate through the early 1970s followed by an upturn in the rest of the decade mirrors a similar pattern found in the United States generally.

Contrary to commonsense expectations, the decline in U.S. prison admissions through the 1960s occurred during a period of rapidly rising crime, while the increase of admissions in the 1970s accompanies much slower increases in crime.[22] Based only on the incidence of crimes and related arrests, the opposite relationship would have been expected. Decreasing prison populations during a period of rapidly rising crime, however, can be attributed to the changing demographic composition of the population. In particular, as the post-war baby boom generation was moving into the high-crime ages in the 1960s—hence causing substantially more crime—they were still juveniles or "first offender" adults and were not likely to go to prison even if convicted. Only when a sizable portion of these offenders became old enough to

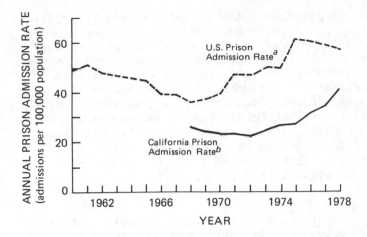

[a]The U.S. rate from 1960 to 1970 is available in U.S. Bureau of Census (1976). The rate for 1971 to 1977 is available in U.S. Bureau of Census (1979). The 1978 rate was obtained from U.S. Bureau of Census (1980).

   In addition to new commitments from court, the published rates for 1972 and 1973 also include parole and other conditional violators returned and escapees returned under old sentence. Based on the distribution of new commitments among this total in 1974 to 1978, the rates of new commitments alone for 1972 and 1973 presented here were estimated as 81.5 percent of the total.
[b]The California rate for males only from 1968 to 1972 is derived from Lipson and Peterson (1980: Figure 1). The total rate for 1973 to 1978 is available in Brewer et al. (1980:Table 5). To make the two periods comparable, an annual admission rate of 2.5 for females was added to the male rates for 1968 to 1972.

FIGURE 7-7 Prison Admission Rate in the United States and California--New Commitments Received From Court During the Year Per 100,000 Population

have developed adult criminal records in the 1970s was there any significant increase in prison commitments. Furthermore, even if crime itself starts to decline in the future because of the continued aging of the baby boom generation and the considerably smaller birth cohorts that followed it, the prison population is likely to continue to increase for a time, since prison-prone ages are older than high-crime ages.

   Analysis of Pennsylvania, a state with an aging population, suggests that total arrests in Pennsylvania will increase to the year 1980 and then begin to decline. The increases in prison commitments will continue to about 1985, and prison populations will not decline until after 1990 (Blumstein et al., 1980). In addressing the question of projections of future prison

populations in California, Lipson and Peterson (1980:39)
indicate that population projections for California show
continued high in-migration to the state of persons ages
18-29. This is likely to delay any substantial decreases
in the population of the state of ages 18-35 and also
delay any reversal of the upward trend in prison
commitments and prison populations. A generally younger
adult population in California than found in the United
States as a whole would also explain the observed delay
in California's upturn in the prison admissions rate
beginning in 1972 compared with that of the United
States, which began in 1968 (Figure 7-7).

Increases in Punitiveness It is also possible that the
increases in prison use in California reflect a real
shift toward increased punitiveness. One would expect
such an increase in punitiveness to be reflected in
changes in the crime-type mix of persons committed to
prison and in time served, especially for less serious
crimes.[23]

Ku (1980) addresses the crime-type mix issue, reporting that robberies exceeded burglaries among prison
commitments in every year from 1969 to 1977. In particular, robberies represented 23 and 25 percent of commitments in 1974 and 1975, while burglaries accounted for 17
percent of commitments in both years. For the spring
quarter of 1978, by contrast, the State Judicial Council
reports that only 10 percent of prison sentences were for
robbery, while 22 percent were for burglary. Ku takes
this as evidence of the emergence of a new lower threshold of seriousness for prison use following DSL. Other
evidence suggests a less dramatic shift to less serious
crimes. Table 7-31 presents data for new commitments
received by the Department of Corrections in 1975, 1976,
and fiscal year 1977-1978. These are supplemented by
court-based Bureau of Criminal Statistics data on prison
sentences for 1979. In these data the post-DSL years are
generally compatible with pre-DSL years; robbery commitments exceeded burglary commitments. Nevertheless, consistent with the possibility of increases in punitiveness,
there was a trend toward increased representation of the
less serious offense of burglary, although it is nothing
like the dramatic shift suggested by the quarterly state
Judicial Council data.

Apparently this increase in burglaries among prison
commitments cannot be accounted for by a shift to more

TABLE 7-31 Crime Type Mix Among Prison
Commitments

Year	% Robberies	% Burglaries
ISL		
1975[a]	27.0	18.5
1976[a]	24.7	20.4
DSL		
1977-1978[a]	27.7	23.9
1979[b]	24.2	22.3

[a]Brewer et al. (1980:Tables 3 and 4). In
calculating crime type percentages,
commitments for homicide and parole violators
returned with new terms are excluded.
[b]California Department of Justice (1980:84).
To be compatible with Department of
Corrections data, sentences for homicide have
been excluded. The status of parole violators
returned with new terms is unclear in the
Department of Justice data.

serious, and thus more prison-prone, types of burglaries
by offenders. Using finer controls for case attributes,
Utz (1981) examined the composition of burglary offenders
sentenced to prison by offense seriousness. As indicated
in Table 7-32 there was very little change in the
seriousness mix of offenses for offenders sentenced to
prison after original charges for burglary. If anything
there was a slight increase in the representation of less
serious offenses, especially in Sacramento.

It has been suggested that any increases in prison use
as a result of DSL are most likely to come from those
marginal prison cases previously sentenced to local jails
or probation. Casper et al. (1981) explicitly addresses
this question through consideration of the ratio of
prison sentences to all incarceration sentences (prison
and jail). Casper found little evidence of any shift
from jail to prison in individual counties either for all
offenses (see Figure 7-8), or for robbery or burglary
(Casper et al., 1981:5-21 to 5-22). Only San Francisco

TABLE 7-32 Offense Seriousness Among Offenders
Sentenced to Prison After Originally Charged With
Burglary

Jurisdiction and Period	Number to Prison	Percent of Cases Sentenced to Prison by Seriousness[a]		
		Low	Moderate	High
Alameda				
ISL-1976	41	7.32	31.71	60.98
DSL-1978	90	11.11	25.56	63.33
Sacramento				
ISL-1976	50	14.00	44.00	42.00
DSL-1978	43	20.93	39.53	39.53

[a]Offense seriousness was scored on the basis of the
attributes of the offense, including whether the
offense was a burglary of a residence, whether there
was confrontation with a victim, whether threat of
force was used, whether the victim was harmed, the
value of the property taken, whether the offense
displayed special criminal sophistication, and whether
the offender was implicated in multiple offense
incidents.

SOURCE: Derived from data in Utz (1981:Tables 44 and
45).

and San Bernardino showed slight increases in prison use
relative to jail, but the increases there predate DSL.
Extending Casper's data to 1979, the increases in San
Francisco and San Bernardino continued. Using data on
sentence outcomes reported in Brewer et al. (1980:Table
5), the same general pattern was observed statewide for
all offenses (also displayed in Figure 7-8). There was a
definite increase in prison use relative to jail, but the
increase predated DSL implementation, continuing a trend
that began in 1975.

In another analysis, Sparks (1981) examined the
changes in prison use after conviction in superior court
by crime type, prior criminal record, and legal status at
the time of the offense. In each instance, the greatest

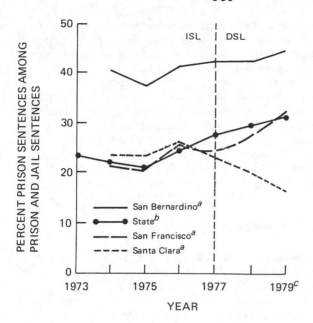

[a]Casper et al. (1981:Figures 5-8 to 5-10).
[b]Brewer et al. (1980:Table 5).
[c]The data for 1979 were obtained from California Department of Justice (1979).

FIGURE 7-8   Percent Prison Sentences Among Prison and
Jail Sentences for California Superior Court
Dispositions—All Offenses

increases in use of prison occur for less serious
offenders. Between 1976 and 1978, the proportion
sentenced to prison increased by more than 50 percent
among convictions for fraud, forgery, auto theft, and
larceny, while prison use increased by only 15 percent
for robbery convictions. Similarly, prison use increased
most for offenders with no prior imprisonments or only
one prior imprisonment, and for those who were under no
commitment or on probation at the time of their offense.
These changes served to narrow the differences in the
likelihood of prison after conviction for cases of
differing seriousness. In all cases, however, this
pattern of increasing punitiveness for less serious cases
began before DSL.

The weight of all the evidence considered here
regarding DSL effects on the decision to imprison or not

falls decidedly on the side of no perceptible change in prison use as a result of DSL. The increases in prison use in superior courts and associated shifts away from probation and jail sentences evident after DSL implementation are best viewed as continuations of preexisting trends. These trends toward increased prison use are consistent with and probably reflect the effects of some combination of increased punitiveness, general increases in the seriousness of cases handled at all levels of the criminal justice system, shifts of less serious cases from superior to municipal court, and changes in the age structure of the population.

Impact on Length of Terms

Two issues are of central concern in considering the effect of DSL on prison terms: (1) changes in the average severity of prison terms reflected in either increases or decreases in mean or median time served and (2) changes in the variability or disparity in time served for similar cases.

The impact of DSL on average prison terms was difficult to anticipate prior to implementation. As originally enacted, the base terms were chosen to reflect recent past experience of time actually served under Adult Authority releasing policies (Nagin, 1979:81; Lipson and Peterson, 1980:4; Casper et al., 1981:2-10). The good-time provisions, which allowed for a maximum of one-third off the sentence, and the application of separate enhancements, whose impact on time served was presumably already reflected in the designation of base terms for each conviction offense, however, contributed to uncertainty in predictions about changes in average time served under DSL. The subsequent enactment of amendments to increase base terms further complicated these predictions.

There was less ambiguity about the expected impact of DSL on the variation or spread of prison terms. A principal purpose of DSL was to introduce greater uniformity in sentences for offenders convicted of the same offense (Lipson and Peterson, 1980:4; Casper et al., 1981:2-9). This was to be achieved through the narrow range of sentence lengths available in the three base terms for any conviction offense. DSL also provided for routine review of all sentences for disparity (i.e., excessive deviation from the distribution of previous sentences for that conviction offense) by the Board of Prison Terms. Both these mechanisms were expected to considerably reduce the range of sentences imposed for the same conviction offense.

All the evidence points to a definite decrease in sentence lengths after DSL. Just as with prison use, however, the changes are part of a continuing trend that began before DSL was implemented. There was also a tendency toward greater uniformity in sentences under DSL. Specifically, most measures of sentence variation or dispersion declined, and the differences in the sentences of men and women were essentially eliminated. Despite this decline and the narrow range of sentence length options provided by base terms, the range of sentences imposed for individual convicted offenses remained surprisingly broad.

Length of Prison Terms

Studies comparing the average length of terms under ISL and DSL use both actual sentences imposed under DSL and adjusted DSL terms reflecting credits for jail time already served, good time off the sentence, or both.[24] The average length of terms served under ISL was estimated from the actual time served by offenders recently released under ISL. These comparisons generally found decreases in mean or median time served under DSL, especially when allowing for jail and maximum good-time discounts from the term actually imposed at sentencing.

Based on Department of Corrections data on receptions and releases statewide, Brewer et al. (1980), for example, report that the mean time that would be served for all offenses, without allowance for credits, increased very slightly from ISL to DSL (40.0 to 41.4 months), using the actual sentence imposed under DSL (Table 7-33). Allowing for maximum good-time credits, however, the adjusted DSL mean time served was considerably lower at 28.7 months. Similarly for robbery, the mean time that would be served for actual DSL sentences, without credits, was higher at 51.8 months compared with 44.8 months for ISL releases. The mean DSL time to be served for robbery, however, dropped to 35.7 when adjusted for good time. For burglary, both the mean time served from actual DSL sentences and the mean from adjusted DSL sentences were lower after DSL than the mean time served found for ISL releases. This same pattern was found when statewide

TABLE 7-33 Length and Variability of Prison Terms in California: ISL Versus DSL

Jurisdiction and Period	Prison Terms (months) All Offenses				Robbery				Burglary (2d Degree)			
	Mean	S.d.	Median	(n)	Mean	S.d.	Median	(n)	Mean	S.d.	Median	(n)
Statewide (Men Only)[a]												
ISL: 1972-1976	40.0	32.8	35	(22,546)	44.8	25.1	41/34[b]	(5,263)	45.4	28.3	37	(3,135)
DSL: 1977-1978												
Actual sentence	41.4	22.9	36	(2,457)	51.8	20.8	48	(643)	26.3	8.7	24	(436)
Adjusted sentence[c]	28.7	15.4	25	(2,452)	35.7	14.0	33	(642)	18.4	5.9	17	(435)
1979: actual sentence[d]	43.1	28.4	36	(10,395)	56.9	28.8	48	(2,216)	27.5	10.5	24	(1,787)

	All Offenses			Robbery			Burglary (2d Degree)		
Statewide[e]	Median	Mid-50% Range	Mid-75% Range	Median	Mid-50% Range	Mid-75% Range	Median	Mid-50% Range	Mid-75% Range
ISL: Composite[f] (1966-1974)	28	17-48	9-60	32	22-42	17-53	23	15-29	8-37
DSL: 1977-1978[c] adjusted sentence	22	12-29	7-43	34	25-41	20-49	14	7-22	4-27

Statewide[g]	Median	Mid-80% Range	Range	Median	Mid-80% Range	Range
ISL: 1975	43	29-66	n.a.	33	21-61	n.a.
DSL: 1978-1979						
Actual sentence	48	36-84	16-240	24	16-48	16-112
Adjusted sentence	32	24-56	11-160	16	11-32	11-75

[a]SOURCE: Brewer et al. (1980:Table 7).
[b]The first number is the median for first-degree robbery and the second is the median for second-degree robbery.
[c]Actual sentences imposed are adjusted to exclude maximum good-time credits (one-third off sentence).
[d]Board of Prison Terms (1981:Table III).
[e]Ku (1980:Figure 4.2).
[f]Refers to release experiences in 1975 for cohorts admitted to Department of Corrections in years 1966 through 1974.
[g]Casper et al. (1981:Table 5.2). No data for "all offenses."

medians were compared in Brewer et al. (1980) and Casper et al. (1981).[25]

Brewer et al. (1980) indicates very different post-DSL changes in time served for men and women (Table 7-34). Time served on discounted DSL sentences for men was shorter than ISL time served for every offense category. For women, however, even the discounted DSL terms for person offenses were longer than ISL time served, and they were about the same for property offenses. DSL thus created greater uniformity in time served across sexes. This was accomplished by introducing a greater differential between person and property offenses in women's terms, with terms for person offenses increasing for women and terms of property offenses remaining about

TABLE 7-34 Changes in Length of Prison Terms by Sex Based on Statewide Data

Offense	Mean Prison Term (Months)		
	Men	Women	Women/Men
All Offenses			
ISL: 1972-1976	40.0	23.7	.59
DSL actual: 1977-1978	41.4	35.3	.85
DSL adjusted: 1977-1978	28.7	24.8	.86
2nd Degree Burglary			
ISL: 1972-1976	30.0	19.5	.65
DSL actual: 1977-1978	26.3	22.3	.85
DSL adjusted: 1977-1978	18.4	16.0	.87
Robbery			
ISL: 1972-1976	44.8	26.7	.60
DSL actual: 1977-1978	51.8	42.8	.83
DSL adjusted: 1977-1978	35.7	29.6	.83
Assault with a Deadly Weapon			
ISL: 1972-1976	40.9	22.3	.55
DSL actual: 1977-1978	47.7	49.7	1.04
DSL adjusted: 1977-1978	32.9	34.7	1.05

SOURCE: Derived from Brewer et al. (1980:Tables 7 and 8).

for women and terms of property offenses remaining about
the same. As indicated in Table 7-34, while women's terms
under ISL were much shorter than those of men, averaging
from 55 to 65 percent of men's terms, even when controlling for crime type, under DSL the lengths of women's
terms were much closer to those of men; women's terms
increased to exceed 80 percent of the length of men's
terms.

When the observation period was increased to include
multiple observations, Lipson and Peterson (1980) found
that the general decline in time served evident after DSL
was consistent with a preexisting trend toward shorter
terms that began several years before DSL implementation.
As evident in Figure 7-9, median ISL prison terms between
1968 and 1976 for all offenses were consistently longer
(at about 3 years) than found in the preceding 23 years,
when prison terms averaged about 26 months. Beginning in
1975, however, the length of terms began to decline again
and reached previous levels in 1978. The shorter DSL
terms after discounting for jail and maximum good-time
credits were fully consistent with this recent decline in
time served. The same trend toward shorter terms is

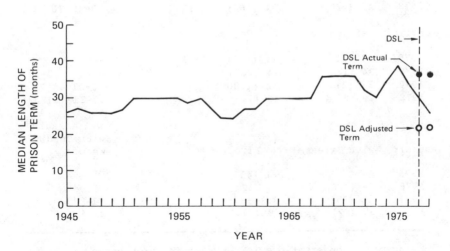

SOURCE: Lipson and Peterson (1980:Figure 4 and Table 5).

FIGURE 7-9 Median Length of Prison Terms Under ISL and
DSL

evident at all levels of seriousness for robbery, burglary, and assault (Table 7-35).[26]

So far the analysis of changes in time served has considered aggregate statewide data with only limited controls for crime type. Using data on burglary cases before and after DSL, Utz (1981) found differences between counties with time served for burglary cases declining after DSL in Alameda and increasing in Sacramento (Table 7-36). Recognizing that a simple two-point comparison of average prison terms may be

TABLE 7-35   Trends in Lengths of Prison Terms By Crime Type

	Median Prison Terms (months)			
	ISL			DSL
Robbery	1st Degree with Firearm	1st Degree	2nd Degree	All
1975	--	45 (1,001)[a]	38 (565)	--
1976	--	39 (818)	30 (417)	--
1977	48 (190)	35 (772)	29 (411)	29-44[b] (756)
1978	45 (220)	34 (664)	27 (380)	29-45 (1,524)
Burglary	1st Degree	2nd Degree		
1975	43 (213)	31 (961)		--
1976	34 (175)	24 (782)		--
1977	31 (243)	22 (1,002)		13-21 (597)
1978	29 (260)	19 (1,249)		13-21 (1,283)
Assault	with Firearm	No Firearm		All Assault with Deadly Weapon
1975	--	41 (455)		--
1976	--	34 (324)		--
1977	40 (35)	33 (367)		21-33 (312)
1978	37 (52)	29 (376)		29-45 (683)

[a]The number of observations is reported in parentheses.
[b]The upper number reflects credit for jail time before prison; the lower number includes both jail time credits and maximum good-time credits.

SOURCE: Lipson and Peterson (1980:Tables 6-8).

TABLE 7-36 Changes in Time Served in Burglary Cases by Jurisdiction

Jurisdiction	Prison Term (months)	
	Mean	Median
Alameda		
ISL: 1976	27.2	24
DSL: 1978 adjusted sentence[a]	24.3	16
Sacramento		
ISL: 1976	23.7	20
DSL: 1978 adjusted sentence[a]	28.6	24

[a]Actual DSL sentences imposed are adjusted to exclude both credit for jail time and maximum good-time credits (one-third off sentence).

SOURCE: Utz (1981:Table 34).

confounded by differences in offense attributes both across jurisdictions and over time, Utz introduced multivariate controls for a variety of indicators of offender and offense seriousness.[27]

With controls for case seriousness, the regression of prison terms on jurisdiction (Sacramento = 1) and time period (DSL = 1) indicates that the effect of DSL was to decrease time served for low-seriousness conviction counts and to increase time served for high-seriousness conviction counts. When controlling for case attributes Sacramento also had more severe prison terms than Alameda; prison terms for "like" cases were 3.5 months longer in Sacramento. The only significant variables among the control variables are all indicators of offense seriousness.[28] No prior record variables were significant for the length of term decision.

Based on these results, the higher prison terms in Alameda under ISL can be attributed to a greater representation of serious cases in Alameda County. The DSL difference between counties of 4.3 months was quite close to the estimated county differential of 3.5 months, suggesting that cases in the two counties were much closer in seriousness in the DSL sample.[29]

The level of control for case differences--including jurisdiction, crime type and other more specific indicators of case seriousness--makes Utz's analysis superior to the other studies considered here. There are, nevertheless, reasons for caution in accepting these results. The main reason for concern is the failure of the regression model to allow for jurisdictional differences in the effects of both DSL and the other control variables.

Certainly, the estimated jurisdictional difference in time served of 3.5 months makes sense in the context of DSL because individual jurisdictions could vary in the severity of sentences imposed. Utz (1981:161), however, is rightly puzzled by the reasons for the same difference between jurisdictions under ISL, when time served was determined by a centralized state agency without explicit regard for sentencing jurisdiction. This result is likely to be an artifact of the way the model was posed, with no allowance for interaction between jurisdiction and time. In this event, jurisdiction necessarily had the same estimated effect in both time periods. This artifact could have been avoided by including an interaction variable for jurisdiction and time period, to allow for the possibility of different jurisdictional differences under ISL and DSL.[30]

Similarly, the model does not address the potential changes in the role of offender and offense variables as the locus of decisions about time served moved from a centralized state agency under ISL to decentralized local courts under DSL. Nor does it allow the effects of the control variables to vary across jurisdictions. As specified the control variables are assumed to have the same effects across jurisdiction and over time. A significant presence of any of these interaction effects would certainly bias the resulting estimates from the homogeneous model posed by Utz.[31] Unfortunately, the data available to Utz, which involve relatively small samples as one focuses only on those cases resulting in prison sentences, do not permit adequate consideration of these issues.

Variability in Prison Terms

Consistent with the emphasis on retribution as a primary purpose of sentencing embodied in DSL, similarly convicted offenses should result in similar sentences. To the extent that this objective is met, one would expect

reductions in the level of variation in prison terms for
"like" offenses.

Several of the studies explicitly address reductions
in the variation, or dispersion, of prison terms after
DSL. Whether measured by the standard deviation around
the mean or the breadth of various mid-ranges around the
median,[32] various studies report reductions in the
spread of prison terms after DSL, when controlling for
convicted offense (Table 7-33). These decreases were
especially pronounced when discounted DSL terms were used.

Because of the associated declines in the means and
medians, however, these decreases in variation must be
regarded cautiously in most cases. Any decrease in the
mean or median increasingly constrains the possible distribution of prison terms below that "midpoint," thus
limiting the range of potential variation. This problem
potentially plagues all ISL-DSL comparisons involving
discounted DSL terms. The comparisons for men of DSL
terms actually imposed with ISL time served in Brewer et
al. (1980:Table 7) provide some more reliable indications
of a real substantive decrease in prison term variation.
Of those crime types with a sufficient number of DSL
cases (more than 75), the standard deviation decreased
from 20 to 50 percent for five of the seven crime types
that experienced increases in means.[33]

While this greater uniformity within conviction
classes was an objective of DSL, the law also provides for
various enhancements to the base term that permit finer
discrimination for differences in seriousness within a
convicted offense class. Consistent with this approach,
Casper et al. (1980:5-33 to 5-34) note that the range of
DSL sentences actually imposed was quite broad (Table
7-33). Before applying any good-time discounts, DSL sentences for robbery ranged from 1 to 20 years and for burglary from 1 to 9 years. These wide ranges were observed
despite the correspondingly narrow range of sentences
available across base terms for each convicted offense,
with maximum differences of only 5 and 2 years for robbery and burglary, respectively. Thus, the availability
of enhancements and consecutive terms on multiple charges
introduced the potential for considerable variability in
sentences for offenders convicted of the same crime type.

Implications for the Size of the Prison Population

Several studies considered the implications of changes in
prison commitments and prison terms for future prison

populations. Both Ku (1980) and Lipson and Peterson (1980) note the important role of the Adult Authority's releasing policies in influencing prison populations in the past. As indicated in Figure 7-10, the large increases in the number of releases from prison in 1970-1971 and again in 1975 were associated with corresponding declines in the size of the prison population. The 1975 increase in releases was particularly important in offsetting the impact of a trend toward increased receptions beginning in 1975.

During the period of relative stability from 1958 to 1968, when annual receptions averaged about 5,250 inmates per year and annual releases averaged about 4,700 inmates per year, the prison population grew at an average of 550 additional inmates per year. Without the discretionary releasing authority of the Adult Authority, a continuation of releases at the stable pre-1968 levels in the face of the increases in receptions experienced during the 1970s would have resulted in unchecked growth in the prison population through the 1970s, reaching over 30,000 inmates by 1978.

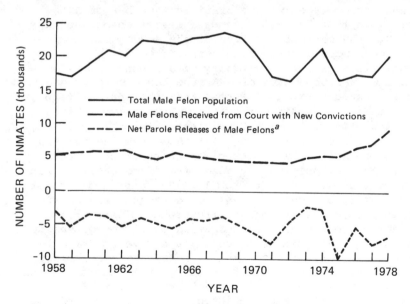

*a*Parole releases and discharges minus parole revocations.

SOURCE: Lipson and Peterson (1980:Figure 5).

FIGURE 7-10 Movement of Male Felons in California Prisons 1958-78

In the absence of some form of safety valve releasing authority, both Lipson and Peterson (1980) and Brewer et al. (1980) have anticipated that the continuing increases in prison commitments and only moderate decreases in time served evident under DSL are likely to result in rapid growth in California's prison population. Indeed the California Department of Corrections projected an increase from 18,502 adult felons in 1978 to 27,020 in 1988 (Brewer et al., 1980:20). The potential exists for even greater increases, when viewed in the context of legislative increases in time served.

Conclusions

There was widespread judicial compliance in applying the provisions of DSL to sentenced defendants. Nevertheless, DSL did little to limit considerable prosecutor discretion in screening the cases that reached superior court and in influencing the charge structure of those cases available for sentencing.

Despite the magnitude of the change in sentencing procedures under DSL, we found no compelling evidence of substantial changes in sentence outcomes attributable to DSL. While prison use increased and time served decreased after DSL, both changes represented continuations of trends that began several years before DSL was implemented. Rather than a major factor in changing sentencing, DSL is perhaps best viewed as a manifestation of a more general shift in sentencing practices in California.

Whatever impact DSL had was largely limited to changes in case processing. DSL did not induce sentence bargaining where it did not exist before; it did, however, expand the scope of already existing sentence bargaining to include explicit reference to the length of prison terms in bargained sentence agreements. DSL provisions for enhancements and probation ineligibility functioned as important bargaining chips for the prosecutor in obtaining agreement to a prison term. Furthermore, while aggregate guilty plea rates changed little, there is evidence that early guilty plea rates did increase.

SENTENCING GUIDELINES

Sentencing guidelines have been developed as a means of structuring judicial sentencing discretion by providing

judges with reasonably specific guidance about the
appropriate sentence for a particular case. Guidelines
have arisen primarily in response to the criticism that
current sentencing provisions permit such wide latitude
for judicial discretion that very similar cases often
receive different sentences (e.g., von Hirsch, 1976;
Frankel, 1972). Although guidelines are only one of
several responses to unwarranted sentencing variation,
the guideline approach has received special impetus from
the application of guidelines to parole decisions by the
Federal Parole Commission (Gottfredson et al., 1978).
The feasibility demonstrated by the parole guidelines
makes guidelines particularly attractive as a means of
structuring sentencing without usurping the proper
exercise of judicial discretion.

Although many types of guidelines have been proposed,
they share certain characteristics. First, guidelines
classify cases into groups based on attributes relevant
to sentencing, such as the seriousness of the current
offense and the offender's prior record. Cases within
the same group are assumed to be sufficiently similar to
each other in terms of the relevant sentencing attributes
to warrant similar sentences. Second, the guidelines
specify a recommended sentence or range of sentences for
each group of offenders. In so doing, guidelines explicitly define sentencing policy by intentionally specifying the desired variation in sentences across different
groups and intentionally specifying limits on acceptable
variation within each group. Underlying this process is
the presumption that the variation in sentences across
groups is warranted (i.e., that differences in the sentencing attributes warrant different sentences), that
most sentence variation among offenders within the same
group is unwarranted, and that the combination of cross-
group variation and limited within-group variation establishes equity in sentencing. Third, some official body,
usually a sentencing guideline commission authorized by
the legislature or the judiciary, is established to construct and promulgate the guidelines. The sentencing
commission is responsible for identifying what attributes
will be used to classify offenders into groups, thereby
indicating the attributes that are most appropriate for
the sentencing decision. In this process the criteria
that define "like" cases are made explicit. In addition,
the commission is responsible for setting sentencing
policy by establishing the recommended cross-group and
within-group variation in sentences.

Implicit in the notion of guidelines is the expectation that judges will be under some degree of obligation to follow the guideline recommendations. This responsiveness will, of course, vary with the legitimacy of the commission, the reasonableness of the commission's recommendations, and the enforcement powers available when sentences fail to adhere to the guideline recommendation. To the extent that guidelines result in changes in judges' sentencing practices that agree with the guideline recommendations, there is "compliance" with the guidelines. Such compliance is expected to reduce unwarranted variation as sentences conform to the recommended cross-group and within-group variation in sentences.

Several examinations of the construction and impact of sentencing guidelines are available: Rich et al. (1981) assessed the construction and subsequent impact of judicially adopted guidelines in Denver and Philadelphia; Sparks et al. (1982) reviewed the construction of guidelines in Massachusetts in depth and those in other jurisdictions in less detail; Cohen and Helland (1981) examined guidelines in Newark; Knapp (1982) and Minnesota Sentencing Guidelines Commission (1982) report on guideline development and impact in Minnesota. The primary consideration in this review of guideline evaluations is their impact on sentencing outcomes and case processing. Only the sentencing guidelines in Minnesota were found to have demonstrably altered sentencing practices after implementation.

Guideline Types

To date, sentencing guidelines have taken two very different forms. One critical dimension that distinguishes the different types of guidelines is the basis of construction, which refers to the process used in choosing the relevant sentencing attributes, classifying offenders in terms of these attributes and establishing sentence recommendations for each offender group. The basis for constructing guidelines can vary along a continuum from descriptive to prescriptive.

A primarily descriptive approach is discussed in Gottfredson et al. (1978) and Wilkins et al. (1976). Descriptive guidelines are intended to articulate past sentencing practices without substantially altering those practices for the court as a whole. By establishing a range of sentences that accommodates a substantial portion of current cases (e.g., 80 percent), the guidelines are intended to provide judges with a description of prevailing sentencing practices in their jurisdiction to serve as a standard in their individual sentencing decisions. This explicit description of past practices may also serve as a basis for possible reconsideration of those practices in an iterative process of description, evaluation, and modification of the guidelines. Descriptive guidelines have been implemented in Denver, Philadelphia, and Newark.

At the other end of the continuum are prescriptive guidelines. These guidelines reflect the values and principles of sentencing that emerge in guideline development and need not relate to current practice. Indeed, the guidelines may represent a deliberate departure from past sentencing practices, as exemplified by the guidelines for the state of Minnesota.

In descriptive guidelines the primary intent is to create consistency across judges. The goal is to change the practices of those judges who deviate by sentencing too leniently or too severely relative to the sentencing practices of the court as a whole. Descriptive guidelines are expected to reduce the variation in sentencing among different judges without shifting the standard sentences of the court. In prescriptive guidelines, by contrast, the goal is to shift the sentencing standards of the entire court to the new standards defined by the guideline recommendations. Consequently, prescriptive guidelines may require that all judges, not just the deviant judges, change their sentencing practices.

Success in achieving the intended guideline effects is determined in part by the degree of obligation judges feel toward the guidelines. Like the basis of construction, the degree of obligation can usefully be viewed as a continuum ranging from voluntary to presumptive. With voluntary guidelines, the guideline sentences are viewed merely as advisory, designed to assist judges by providing a set of standard sentences. If an actual sentence deviates from the guidelines, the judge may justify the deviation, but the justification is intended to serve primarily informational purposes in subsequent reconsideration of guidelines (e.g., Wilkins et al., 1976). The guidelines in Denver, Philadelphia, and Newark were voluntary.

With presumptive guidelines, judges are expected to impose the recommended sentence. The Minnesota sentencing guidelines are an example of presumptive guidelines. Departures from the guidelines are permitted in the presence of substantial and compelling circumstances. In cases of departures, the judge must prepare a written justification for the deviation and the merits of that justification are the basis for appeal by the defense or prosecution.

The impact of guidelines on sentencing practices can be expected to vary with the type of guideline. Descriptive/voluntary guidelines are likely to involve the smallest impact on sentencing. Since descriptive guidelines recommend essentially no departure from current practice for the court as a whole, only those judges who deviate widely from current practice are expected to change their sentences. Because of the voluntary nature of the guidelines, however, very little compliance is expected from these few deviant judges. To the extent that prescriptive guidelines depart from current practices, compliance with the guidelines will require widespread changes in sentencing practices. As implemented in Minnesota, such compliance is likely to be high because of the presumptive authority of those guidelines.

Formal Compliance

Because of the descriptive nature of many sentencing guidelines, it is particularly important to distinguish compliance from agreement with guidelines. Agreement is the extent to which actual sentences are the same as recommended sentences. Compliance, on the other hand, is the increase in the level of agreement in sentencing done with guidelines compared with that done without guidelines. The increase indicates the extent of change in practices in a direction consistent with the guideline recommendations. Simply noting a high level of agreement after guideline implementation may not indicate an effect of guidelines on sentencing practices. This is especially true for descriptive guidelines, which are designed largely to accommodate past sentencing practices.

Voluntary/Descriptive Guidelines

There is little evidence of formal compliance with voluntary/descriptive guidelines in the jurisdictions studied. Rich et al. (1981) found that, in the aggregate, judicial decisions to incarcerate were consistent with guidelines in about 70 percent of cases, both before and after guideline implementation in Denver and Philadelphia. Agreement in terms of sentence length was lower, at about 40 percent after guideline implementation in those two cities. Agreement on both decisions occurred in only about half of all cases in Philadelphia and Denver. Similar results were found in Newark (Cohen and Helland, 1981), with about 78 percent agreement with incarceration sentences and 40 percent agreement with sentence length recommendations before and after guideline implementation.

The Denver evaluation (Rich et al., 1981) used data on 632 cases sentenced in the 18 months before guideline implementation in November 1976 and 1,451 cases sentenced in the 30 months after guidelines were implemented.[34] The Philadelphia analysis (Rich et al., 1981) was based on a 10-percent random sample of cases sentenced in the 39 months before guidelines were implemented on March 5, 1979, and a 45-percent random sample of cases sentenced in the first six months after guideline implementation.[35] The Newark evaluation (Cohen and Helland, 1981) used data on 1,446 cases with presentence reports prepared over a total of 15 months before guideline implementation and another 634 cases sentenced in the first six months after guidelines were implemented in July 1977.[36] Except for those in the Denver evaluation, the follow-up periods after guideline implementation were quite short at 6 months, and it was therefore difficult to sort out long-term impact from start-up effects.

The lack of any significant changes in agreement after descriptive guidelines were implemented in these jurisdictions is consistent with the intent of descriptive guidelines. This finding of no compliance for the court as a whole, however, provides no indication of whether guidelines had the intended effect in changing the sentencing behavior of individual deviant judges. A finding of no overall compliance could occur whether or not deviant judges comply with guideline recommendations. Data on the sentences of individual judges are crucial to evaluating the primary impact of descriptive guidelines on individual judges. None of the evaluations reviewed here includes the necessary analyses of individual judge data.

The low levels of agreement found with sentence length recommendations are noteworthy. Despite claims that the

guidelines were descriptive, the recommendations on
length were more prescriptive in character: They
represented a substantial reduction in the range of
sentence lengths from that observed in past practices.
There was, however, no evidence of compliance by the
court with these narrowed ranges. The degree of
obligation to comply with these voluntary guidelines was
apparently not sufficient to affect judges' sentencing
behavior.

Lawyers and judges interviewed in Philadelphia and
Denver indicated that few judges made significant efforts
to comply with the guidelines. This indifference to the
guidelines was evident in the widespread failure to
comply with their procedural requirements. In Denver the
guideline worksheets for determining the guideline
sentence in each case were available for only a fraction
of the cases sentenced after guidelines were
implemented. An important feature of descriptive
guidelines is the expected role of departures from
guideline sentences in a continuing process of guideline
evaluation and modification. In Denver, however, the
requisite written reasons were provided in only 12
percent of cases involving departures.

Presumptive/Prescriptive Guidelines

Minnesota is the only jurisdiction that has, at the time
of this writing, implemented sentencing guidelines that
are both presumptive and prescriptive.

The Minnesota Sentencing Guidelines Commission was
established by the state legislature in 1978 and charged
with developing presumptive sentencing guidelines for the
state. These guidelines were accepted by the legislature
and were to be used for sentencing all felonies committed
after May 1, 1980. The guidelines articulate and embody
a number of principles of sentencing. These standards
for sentences have served as the basis for appellate
review and the emergence of case law governing the choice
of appropriate sentences. Two principles in particular
have been affirmed in various Minnesota supreme court
rulings: (1) that the sentence be based on the
conviction offense and not on alleged but unproved
offenses and (2) that the severity of the sentence be
proportional to the seriousness of the offense when
compared with other offenses (Minnesota Sentencing
Guidelines Commission, 1982).

The guidelines identify two criteria for sentencing decisions: the seriousness of the offense, reflected in an offense score for different statutory offense types, and the offender's prior criminal history score. Personal attributes of the offender are explicitly excluded from consideration. In developing the guidelines the sentencing commission adopted a prescriptive approach. The recommended sentences represented a deliberate departure from past sentencing practices. Emphasizing retribution as the principal goal of sentencing, the guidelines recommended increased use of prison for violent offenders, including those with low criminal histories, and decreased use of prison for property offenders, regardless of their prior criminal histories.

The Minnesota guidelines are expressed as a grid with offense score on one axis and offender criminal history score on the other. The recommended sentence for a case is found by locating the appropriate cell of the guideline grid. The guidelines distinguish two types of sentences, INs and OUTs. Those cases with an IN recommendation are expected to receive a state prison sentence within the recommended range of terms. Cases with OUT recommendations are not expected to be sentenced to state prison (i.e., the state prison term is stayed); instead OUTs may be sentenced to probation or to terms in local jails.

Internal evaluations of the impact of the Minnesota guidelines found substantial formal compliance by judges in both the decision to incarcerate and the decision about sentence length (Knapp, 1982; Minnesota Sentencing Guidelines Commission, 1982). Table 7-37 shows the percentages of cases in the 1978 baseline sample that would have been sentenced consistently with the pre-sumptive IN and OUT sentences had the guidelines been in effect in 1978 and the percentages of cases sentenced consistently with the presumptive sentences under the guidelines in 1980-1981. For both IN and OUT decisions there were marked shifts in sentences consistent with the guidelines. As Table 7-38 reveals, these shifts in sentencing were often greater when individual cells in the guideline grid are examined than is apparent overall.

The relatively low consistency before guideline implementation in Tables 7-37 and 7-38 illustrates the extent to which the guidelines departed from previous sentencing practices in Minnesota. The increases in agreement in individual cells of the guidelines in Table 7-38 indicate

TABLE 7-37 Percentage of Cases Sentenced Consistently
with Presumptive Sentences for Minnesota Sentencing
Guidelines

	Presumptive OUTs Who Were Sentenced "Out"	Presumptive INs Who Were Sentenced "In"
1978 baseline cases	86	44
1980-1981 sentences imposed	96	77

NOTE: These figures were estimated from data provided by
Knapp (1982). The figures are not precise because some
cases that appear among the presumptive OUTs are actually
treated as presumptive INs under separate statutory
provisions for mandatory sentencing.

the high rates of compliance by judges with the new
policy for low-history violent offenders and high-history
property offenders.

Before implementation of the Minnesota guidelines,
sentence length was determined exclusively by the
paroling authority, so a before-and-after comparison for
length decisions would not be meaningful. Departure
rates after guideline implementation, however, indicate
substantial use of the narrow sentence ranges provided in
the guidelines. Of 827 cases committed to prison after
guideline implementation during 1980-1981, 76.4 percent
were within the guideline range, with 7.9 percent
receiving longer sentences and 15.7 percent shorter
sentences (Knapp, 1982; Minnesota Sentencing Guidelines
Commission, 1982).

Furthermore, the monitoring and follow-up by the
Minnesota Sentencing Guidelines Commission resulted in
strong compliance by judges in submitting the required
written justifications for departures from the guideline
sentence. The appellate review of sentences in Minnesota
has generally upheld the presumptive nature of the
guideline sentences, and case law is now emerging on
acceptable grounds for departures from the presumptive
sentence.

TABLE 7-38 Percentage of Cases Sentenced Consistently with Presumptive Sentences Within Individual Cells of Minnesota Sentencing Guidelines

| | | | Percent Actually Sentenced "Out" | |
			1978 Baseline Cases	1980-1981 Sentenced Cases
Offense 5,	history	1	60.7	95.0
5		2	21.8	74.2
3		3	45.4	80.3

| | | | Percent Actually Sentenced "In" | |
			1978 Baseline Cases	1980-1981 Sentenced Cases
Offense 7,	history	0	39.1	71.8
8		0	41.9	85.4
8		1	29.1	75.0

SOURCE: Knapp (1982).

Variability in Sentences

One of the purposes of sentencing guidelines has been to reduce the variation in sentences for otherwise "like" cases. The guidelines make explicit the criteria for identifying "like" cases and recommend a sentence for those cases. The degree to which guidelines reduce variation in sentences depends partly on the range of variation permitted by the guideline recommendation. The narrower that range, the greater the reduction in variation that can be expected.

In an effort to accommodate large portions of past sentencing practices, voluntary/descriptive guidelines have generally preserved wide ranges on recommended sentences. Assessments of these guidelines have generally found little effect on the extent of variation in sentences imposed on like cases (as classified by the guidelines).

Using regression analysis, Rich et al. (1981) found little change in the proportion of total variance in sentence outcomes that was accounted for by the guideline variables. It is also worth noting that the amount of variance explained was always quite small--25 percent or less in both Denver and Philadelphia. As a further test of sentence variability, Rich et al. (1981) examined the neutrality of sentencing with respect to nonguideline variables, such as race and sex of the defendant. Including these variables with the guideline variables in a regression on sentence outcomes, they found little evidence that these variables affected sentence length decisions. When they did influence IN/OUT decisions, with males more likely to be sentenced to prison in both Denver and Philadelphia and blacks more likely to be sent to prison in Philadelphia, introduction of the guidelines did not reduce the observed racial and sexual disparity in sentences.

In Newark, Cohen and Helland (1981) found little detectable change in the proportions of cases sentenced to IN and OUT sentences in different guideline categories, and thus no evidence of a reduction in the variance of these sentences. Despite the general lack of compliance with sentence length recommendations in Newark, there was a trend toward reduced variance in sentence lengths within guideline categories. This suggests that guidelines may have reduced variance by moving extreme sentences in the direction of the guideline range without necessarily moving the sentence into the recommended range. No analysis of the role of personal attributes of offenders is provided for Newark.

In contrast to the voluntary/descriptive guidelines, the Minnesota guidelines make strong recommendations on IN and OUT sentences and pose relatively narrow ranges for the length of state prison terms to be imposed. As was evident in Table 7-38 there has been strong compliance with the explicitly prescribed IN and OUT sentences. As the proportion receiving the recommended sentence increased toward 100 percent, the variance in IN/OUT sentences also decreased. With a maximum possible variance in IN/OUT sentences of .25 the variance decreased 52 percent, from .1041 in the 1978 baseline data to .0499 in 1980-1981 (Knapp, 1982; Minnesota Sentencing Guidelines Commission, 1982). There were only 23.6 percent departures from the narrow range of sentence lengths provided by the guidelines. Since the paroling authority determined the length of prison terms before the sentencing guidelines were implemented, the only comparison for decisions on length of term is departures from the parole guidelines. In 1979 there were 24 percent mandatory and discretionary departures from the parole guideline term and an addtional 14 percent adjustments under administrative rules. In 1980 combined departures and adjustments represented 46 percent of parole cases.

An important principle articulated in the Minnesota guidelines is that sentences should be neutral with respect to the race, sex, and socioeconomic status of the defendant. One indicator of the success of the guidelines in achieving more uniform sentencing is the rate of departure of sentences from the guidelines for different demographic groups. The data in Table 7-39 indicate that considerable variations in sentences

TABLE 7-39 IN/OUT Departure Rates for Cases Sentenced Under Minnesota Sentencing Guidelines

Demographic Group	Percent Departures over All Cases	Percent Severe Departures Among Total (Presumptive OUTs Who Were Sentenced IN)	Percent Lenient Departures Among Total (Presumptive INs Who Were Sentenced OUT)
Total	6.2	3.1	3.1
Race			
White	5.2	2.6	2.7
Black	9.6	4.9	4.7
Native American	12.4	7.5	4.9
Sex			
Male	6.5	not reported	not reported
Female	3.1	not reported	not reported
Employment			
Employed	3.4	0.2	3.2
Unemployed	8.9	5.0	3.9

SOURCE: Knapp (1982); Minnesota Sentencing Guidelines Commission (1982).

remained after implementation of the guidelines. The number of IN/OUT departures was reduced in the aggregate of all cases from 19.4 percent in 1978 to 6.2 percent in 1980-1981, and similar reductions were found for all demographic groups. Nevertheless, minority, male, and unemployed offenders continued to experience more departures from the presumptive sentences, and these departures tended to be in the direction of more severe sentences (i.e., presumptive OUTS who were in fact sentenced to the state prison).

The distribution of types of cases differed sharply across demographic groups, with cases of whites, females, and employed offenders more likely to be for low-severity offenses and low criminal history scores. Departure rates were also generally lower for these cases; the typical reasons for departures related to the extent of injury to victims--conditions that do not apply in low-severity property offenses. These differences in the representation of cases with low departure rates could affect the comparisons of departure rates across demographic groups. As a minimum control for the potential influence of differences in the distribution of cases, departure rates were estimated separately among presumptive INs and presumptive OUTs. As indicated in Table 7-40, the differences across race and sex remain after minimally controlling for case distribution and the differences between employed and unemployed offenders are increased.

The actual departure rates were compared with an independent assessment by commission staff of justified departures for a sample of cases from eight counties. The commission staff assessment was conservative in the sense that there was a strong presumption in favor of the guideline sentence. The departure rates in the independent assessment reported in Table 7-41 are thus uniformly lower than those observed in actual sentences. Based on the independent assessment, blacks were 73 percent more likely and Native Americans were 3.3 times more likely than whites to merit severe departures. Thus the actual differential between blacks and whites in Table 7-40 is somewhat higher than expected from the independent assessment. Relative to whites, blacks and Native Americans also received lenient departures from presumptive IN sentences more often than expected. The observed difference between men and women is fully consistent with that expected from the differences in case seriousness as reflected in the independent assessment.

TABLE 7-40 Departure Rates Among Presumptive INs and
Presumptive OUTs for Cases Sentenced Under Minnesota
Sentencing Guidelines

Demographic Group	Percent Sentenced IN Among Presumptive OUTs[a]	Percent Sentenced OUT Among Presumptive INs
Race		
White	3.1	15.4
Black	6.8	10.7
Native American	9.5	17.2
Sex		
Male	4.0	14.2
Female	1.6	25.9
Employment[b]		
Employed	0.2	46.4
Unemployed	6.3	18.8

[a]Severity level VI offenses are excluded from the
presumptive OUTs because some of these offenses are in
fact presumptive INs under the terms of separate
mandatory sentencing.
[b]The departure rates by employment status are estimated
from data on departure rates and the distribution of
cases for different categories of offenders available
from the Minnesota Sentencing Guidelines Commission.
The figures reported here are only approximations based
on estimates of both the number of departures and the
total number of cases in each category. They include
severity level VI offenses among presumptive OUTs.

SOURCE: Minnesota Sentencing Guidelines Commission
(1982).

No independent assessment is available by employment
status. On the basis of this analysis, it is evident
that differences in case seriousness account for much of
the difference in departures across demographic groups.
The greater than expected incidence of severe departures
for blacks relative to whites nevertheless remains a
matter of some concern.

TABLE 7-41 Expected Departure Rates Among Presumptive
INs and Presumptive OUTs Based on Independent Assessment
of Case Attributes

Demographic Group	Percent Expected to be Sentenced IN Among Presumptive OUTS[a]	Percent Expected to be Sentenced OUT Among Presumptive INs
Total Cases	2.7	2.0
Race		
White	2.2	2.9
Black	3.8	0.7
Native American	7.2	0.0
Sex		
Male	3.0	1.9
Female	1.1	4.8

NOTE: The independent assessment was made by Minnesota
Sentencing Guidelines Commission staff on a sample of
1,728 cases from eight counties in 1980-81.

[a]Severity level VI offenses are excluded from the
presumptive OUTs because some of these offenses are in
fact presumptive INs under the terms of separate
mandatory sentencing.

SOURCE: Minnesota Sentencing Guidelines Commission
(1982).

Case Processing

The Rich et al. (1981) evaluation of voluntary/
descriptive sentencing guidelines systems attempted to
study the effects of the guidelines on plea negotiations.
Interview data from Philadelphia, Chicago, and Denver
indicate that lawyers did not consider the guidelines to
be important and accordingly did not take them into
account when negotiating plea agreements. Because
Minnesota's presumptive sentencing guidelines have legal
force and prescribe narrow ranges from within which
prison sentence lengths must be selected, some guideline

critics have suggested that counsel would incorporate the guidelines into their plea negotiations. Since the applicable guideline range is based on conviction offenses, charge bargains would consequently permit counsel to determine the applicable guideline sentence. Some evidence was found of changes in charge reduction patterns for cases in which aggravated robbery was the most serious charge (Knapp, 1982; Minnesota Sentencing Guidelines Commission, 1982). As evidenced in Table 7-42, the proportion of charge reductions increased for cases with low criminal history scores--fewer cases were actually convicted of aggravated robbery. There were apparently adjustments in case processing to avoid imposing the prescribed prison term for marginally serious defendants when prison was not deemed appropriate in every case by court personnel. With high criminal history scores, however, the proportion of charge reductions declined, and more cases ended in convictions for aggravated robbery. This pattern suggests that prosecutors and judges were operating to preserve distinctions among cases on the basis of criminal history despite the explicit guideline policy of uniformly prescribed prison terms for all these cases.

It was also anticipated by some that the guidelines would result in increases in the rate of trial. No such

TABLE 7-42 Changes in Charge Reductions After Implementation of the Minnesota Sentencing Guidelines

| Criminal History Score | Percent of Cases Convicted of Aggravated Robbery When Aggravated Robbery was the Most Serious Charge | |
	1978 Baseline Cases	Cases Sentenced Under Guidelines, 1980-1981
0	59	49
1	75	60
2	64	66
3	54	70
4	58	70

SOURCE: Knapp (1982); Minnesota Sentencing Guidelines Commission (1982).

increase was observed during the first year after full implementation of the guidelines; the trial rate among felony convictions was 5 percent in 1978 and 4 percent among 5,500 cases disposed under the guidelines (Knapp, 1982). However, in assessing the impact on trial rates it is important to also examine disposition time. If disposition time from arrest to sentence increased, especially for trial cases, increases in trial rates might not be evident during the early guideline implementation period. This remains an issue for further exploration in the continuing evaluation of the impact of the Minnesota guidelines. In addition, although the Minnesota Sentencing Guidelines Commission is now conducting an assessment of the impact on plea negotiations, only preliminary findings on aggravated robbery are available.

Prison Use

The Minnesota guidelines included an explicit policy choice to increase the use of prison for serious offenses against persons by offenders with limited criminal histories while decreasing prison use for property offenders regardless of their prior criminal history. Consistent with the guidelines, the portion of offenders committed to state prisons for person offenses increased from 32 percent to 46 percent. There was no similar shift in offense types among convictions, with cases with presumptive prison sentences representing about 13 percent of convictions before (1978) and after (1980-1981) guideline implementation. Table 7-43 provides further evidence of the effectiveness of the guidelines in shifting prison sentences from property to personal offenses. The portion sentenced to prison of low-history offenders in serious offenses increased sharply, from 45 percent to 77 percent after implementation of the guidelines, while the portion sentenced to prison of high-history offenders in the least serious felonies decreased from 53 percent to 16 percent (Knapp, 1982; Minnesota Sentencing Guidelines Commission, 1982). This change is an instance in which the sentencing reform, through its explicitly prescribed IN and OUT sentences, has effectively increased the difference between cases that were previously treated similarly.

The impact of guidelines on the overall size of the prison population was also an overriding concern of the Minnesota Sentencing Guidelines Commission. The guide-

TABLE 7-43 Shift in Prison Sentences from Property to
Persons Offenses under Minnesota Sentencing Guidelines

Offense Severity Level	Criminal History Score	Percent of Cases Sentenced to State Prisons	
		1978 Baseline Cases	Cases Sentenced Under Guidelines, 1980-1981
VII, VIII, IX (High)	0, 1 (Low)	45	77
I, II (Low)	3, 4, 5 (High)	53	16

SOURCE: Knapp (1982); Minnesota Sentencing Guidelines
Commission (1982).

lines were explicitly developed with an eye to the
existing capacity of state prisons. Through the end of
1981 the average prison population was at the expected
level at 96 percent of capacity. In assessing the
anticipated effect of guidelines on the prison
population, the commission used the baseline distribution
of court cases in 1978 with minor adjustments for expected changes in the demographics of the state. The
impact assessment did not allow for changes in case mix
that might result from changes in crime rates or in
arrest and charging practices. To the extent that such
changes do occur, the projections of impact on prison
population could be seriously in error. For this reason
the commission continually monitors the size and
composition of the state prison population.

While the prison population has remained relatively
stable in size since implementation of the guidelines,
the population in local jails has increased. This is
partly due to increased use of jail as a condition of
stayed prison sentences. In 1980-1981 after the
guidelines 46 percent of convicted felons were committed
to jails, compared with 35 percent to jail in the
baseline year 1978. Of this 11 percentage point
increase, about half can be attributed to the reduction
of 4 to 5 percent in prison use at sentencing. The

remainder of the increase is part of a continuing trend
toward increased use of jails that began in 1974
(Minnesota Sentencing Guidelines Commission, 1982:63).

Conclusion

There is little evidence that voluntary/descriptive
guidelines have had any demonstrable impact on sentencing
practices for the court as a whole, either in terms of
compliance or in reductions in variation in sentences.
This is not surprising, however, because the principal
intent of these guidelines has been to increase the
consistency of sentences across individual judges. Thus
far, the crucial data on sentencing by individual judges
that are necessary for examining compliance by individual
deviant judges has not been examined, and the impact of
these guidelines on individual judges remains largely
unknown.

In sharp contrast, the case of the Minnesota
sentencing guidelines, which were prescriptive and
presumptive in authority, have indicated that it is
possible to achieve substantial compliance resulting in
major policy shifts through the use of guidelines. The
key factors in achieving this impact in Minnesota appear
to have been: the legal authority of the guidelines
manifested in the legislative mandate; the careful
implementation of the guidelines involving many facets of
the community as well as criminal justice system
participants; and the enforcement of the guidelines
through monitoring of sentences by the commission staff
and affirmation of the guideline sentences in Supreme
Court decisions on appeals.

PAROLE REFORMS

Parole Abolition

On May 1, 1976, Maine became the first state in modern
times to establish a determinate sentencing system and
abolish parole. The climate for this change included
emerging sentiment for harsher sentencing, particularly
in rural areas; a widespread belief that the public felt
the parole board was too lenient; and skepticism about
rehabilitative programs among members of the Law Revision
Committee. Sentencing became determinate in the sense

that the duration of prison sentences was calculable at the time of sentencing. "Good time" accrued at a rate of 10 days a month, and "gain" time at a rate of two days a month. Assuming maximum credits, defendants could expect to serve 60 percent of the nominal prison sentence.

The National Institute of Justice has supported two evaluations of Maine's innovations. The first, conducted by a group at Pennsylvania State University, assessed the impact of the new regime during its first 12 months and was completed in late 1978 (Kramer et al., 1978). The second, directed by Donald Anspach of the University of Southern Maine, has generated one lengthy "Interim Report" (Anspach, 1981)—it is primarily a content analysis of changes in Maine's substantive criminal law—and is expected to culminate in a comprehensive final report. Neither study has produced credible findings, although the Southern Maine project may yet do so.

There are several general reasons why the Maine experience is not likely to produce credible evaluation results. First, Maine's small and not especially criminous population does not generate enough cases to permit meaningful statistical analyses of year-to-year changes. Second, simultaneous changes in the substantive criminal law and the sentencing system confounded efforts to isolate the effects of either separate set of changes.

Before 1976, Maine's criminal law consisted of a large number of individual statutes that had been enacted over two centuries and were often inconsistent and overlapping. There were, for example, nine different forgery statutes; the new statutory forgery formulation incorporated "over sixteen different but related statutes" (Anspach, 1981:24, 8). There was no compelling logic to the sentences authorized for different offenses. There were more than 24 different maximum prison terms authorized for different offenses and 60 different statutory sentencing provisions (Anspach, 1981:10; Zarr, 1976:118).

The statutory changes that affected sentencing included the separation of all substantive offenses into five offense classes, each authorizing a maximum term of imprisonment and probation and a maximum fine. Other critical changes included the abolition of the parole board, the establishment of appellate sentence review, and the creation of a procedure by which the corrections commissioner can petition the courts for resentencing of prisoners who receive sentences longer than one year.

The abolition of parole, without simultaneous creation of criteria for judicial sentencing, gave rise to a number of hypotheses about likely effects. One might expect greater disparity, following abolition, in the lengths of prison terms actually served, because there is no parole board to even out gross anomalies. Prison sentences might become longer because judges are accustomed to dealing in inflated terms and may not reduce the lengths of sentences imposed fully to account for parole deflation (see von Hirsch and Hanrahan, 1979:88-90). By contrast, one might hypothesize a real reduction in sentence severity, because judges may have been consciously increasing past prison sentences to discount for parole release and no longer need to do so and because, without a parole board, judges may be chastened by the sole responsibility for punishment decisions and impose less severe sentences (see, e.g., Kramer et al., 1978:62-64).

Maine regrettably was the wrong state in which to test such hypotheses. It is thinly populated and there are relatively few prosecutions or convictions. In the six counties from which the Penn State study included the universe of convictions in the first year after implementation, there were 957 convictions, two-thirds of which were for misdemeanor equivalents. There were 441 convictions for Class A, B, or C felonies in the six counties in the first 12 months of the new law, nearly half of which resulted in nonincarcerative sentences (n = 207). The number of persons convicted of any particular offense in any one year was too small to permit meaningful statistical analysis of changes in sentence by offense type. Moreover, most of the definitions of substantive offenses were changed in the new criminal code, making it difficult to compare the handling of particular offenses before and after the statutory change.

The Penn State evaluation concluded that the 1976 sentencing changes caused (1) a decrease in the use of incarcerative sentences, (2) reduced sentence lengths for persons convicted of Class B and C offenses and longer sentences for persons convicted of Class A offenses, and (3) an increase in sentence disparities. Some or all of those things may have happened, but major defects in research design make the report's conclusions less than persuasive. Before discussing those defects it may be helpful to describe the general research strategy.

Data were collected on all convictions in the superior courts of 6 of Maine's 16 counties for the fifth through second years preceding the changes (May 1970 to April 1974). The sample included five of the six busiest superior courts and encompassed more than 70 percent of Maine's criminal prosecutions. Data were also collected on all convictions in those counties during the first 12 months after implementation. Because prison records were centrally located and easily accessible, data were collected on all persons released from Maine's prisons without regard to county of conviction for the periods May 1971-April 1972, May 1973-April 1974, and May 1976-April 1977. The analysis consisted of a series of comparisons of outcomes of sentences imposed during the 4-year preinnovation period and the 12-month postimplementation period, and comparisons between the durations of sentences served by prisoners released prior to implementation and the sentences to be served by persons convicted during the 12-month postinnovation period, assuming they receive the maximum 12 day credit for good time per month.

There are seven reasons why the Penn State study's findings are not credible. First, changes in substantive offense definitions make the comparability of precode and postcode convictions unclear. The study relied on a "conversion table" to match offenses developed by the Maine Department of Mental Health and Corrections, but there is no way readers of the report can determine how reliable that conversion table is. Any conversion system would require highly substantive judgments, and this one had the added difficulty that "there are pre-code offenses for which there is no corollary in the new code and vice versa" (Kramer et al., 1978:26).

Second, because the percentage of cases involving more than one charge increased from 5.5 percent precode to 21.3 percent postcode, all multiple conviction cases were deleted from the conviction samples. The rationales for that deletion were:

(1) multiple offenders were systematically treated more harshly than single offenders;
(2) the proportions of multiple offenders in the precode and postcode samples of imprisoned offenders were strikingly different (e.g., 12.7 percent of those incarcerated at Maine State Prison precode and 35.6 percent postcode);
(3) coding problems were generated by the impossibility of knowing which offense accounts for what part of the sentence; and

(4) the number of multiple offense cases was too small
    to permit independent analysis (Kramer et al.,
    1978:31).

While the problems noted are not inconsiderable, the
substantial increases in multiple charge convictions and
among Maine State Prison incarcerations[37] may have been
important consequences of the law changes, yet they were
defined out of the sample. Moreover, the deletion of
cases producing 35.6 percent of Maine State Prison
commitments creates a systematic and substantial
underrepresentation of serious cases in the sample.
(This may account for the conclusions that the frequency
of incarcerative sentences declined and sentence severity
declined for Class B and C offenders postcode).

Third, all Class D and Class E convictions were
deleted from the conviction samples, in part for the
logistical reason that case records for these
misdemeanor-equivalent offenses were located at 34
municipal court sites throughout the state. Moreover,
"for purposes of this study, it was felt that these
misdemeanor offenses involved sanctions less important
from a national perspective than the felony offenses;
therefore, we opted for studying sentencing and outcome
data for Class A through C offenders only" (Kramer et
al., 1978:27). The difficulty here is that changes in
charging or bargaining patterns under the new law may
have led to the prosecution of cases as Class C offenses
postcode that were prosecuted as Class D equivalents
precode, or vice versa. Given that almost half of the
postcode Class A, B, and C sentences were
nonincarcerative, and that prison sentences up to 12 and
6 months may be imposed on Class D and E offenses, that
sort of offense drift is not unlikely and it represents
one of the changes that an evaluation should try to
investigate. Whether offense drift occurred, or in which
predominant direction (A,B,C, to D,E, or the reverse) is
unclear, but exclusion of all D and E offenses ensured
that the study would fail to account or control for those
changes.

Fourth, the precode conviction cases were drawn from a
four-year period and aggregated into one precode sample
against which postcode cases were compared, thereby
homogenizing any precode trends into an aggregate. If
the study's conclusion that use of incarceration declined
is right, it is entirely possible that a trend in that
direction had been under way for several years. The

four-year aggregation would mask any such trend and thus risk attributing changes to the new law that predated it.

Fifth, outcome data on prison release dates were not obtained on 45 cases in the precode sample of Maine Correctional Center commitments and on 31 Maine State Prison cases. The aggregate three-year sample of precode release cases for which records were found totals 431. The 76 missing cases would increase the precode release sample by almost 20 percent. "While there is no reason to expect that missing MCC cases are systematically different from those in our sample" (Kramer et al., 1978:28), there is no reason not to make that assumption. Of the missing 31 Maine State Prison cases, some had not been released at the completion of data collection; their absence systematically reduces average sentence severity in the precode sample. Other files that were lost concern prisoners whose sentences had expired. Still others were under life sentence and were excluded from the sample. Perhaps ironically, five of the missing Maine State Prison cases involved prisoners serving prison terms for offenses that have retrospectively been characterized as Class D offenses and therefore were excluded from the study.

Sixth, the analyses aggregated conventional Maine Correctional Center and Maine State Prison incarcerative sentences with short-term local jail sentences and "split" sentences. Doing so would obscure changes in the imposition of long sentences. The use of split sentences (probation on condition that the defendant serve a short term of incarceration) increased markedly under the new law (7.8 percent of persons sentenced precode versus 22.2 percent postcode). The increased use of split sentences is not surprising: the new law expressly authorized split sentences involving not more than 90 (shortly thereafter increased by amendment to 120) days of incarceration.

Seventh, there were apparently few if any interviews conducted with lawyers, judges, and courtroom personnel. Given many of the difficulties of conducting a statistically rigorous evaluation in Maine, a qualitative study of work-group reactions to the new law and perceptions of its operation might have been enlightening.

Taken together, these various tactical decisions make the precode and postcode samples of persons convicted and persons serving prison terms noncomparable and the results of the research unpersuasive.

The Southern Maine Interim Report adds nothing to our knowledge of what happened in Maine when parole was abolished. The Interim Report addresses itself to

"sociologists of deviance" and "students of the sociology
of law." The changes in substantive offense definitions
in Maine and sentencing reform are "subjects of a critical analysis of value-laden social construction"
(Anspach, 1981:82). This content analysis of substantive
law changes casts little light on the impacts of the
statutory changes. Perhaps the final report from this
project will provide more useful insights.

Neither of the available reports of the evaluations on
the impact of Maine's abolition of parole provides credible findings. Maine's prison population increased
greatly from 1976 to 1980. Whether that increase is
partly attributable to law reform efforts, notably the
abandoned administrative release powers of the parole
board, is worth knowing. Unfortunately, the evaluations
cast little light on this issue.

Parole Guidelines

There have been three major recent evaluations of the
operations of parole guidelines systems. Arthur D.
Little, Inc. (ADL, 1981) examined the U.S. Parole Commission's parole guidelines system and state guideline
systems in Washington, Oregon, and Minnesota. Mueller and
Sparks (1982) studied the operation of the Oregon parole
guidelines. The General Accounting Office released a report in 1982 on the operation of the federal parole guidelines system. Four primary questions have been studied:

(1) Severity--the effect of sentencing guidelines on
    the overall severity of prison sentences;
(2) Accuracy--the extent to which parole guidelines are
    correctly applied in prison release decisions;
(3) Variability--the extent to which parole release
    decisions are consistent with apparently applicable
    guidelines; and
(4) Disparity reduction--the extent to which parole
    guidelines serve to reduce disparities in punish-
    ment compared with parole release without guide-
    lines and compared with the distribution of
    sentences imposed by judges.

Severity

Mueller and Sparks (1982:15-20) investigated severity--
whether the overall severity of prison sentences served

in Oregon increased between 1974, before guidelines were implemented, and 1978, when guidelines had been in effect for several years. They concluded that there was "an overall increase in severity of terms" (p. 20), but cautioned, as we do with regard to the evaluations of California's Determinate Sentence Law, against concluding that "the guidelines caused the observed changes" (Mueller and Sparks, 1982:1, emphasis in original). The other studies did not assess severity changes.

Accuracy

The Arthur D. Little and General Accounting Office studies investigated accuracy--the consistency with which different decision makers would apply the guidelines to individual cases. This was tested by having researchers or (in the General Accounting Office study) parole hearing examiners calculate guideline sentences on the basis of case files for cases already decided, and compare the researchers' sentences to those actually imposed.

In Minnesota (where the parole guidelines have since been abandoned), Arthur D. Little researchers, working with case files for a sample of prisoners released in 1979, concluded that the parole board "applies parole decision guidelines in a highly consistent manner" (ADL, 1981d:97). By contrast, both the General Accounting Office and the Arthur D. Little studies of the U.S. Parole Commission's guidelines found serious accuracy problems. Arthur D. Little researchers--using a method in which two individuals separately evaluated each file, reconciled their decisions, and compared them with the actual case decisions--were in agreement with the actual Parole Commission offense severity and salient factor calculations in only 61 percent of the cases studied (ADL, 1981b:49). The General Accounting Office (1982) study found great inconsistencies in release date calculations when it had parole examiners calculate guideline sentences for 30 prisoners previously released. The guideline calculations of Arthur D. Little researchers in Oregon were completely consistent with parole board calculations in two-thirds of the cases studied (ADL, 1981a:8). The complete agreement rate in Arthur D. Little's Washington study, by stark contrast, was only 13 percent (ADL, 1981c:2). The evaluators point out that their analyses may, for several reasons, overstate discordance. Nonetheless, for all but Minnesota's "simple and explicit" system, all of the guidelines systems appear highly subject to calculation errors, owing to various combinations of inherent complexity, poor quality control procedures, insufficiently specific policy rules, and problems of missing and unreliable data.

Variability

Variability concerns the extent to which release dates are consistent with the apparently applicable guideline (that is, the guideline that the examiner determined was applicable, which often, as noted above, was an inaccurate determination). Two important caveats must be noted. First, all parole guideline systems authorize examiners to depart from the guidelines in exceptional cases. Thus a release date not authorized by the guidelines does not necessarily mean that it is not in compliance with the guidelines system, nor is a release date from within the applicable guidelines necessarily compliant. Second, rates of compliance with guidelines are not especially informative without knowledge of the widths of the guideline ranges and the specificity of guideline criteria. A 90 percent compliance rate with 3-to-6 year ranges may be less meaningful than a 50 percent compliance rate with a 56-to-58 month range. The discretionary "departure rates" under the U.S. Parole Guidelines have varied between 10 percent and 20 percent. Under the Minnesota guidelines the overall discretionary departure rate in 1977-1979 was less than 10 percent (ADL, 1981d:40). Compliance with Washington's first set of guidelines occurred in about 30 percent of the cases (ADL, 1981c:8), but those guidelines were later repealed and replaced with guidelines expressed in a different format: Arthur D. Little found that in 1979-1980, release dates were set within the guidelines 74 percent of the time (ADL, 1981f:14).

These guideline systems vary substantially in the widths of guideline ranges (Minnesota's were quite narrow; the U.S. Parole Commission's were quite broad). Yet compliance rates exceeded 75 percent in the jurisdictions studied, except under the original, quickly abandoned Washington guidelines. Thus it would appear that parole boards are capable of achieving considerable accountability in parole release decision making (assuming that "accuracy" problems are surmountable).

Disparity Reduction

All of the studies reviewed that assessed the impact of
parole guidelines on disparity found evidence that the
guidelines reduced sentencing disparities. Mueller and
Sparks (1982:20-21, 36) concluded that controlling for
offense severity and using the Oregon Parole Board's offender scoring system, the variability of prison terms was
less in 1976 and 1978, under guidelines, than in 1974 before guidelines were implemented. The Arthur D. Little
study of the impact of the U.S. parole guidelines on disparity compared actual times served by prisoners convicted
of robbery and selected property offense who were released
in 1970 (preguidelines) and 1979 (postguidelines) and
found "measurably less dispersion in the distribution of
actual time served" for the 1979 releases that could not
be explained by reduced variability in sentences imposed
by judges (ADL, 1981e:3). Finally, for Minnesota, Arthur
D. Little found that for persons convicted of aggravated
robbery "offenders released in 1979 under the guidelines
system tended to serve more nearly the same amount of time
. . . when stratified into subgroups based upon prior
history" than did aggravated robbery prisoners who were
released preguidelines in 1974 (ADL, 1981e:63). Thus it
appears that well-managed parole guideline systems can
operate to reduce sentence disparity among persons imprisoned.

CONCLUSION

Substantive Findings

Almost all the studies reviewed found, in the most trivial sense, formal compliance with the procedural requirements of reform. Prosecutors refrained from bargaining,
judges imposed the mandated sentences on convicted offenders, and parole boards released according to guideline requirements. This behavioral change, however,
usually represented compliance more in form than in substance. Participants routinely attempted to circumvent
changes by filtering cases out earlier. One result thus
dominates the studies of sentencing reform impact: Regardless of the type or locus of the procedural change,
no appreciable changes were found in the use of prison;
whatever system changes occurred were limited largely to
modifications of case-processing procedures.

Procedural Compliance

The mechanisms for achieving compliance were quite
different in different contexts. Plea bargaining and
parole reforms were successfully achieved through
administrative orders, executed by system participants
who were usually agents of, and sometimes employees of,
an administrative agency and who shared an organizational
orientation. When prosecutors wanted to abolish plea
bargaining in general or in a particular form and were
serious about it, they were able to do so. All three
plea bargaining evaluations so attest. In the Michigan
county in which charge bargaining was forbidden in drug
sale cases, the percentage of convictions resulting from
guilty pleas to reduced charges declined from 80 percent
in 1973, the year before the ban, to 0 in sample cases
disposed in 1974 after the ban. All the evidence in
Alaska suggests that the plea bargaining ban was
generally followed. In Detroit, the firearm plea
bargaining ban also appears to have been followed.

In general, assistant prosecutors working in systems
in which plea bargaining had been restricted much
preferred the new regime. To some extent, their work
loads were reduced (there was much less haggling). To
some extent, they had to work harder, but at work that
enhanced their self-images by calling on them to try
cases and to prepare them for trial or generally to
behave more "professionally."

Conversely, defense lawyers tended to dislike the
bans. While their objections were often expressed as
concern that inflexibility caused injustice, their
objections appeared at least in part to be self-serving.
The economics of defense practice often place a premium
on quick resolution of a high volume of cases. The bans
impeded realization of that goal; the only solutions were
for defense counsels to work harder on each case or to
represent their clients less effectively. No doubt the
trade-off between reduced income and reduced effectiveness was resolved differently by different lawyers.
However it was resolved, the dilemma was one that made
defense counsel uneasy.

Achieving the compliance of judges was another matter
entirely. Judges traditionally operate as independent
agents whose official actions are bound only by the rule
of law. Being elected or appointed to the position,
usually for long terms, they are less subject to
administratively imposed changes and relatively imper-

vious to organizational controls. In all the studies, judicial compliance with new sentencing provisions was only achieved when mandated by statute, as found in cases of mandatory and determinate sentences, and for the Minnesota Sentencing Guidelines. Administratively imposed changes, not backed by the force of law, as found in most cases of sentencing guidelines, were advisory at best.

Adaptive Responses

In every case of procedural compliance, the studies also found evidence of increased screening or other early disposition of cases, effectively avoiding application of the procedural change in many cases.

In Alaska the portion of felony arrest cases screened out early increased by at least 2.9 percentage points, and perhaps as much as 6.4 percentage points, from a rate of 10 percent. In Boston and Detroit there was evidence of earlier disposition of moderate severity cases to avoid the impact of the mandatory sentence laws.

In Boston district courts, defendants charged only with violation of the illegal firearms carrying statute were more than twice as likely to be acquitted after the law took effect: 16 percent of court dispositions before and 36 percent after. Of those convicted and sentenced in the lower court, the likelihood of appeal to a trial de novo (and hence another opportunity at escaping the prison sentence) increased dramatically: Before the law, 52 percent of defendants were convicted, of whom a quarter--12 percent of all dispositions--appealed; afterward, 39 percent of dispositions were convictions and virtually all of them (38 percent of all dispositions) appealed.

In Detroit the likelihood that "other assault" cases would be dismissed or result in acquittal increased from 36 percent before the mandatory sentencing law took effect to 50 percent afterward; recall that an effective ban of plea bargaining occurred simultaneously, which may make the shift more striking because new ways had to be found to achieve the increased dismissal rate.

In New York, notwithstanding significant declines in drug felony arrests statewide (1972: 19,269; 1975: 15,941), which should have increased the "quality" of arrests, there were steady declines in indictment rates, given arrest, and in conviction rates, given indictment.

In New York City, drug felony arrests declined by
one-third (1972: 11,259; 1975: 7,498), yet indictment
rates, given arrest, declined and dismissal rates tripled.

In California early guilty pleas increased immediately
after the determinate sentencing system took effect, from
32 percent of all guilty pleas in 1976 to 43 percent in
1978. There is also evidence that cases were increasingly disposed in lower courts, with dispositions in
superior courts declining from 71 percent in 1968 to only
30 percent by 1979.

One irony about sentencing reforms is that their
implied invitation to circumvention meant that while the
severity of prison sentences actually imposed sometimes
increased, the number of defendants imprisoned often
declined. In New York, the likelihood of imprisonment
given arrest was approximately 11 percent in both 1972
and in the first half of 1976, but the arrest base was
much smaller, meaning that there were fewer prison
sentences imposed overall. If, as is widely believed,
the deterrent effectiveness of criminal laws depends more
on certainty and celerity than on severity, the New York
drug law appears to have achieved exactly the opposite
balance.

Marginal Cases

One theme running through almost every evaluation
considered is that the greater rigidity of a system in
which plea bargaining has been controlled or in which
sentences have been prescribed, the more people worried
about possible undue severity in marginal cases. In
California, Casper et al. (1981) noted a widespread
belief that DSL would increase the number of marginal
offenders receiving prison sentences. Under ISL, a judge
who wanted to send an offender to prison for two years
would hesitate to do so from apprehension that the Adult
Authority might hold the offender much longer.
Accordingly, such offenders were often given local jail
sentences or probation, even though the sentence was less
severe than the judge would have preferred. Under DSL,
that problem no longer existed. A 2-year sentence, given
good-time, meant 16 months, and one need not worry about
the Adult Authority.

In each evaluation in which participants were
interviewed, both prosecutors and defense lawyers were
quoted as expressing concern that defendants with minor

records or those accused of minor offenses, who in the
past received modest, generally nonincarcerative sentences, might become enmeshed in the rigidity of the new
scheme.

Virtually every study provides some evidence that
those marginal offenders not protected by means of early
filtering decisions were subject to harsher sentences.
In Alaska there were selected increases in sentence
length for drug cases and low-seriousness theft cases.
In Detroit offenders charged with "other assaults" experienced increases in both the probability of prison
after conviction and the length of prison terms. In
California, continuing an existing trend, the portion of
persons convicted of burglary found among prison commitments increased steadily relative to robbery.

Methodological Concerns

A number of key methodological issues have emerged as
fundamental to adequate impact evaluations of criminal
justice reforms generally and of sentencing reforms particularly. To some extent these issues derive from
unique features of criminal case processing; when formulated more generally, however, they are likely to characterize any complex flow system in which inputs at one
point are transformed into outputs at some other point in
the system. Most generally, these concerns relate to the
length and scope of observation and to the level of control for differences between individual cases.

The Necessity for Extended Observation Periods

Many of the impact evaluations reviewed here involved
simple two-point designs with single observations before
and after the reform. These were inadequate for a number
of reasons.

As demonstrated by several studies (e.g., Casper et
al., 1981; Lipson and Peterson, 1980; Joint Committee,
1977) there is considerable value to having multiple observations of outcomes before implementation of the change
under study. These allow one to distinguish discrete
changes or impacts associated with a reform from the continuation of existing trends. The presence of such trend
evidence is crucial to the conclusion that introduction
of determinate sentencing in California resulted in no

substantial changes in sentencing outcomes there. Prison use had been increasing and time served decreasing for several years before DSL.

Ideally the postreform observation period should also extend for multiple observations beyond the reform to permit sufficient time for the full impact of the reform to be realized. Case processing is obviously far from instantaneous in criminal justice systems. It is not uncommon to find mean times to final disposition as long as six months or more. Thus a sentencing reform that is to apply to all cases involving offenses committed after January 1 may not be applied to any substantial number of cases until well into the second year after the reform is implemented. And a reform that itself contributes to increased processing times through the system will only further delay full realization of impact. To the extent that cases disposed early under the reform differ in important ways from cases that take much longer to resolve, evaluations of early impact are likely to be biased, sometimes evidencing opposite effects from later impacts.

The possibility of delayed impact was strongly suggested in the case of the New York drug law: Median disposition times doubled in New York City (1973: 172 days; January to June 1976: 351 days) as defendants increasingly requested trials and postponements (Joint Committee, 1977:103-5). Conviction rates and imprisonment rates for drug felonies fell considerably immediately after the law went into effect and then increased steadily to slightly exceed prelaw rates in the first half of 1976 (Joint Committee, 1977:Tables 24, 27, 29). Based only on early performance, the reform appears to have achieved the exact opposite of its intended effect--sanctions decreased for felony drug defendants. However, following the process for a longer postlaw period, sanction rates increased up to then slightly exceeded prelaw rates. Because of processing delays it may well be that we would not have observed the full impact of the drug law until 1976 or later.

To avoid possible spurious findings of impact arising from delays, evaluations should routinely include measures of case-processing times and changes in work load and backlog. These variables are important not only as direct indicators of impact but also for identifying necessary follow-up periods.

The potentially extended time periods necessary for adequate evaluations of impact have direct implications both for the structure of research funding and program

design and for strategies to implement reforms. If
impact evaluations are not to be limited to retrospective
analysis of easily accessible summary statistics or
automated record systems, field work will be needed
throughout the extended follow-up period both to
continually search current records and to measure changes
in participant reactions over time. This requires
long-term commitments to continued funding of research
efforts over extended periods of time. One- or two-year
funding arrangements with limited options for renewal or
continuation do not encourage this type of research.
With regard to promulgating innovative and promising
reforms, one must weigh the trade-offs between timeliness
in obtaining feedback on the impact of new innovations
against the benefits, largely in terms of credibility and
rigor, of the results derived from a more protracted
evaluation that distinguishes between short-term and
long-term effects.

The Necessity for Outcome Measures
at All Levels of Case Processing

All too frequently evaluations are limited to those
aspects of the process most directly affected by a reform
and fail to address processing at earlier or later
stages. For example, if prison terms are changed, only
impacts on the lengths of terms of sentenced defendants
and perhaps sentences for convicted offenders might be
considered (Kramer et al., 1978). The evaluations of a
ban on plea bargaining (Beha, 1977) and of a mandatory
sentencing law (Church, 1976) failed to include data on
sanctions imposed on convicted offenders. All the
evaluations of the California Determinate Sentencing Law
considered in this review are limited to cases disposed
in superior court; earlier charging and lower court
decisions that screen cases out of superior court were
not examined.

This narrowness of focus fails to acknowledge the complexity of criminal case processing and the many opportunities for the exercise of discretion that it affords.
While in a literal sense criminal sentences are limited
to the sanctions imposed by the court on convicted
offenders, the character of these sentence outcomes is
substantially influenced by factors that determine which
cases are actually available for sentencing.

For example, by effectively weeding out those cases least likely to end in a prison sentence if convicted--through some combination of screening of initial charging, prosecutor nolles, case dismissals, or shifting final disposition from upper to lower courts--the cases that reach the upper courts will be increasingly restricted to the more likely prison cases. In this event the resulting increased use of prison among upper court convictions is more apparent than real; it derives from a change in the mix of cases at the upper court and not from a real change in sentencing policy to extend prison use to cases previously sentenced to nonprison outcomes.

The significance of the filtering process was highlighted in the evaluations of the New York drug law (Joint Committee, 1977) and the mandatory sentencing law for firearms violations in Detroit (Heumann and Loftin, 1979). In both jurisdictions prison use among convictions increased dramatically after the reform, rising from 34 percent in 1972 to 55 percent in the first half of 1976 for drug felonies in New York (Table 7-14) and from 57 percent to 83 percent following reform for "other assaults" in Detroit (Table 7-10). At the same time, however, there was virtually no change in prison use for cases entering the system; prison use for those arrested for drug felonies in New York remained stable at approximately 11 percent and went from 37 percent to 43 percent for persons charged with "other assaults" in Detroit.

The considerable opportunities for filtering cases before they reach the sentencing stage cannot be ignored. The studies reviewed here are replete with references to potential confounding effects of unobserved changes in the filtering process. The need to address the impact of filtering changes adequately is one of the most important lessons to be learned from previous impact evaluations.

The Necessity for Adequate Controls
for Changes in Case Attributes

General changes in the character of cases--particularly changes in the seriousness of cases--are related to but certainly not limited to the filtering process. Case attributes relevant to sentencing outcomes might also be affected by general changes in offending patterns involving shifts to more or less serious offending. Demographic changes increasing the representation of "older" offenders (ages 25 to 35) might also alter the extent and nature of prior criminal records for offenders. Failure to control for any resulting changes in case attributes before and after a reform can seriously jeopardize the validity of conclusions about the impact of that reform on case outcomes at various stages, particularly sentencing outcomes.[38] This issue of adequate controls is especially troubling in the impact studies reviewed here, in which there was little control beyond the crime type category.

The Necessity for Qualitative Analysis
of System Functioning

Many evaluations are limited entirely to statistical analysis of abstracted case processing data, often available from centralized automated data systems. Such analyses are particularly useful for providing aggregate average characterizations of case processing for large numbers of cases. However, quantitative data alone, while often necessary, are seldom sufficient if we are to understand the impacts of change on what goes on in courts. To gain a fuller appreciation of the complexity of the process, with its interleaved discretions, the analysis should also include more qualitative approaches, including participant observation and systematic interviewing. These qualitative approaches can often illuminate what seem like anomalous results in the statistical analysis. No one approach by itself will suffice. Together, the diverse methods may permit a diversity of perspectives and knowledge from which credible findings can emerge.

NOTES

1. The following illustrates an example in which guilty plea rates for defendants decline from 80 percent to 68 percent, but guilty pleas among "cases" remain stable at a 40 percent rate:

	Single Charges	Multiple Charges	Total	Number Guilty Pleas	Percent Guilty Pleas

Year 1: 80 percent of All Defendants Plead Guilty to a Single Charge

Defendants	60	40	100	80	80
		(@ 3.5 ea.)			
Charges	60	140	200	80	40

Year 2: To encourage continued guilty pleas, the prosecutor shifts some multiple charges to a single charge at initial charging stage.

Defendants	80	20	100	68	68
		(@ 4.5 ea.)			
Charges	80	90	170	68	40

2. The sample sizes in Juneau were very small, even when the six-month periods were aggregated to form whole-year samples. This increases the likelihood that large variations are due to chance.

3. The ambiguity arose from the attorney general's effort to distinguish charge reductions to induce guilty pleas, which he wanted stopped, from unilateral charge dismissals and reductions resulting from professional judgments about the strength of evidence, problems of proof, and the like.

4. The marginal offender hypothesis is supported by each of the plea bargaining and mandatory sentence evaluations. Jonathan Casper develops the converse hypothesis to support a prediction that more minor offenders would be imprisoned under California's Determinate Sentencing Law. Under the Indeterminate Sentencing Law, a judge who wanted to impose, say, a two-year sentence but no more could not do so. A significant chance existed that the defendant would be held for a longer period. Judges were unwilling to expose such defendants to that risk and instead sentenced them to local sanctions. Under the new law, prison sentences

were determinate and a judge who wanted to impose a short prison sentence could do so (Casper et al., 1981:12).

5.   If one conservatively estimates that the "true" number of felony arrests remained stable at 1,776, the adjusted screening rate would be 4 percent plus 2.9 percent of 1,707, which represents 2.4 percent of 1,776, a total of 6.4 percent.

6.   This impact of excluded cases was potentially greatest in Juneau. When only those cases finally disposed of were considered, trial cases in Juneau appeared to decrease from 6.3 percent to 2.2 percent of all cases disposed after screening. Juneau, however, also experienced a 26 percent decrease (from 127 to 94) in the number of cases disposed after screening. To the extent that this decrease is associated with cases that were excluded from the sample because they were not disposed by the end of 1977, the excluded cases could substantially increase the postban trial rates in Juneau.

7.   Hampton County is a pseudonym used by the researcher to conceal the identity of the research site.

8.   The charges examined because of their frequent association with gun use include firstand second-degree murder, armed robbery, felonious assault, and other major assaults.

9.   The following discussion of data in Table 7-10 is based on the assumption that the cases in the before and after samples are comparable; in fact, we have reason to doubt that (see discussion above).

10.   Because the dependent variable is truncated at zero, maximum likelihood TOBIT estimators were used. In addition to dummy variables reflecting gun use and the observation period (before and after implementation of the gun law), the model includes an interaction variable of gun use and period.
    This interaction variable is taken to indicate the changes in sentences unique to the gun law. As the authors note, to the extent that factors other than the gun law affected the postlaw gun cases selectively, these other effects would be confounded in the above estimates. The authors note in particular a "crash program" to decrease court backlog beginning about the same time as the

implementation of the gun law. The authors' conclusion to the contrary notwithstanding, such a program might very well selectively affect sanctions in gun cases if other cases were more likely to be dismissed in clearing the backlog.

11. This could be verified by comparing the processing times of trial cases with those of other disposition types. To ensure greater comparability between the two samples, the preperiod sample could be restricted only to those cases initiated and disposed in the six-month period July 1, 1976, to December 31, 1976.

12. These expectations are discussed at length in Messinger and Johnson (1978), Cassou and Taugher (1978), Nagin (1979), Brewer et al. (1980), Lipson and Peterson (1980), and Casper et al. (1981).

13. The same pattern is reported for 1977-1978 by Lipson and Peterson (1980) using Judicial Council data on sentences imposed in court between July 1, 1977, and September 30, 1978; 60 percent of all sentenced cases received the middle term (Lipson and Peterson, 1980:Table 10). The court sentencing data, however, show slightly higher use of the upper base term than was indicated by the corrections statistics, perhaps reflecting a greater likelihood that defendants receiving the aggravated upper base term will appeal conviction and thus delay their reception in prison.

14. The crime types directly affected by SB709 were first-degree burglary, robbery, voluntary manslaughter, rape, crimes against children, and oral copulation. Both the middle and upper terms were increased for all these offenses except robbery, for which only the upper term was increased.

15. The 1977-1978 data are available in Brewer et al. (1980:Tables 7 and 8); comparable data for 1979 are found in Board of Prison Terms (1981:Table III).

16. Because of the way the model is specified with no interaction between jurisdiction and law period, we cannot sort out whether the jurisdiction differences vary for the different periods of law.

17. Lipson and Peterson (1980:21-22) report that for the state as a whole there was definite evidence of less

serious felonies shifting to municipal court between 1971 and 1976. During this period, while the number of defendants sentenced to prison or to both probation and jail remained relatively constant, these cases constituted an increasing proportion of superior court sentences as fewer felony arrests reached superior court. The above conclusion rests on the assumption that the less serious felony cases shifting to municipal court were also more likely to plead guilty early.

18. Utz (1978) describes this cooperative process of "settling the facts" as a principal means for achieving "substantive justice."

19. The influence of this legislative change on case mix in superior court is noted in Lipson and Peterson (1980:21) to account for increases in use of prison among superior court convictions through the early 1970s.

20. Data on lower court prosecutions were not available after 1973.

21. An ordinal variable was used to represent the dependent sentence type variable where "prison" = 4, "California Youth Authority" = 3, "jail" = 2 and "no jail" = 1. The estimated model is

$$S = aJ + cT + bX + \varepsilon$$

where S is sentence type, J is jurisdiction (Sacramento = 1, Alameda = 0) and T is the time period (post-DSL = 1, pre-DSL = 0). X includes a number of case attribute variables, reflecting whether the offense was a residential burglary or not, weapon use, physical harm to victim, presence of a vulnerable victim, sophistication in committing the offense, prior record of offender, weight of conviction charges, and race and sex of offender. Only race and weight of conviction charges were not statistically significant; all other variables, except sex (female = 1) were found to have a positive contribution toward a prison outcome.

In this model "a" represents the pre-DSL difference between jurisdictions, and a + c is the post-DSL difference between jurisdictions with c being the ISL to DSL change in sentence outcomes, regardless of jurisdiction. In the estimate of the model both a and c are positive and significant.

As formulated the model does not permit separately
identifying different effects of DSL in the two
jurisdictions; instead, both jurisdictions are assumed to
experience the _same_ change in sentence type outcomes
after DSL, namely, c. Inclusion of a simple interaction
variable combining jurisdiction with time period (J x T =
1 for post-DSL period in Sacramento, and 0 otherwise)
would have permitted isolating separate DSL effects in
each jurisdiction. For d the coefficient of J x T, the
ISL to DSL change is c in Alameda and d + c in Sacramento.
While a number of different models containing various
interaction terms were estimated, none of them included
an interaction of jurisdiction with time period.

22. In the eight years from 1962 to 1970, the FBI's
reported index crime rate rose 97.3 percent: from
2,019.8 to 3,984.5 per 100,000 population. From 1970 to
1978 this rate rose only 28.2 percent: from 3,984.5 to
5,109.3 per 100,000 population (U.S. Bureau of Criminal
Statistics, 1981).

23. The issue of changes in time served is discussed in
detail in the next section.

24. Since most of the studies were undertaken in the
first few years after implementation of DSL, the number
of individuals sentenced and subsequently released under
DSL was quite small. Information from the Department of
Corrections indicates that in the early years of DSL,
with the admittedly limited experience of implementation
of the early-release, good-time provisions, most
prisoners were released with maximum good time off their
sentences (Lipson and Peterson, 1980:25; Brewer et al.,
1980:14-15; Utz, 1981:150).

25. The results from Ku (1980) were consistent for all
offenses and for burglary; robbery, by contrast,
increased slightly from ISL to DSL. Ku's estimates of
the medians were consistently lower than comparable
medians reported in Brewer et al. (1980) and Casper et
al. (1981). The difference between these estimates lies
in Ku's use of the population remaining in prison on
December 31, 1975, while the other estimates were based
on time served by persons released during 1975.
     For Ku, the proportion of inmates with time served of
at least one to two years was derived from the admissions
during 1974 who are still in prison on December 31,

1975. When releases during 1975 were used (Brewer et
al., 1980, and Casper et al., 1981), time served of at
least one to two years derives from admissions on or
before January 1973 to January 1974 for January 1975
releases, and so on, to admissions on or before December
1973 to December 1974 for December 1975 releases.

Thus, there is greater representation of earlier
admission cohorts in the estimates based on releases. To
the extent that time served has been decreasing for more
recent cohorts as suggested in Figure 7-9, the estimates
of time served based on more recent cohorts from data on
remaining populations will be lower.

26. In comparing ISL to DSL, Lipson and Peterson
(1980:Table V) concluded that there were substantial
reductions in time served under DSL for burglary, but
only slight reductions for the persons offenses of
robbery and assault. This imputed difference between
crime types was then the basis for the authors to
conclude that the overall decrease in prison terms was
largely the result of a greater representation of minor
convictions previously sentenced to jail but now
appearing among prison commitments with shorter terms on
average.

This seems an excessively strong conclusion to draw
from these data. Allowing for maximum credit for good
time, as they do for burglary, the combined 1977 and 1978
reductions for robbery (from 35 to 29 months) and assault
(from 31 to 26 months) are comparable to those for
burglary (from 21 to 13 months).

27. The control variables include whether the offense
was a residential burglary or not, weapon use, physical
harm to victim, presence of a vulnerable victim,
sophistication in committing the offense, several
indicators of prior record of the offender, weight of the
conviction charges, and race and sex of the offender.

28. Only three control variables were significant:
physical harm to victim, an interaction variable of
weight of conviction counts and time period, and number
of conviction counts. Neither race nor sex was
significant.

29. These results are consistent with the independent
assessment of differences in case seriousness in the two
counties (Utz, 1981:22-27).

30. If T = a + b Jurisdiction + c (Jurisdiction x Time) + dX + ε then the total effect of jurisdiction is given by (b + c Time) x Jurisdiction. When Time = 0 (ISL) the jurisdictional difference is only b; for Time = 1 (DSL) this difference is b + c.

31. For example, as specified, the model includes an interaction between time period and the weight of the conviction charges. To the extent that conviction charges and jurisdiction were negatively correlated, with the Sacramento sample, tending to have offenses of lower seriousness, the differential effect of DSL found for different levels of seriousness might be reflecting a difference in DSL effects in the two counties, with prison terms decreasing more under DSL in Sacramento than they do in Alameda.

32. The 80 percent mid-range, for example, is the range of prison terms that includes 40 percent of cases below the median and 40 percent above the median.

33. The seven crime types include second-degree murder, robbery, assault with a deadly weapon, first-degree burglary, receiving stolen property, forgery and checks, and rape. The standard deviation decreased for all but assault with a deadly weapon and rape.

34. The Denver data file included all cases for which charges were filed in district court between May 1, 1975, and October 31, 1978, and sentences were imposed by April 30, 1979. These included 1,208 cases sentenced before guideline implementation and 2,397 cases sentenced after guideline implementation. However, many of these cases could not be used because of missing data, and there is little basis for assessing the representativeness of those cases that were used.

35. There is no indication of the extent of missing data in Philadelphia. The cases actually used in the impact analysis number 920 before and 429 after guideline implementation.

36. The preguideline data include randomly selected presentence reports prepared in calendar year 1975 and all presentence reports during January, February, and March 1977. Of a total of 1,704 preguideline cases, 258 were deleted because of missing data. The postguideline

data include 702 cases in which guidelines were used from July 1977 through January 1978; 68 cases were excluded because of missing data. Guidelines were not used in all cases sentenced after July 1977, and there is no information available on the basis for selecting cases for guideline use.

37. Maine State Prison is the long-term prison; prisoners sent to the Maine Correctional Center are under sentences of three years or less.

38. This issue is discussed at length in the context of discrimination in sentencing in the paper by Klepper et al. (in this volume).

REFERENCES

Anspach, Donald F.
   1981 Crossroads of Justice: Problems With Determinate
        Sentencing in Maine. University of Southern
        Maine, Portland, Maine (April 1, 1981).
Arthur D. Little, Inc., and Goldfarb, Singer, and Austern
(ADL)
   1981 An Evaluation of Parole Guidelines in Four
        Jurisdictions. Unpublished document prepared for
        the National Institute of Corrections by Arthur
        D. Little, Inc., Washington, D.C.
   1981a Consistency: An Analysis of the Parole Decision
        Guidelines of the Oregon Board of Parole. In ADL
        (1981).
   1981b Consistency: An Analysis of the Parole Decision
        Guidelines of the U.S. Parole Commission. In ADL
        (1981).
   1981c Consistency: An Analysis of the Parole Decision
        Guidelines of the Washington State Board of
        Prison Terms and Parole. In ADL (1981).
   1981d The Parole Guidelines of the Minnesota Corrections
        Board. In ADL (1981).
   1981e The Parole Guidelines of the U.S. Parole Commis-
        sion: An Analysis of Disparity. In ADL (1981).
   1981f Washington State Board of Prison Terms and
        Paroles: An Analysis of Release Decision-Making
        Under Guidelines. In ADL (1981).
Beha, James A.
   1977 "And nobody can get you out"--the impact of a

mandatory prison sentence for the illegal carrying of a firearm on the use of firearms and on
the administration of criminal justice in Boston.
Boston University Law Review 57:96-146(Part I),
289-333(Part II).

Blumstein, A., J. Cohen, and D. Nagin
1978 Deterrence and Incapacitation: Estimating the
Effects of Criminal Sanctions on Crime Rates.
Panel on Research on Deterrent and Incapacitative
Effects, Committee on Research on Law Enforcement
and Criminal Justice. Washington, D.C.:
National Academy of Sciences.

Blumstein, A., J. Cohen, and H. Miller
1980 Demographically disaggregated projections of
prison populations. Journal of Criminal Justice
8:1-26.

Board of Prison Terms
1981 Sentencing Practices: Determinate Sentencing
Law. California Board of Prison Terms, February
11, 1981.

Brewer, D., G.E. Beckett, and N. Holt
1980 Determinate Sentencing in California: The First
Year's Experience. California Department of
Correction, Chino.

California Department of Justice
1980 Criminal Justice Profile--1979. Bureau of Criminal Statistics and Special Services, California
Department of Justice.
1981 Criminal Justice Profile--1980. Bureau of Criminal Statistics and Special Services, California
Department of Justice.

Casper, J.D., D. Brereton, and D. Neal
1981 The Implementation of the California Determinate
Sentencing Law. Draft final report to National
Institute of Justice.

Cassou, A.K., and B. Taugher
1978 Determinate sentencing in California: the new
numbers game. The Pacific Law Journal 9(1):2-106.

Church, Thomas, Jr.
1976 "Plea" bargains, concessions, and the courts:
analysis of a quasi-experiment. Law & Society
Review 10:377-401.

Cohen, J., and J. Helland
1981 Methodology for Evaluating the Impact of Sentencing Guidelines. Unpublished paper, School of
Urban and Public Affairs, Carnegie-Mellon
University.

Frankel, M.E.
   1972 Criminal Sentences: Law Without Order. New
         York: Hill and Wang.
General Accounting Office
   1982 Federal Parole Practices: Better Management and
         Legislative Changes are Needed. Washington,
         D.C.: U.S. Government Printing Office.
Gottfredson, D.M., L.T. Wilkins, and P.B. Hoffman
   1978 Guidelines for Parole and Sentencing. Lexington,
         Mass.: Lexington Books.
Hay, Douglas, P. Linebaugh, J. Rule, E.P. Thompson, and
C. Winslow
   1975 Albion's Fatal Tree. New York: Pantheon.
Heumann, Milton, and Colin Loftin
   1979 Mandatory sentencing and the abolition of plea
         bargaining: the Michigan Felony Fire Arm
         Statute. Law & Society Review 13:393-430.
Hubay, C.
   1979 Study of robbery cases in Alameda County funded
         as part of Research Agreements Program of the
         National Institute of Justice to the Rand Cor-
         poration, Santa Monica, California.
Iowa Law Review
   1975 The elimination of plea bargaining in Black Hawk
         County: a case study. Iowa Law Review 61:1053.
Joint Committee on New York Drug Law Evaluation
   1977 The Nation's Toughest Drug Law: Evaluating the
         New York Experience. Washington, D.C.: U.S.
         Government Printing Office.
Knapp, K.
   1982 Impact of the Minnesota Sentencing Guidelines on
         Sentencing Practices. Hamline Law Review
         5(June):237-256.
Kramer, J.H., F.A. Hussey, S.P. Lagoy, D. Katkin, and
C.V. McLaughlin
   1978 Assessing the Impact of Determinate Sentencing
         and Parole Abolition in Maine. Draft report to
         National Institute of Justice.
Ku, R.
   1980 American Prisons and Jails: Vol. IV Supplement
         Report--Case Studies of New Legislation Governing
         Sentencing and Release. National Institute of
         Justice. Washington, D.C.: U.S. Department of
         Justice.
Lipson, A.J., and M.A. Peterson
   1980 California Justice Under Determinate Sentencing:
         A Review and Agenda for Research. Report

#R-2497-CRB to the California Board of Prison
Terms. Santa Monica: Rand Corporation.

Loftin, C., and D. McDowall
1981 "One with a gun gets you two": mandatory sentencing and firearms violence in Detroit." The
Annals of the Academy of Political and Social
Science 455(May 1981):150-167.

Messinger, S., and P. Johnson
1978 California's determinate sentencing statute:
history and issues. In National Institute of Law
Enforcement and Criminal Justice, Determinate
Sentencing: Reform or Regression. Proceedings
of the Special Conference on Determinate Sentencing, June 2-3, 1977. Washington, D.C.: U.S.
Department of Justice.

Messinger, S.L., A. von Hirsch, and R. Sparks
1981 Strategies for Determinate Sentencing. Draft
final report submitted to National Institute of
Justice.

Michael, Jerome, and Herbert Wechsler
1940 Criminal Law and Its Administration. Boston,
Mass.: Little, Brown and Co.

Minnesota Sentencing Guidelines Commission
1982 Preliminary Report on the Development and Impact
of the Minnesota Sentencing Guidelines. Report
prepared by Minnesota Sentencing Guidelines
Commission, Suite 284 Metro Square Building, 7th
and Robert Streets, St. Paul, Minn. 55101.

Mueller, Julia M., and Sparks, Richard F.
1982 Strategy for determinate sentencing--some statewide statistical results (Oregon). In S.L.
Messinger et al., Report on Strategies for Determinate Sentencing. Unpublished document prepared
for the National Institute of Justice, U.S.
Department of Justice.

Nagin, D.
1979 The impact of determinate sentencing legislation
on prison population and sentence length: a
California case study. Public Policy 27(1):69-98.

Rich, W.D., L.P. Sutton, T.R. Clear, and M.J. Saks
1981 Sentencing Guidelines: Their Operation and
Impact on the Courts. Williamsburg, Va.:
National Center for State Courts.

Rubinstein, Michael L., Steven H. Clarke, and Teresa J.
White
1980 Alaska Bans Plea Bargaining. National Institute
of Justice. Washington, D.C.: U.S. Department
of Justice.

Sechrest, L., S.O. White, and E.D. Brown
  1979 The Rehabilitation of Criminal Offenders: Prob-
        lems and Prospects. Panel on Research on Reha-
        bilitative Techniques, Committee on Research on
        Law Enforcement and the Administration of Jus-
        tice. Washington, D.C.: National Academy of
        Sciences.
Sparks, Richard F.
  1981 Sentencing before and after DSL: Some statis-
        tical findings. In S.L. Messinger et al., Report
        on Strategies for Determinate Sentencing. Unpub-
        lished document prepared for the National Insti-
        tute of Justice, U.S. Department of Justice,
        Washington, D.C.
Sparks, Richard F., Bridget A. Stecher, Jay Albanese, and
Peggy L. Shelly
  1982 Stumbling Toward Justice: Some Overlooked
        Research and Policy Questions About Statewide
        Sentencing Guidelines. Final report of the
        Evaluation of Statewide Sentencing Guidelines
        Project, National Institute of Justice, U.S.
        Department of Justice.
U.S. Bureau of the Census
  1976 Historical Statistics of the U.S. From Colonial
        Times to 1970. Washington, D.C.: U.S.
        Department of Commerce.
  1979 Statistical Abstracts of the U.S.--1979.
        Washington, D.C.: U.S. Department of Commerce.
  1980 Prisoners in State and Federal Institutions--
        1978. Washington, D.C.: U.S. Department of
        Commerce.
U.S. Bureau of Criminal Statistics
  1981 Sourcebook of Criminal Justice Statistics--1980.
        Washington, D.C.: U.S. Department of Justice.
Utz, P.
  1978 Settling the Facts: Discretion and Negotiation
        in Criminal Court. Lexington, Mass.: Heath.
  1981 Determinate sentencing in two California courts.
        In S.L. Messinger et al., Report on Strategies
        for Determinate Sentencing. Unpublished document
        prepared for the National Institute of Justice,
        U.S. Department of Justice, Washington, D.C.
von Hirsch, A.
  1976 Doing Justice: The Choice of Punishments. New
        York: Hill and Wang.

von Hirsch, Andrew, and Kathleen J. Hanrahan
   1979 The Question of Parole. Cambridge, Mass.:
       Ballinger.
Wilkins, L.T., J.M. Kress, D.M. Gottfredson, J.C. Calpin,
and A.M. Gelman
   1976 Sentencing Guidelines: Structuring Judicial Dis-
       cretion. Final Report of the Feasibility Study.
       Albany, N.Y.: Criminal Justice Research Center.
Zarr, Melvyn
   1976 Sentencing. Maine Law Review 28(Special
       Issue):117-148.

8

The Impact of Changes in Sentencing Policy on Prison Populations

Alfred Blumstein

THE NEED FOR ESTIMATES

Widespread activity oriented toward structuring sentencing policy[1] has generated a need for the development of improved methodology for estimating the impact of changes in sentencing policies on prison populations.

The need for such estimates is particularly intense today because prisons in the United States are now effectively filled and are likely to get more crowded even in the absence of a policy change. Since changes in sentencing policy tend much more often to be directed at increasing rather than decreasing prison populations, failure to account for the impact of a policy change will result in two kinds of undesirable consequences: (1) Judges will adhere to the policy change, and prisons will become severely overcrowded, with the attendant dehumanization and associated risks of violence, misconduct, riot, and recidivism; and (2) Judges will adhere to existing capacity limits, and will do so by accommodating in ways **they** choose, which may well violate the mandated policies adopted.

If a proposed policy change does involve a need for significant new prison capacity, then it is important that the body adopting the policy, and certainly the legislature, weigh the desirability of the policy change against the cost of that increment of capacity. If the policy change is worth that cost, then the legislature should appropriate the funds for the extra capital cost

and consider the anticipated operating cost of the extra
capacity. If not, then adoption of an empty policy is
likely to serve only to further discredit the criminal
justice system. Thus, finding reliable means for estimating the prison impact—and the corresponding budget
impact—of a sentencing policy is a necessary part of
ensuring responsible consideration of such policies. The
resulting "prison impact statement" and its associated
"budget impact statement" can then be as helpful in this
case as it is with many other kinds of legislation.

In determining sentencing policies, only rarely is any
consideration given to the downstream implications of
such policies by the judiciary or by legislative judiciary committees, perhaps because such considerations of
impact seldom enter their concerns. That limited perspective may have been satisfactory when resources were
available to accommodate any reasonable policy adopted,
when the increment of resources are costless, or when
they can be expanded rapidly and easily to accommodate
the demand imposed by the court. It is certainly not the
situation that prevails in the criminal justice system of
today, and the situation is likely to become even more
severe throughout the decade of the 1980s.

On one hand, such impact estimates are necessary
because those capacity limits, which are being severely
pressed, should enter into any consideration of sentencing policy. A policy that fails to take such considerations into account will simply be violated, but on the
basis of ad hoc considerations of individual judges or
prosecutors in individual cases, rather than on the basis
of the considerations of those responsible for establishing policy. This accommodation could take the form of
shifts in plea bargaining, greater use of mitigating
circumstances, and the development of various "front
door" diversion strategies and "back door" early-release
strategies to accommodate the resource or capacity constraint in prison space.

Even if the body establishing the sentencing policy
chooses to ignore such capacity considerations in reaching their policy choices—and there are many who insist
not only that such considerations can be ignored but also
that they should be ignored—it is necessary to be able
to estimate the impact of their choices on prison
resource requirements. Such estimates enable
legislatures charged with reviewing or adopting such
policies to assess the reasonableness of any sentencing
policy. Then, when a policy is adopted and implemented,

impact estimates are necessary to begin to plan for the resources to accommodate the new policy.

In many cases a body charged with establishing sentencing policy is specifically mandated to establish that policy without generating any increase in prison populations or capacity. The Minnesota legislature, for example, in establishing the Minnesota Sentencing Guidelines Commission, suggested that they "take into substantial consideration . . . correctional resources . . ." and the commission took that suggestion as a constraint, so that any sentencing schedule it adopted would have a zero net aggregate prison impact. The Pennsylvania Commission on Sentencing did not adopt current populations as a constraint on its eventual schedule but did try to keep informed of the estimated effect of the evolving sentencing schedule on Pennsylvania's prison population.

Any impact estimate is associated with a future time after the sentencing policy is adopted and implemented. The impact estimate must therefore use as a baseline a projection of future prison populations under current policies prior to the policy change. The policy change, or alternative changes being considered, can then be viewed as a perturbation to that projected baseline level. The difference between the two projections is the estimated impact associated with the policy change.

In developing the estimate of the impact projection, the time dimension must be taken into account. That is, different policies involve different build-up rates of prison populations, and those differences can be very important. For example, a policy that involves a large increase in numbers of prison commitments will display a more rapid growth in prison populations compared with a policy that involves a similar fractional increase in time served. Even though both policies will require the same capacity eventually, in the latter case, the build-up will take place more slowly over time as release dates are extended.

Any impact estimate must take account of compliance with the planned policy. This requires some behavioral assumptions about how judges, prosecutors, and defense counsel respond to the imposition of the changed policy. The simplest--and most simplistic--assumption is that they will fully comply with the policy. Another simple assumption is that they will ignore the policy and continue their prior practices. Even though this assumption is not so simplistic, the associated impact estimate is zero, and the estimate of future prison populations is merely the baseline projection.

Most often, of course, the response is somewhere between the two extremes. There does tend to be some compliance with a policy change, but it often is less than total compliance. In considering a 5-year mandatory minimum sentencing law for rape, for example, it is entirely possible that introduction of the law will bring about no change in charging behavior by the prosecutor and that everyone charged under the law will be sent to prison with certainty for a sentence no less than the specified 5-year mandatory minimum sentence; this would represent total compliance. It is more likely, however, that under the new law a larger fraction of the rape arrests would appear as assault cases, or that judges faced with a rape indictment would be more likely to dismiss the charge or to find mitigating circumstances that would enable them to assign probation if the only available prison sentence is 5 years or more. These kinds of accommodation behaviors must somehow be reflected in any impact assessment that is made.

In discussing impact assessment, therefore, we begin first with a discussion of approaches to the projection of future prison populations, then consider means of incorporating policy changes into those projections.

PROJECTION OF FUTURE PRISON POPULATIONS AS A BASELINE FOR THE IMPACT ESTIMATE

In considering approaches to estimating future prison populations, it is useful to organize them roughly in order of increasing complexity of the projection model and the associated increase in the richness or subtlety of the assumptions involved in generating a projection.

Naive Projection--Current Situation as a Baseline

The simplest, most simplistic projection is the naive one that suggests that any subsequent year's prison population will be the same as that of the current year. This has the obvious benefit of requiring only one assumption (however gross), instead of many more complex and challenging, subtle and simple ones. (Clearly, the number of assumptions is not necessarily a good indicator of the parsimony of a model).

Such an assumption can be invoked even in the absence of any conviction that it represents a good approximation of reality. This form of projection is implied, for example, when current practice is used as a baseline on which to estimate the impact of a policy change. This clearly avoids the many concerns that arise in attempting to project the baseline to reflect continuation of current practice in the absence of a policy change. This is probably a very reasonable approach when there are no external changes affecting criminal justice operations. When there are such important influences in progress-- demographic shifts, for example--then it does become important to have an accurate baseline projection, especially when saturation of prison capacity becomes relevant. If current practice results in a prison population well below current prison capacity, and if the external changes in the absence of policy shifts would generate prison populations that exceed prison capacity, then it is important to have that baseline estimate to plan future resource requirements. The cost of a policy is appreciably greater if it requires creating new capacity than if it can be accommodated within existing capacity.

This approach of using current practice as the baseline level was used by the Pennsylvania Commission on Sentencing in estimating the impact of its sentencing schedule. The commission collected a sample of conviction cases in Pennsylvania in 1977 and assigned each case to the appropriate cell of the sentencing guideline grid.[2] Then, with N_i cases assigned to the ith cell in the sentencing grid and M_i of them given prison sentences, the sentences imposed in that sample of cases provide estimates of the principal sentencing parameters in each cell, Q_i, the probability of imprisonment, and S_i, the sentence served. The probability of imprisonment, Q_i, is estimated as $Q_i = M_i/N_i$, and the mean sentence, S_i, is estimated as

$$S_i = \sum_{j=1}^{M_i} S_{ij} ,$$

where S_{ij} is the sentence assigned to the jth case (j = 1, 2, . . . , M_i) that falls in the ith cell. The prison capacity associated with cell i in the baseline case is then

$$C_i = N_i Q_i S_i ,$$

and the total prison capacity required would be

$$C = \sum_{i=1}^{n} c_i = \sum_{i=1}^{n} N_i Q_i S_i \; ,$$

where the summation is taken over the n cells in the sentencing grid.

The impact of a recommended guideline structure can then be estimated as a change in this baseline. If a prison sentence of S_i' years is recommended for cell i (with $S_i' = 0$ for cells in which no imprisonment is recommended), then the prison capacity for cell i under the recommended schedule is

$$C_i' = N_i S_i' \; ,$$

and the total capacity required is

$$C' = \sum_{i=1}^{n} N_i S_i' \; .$$

If the sentence recommendation for cell i is a range, $S_{i0} - S_{i1}$ (e.g., 3-4 years), then one can generate a conservative estimate of capacity requirements by using the upper S_{i1} value in each cell, a risky estimate by using the lower S_{i0} value, or a median estimate by using the average,

$$(S_{i0} + S_{i1})/2 \; .$$

For a heterogeneous jurisdiction with diverse sentencing practices across its counties (as is certainly the case in Pennsylvania), a better estimate can be obtained by assuming that the lower values are applied in the metropolitan counties and the upper values in the rural counties. This additional refinement--as is the case with most refinements--requires additional information. The extra information required is the distribution of cases across counties, N_{ik}, the number of cases falling within cell i from the kth type of county.

Extrapolation of the Time Series of Prison Populations

One of the least helpful approaches to projecting future prison populations is linear extrapolation of recent trends. After a number of years of fairly steady increases (or decreases) in prison populations, it can be particularly tempting to simply draw a line through the points and extrapolate that line into the future.

This approach has a number of serious pitfalls. If the points were following a downward trend, even the most naive extrapolator would know enough not to draw that line far enough so that it took on negative values for prison population. Projecting an increasing trend does not yield such obviously absurd results, but it could be equally inaccurate. Simple linear extrapolation--even though widely used--fails to recognize the fact that most trends at some point saturate and reverse themselves, and are certainly more likely to do that than to continue indefinitely. While a linear extrapolation may be reasonable for a short-term projection of one or two years, going beyond that can be very risky.

The underlying model of the linear extrapolation is:

$$Y_t = a_0{*} + a_1{*}t , \tag{1}$$

where t represents time, Y_t represents the prison population at time t, and $a_0{*}$ and $a_1{*}$ are two parameters to be fit from recent data. Here, a_0 is the prison population in the year when t is set at 0, and a_1 is the average annual increase in prison population.

So simple a model, of course, invokes only one variable, time, and no other information about the other factors influencing imprisonment. Most important, from the viewpoint of using this projection as a policy tool for impact estimation, such a model contains no policy variables, reflecting sentencing practice (the Q_i and S_i of the previous section) whose impact on prison population can be directly measured.

If the time series of imprisonment has been moving in other than a linear way, one might become somewhat more elaborate in the extrapolation by adding additional terms involving higher powers of t, for example, by adding a term, $a_2{*}t^2$, to equation (1). Such an elaboration of fitting a higher-degree polynomial to the data can be very risky. Even though adding terms can give a closer fit to the data, that higher-degree polynomial is much more vulnerable to radical deviation outside the fitted data points. In contrast, one of the virtues of the linear equation is the severe limitation on how rapidly it can change.

A much more sophisticated form of extrapolation involves the use of ARIMA models, introduced by Box and Jenkins (1976; see also McCleary and Hay, 1980), as a

means of using data on a time series $(Y_1, Y_2, \ldots, Y_t)$
to forecast future values, $(Y_{t+1}, Y_{t+2}, \ldots, Y_{t+k})$.
The basic approach in developing such a forecast involves
first identifying the form of the underlying process that
generated the original series, then estimating the parameters of that process, and finally, by assuming that the
same underlying process continues into the future, generating estimates of the expected future values of the
series. As with all such forecasts, the farther the look
into the future, the more sources of error there are that
can lead to an erroneous forecast, and the more likely it
becomes that the underlying assumption of a continuation
of the prior underlying process will be violated by a
distortion of the process.

Such univariate time series have the limitation that
they do not include the relevant policy variables.
Multivariate ARIMA processes, which are used to establish
the link between two or more time series--for example,
prison population Y and the sentencing policy variables,
Q (the probability of imprisonment given conviction) and
S (the average sentence imposed)--can then be used to
test the effect of a change in one of those policy
variables.

Multivariate Regression

One can go beyond models that use only the single variable time as an exogenous determinant of future prison
populations by invoking a variety of other variables
known to be causally related to prison populations. This
equation takes the following form:

$$Y_t = a_0 + a_1 x_{1t} + a_2 x_{2t} = \ldots + a_n x_{nt} , \qquad (2)$$

where Y_t is the prison population in year t and the $\underline{x}$
vector,

$$\{x_{it} \mid i = 1, 2, \ldots, n\} ,$$

includes exogenous determinants of prison population in
year t. Factors that have been proposed for $\underline{x}$ include
unemployment rates (see Greenberg, 1977, for example)
consumer price index (see Fox, 1978,), or demographic
variables (e.g., population of men ages 20-30) and other
such variables. They could also include sentencing
parameters, Q_t (the probability of imprisonment in year
t) and S_t (average sentence imposed in year t).

Such a model could be estimated by collecting data on the specified x_t variables and on the associated Y_t over a period of years, using standard multivariate techniques to estimate the values of the coefficients $(a_0{}^*, a_1{}^*, a_2{}^*, \ldots, a_n{}^*)$.

Using such a model for projecting future prison populations obviously requires projections of the values of the $\underline{x}$ vector $(x_1, \ldots, x_n)$. For many variables that would be important candidates for inclusion in $\underline{x}$, it may be far more difficult to generate a projected estimate of that variable than of prison population itself. If that is the case for the unemployment rate, for example, then a model that depends strongly on a projection of the unemployment rate contributes little to the capability of projecting prison population (Y).

Some variables, such as demographic variables, are more easily projected. For example, the number of men in a particular high-imprisonment age group (for example, ages 20-29), is relatively easy to project for at least 20 years into the future. Aside from migration, all individuals who will be in that age group are already born, so the only uncertainty is that associated with death and migration. Death rates are fairly small for ages 1-20 and are also reasonably predictable. Migration can be a major distorting factor in a small region like a city or in a rapidly growing state, and it must certainly be taken into account in projecting the demographic variables.

Some variables can reasonably serve as leading indicators of Y (e.g., x_{t-k} is one of the components of the $\underline{x}_t$ vector in equation (2) for Y_t). When that is the case, then such a variable can be helpful for projecting as many as k years ahead.

An important limitation of the multivariate regression approach, especially for estimating the effect of changes in the sentencing policy variables, is the anticipated insensitivity of the regression equation to those variables. First, as with most complex phenomena, one can expect only limited success in accounting for the factors contributing to the variation in prison population through a linear regression equation.

Second, the regression of Y_t on the sentencing policy variables, Q and S, must involve, in addition to Q_t and S_t, $(Q,S)_{t-1}$, $(Q,S)_{t-2}$, etc., since the prison population in year t (Y_t) includes people sentenced one or more years earlier, and so was determined by sentencing policies more than several years prior to t. One might try to avoid this complexity by considering only commitments during t, but that strategy would fail to recognize the effects of sentence length, S, or changes in S.

Finally, in the context of the other exogenous political, demographic, and socioeconomic factors that influence prison populations, each of which is difficult to capture totally, it is likely to be very difficult to discern the separate effects of sentencing policy through a multiple regression model. Thus one cannot have strong confidence that the coefficients associated with the sentencing policy variables will be reliably estimated.

Projections Based on
Demographic-Specific Incarceration Rates

It is well known that different age, race, and sex groups differ markedly in many aspects of their involvement with the criminal justice system. This is particularly true in prison populations: in 1979 females made up only 4 percent of the total state prison population; the incarceration rate for males (i.e., prisoners per capita) was disproportionately large by a factor of 25 to 1 compared with females; black males made up 46 percent of the total U.S. male prison population, a disproportionate representation of 6.7 to 1 compared with white males; and the incarceration rate by age was also markedly different across the different age groups.[3]

Table 8-1 shows the incarceration rate by race and age for males in U.S. state prisons in 1979.[4] The peak incarceration rate for white males occurs at age 23 and is 2.2 times that at ages 35-39 and 8.8 times that at age 40 or older. The incarceration rate for black males reaches its peak at ages 25-29 and is 7.5 times the peak for white males (at age 23). The age falloff for blacks is comparably fast, the peak being 2.5 times the rate at ages 35-39 and 9.1 times the rate at age 40 or older.

These striking age, race, and sex differences suggest another approach to projecting prison populations. The current prison population can be partitioned into demographic subgroups and the incarceration rate calculated for each subgroup; if that rate is assumed constant (or projected), that incarceration rate can then be applied to any projection of the general population.

Thus, for example, one can generate a vector of incarceration rates,

$$g_i = Y_i/N_i \ ,$$

TABLE 8-1 Demographic-Specific Incarceration Rates (prisoners per 100,000 population) in 1979 for U.S. Males by Race and Age

Age	Total U.S.	White	Black
18-19	432	242	1,657
20	678	427	2,234
21	734	436	2,826
22	819	476	3,208
23	889	513	3,485
24	831	465	3,543
25-29	796	416	3,856
30-37	526	280	2,716
35-39	362	233	1,515
40+	92	58	424
Total	254	145	1,062

NOTE: Incarceration rates were calculated from Y_i/N_i, where Y_i is the number of prisoners in demographic group i at time of the 1979 survey of the Bureau of Justice Statistics and the Bureau of the Census, and N_i is the number of persons in the general population in demographic group i in 1979.

SOURCE: U.S. Bureau of the Census (1980).

where Y_i is the number of prisoners in the ith demographic group, N_i is the number in the general population within the ith demographic group, and g_i is the incarceration rate for the ith subgroup. Then, if one has a demographic projection of the population for time t', say, $N_i^*(t')$, then the estimate of the prison population in demographic group i at time t' is given by

$$Y_i^*(t') = g_i N_i^*(t')$$

and

$$Y^*(t') = \sum_i Y_i^*(t') \ .$$

The crucial assumption is that the incarceration rate, g_i, remains fairly constant within any demographic group over time. That is not necessarily the case, as is suggested by Table 8-2, which presents estimates of the incarceration rates based on two estimates of prisoner demographics[5] from two surveys, one in 1974 and one in 1979. It is striking to note the significant growth in incarceration rates between the two surveys. The aggregate growth is 40 percent over the entire population and is between 20 and 40 percent for most age groups. In addition, there does not appear to be important differences between the growth rate for blacks and that for the population generally.

If values of incarceration rates were available at several points in time, and if those values displayed a trend instead of a constant rate, then one might try to extrapolate the incarceration rates to generate estimates $g_i^*(t')$ for time t'. One would expect $g_i(t)$ to be more stable than $Y_i(t)$ [because $Y_i(t)$ also reflects demo-

TABLE 8-2   Age-Specific Incarceration Rates (prisoners per 100,000 population) Estimated for U.S. Males in 1974 and 1979

| | 1974 Rates | | 1979 Rates | | Percentage Increase 1974-1979 | |
Age	Total U.S.	Black	Total U.S.	Black	Total U.S.	Black
18-19	825	3,497	902	3,600	9	3
20	720	3,009	885	3,391	23	13
21	664	2,627	889	3,734	34	42
22	724	3,286	944	3,602	30	10
23	698	3,078	941	3,912	35	27
24	580	2,620	849	3,676	46	40
25-29	455	2,168	681	3,211	50	48
30-34	307	1,368	408	1,868	33	37
35-39	231	901	303	1,158	31	29
40+	58	263	70	324	21	23
Total	182	771	254	1,062	40	38

graphic shifts occurring in $N_i(t)$], and if that stability
is displayed, then extrapolating $g_i(t)$ may be reasonable.
If $g_i(t)$ follows a trend, however, all the cautions
necessary in extrapolating a trending variable (see the
section on time series above, for example) must be taken
into account.

This projection approach based on demographic-specific
incarceration rates is particularly attractive when the
incarceration rates, especially for the high-rate demographic groups (e.g, males in their 20s), are found to be
fairly constant over time. This approach is particularly
important when significant demographic changes are taking
place in the high-rate groups and when one has fairly
reliable projections of those demographic changes. This
approach allows anticipation of the effects of the
demographic changes.

An important shortcoming of this approach, as with the
others involving extrapolation of prison population
estimates, is the absence of any sentencing policy variables from the projection model. This could be remedied
by generating instead a demographic-specific conviction
rate by offense, then applying the corresponding sentencing variables, Q and S, to those conviction rates. (This
is the basic approach associated with flow models, and
these are developed in more detail in the next section.)
Unfortunately, while the data systems in most jurisdictions will support calculation of incarceration rates
because of good records on prison populations, the data
based on court records are sufficiently inadequate that
estimates of demographic- and offense-specific conviction
rates will be extremely difficult to generate.

Disaggregated Flow Models

The data problems become much more manageable in those
jurisdictions in which some form of offender-based transaction statistics (OBTS) system is operational. These
data permit a much more detailed and disaggregated examination of prison population projections. In the OBTS
system, an individual record is created at each arrest or
court filing, and that record is augmented by each subsequent transaction as the case moves through successive
processing stages in the criminal justice system. Collection of these individual records of terminated cases
at the end of a year permits highly disaggregated estimates of the processing parameters through the system.

With the support of such a data base, highly detailed
flow models of the criminal justice system become possible. One such illustration is the JUSSIM model[6] that
has seen fairly widespread implementation. In this
program the criminal justice system is represented as a
sequence of stages processing defendants or "units of
flow." These flow units impose work loads, consume
various types of resources, and incur costs at each
processing stage. The flow through the processing network can be represented by a matrix of "branching ratios"
or transition probabilities,

$$\{p_{ij}(v); \sum_j p_{ij}(v) = 1\} ,$$

representing the fraction of the cases at stage i that go
to stage j next: these transition probabilities are
disaggregated by crime type v (or any other relevant
attribute of the units of flow that influences the flow
process), since different crime types generally flow
differently through the system.

For reasons of simplicity, the JUSSIM model was designed as a steady-stage flow model that takes no account
of the passage of time but simply averages the flow
through any stage in any year. It is thus somewhat too
simplistic for dealing with the time accumulation of
prisoners in prison, although an extension to incorporate
that feature has been introduced by Lettre et al. (1978).
Another important limiting feature is the fact that the
parameters of the model (e.g., the branching ratios) are
treated deterministically in the model as fixed quantities rather than as functions of state variables
describing the condition of the criminal justice system.

The model is designed to operate interactively. The
user can then change any of the parameters, but must
decide which parameters to change and by how much. Thus,
if any of the parameters is trending over time, that
trend can simply be projected. In particular, there is
no behavioral model built into the program that, as the
prison population builds up beyond the prison's capacity,
reduces the flow rate from a sentencing stage to prison
(by reducing the probability of prison given conviction),
even though such accommodation is likely. The problem in
doing that lies in the difficulty of learning the nature
of the behavioral response and incorporating its consequences.

One approach to the use of such flow models involves
treating the flow structure of the criminal justice

system rather simply and directing attention to achieving greater disaggregation of the demographic structure of the offenders. Then, by focusing particular attention on the sentencing stage of the process, an effective and valuable sentencing-impact-assessment instrument can be developed.

This demographic disaggregation becomes particularly necessary when demographic changes are important factors influencing prison populations, as they certainly are in many regions of the United States and in other countries experiencing the postwar baby boom of 1947 to 1962. Thus, a flow model like JUSSIM, augmented by retaining demographic disaggregation of processing parameters, could be used to generate a projection of prison populations that was sensitive to demographic shifts.

Such a model was formulated and estimated by Blumstein et al. (1980). They found, using data for Pennsylvania for 1970 through 1975, that most of the criminal justice processing parameters (i.e., arrest rates, probability of indictment given arrest, and probability of being sentenced to prison given conviction) were fairly constant within demographic groups and offense types. Their model first estimated commitments to prison by

$$C_{tjo} = N_{tj} \times a_{tjo} \times c_{tjo} \times Q_{tjo} , \qquad (3)$$

where:

C_{tjo} = number of commitments to prison in year t for offense o of people in demographic group (age, race, sex combinations) j;

N_{tj} = number of people in the general population in year t in demographic group j;

a_{tjo} = demographic-specific arrest rate for offense o in year t;

c_{tjo} = probability of conviction given arrest; and

Q_{tjo} = probability of commitment to prison given conviction.

Then, P_t, the number of prisoners in any year t, depends on the number of prisoners in the previous year, P_{t-1}, the average time served per commitment, S, and the number of commitments, C. The basic equation for their model thus consists of two terms, one to account for last year's prisoners still serving time and one for the current year's commitments still left at the end of the year. Carrying the same subscripts forward, P_{tjo} is given by

$$P_{tjo} = P_{(t-1)jo} \times e^{-1/S_{tjo}} + C_{tjo} \times S_{tjo} \times (1 - e^{-1/S_{tjo}}) . \tag{4}$$

The total prison population is then found by summing over the offense types and demographic groups:

$$P_t = \sum_j \sum_o P_{tjo} . \tag{5}$$

Their analyses provided a basis for projecting numbers of arrests, commitments to prison, and prison populations to the year 2000. Those projections reflected the strong effects of the postwar baby boom on the criminal justice system as the trailing edge of that group (the 1962 birth cohort) moves out of the high-crime ages of 16-18. The results suggested that arrest rates should reach a peak about 1980. They projected, however, that prison commitments would not reach their peak until 1985: They are lagged because juveniles are rarely sent to prison, and most adult arrestees do not go to prison until they have accumulated several convictions, by which time they are in their mid-20s. They also projected that prison populations would peak about five years later still, about 1990; this lag reflects the fact that prison population will still accumulate even after the input flow has peaked because it will take several more years before the departure rate (reflecting time served) exceeds the declining arrival rate.[7]

This projection of prison population pointed out that Pennsylvania was expected to exceed the prison capacity in 1979[8] and to reach a peak in 1990 of 10,200, about 25 percent in excess of the 1977 capacity.[9] In making these projections, the model ignores the effects of such saturation by keeping the behavioral parameters unchanged through that saturation period. It is likely, of course, that some form of behavioral response would result. The capacity could be increased by constructing additional cells (and that would take several years to accomplish), or by expanding the nominal capacity by crowding more prisoners into the same number of cells. Alternatively, if the capacity is kept fixed, then adaptation could occur by introducing diversion programs (i.e., reducing Q) or by lowering time served (i.e., reducing S) through shorter sentences or earlier parole release. Since the nature of the choice among such behavioral responses is

extremely difficult to predict, and since the actual
choice in any case will be idiosyncratic to a particular
jurisdiction or to a particular decision maker, it is
extremely difficult to incorporate them into the projection model. The role of the projection analysis in such
a situation is to call attention to the impending saturation and thereby to highlight the need for some form of
response: Either capacity must be increased or policy
must be changed to accommodate to the existing capacity.
After that, the issue is one of political decision
making. The model can help in that process, however, by
helping to illuminate the impact of those choices on
prison populations.

This approach of analyzing the demographically disaggregated flow process is particularly attractive because
of the disaggregation of the flow units (by the changing
demographic variables of age, race, and sex as well as by
crime type) and because of the potential for isolating
whatever processing stages in the criminal justice system
are available for policy control. In particular, the
model of equation (4) contains the primary policy variables: $Q,^{10}$ the probability of imprisonment given
conviction, and S, the time served for those who are sent
to prison. Here, Q and S are disaggregated by crime type
and by demographic group (which might be related to prior
record) for independent testing of alternative policy
changes.

Microsimulation Models

The flow models discussed in the previous section simply
treat average flow rates at each stage of the criminal
justice system and examine the distribution of those
units of flow across the processing network. This is
efficient computationally, but it looks only at average
statistics. Estimates of total distributions can be
developed by simulating the flow of individual offenders
through the system and combining their individual experiences to generate aggregate statistics. In this
approach, a sample of individual simulated offenders are
generated with their individual demographic attributes:
type of current offense, prior record, and any other
attribute relevant to their processing through the criminal justice system. One could generate this sample of
offenders by taking a group of actual case records,
extracting their relevant attributes, and using those as

the simulated sample.[11] If the demography of the
population was anticipated to be undergoing a shift (for
example, more blacks), that subset of the sample could be
replicated at an appropriate rate to match whatever
future mix was projected. Alternatively, one could
collect statistics on the joint distribution of offender
attributes and use Monte Carlo sampling methods to synthesize a simulated sample of offenders from that distribution.

The former method has the benefit of avoiding explicit
worry about the particular joint distribution of offender
attributes; the sample of cases provides that distribution directly. The latter approach has the flexibility
of permitting the joint distribution, or any aspect of
it, to be changed analytically, something that can be
done easily.

In the operation of such a simulation, the sentencing
policy decision rules (including the possibility of a
probabilistic choice that would be realized by the
results of a process of random-number generation) would
be established, and the sentences would be imposed on
each of the simulated cases that arrive for sentencing.
Then, the aggregate consequences in terms of impact on
prison populations of any sentencing policy can be
examined over the years that policy is expected to be in
effect.

IMPACT ESTIMATION

In the discussion of the projection of prison populations
in the previous section, some attention was focused on
manipulating the sentencing policy variables, Q and S, in
order to estimate the consequences of those changes in
sentencing policies on prison populations. Even though a
number of models can project prison population reasonably, only the subset that specifically contains the
sentencing policy variables Q and S can also serve the
policy-impact-estimation function. The approaches that
are most appropriate are likely to be the disaggregated
flow models and the microsimulations.

Development of such an impact involves four basic
steps:

1. Characterizing the subset of court cases to which
   the policy applies;
2. Translating the policies into corresponding values
   of the policy variables in the projection models;

3. Formulating the behavioral model characterizing the response of the court to the sentencing policy; and

4. Calculating the projected change in prison population resulting from the response to the changed policy.

Identification of Population Subsets

Any sentencing policy ordinarily specifies at least the following attributes of those to whom it applies: (1) offense type; (2) particular aspects of the offense type (e.g., use of a weapon, causing of bodily harm, vulnerabilities of the victim such as age); and (3) prior record of the offender.

If one had a rich data base characterizing each case in terms of each of the attributes invoked in the policy, then it would be easy to identify each case in terms of whether each specific provision of the policy applied. Each case could then be assigned the specified imprisonment policy associated with its attributes, and the consequences under the old and the new policies could be compared. In the sample-case simulation, this requires that the records associated with each of the sampled cases include each of those attributes. In the flow model, it requires that the units of flow be adequately characterized in terms of each of the attributes invoked in the sentencing policy.

Since it is almost always the case that the available data set is not sufficiently rich and satisfactory, then other approaches must be used as an approximation. First, for those relevant variables that are available, the data set can be partitioned according to those variables. Then, within those variables, some independent sampled estimates must be obtained to estimate the joint distribution with the variables already recorded of the variables not adequately recorded. This can generate the fraction associated with each of the other policy variables.

Establishment of Values of Policy Variables

With a sufficiently fine characterization of the offenders into identified subsets, $\{G_i\}$, the task in characterizing a sentencing policy for analysis lies in determining for each such $\{G_j\}$ the corresponding sentencing variables, Q_i and S_i. For example, those groups for whom a policy calls for mandatory imprisonment should have Q_i set equal to 1.0. For those groups that remain unaffected by the law or policy, then Q_i can remain at its prior value.

A similar approach pertains to sentence under a mandatory minimum sentencing policy. For those offenders whose prior sentence was below their mandatory minimum, S_{oi}, their sentences should be moved up to the mandatory minimum itself. Those whose sentence is above the mandatory minimum would presumably remain unaffected. Those subgroups whose offense is not addressed by the mandatory minimum law should remain unaffected. Thus, using (Q_i', S_i') to denote the sentence of group i under the new policy and (Q_i, S_i) under the old, we can summarize:

$$(Q_j', S_j') = (Q_j, S_j) \text{ for groups j unaffected by the mandatory minimum law;}$$

$$Q_i' = 1 \text{ for groups i for whom imprisonment is mandatory;}$$

$$S_i' = S_{oi} \text{ for groups i affected by the law if } S_i < S_{oi};$$

$$S_i' = S_i \text{ for groups i affected by the law if } S_i \geq S_{oi}.$$

Behavioral Response to the New Policy

The previous discussion has attempted to translate into the policy the Q and S variables precisely as prescribed by the policy. Actually, however, there are likely to be many forms of adaptation by the practitioners within the court work groups. Some examples follow:

1. The judge, faced with imposing an excessively large mandatory minimum sentence on someone who might otherwise have received a shorter prison term might conform to the law (i.e., raise S_i to S_{oi}), or the judge might decide to assign such an individual to probation instead.

2. The judge could adhere to the minimum for all who are sent to prison (i.e., if $Q_i = 1$, then $S_i' \geq S_{oi}$) but could ignore the mandatory requirement by retaining probation when that was done before (i.e., $Q_i' = Q_i$).

3. The prosecutor could revise charging behavior so that individuals for whom the mandatory minimum sentence seems excessively severe could be charged under one of the many related offense types, thereby decreasing the fraction charged with a prescribed offense and correspondingly increasing some of the other offenses.

In all of these cases, the response could be characterized in terms of a corresponding change in Q_i or S_i as well as in changes in the number of persons associated with each subset, $\{G_i\}$.

Calculation of the Effects of the Sentencing Policy Change

Once the parameters in the estimation models have been formulated to generate estimates of the numbers in each subset, $\{G_i\}$, and their associated Q_i and S_i under each of the alternative sentencing policies being considered, and for each of the behavioral adaptation assumptions, it then becomes possible to calculate the prison populations associated with each sentencing policy. That calculation could be accomplished using a disaggregated flow model (equations (3) to (5)) or a microsimulation, each with the appropriate sentencing policy variables, Q_i and S_i. By comparing P_t', the prison population in year t under the new policy to the corresponding P_t under the old, the difference $(P_t' - P_t)$ represents the incremental cost (or savings) associated with the policy change.

Estimation of the Impact of a
Mandatory Minimum Sentencing Bill

In order to illustrate some of the methodological issues discussed earlier and also to convey some of the substantive insights that emerged, this section summarizes the results of an impact analysis[12] in Pennsylvania, building on projections of prison populations in Pennsylvania through the demographic-specific flow model discussed above.

The particular policy change examined is a mandatory minimum sentencing bill, S.B. 995, that was one of several such bills being considered by the Pennsylvania legislature during its 1976 session. The bill addressed 10 felony offenses ranging from murder to sale of nar-

481

cotics and burglary. Recidivists with one prior conviction were to receive a one-year mandatory minimum
sentence upon reconviction, and those with two or more
prior convictions were to receive a two-year minimum.[13]
If a firearm was used in the current offense, an additional year was to be added to the minimum sentence.

These provisions of the bill provided the necessary
guidance for generating the offense and offender subsets
that fall under its provisions. The relevant offenses
were clearly specified in the bill and also were available in the court OBTS records. The prior record provisions were clear in the bill but, as is often the case,
were not available in the individual records from the
court; court records, at best, might include a single
number (such as prior felony convictions) but are not
likely to provide more detailed information on convictions for a specified group of felonies. Thus it became
necessary to draw a separate sample of convicted persons
and to examine their prior records in detail in order to
determine the fraction associated with each combination
of current offense type and prior record that were specified by the bill. A similar partition was conducted for
the offenses involving firearms.

This information provided the basis for partitioning
convicted offenders in any year into appropriate subsets,
$\{G_i\}$, corresponding to each of the combinations of
conditions specified in the bill. For each such group,
the fraction of cases involved and the sentencing pattern
prior to enactment of the bill, Q_i and S_i, could be
determined. For each such group, the provisions of the
bill indicated Q_i' (either $Q_i' = Q_i$ if the group was not
relevant to the bill or $Q_i' = 1$ if imprisonment was
mandatory). The average sentence under the bill, S_i',
depended on the distribution of sentences in prior
practice. For the groups not addressed by the bill,
$S_i' = S_i$. For those for whom prison was mandated, the
lower tail (below S_{oi}, the group's relevant mandatory
minimum) of the sentence distribution was set at S_{oi},
those previously assigned to probation were set at S_{oi},
and the upper tail of the sentence distribution (above
S_{oi}) remained unaffected.

These statements reflect literal interpretation of the
bill's provisions. The next step involved characterizing
the judges' behavioral responses to those provisions.
Since the bill afforded judges the opportunity to avoid
imposing a sentence if they found that mitigating factors
warranted such an action, three possible scenarios were
considered:

1. Mandatory Prison Scenario: Literal interpretation of the bill so that anyone who satisfied the conditions of the bill was sent to prison for the specified mandatory minimum sentence.
2. Conforming to Minimum Only Scenario: Only those who formerly were sent to prison but served less than the specified minimum had their sentences raised to the minimum; others--and particularly those who formerly were assigned to probation-- remained unaffected by the bill.
3. Undermining Scenario: Those who were formerly sent to prison for a sentence less than the mandatory minimum were put on probation in order to avoid having to increase their sentences; others remained unaffected by the bill.

Analysis was carried out only on the first two of these scenarios, and their effects on state prison populations were examined. Since the impact will accumulate over a number of years as new offenders are convicted under the new bill, the impact estimate was calculated over time as a perturbation to the population projections assuming continuation of current practice. These effects under the two scenarios, reflecting the different behavioral responses to the bill, are shown in Figure 8-1. The striking observation is that full implementation of the legislation as written (the mandatory prison scenario) would have involved an increase of about 50 percent in prison populations at the peak. A much less dramatic change is associated with the conforming to minimum only scenario, in which the prior probation decisions remain unaffected. Under this scenario, prison population would increase only about 10 percent, certainly well within any forecasting or impact estimation error and certainly a tolerable impact on any prison system. This also indicates that the major change called for by the bill is the increase in the use of imprisonment for people who otherwise are put on probation, and it does not call for major increases in time served by those who already do go to prison.

These two scenarios undoubtedly encompass the judicial response that would be anticipated. The results also suggest that if the bill were passed, most judges would probably invoke the mitigating factors option, at least for a sizable fraction of the cases they had formerly put on probation.

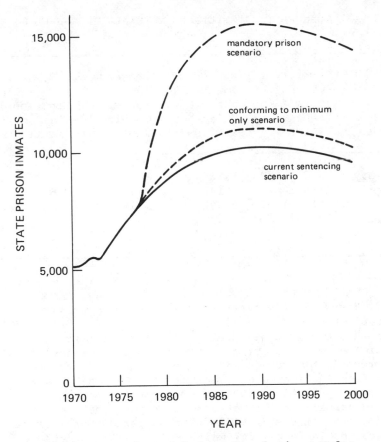

FIGURE 8-1 Projected Prison Populations Under Alternative Sentencing Scenarios (S.B. 995)

It was also interesting to identify the offenses that contributed to the major growth in prison populations under the mandatory minimum scenario. The changes in the number of commitments for five offense categories are shown in Table 8-3. It is clear from the table that the bill would have very little effect on those convicted of murder and rape--virtually all of them go to prison already. The major influence would be on those convicted of relatively minor offenses, burglary in particular. The predominant portion of those new commitments would be those convicted of burglary with relatively few prior

TABLE 8-3 Changes in Commitments to State Prison Under
S.B. 995

Offense	Number of Current Commitments (1975)	Number of Commitments Under S.B. 995	Increase in Number of Commitments	Percentage Increase in Commitments
Burglary	685	1,626	941	137
Robbery	686	1,148	462	67
Drugs	401	582	181	45
Murder	406	436	30	7
Rape	120	145	25	21

convictions, largely because they were not committed under prior policy.

In view of the considerable disparity in sentencing practice across a state as heterogeneous as Pennsylvania, the predominant increase in sentences to state prison comes from Philadelphia. For example, Philadelphia would provide 58 percent of the new commitments for robbery. This is partly a result of the disproportionate number of robbery convictions in Philadelphia, partly a result of the greater leniency with which Philadelphia treats robbery—many of its convicted robbers go to the county jail for sentences less than the mandatory minimum, and S.B. 995 would require that they be sent to the state prison.

The results of this analysis were presented in testimony to the Pennsylvania legislature in 1977 and in 1978, when it was considering a number of mandatory minimum bills, along with a proposal to create a sentencing commission. The sentencing commission was intended, at least in part, as a means of heading off the politically attractive mandatory minimum bills. The magnitude of the estimated impact estimate of S.B. 995 was surprising to many of the legislators; that provided one basis for arguing for the necessity of formulating sentencing policy in a forum like a sentencing commission, which they hoped would be more deliberative than is normally the case on the floor of a state legislature. The sentencing commission bill was passed with a majority of only one vote.

SUMMARY AND FURTHER RESEARCH NEEDS

This paper has focused on the importance and the feasibility of providing estimates of the impact on prison populations of proposed changes in sentencing policy and of the need to develop improved methods for generating them. Such estimates are necessary to ensure that the debate over sentencing policy is balanced and that the political attractiveness of a tougher policy is responsibly weighed against the costs of such a policy.

This issue will be particularly important in the coming decade, when prisons, already largely filled to capacity, can expect significant growth in sentenced populations. It is also important that the impact be examined in the context of projections of prison populations over an interval of at least 20 years in order to estimate the degree to which the anticipated future prison population growth warrants provision of additional prison capacity. At least in those states of the Northeast and the Midwest in which prison populations can be expected to reach a peak and to decline after about 1990, there may be a serious question about the advisability of creating that extra capacity, especially if one considers the limited excess demand after it is finally constructed. The availability of impact estimates provides legislatures and the public generally the opportunity to make responsible and explicit trade-offs between the desired level of punitiveness and its cost.

There are a number of research approaches that could make important contributions to the ability to develop such impact estimates:

1. A number of readily available models for calculating prison impact should be formulated and made available to criminal justice planning agencies for their use in assisting a legislature or sentencing commission in estimating the impact of their policy choices.
2. Some pilot trials ought to be undertaken in states with OBTS systems to develop good means for projecting future prison populations and to estimate impacts.
3. In jurisdictions that have adopted significant new sentencing policies, the impact should be estimated

using data that were available prior to the policy changes, and these projections should be compared with the changes that actually occurred.

4. Cross-jurisdictional studies should be conducted to discern how judges respond to changes in sentencing policy. It is particularly important to be able to compare courts in jurisdictions in which the prison system is fully saturated with those in which there is slack capacity in the prison.

NOTES

1. In this paper, the term sentencing policy is used generically to refer to guidance or mandates to sentencing judges, whether that guidance is established by a legislated determinate sentencing schedule as embodied in California's SB-42, by a mandatory minimum sentencing law, or by sentencing guidelines established by a judicial council or by a legislatively created sentencing commission. Statutory sentence maximums are also a form of sentencing policy, but they are largely ignored in this paper, partly because their role in the courtroom is insignificant, but primarily because the questions of prison impact addressed here are much more related to concerns over the effects of sentences that are constrained from below than from above.

2. The grid was created by generating an offense score of 12 levels based on a ranking of offense seriousness and an offender score of 7 levels based on the prior conviction history of the defendant.

3. The estimates of number of prisoners by sex and race are based on Tables 2 and 3 (for sex) and Table 7 (for race of males) of U.S. Department of Justice (1981). The general population estimates are based on U.S. Bureau of the Census (1980:Table 2).

4. The rates in Table 8-1 were calculated on the basis of the age and race of the male prisoners responding to a survey in 1979 conducted by the U.S. Bureau of the Census (1980) for the Bureau of Justice Statistics, and the demographic composition of the U.S. population was determined from U.S. Bureau of the Census (1980).

5. These are not the same incarceration rates presented in Table 8-1. The values in Table 8-2 are based on the demographic features of interviewed prisoners at the time of their admission to prison. The more appropriate numerators are the demographic features at the time of the survey, which were used in Table 8-1. That numerator, however, was available only for the 1979 survey, and so, for comparability, the less appropriate measure of age at admission is used in Table 8-2.

6. For a description of the JUSSIM model, see Blumstein (1980). That article contains detailed references on the program and its operation.

7. These substantive observations are, of course, precisely true only for Pennsylvania. The important role of the demographic shifts associated with the baby boom, however, is likely to apply broadly to the states of the Northeast and the Midwest, with their numerically stable and aging populations. Even within those states, the large cities would have to be examined separately because of their large rates of migration and the strong effect those migration patterns could have on demographic structures. At the state level, however, the level at which concern over prison population is most relevant, demography is less sensitive to shifting migration patterns. In contrast to the Northeast, the rapid population growth in the West and the Southwest could dominate the age shifts that cause the peaking observed in Pennsylvania.

8. In 1981, Pennsylvania's prison population was about 300 prisoners over capacity.

9. These projections were based on the processing parameters remaining constant throughout the period, a situation that did prevail in the early 1970s. In the late 1970s, however, sentences were observed to increase, thereby intensifying the anticipated saturation.

10. Literally, C enters equation (4), but Q influences C through equation (3).

11. This is the approach used by the Minnesota Sentencing Guidelines Commission in estimating the effect of any guideline sentencing schedule on prison populations, enabling the commission to adhere to the policy it adopted of avoiding any policy that would lead to an increase in prison populations (see Knapp and Anderson, 1981).

12. The details of the impact analysis are reported in Blumstein et al. (1979). The results are summarized in Miller (1981).

13. One interesting indication of the shift in attitudes since 1976 is the fact that the mandatory minimum bills considered by the Pennsylvania general assembly in 1981 call for minimum sentences of five years rather than one or two years.

REFERENCES

Blumstein, Alfred
  1980 Planning models for analytical evaluation. Pp. 237-257 in Malcolm W. Klein and Katherine S. Teilmann, eds., Handbook of Criminal Justice Evaluation. Beverly Hills, Calif.: Sage Publications.
Blumstein, Alfred, Jacqueline Cohen, and Harold D. Miller
  1980 Demographically disaggregated projections of prison populations. Journal of Criminal Justice 8(1):1-25.
Blumstein, Alfred, Harold Miller, Wendy Bell, Deborah Kahn, and Stewart Szydlo
  1979 The Impact of New Sentencing Laws on State Prison Populations in Pennsylvania: Final Report. Urban Systems Institute, Carnegie-Mellon University.
Box, George E.P., and Gwilym M. Jenkins
  1976 Time Series Analysis: Forecasting and Control. San Francisco: Holden-Day.
Fox, James A.
  1978 Forecasting Crime Data: An Econometric Analysis. Lexington, Mass.: Lexington Books.
Greenberg, David F.
  1977 The dynamics of oscillatory punishment processes. Journal of Criminal Law and Criminology 68(4):643-651.
Knapp, Kay A., and Ronald E. Anderson
  1981 Minnesota Sentencing Guidelines Projection Program--User's Manual. Minnesota Sentencing Guidelines Commission, St. Paul. 55101.
Lettre, Michel A., et al.
  1978 A Jurisdiction-Based Description of the Maryland Criminal Juvenile Justice System. Maryland Governor's Commission on Law Enforcement and Administration of Justice.

McCleary, Richard, and Richard A. Hay, Jr.
   1980 Applied Time Series Analysis for the Social
        Sciences. Beverly Hills, Calif.: Sage
        Publications.
Miller, Harold
   1981 Projecting the impact of new sentencing laws on
        prison populations. Policy Sciences 13:51-73.
U.S. Bureau of the Census
   1980 Estimates of the population of the United States
        by age, race, and sex: 1976 to 1979. Report No.
        870, Series P-25, Population Estimates and
        Projections. Washington, D.C.: U.S. Department
        of Commerce.
U.S. Department of Justice
   1976 Survey of Inmates of State Correctional Facili-
        ties 1974. National Prisoner Statistics Special
        Report SD-NPS-SR-Z. Washington, D.C.: U.S.
        Department of Justice.
   1981 Prisoners in State and Federal Institutions on
        December 31, 1979. National Prisoner Statistics
        Bulletin No. NPS-PSF-7, NCJ-73719. Washington,
        D.C.: U.S. Department of Justice, Bureau of
        Justice Statistics.